To Be an Invalid

To Be an

Ralph Colp, Jr., M.D.

The Illness of
Charles Darwin

The University of Chicago Press
Chicago and London

Invalid

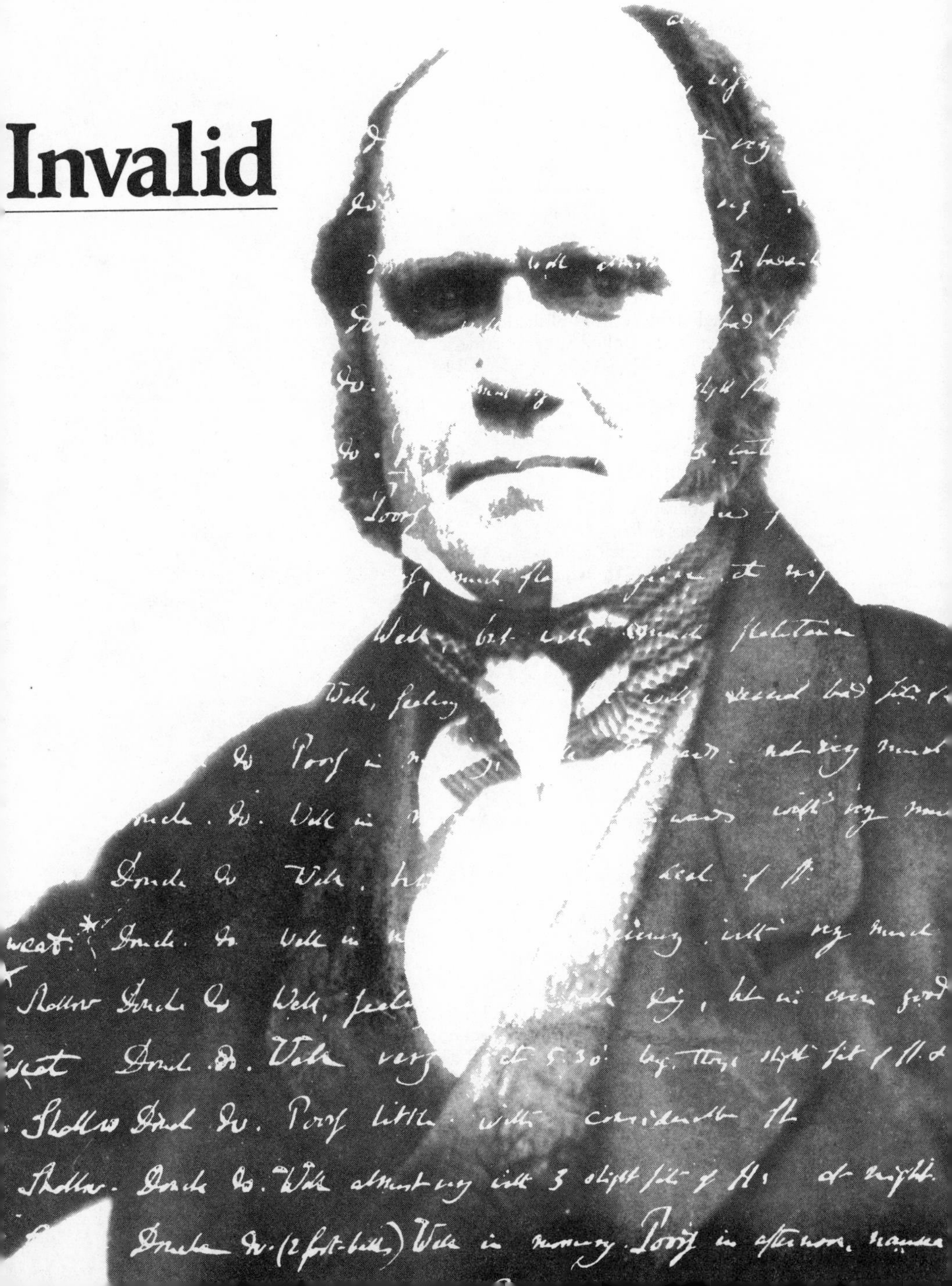

The University of Chicago Press,
Chicago 60637
The University of Chicago Press, Ltd.,
London
© 1977 by The University of Chicago
All rights reserved. Published 1977
Printed in the United States of America
81 80 79 78 77   9 8 7 6 5 4 3 2 1

Library of Congress Cataloging in Publication Data

Colp, Ralph.
  To be an invalid.

  Bibliography : p.
  Includes index.
  1. Darwin, Charles Robert, 1809–1882.
2. Naturalists—United States—Biography.
3. Chronic diseases—Cases, clinical reports,
statistics.   I. Title.
QH31.D2C6   575′.0092′4 [B]   76-17698
ISBN 0-226-11401-5

RALPH COLP, JR., M.D., is.a graduate
of Columbia Medical School and (acting) director of the Psychiatric Section,
Columbia University Health Service.
He has written many articles, several
on Charles Darwin.

To Charlotte, Ruth, and Judy
who lived with me
during the many years
I lived with Charles Darwin

I fear that my head will stand no
thought, but I would sooner be the
wretched contemptible invalid,
which I am, than live the life of an
idle squire.

Charles Darwin

Contents

1

The Illness

2

Acknowledgments

I am deeply indebted to Mr. Peter J. Gautrey, assistant under-librarian, University Library, Cambridge. He has warmly guided me through his library's unrivaled collection of Darwin books and documents. Without his unstinting aid in sending me copies of Darwin's letters and manuscripts, this work would not have been possible.

My debt to Mr. Karl Aschaffenburg is likewise great. Without his expert skill in identifying and analyzing the handwriting of different members of the Darwin family, in entering into the spirit of this family, and in deciphering some passages of Charles Darwin's writing, my manuscript would have been much the worse.

Robin Price, librarian, Wellcome Institute of the History of Medicine, has graciously replied to many letters of inquiry and directed me to sources of information about Victorian medications, treatments, and doctors.

Lieutenant Colonel Charles Casolani (retired) has rendered invaluable service in searching out diverse sources of information.

Paul H. Barrett, professor of natural science at Michigan State University, has shared with me his very great knowledge of Darwin and Darwin manuscripts.

Sir Hedley Atkins, past president of the Royal College of Surgeons of England and curator of the Down House Estate, has replied to many letters, sent me copies of Darwin documents in his possession, and given permission to transcribe The "Receipts" and "Memoranda" Book and to quote from the Diary of Health and the "Henrietta Litchfield manuscript."

Jessie Dobson—past curator of the Hunterian Museum of the Royal College of Surgeons—and Elizabeth Allen—present curator of the Hunterian Museum—have sent me copies of Darwin's medical notebooks and account books and answered my queries.

Mr. Samuel Robinson, former custodian of Down House, has

guided me about Down House and replied to my letters of inquiry. Mr. Philip Titheradge, present custodian of Down House, has replied to my queries and searched out sources of information for me.

Leonard G. Wilson, professor of the history of medicine at the University of Minnesota, has shared with me his information about Sir Charles Lyell, and written me several detailed letters about Lyell, Mrs. Lyell, and Darwin.

I am also indebted to the following: the Syndics of the University Library, Cambridge, for permission to publish Darwin documents in their possession; the Royal College of Surgeons of England for permission to publish The "Receipts" and "Memoranda" Book, and to quote from the Diary of Health and the "Henrietta Litchfield manuscript"; Edmund Berkeley, Jr., curator of manuscripts in the University of Virginia Library, for permission to quote from documents in the "Darwin Evolution Collection, University of Virginia Library"; Gregory A. Johnson, public services assistant in the University of Virginia Library, for sending me copies of documents in the "Darwin Evolution Collection" of his library; Patricia Hall, former librarian in the Gray Herbarium and Arnold Arboretum of Harvard University, for copies of Darwin's letters to Asa Gray; Jeanne Pingree and B. Y. Cormeau, Archives of the Imperial College of Science and Technology, London, for copies of Darwin's letters to Thomas H. Huxley; Brenda Sutton, former librarian of the History of Medicine Library, Woodward Biomedical Library, the University of British Columbia, Vancouver, Canada, for copies of Darwin-Fox letters in the Pearce Collection; Bern Dibner, of the Burndy Library, Norwalk, Connecticut, for copies of Darwin documents and for his encouragement; Murphy D. Smith, librarian, American Philosophical Society Library, for his interest and encouragement, for showing me his library's rich collection of Darwinia, and for copies of Darwin's letters to Charles Lyell; Rita Kecheissen, reference librarian in the Columbia University Library, for her unflagging skill and assistance in locating sources of information; Nancy E. Schroeder and Robert True, of the Interlibrary Loan Service, Columbia University Library, for helping me obtain books from different libraries; Lady Margaret Keynes, for permission to quote from Darwin's "Private Diary"; Sarah Pomeroy, for translating a Latin prescription in The "Receipts" and "Memoranda" Book; Dr. C. P. Courtney, librarian of Christ's College, for answering my questions about the Darwin-Fox letters in his library, and the Master and Fellows of Christ's College, for permission to quote from these letters; Mr. George P. Darwin, for permission to quote from Darwin papers held by the American Philosophical Society; and Dr. Frederick Burkhardt, for informing me about Darwin's health for the period of October 1836 to July 1837.

For helping me obtain many different books and journals, I am grateful to the following librarians at the New York Academy of Medicine: Alice Weaver and Sali Morgenstern in the rare book room; Stephen Carey and Jane Magenheim in the library.

I am further indebted to the following libraries and their staffs for information about Darwin and nineteenth-century medicine: Yale Medical Library; special collections (book division), microfilm department, and math, geology, psychology, and biology libraries of Columbia University Library; the New York Pubic Library; the Library of the New York Museum of Natural History; the Library of the New York Botanical Garden; the National Library of Medicine; the Library of Congress; the British Museum; the Shrewsbury Public Library and the Shrewsbury School Library; the Wedgwood Museum; the Linnean Society of London.

Among the many individuals with whom I have had valuable discussions about Darwin, I should like to mention Lady Nora Barlow, Jerome H. Buckley, Sir Gavin de Beer, P. Thomas Carroll, Loren Eisley, Harold Fruchtbaum, Howard Gruber, Bert Hansen, Elizabeth Jenkins, Dr. Stephen B. Kurtin, Ralph Lewis, H. Lewis McKinney, Gerald Morice, Dr. Leonard Shengold, Sydney Smith, Peter J. Vorzimmer, and Dr. Torben K. With.

Introduction

For most of his adult life, Charles Darwin suffered from an illness the origin and nature of which mystified his contemporaries. In the ninety years since Darwin's death, although there have been studies and interpretations of this illness, our knowledge of its clinical picture is still incomplete, and there is much disagreement about its etiology.[1] "The nature of Darwin's illness," wrote one Darwin scholar in 1971, "is still a mystery."[2]

Ever since the centenary of *The Origin of Species* reminded me how one man changed human thought, I have been studying the published writings by and about Darwin, and the treasury of unpublished Darwin manuscripts. This work is written with two aims. To tell, as fully as possible, the history of the several aspects of Darwin's illness: his symptoms, medications, and treatments; how he experienced his life of invalidism; his relations with his doctors and those family and friends who concerned themselves about his health. And to review and evaluate the many theories about the causes of his illness, and to postulate that the most apparent causes were different psychological stresses—especially stresses from his scientific work and his ideas of evolution. I think that Darwin's illness cannot be understood without understanding two attributes of Darwin the man: his determination to win acceptance for his evolutionary theory, and his anxieties over the difficulties of proving this theory and over some of its ideological consequences.

1

The Illness

1

A Family of Doctors

Charles Darwin grew up in a family of doctors. His paternal grand-father, Dr. Erasmus Darwin, had been one of the most preeminent physicians of the eighteenth century.[1] A brilliant paternal uncle and namesake—Charles Darwin—had died while studying medicine at Edinburgh.[2] His father, Dr. Robert Waring Darwin, was a skilled and respected physician who lived and practiced in Shrewsbury and who had developed one of the largest medical practices outside of London.[3] His older brother, Erasmus Alvey Darwin, studied medicine at Cambridge and Edinburgh. (Erasmus then became ill, depressed, and unable to work.[4])

When Darwin was in his teens he read, and "admired greatly,"[5] Dr. Erasmus Darwin's two-volume magnum opus *Zoonomia; or, The Laws of Organic Life.*[6] This work, published thirteen years before Darwin was born, was still regarded as an encyclopedia of facts and theories of normal and diseased life. Volume 1 (586 pages) discussed the physiology of digestion, circulation, respiration, muscular move-ments, vision, sleep and dreams, temperament, and how the mind produces ideas. One section, "Of Generation," enunciated a theory of evolution. Volume 2 (772 pages) first comprised a "Catalogue" of 474 diseases, frequently with graphic case illustrations, and an account of the treatment of each disease. There was then a part on "Materia Medicine," which was an inventory of eighteenth-century medicines, and an "account of the operation of medicines." *Zoonomia* was largely a book for physicians: it contained practical suggestions for the diagnosis and treatment of all known illnesses, and it enabled a physician to see his efforts against a background of general biology.

When Darwin was sixteen years old, in the summer of 1825, his father began to prepare him to become a doctor. Young Darwin visited some sick women and children in Shrewsbury and reported back to his father. "I wrote down," Darwin recollected, "as full an account as I could of the cases with all the symptoms, and read them aloud to my father, who suggested further enqueries, and advised me what medicines to give, which I made up myself. At one time I had at least a dozen patients, and I felt a keen interest in the work. My father, who was by far the best judge of character whom I ever knew, declared that I should make a successful physician,—meaning by this, one who got many patients." Darwin felt an especial "pride" at successfully treating a whole family with tartar emetic.[7] Dr. Darwin also had his son be present when he examined some poor patients, so that he could demonstrate his medical methods.[8] At this time Darwin may have read Dr. J. A. Paris' *Pharmacologia*, a sixth edition of which had just been published, which discussed the pharmacology and clinical usage of the most important existing medicines.[9]

In the fall of 1825 Darwin enrolled as a medical student in Edinburgh. For the next year he attended courses in "Chemistry and Pharmacy," "Anatomy, Physiology, and Pathology," "Clinical Lectures" (on medical topics), "Principles and Practice of Surgery," and "Materia Medica, Dietetics, and Pharmacy."[10] For his course in Materia Medica, taught by Dr. Andrew Duncan, Jr., he purchased and studied the eleventh edition (just published in 1826) of Dr. Duncan's book, *The Edinburgh New Dispensatory*, which contained sections on materia medica, pharmacy, and pharmaceutical preparations.[11] He also wrote out six pages of notes, entitled "Dr Duncan's Mat. Medica," where he listed the properties and therapeutic indications of about sixty medicines.[12] In eight pages of medical notes he listed the clinical signs, treatments, and prognosis of the following diseases: mania, palsies, apoplexy, typhus, "Rosalia," "Rubeola," "Empresma,"[13] pneumonitis, pleuritis, peritonitis, gastritis, enteritis, and hepatitis. In these notes he cites the medical opinions of "My Father" once, and his grandfather—whom he calls "Dr. D—," "Dr. D," "Dr. Darwin," and "Zonomia Dr. Darwin"—six times.[14] Several months after arriving at Edinburgh he met the aged Dr. Andrew Duncan, Sr., who spoke to him "with the warmest affection" of his uncle Charles Darwin, whom Dr. Duncan had known forty-seven years previously.[15]

During his first year at Edinburgh, however, Darwin lost his desire to become a doctor. With the exception of chemistry he came to dislike all of his courses, especially Dr. Duncan's Materia Medica, and he was "distressed" by the suffering of some of the patients he saw, and deeply disturbed by seeing "two very bad operations."[16] Previously, while a schoolboy at Shrewsbury, he had already come to

regard surgery as "a beastly profession."[17] During his second year at
Edinburgh, although he enrolled in classes of "Practice of Physic" and
"Midwifery," he may not have attended these or any medical classes;
instead he attended lectures on geology and zoology,[18] and he became
a member of the Plinian Society, which consisted of Edinburgh
students who "met in an underground room in the University for the
sake of reading papers on natural science and discussing them."[19]
Then, following the suggestion of his father (who seems to have
become resigned to his not studying medicine), he determined to
become a clergyman. For the next three years he was a pre-divinity
student at Christ's College, Cambridge, and he passed his B.A. degree
exams early in 1831.[20]

Darwin would never regret that he had not become a doctor. For
"many a long year" he woud be "haunted" by memories of "the two
very bad operations,"[21] and his memories of Dr. Duncan's course in
Materia Medica would cause him great mental pain.[22] Yet his early
contacts with medicine left him with a belief in the therapeutic
effectiveness of some medicines, a knowledge of how to observe and
follow the symptoms of an illness, and a pride in the professional
prowess of his father and grandfather.

The youthful Darwin was, in variform ways, omnivorous of life:
gregarious and friendly with a number of young men of his own age;
physically active and partaking of long country walks and cross-
country horse rides; "passion[ate]" for hunting;[23] curious about
natural history (yet without any career goals in this field); and eager
to travel to foreign lands. Although he was, according to his later
recollection, in "excellent health,"[24] he was also susceptible to two
kinds of ill health. First, he had a tendency to become psychically,
and/or psychophysiologically, ill when confronted with unpleasant
events. When he had just turned sixteen, and was living in Shrewsbury, he received a letter from his older brother Erasmus who was in
Cambridge studying to be a doctor. Erasmus wrote him: "I am getting
a little case-hardening in anatomy; for ["yesterday" inserted] seeing a
body ex [rest of word torn off] and being Junior they gave me a deal of
the dirty work, & I was not the least annoyed while an old Physician
also present kept leaving the room perpetually. I don't fancy it wld.
have suited your ["Fancy" crossed out] stomack especially before
breakfast."[25] Several months later, when Darwin had become a
medical student in Edinburgh, his younger sister Catherine wrote him
from Shrewsbury about his dog Sparks: "I must now give you a piece
of news about *your* favourite *child*, which I am afraid will prove a

blow to you; i.e. that Sparks is gone to Overton;[26] at least till your
return next summer, as they were in want of a watch dog, and Czar is
finally going, having bit another person—I am afraid this intelligence
will be a shock to all your nerves, and will spoil a good many
breakfasts; but all I can tell you for your comfort is that Dr. Parker is
very fond of her, and means to take the feeding of her entirely in his
own care."[27] Note how Catherine anticipates that her brother's
reaction to the loss of his beloved dog will be psychic and psychophysiologic: a "shock" to "all nerves," and an upset stomach lasting
for "a good many breakfasts." Both Erasmus and Catherine observe
that their brother's upset stomach (exact symptoms unspecified)
mainly manifests itself during breakfast.

Darwin's second kind of ill health involved his lips and his hands. In
the first half of 1829, when he was twenty and a student at
Cambridge, he complained about his lips in letters to his Cambridge
friend and cousin William Darwin Fox[28] (Fox suffered from chronic
"chest complaints,"[29] and was interested in things medical): 2 January:
"My life is very quiet & uniform & what makes it more so; my lips
have lately taken to be bad, which will prevent my going to
Edinburgh";[30] 1 April: "I find Cambridge rather stupid. ["I" crossed
out] & as I know scarcely any one that walks, & this joined with my
lips not being quite so well has reduced me to sort of hybernation.
Which almost equalls 'poor little Whitmores' melancholy case."[31]

On 4 July he told Fox that he had gone home to Shrewsbury, then
out to hunt beetles: "The first two days I went on pretty well, taking
several good insects, but for the rest of that week my lips became
suddenly so bad, & I myself not so very well, that I was unable to
leave the room & on the Monday I retreated with grief & sorrow back
again to Shrewsbury." He added: "I am sure you will properly
sympathize with my unfortunate situation."[32] Two years later, in a
letter to his sister Susan, he complained about his hands: "My hands
are not quite well, and I have always observed that if I once get them
well, and change my manner of living about the same time, they will
frequently remain well."[33] The exact clinical nature, frequency and
duration, and cause or causes (whether one or a combination of
chemical, infectious, or psychophysiologic factors) of his hand and lip
afflictions are unknown. His hand disturbance may have been caused
by psychological factors—his "manner of living"—and then assuaged
when these psychological factors were changed. His lip affliction
seems to have been accompanied by feelings of shame and depression,
and withdrawal from people.

In 1882, J. M. Herbert wrote this 1828–31 Cambridge recollection of
Darwin: "He had at one time an eruption about the mouth for which
he took small doses of arsenic. He told me that he had mentd. this
treatment to his Father—& that his Father had warned him that the
cure might be attended with worse consequences—I forget what he
said the risk was, but I think it was of [word smudged and illegible]
partial paralysis."[34] This is the only reference to Darwin's actually
taking arsenic; it does not tell the frequency and size of the "small
doses" that he used, whether he took it locally or internally, or how he
came to take it. In February 1829, about the time he had his lip
condition, he spent a day in London with Dr. Henry Holland, who
lent him a horse to ride in the park.[35] Dr. Holland was a socially
prominent London physician—whose work has been described as
"more fashionable than scientific"[36]—and a second cousin of the
Darwins and the Wedgwoods.[37] In the future Darwin would see
Holland socially, and sometimes consult him medically or about his
scientific work. It may be that Holland prescribed arsenic, although
Holland's views on arsenic are unknown.

Another possibility was that Darwin prescribed arsenic for himself,[38] because of the use of the drug then in the fens of Lincolnshire
(near Cambridge)[39] and because of his belief in the therapeutic
effectiveness of medicines, and what he may have read in Dr.
Darwin's *Zoonomia*, Paris' *Pharmacologia*, and Duncan's *The Edinburgh New Dispensatory*.[40] These authors recommended that arsenic
be used externally in cancer and skin diseases, and internally (usually
in the form of Fowler's solution) as the treatment for fevers, headaches, periodical diseases, and "many anomalous diseases of the
skin."[41] It was, however, recognized that arsenic was "one of the most
virulent poisons," and that, taken medicinally, it could cause gastrointestinal upsets, debility and fainting, "tremors and palsies," dropsy,
and skin eruptions.[42] Paris advised that arsenic should be prescribed
with "the greatest circumspection," and only after other remedies have
failed.[43] Duncan quoted a physician on how to give arsenic and guard
against its toxic effects. "From all I have observed, I have little
apprehension of risk in a guarded and judicious use of the arsenical
solution. It will always be proper to begin with the smallest doses, in
order to ascertain how it agrees with the stomach. Having suited the
dose to this, the feeling of swelling and stiffness of the palpebrae and
face, heat, soreness, and itching of the tarsi, or tenderness of the
mouth, are proofs that the medicine is exerting its specific effects on
the constitution; that the dose has been carried to a sufficient length;

and that it is time to decrease the dose, and attentively to watch its future effects. On the appearance of erythema, or salivation, it is time to interrupt, altogether, for a while, the exhibition of arsenic; if necessary, it may be resumed when these symptoms have vanished. If pain of the stomach, nausea, or vomiting supervine; if the head be affected with pain or vertigo; or should a cough, with any signs of irritation of the pulmonary organs, be observed, the use of arsenic should be totally and forever abandoned."[44]

The above accounts may have caused Darwin to desire yet fear arsenic, and then to take it in "small doses" because of its toxicity. After taking arsenic he may have felt better. And when his father warned him about arsenic's toxicity, although he repeated this warning to his friend Herbert, he still—for a time—may have felt inclined to take arsenic if his skin condition worsened.

2

The *Beagle* Illnesses

On 29 August 1831 Darwin was offered a position on H.M.S. *Beagle*, which was preparing to sail around the world. He first accepted; then, mainly because of his father's objection, he refused. When his uncle Josiah Wedgwood persuaded his father to change his mind, he again, and finally, accepted. He later commented that during this time "my mind was like a swinging pendulum."[1] He was torn between his desire to go on the *Beagle* and his apprehension at leaving his English home and friends and opposing his father's objections. "Even if I was to go," he had written on 30 August, "my Father disliking [it] would take away all energy, & I should want a good stock of that."[2]

In September 1831 he went to London to purchase equipment for the *Beagle*, and from there he wrote his sister Susan in Shrewsbury: "I daresay you expect I shall turn back at the Madeira: if I have a morsel of stomach left, I won't give up." It is not clear whether this refers to his tendency to suffer an upset stomach from psychic causes, or a fear that he will become seasick during the *Beagle* voyage (when he wrote this he had not yet been aboard the *Beagle*), or both. In the same letter, mentioning his previously quoted account of his hand being "not quite well," he queried Susan: "Ask my Father if he thinks there would be any objection to my taking Arsenic for a little time.... What is the dose?"[3] Thus, despite his father's warning, he is tempted to take arsenic; yet he will only take it for "a little time," and only with paternal approval. When his father, apparently, disapproved he then informed Susan: "I do not think I shall take any Arsenic."[4] Over the next four months he makes no mention of any medications or hand complaints.

On 24 October he moved from London to Plymouth where the *Beagle* was preparing to depart. Then, when the *Beagle* twice attempted to sail but was driven back by heavy gales, there was a delay of two months. During these months, which he would describe as "very miserable"[5] and "the most miserable which I ever spent,"[6] he suffered old and new anxieties because of the following immediate and anticipated hardships: the smallness of his ship quarters ("The absolute want of room is an evil, that nothing can surmount"[7]) and his close contact with some of the *Beagle* crew;[8] the prospect "of leaving all my family and friends for so long a time";[9] and the fear of being killed by infectious diseases or hostile natives.[10] Aboard the *Beagle* he became seasick. He then feared that this seasickness would persist throughout the *Beagle* voyage, and that it would cause him to become "incapacitated" and unable to do active work.[11]

In addition to being anxious he became psychically depressed. The weather seemed to him "inexpressibly gloomy."[12] Daily ordinary actions of reading, washing his hands, and conversations with acquaintances seemed futile and burdensome.[13]

He later revealed that "I was also troubled with palpitations and pain about the heart, and like many a young ignorant man, especially one with a smattering of medical knowledge, was convinced that I had heart disease. I did not consult any doctor, as I fully expected to hear the verdict that I was not fit for the voyage, and I was resolved to go at all hazards."[14] His cardiac palpitations (perhaps experienced for the first time) were probably a psychophysiologic symptom caused by his *Beagle* anxieties. These palpitations—ordinarily fearsome by their very nature—then caused him a succession of new fears: that he had heart disease; that this would interdict his going on the *Beagle*; and that, therefore, he must conceal his palpitations from doctors and everyone, including (probably) his father. There is no mention of palpitations in his letters or *Beagle* diary. His new apprehensions may have intensified his palpitations.

On 27 December 1831 the *Beagle* sailed from Plymouth and across the North Atlantic, and by 5 January 1832 Darwin's symptoms of depression, and probably his cardiac palpitations, had ceased.[15] Over the next (almost) five years, as the *Beagle* voyaged to different places,

Darwin overcame—or attenuated—most of his pre-voyage misgivings, was usually interested and enthusiastic in what he saw, and
worked hard in all branches of natural history, especially geology. He
always had feelings of homesickness, but these were never as severe
and protracted as he had feared. He was happy when he heard from
his sisters that his father approved of what he was doing. He
developed warm friendships toward his *Beagle* shipmates, and his
cramped ship quarters forced him to develop "methodical habits of
working."[16]

Aboard the *Beagle* he suffered from seasickness, which caused him
"excessive" misery,[17] and which worsened toward the end of the
voyage.[18] Whether this sickness was related to his tendency to suffer a
psychically upset stomach cannot be determined. He first treated his
seasickness by a diet of biscuits and raisins (the latter prescribed by his
father),[19] and by eating unspecified amounts of a very hot mixture of
"Sago,[20] with wine & spice."[21] Later he may have taken, separately or
in different combinations, peppermint, hops, carbonate of soda,
laudanum, and lavender water.[22] The treatment that he found "the
only sure thing,"[23] and used constantly, was to lie in the horizontal
position, preferably in a hammock. His shipmate, John Lort Stokes,
recollected how Darwin would work for about an hour at a table in
the poop cabin of the *Beagle*; then he woud say to Stokes, "Old
fellow, I must take the horizontal for it," and he would stretch out on
one side of the table for a time. He would then resume his labors, and
after a while again have to lie down.[24] Referring to this treatment he
wrote: "It must never be forgotten the more you combat the enemy
the sooner he will yield."[25] With this treatment he was able to
accomplish a good deal of work while at sea.

During his sojourns in different lands he displayed physical courage
and physical endurance, and his health was robust, except for the
following episodes of infectious and febrile illness. During his
February to July 1832 stay in Brazil he had severe inflammations of his
knee, and then of his arm, each of which lasted about one week and
then cleared.[26] He observed that "any small prick is very apt to
become in this country a painful boil."[27] On 11 April 1832, while
journeying through a Brazilian forest, he began "to feel feverish,
shivering. and sickness—much exhausted: could eat nothing...."[28]
"Sickness" probably refers to vomiting. He stayed for the night in a
Brazilian country house, feeling sick and fearful of more sickness. "It
did not require much imagination," he wrote, "to paint the horrors of
illness in a foreign country, without being able to speak one word or

obtain any medical aid."[29] In the morning he treated himself by "eating cinnamon & drinking port wine."[30] He then reported that this "cured me in a wonderful manner."[31] He noted that in the Brazilian house there was "dreadful ... difficulty in procuring surgical aid," but "plenty of ... medicines." His choice of medicines for his fever may have been influenced by his father, who prescribed port wine for fevers in children, and cinnamon teas as a daily drink.[32]

After he returned to Rio de Janeiro he walked to the Botanic Garden and studied the "trees" of camphor, sago, cinnamon, tea, cloves, and pepper. He was interested in these plants because of their medicinal use—what he called their "notorious ... utility"—and he smelled and tasted some of their leaves.[33]

On 6 June 1832, he wrote his family in Shrewsbury some "calamitous" news. "A large party of our officers and two sailors before leaving Rio, went a party in the Cutter for snipe shooting up the bay. Most of them were slightly attacked with fever: but the two men and poor little Musters[34] were seized violently and died in a few days.... What numbers snipe shooting has killed and how rapidly they drop off."[35] Before receiving this news he had "very nearly" joined another snipe-shooting party: "My good star," he commented, "presided over me when I failed."[36] For the next sixteen months he remained free of illness.

On 2 October 1833, while horseback riding from Buenos Ayres to Santa Fe in Argentina, he began to feel "very weak from great heat,"[37] and "unwell and feverish, from having exerted myself too much in the sun."[38] This may have been a heat stroke.[39] He reached Santa Fe on 3 October, feeling "very unwell"[40] and with a "headache";[41] he got himself into a house and a bed there. He later recollected how he was cared for by "a goodnatured old woman," who wanted to treat him by placing an orange leaf or a bit of black plaster to each of his temples, and/or by splitting a bean into halves and placing one on each temple.[42] "Many of the remedies used by the people of the country are ludicrously strange, but too disgusting to be mentioned. One of the least nasty is to kill and cut open two puppies and bind them on each side of a broken limb. Little hairless dogs are in great request to sleep at the feet of invalids."[43] On 5 October he was well enough to move out of his Santa Fe house and bed. Then, "not being quite well"[44] and "unable to ride" a horse,[45] he returned to Buenos Ayres in a small boat.

On 16 November 1833, while in Montevideo, Uruguay, he felt "not ... quite well"[46] and "stomach disordered,"[47] and he stayed for a day in a house. The following day he had no complaints and was able to travel.

On 11 January 1834, the *Beagle* anchored at Port Saint Julien, in Southern Argentina, and Darwin, FitzRoy, and a group from the *Beagle* went on a walk into the interior country. The day was very hot, the group became "excessively tired"—several collapsed and were unable to walk—and suffered "a most painful degree of thirst." After some hours they were able to obtain some water and returned to the *Beagle*. During this time Darwin showed more endurance and was able to be more physically active than the others; he was one of the first to reach the *Beagle*'s boat, and reported that he felt "not much tired." However, for the next two days he was "very feverish in bed"; this was in contrast to the other members of the *Beagle* group who suffered no ill aftereffects.[48] This may have been another episode of heat stroke. By the third day he felt well and "went out walking."[49]

In September 1834, while visiting a gold mine in Chile, he drank some Chichi wine. "This half poisoned me," he wrote his father and sisters, and "I staid till I thought I was well; but my first day's ride, which was a long one, again disordered my stomach & afterwards I could not get well; I quite lost my appetite & became very weak. I had a long distance to travel & I suffered very much."[50] He became so exhausted that he was unable to ride his horse, and had to hire a carriage to carry him back to the Chilean port of Valparaiso, where the *Beagle* was.[51] At Valparaiso he was cared for in the home of Mr. Richard Corfield—an Englishman who had lived in Shrewsbury—and he was seen by Mr. Benjamin Bynoe, the *Beagle*'s surgeon, who treated him with rest and "a good deal of Calomel."[52] Calomel was then a much used medication, prescribed by Dr. Robert Darwin for some fevers,[53] and in 1833 Darwin had made a note to buy "medicine, Calomel."[54] Darwin's illness lasted about a month, disturbed "every secretion of his body," and then waned, and was never diagnosed.[55] Early in November 1834 he felt "quite well again,"[56] and rejoined the *Beagle* while it cruised along the Chilean coast. Then on 10 March 1835, while the *Beagle* was preparing to stop at Valparaiso, he wrote Caroline: "I am very glad of this spell on shore; my stomach, partly from sea-sickness & partly from my illness at Valparaiso, is not very strong. I expect some good rides will make another man of me."[57] He then went on strenuous excursions to the Andes and the interior of Chile; and (aside from seasickness) he made no further complaints about his stomach for the rest of the *Beagle* voyage.

When Dr. Robert Darwin, living with his three daughters—

Catherine, Caroline, and Susan—in his home in Shrewsbury, read Darwin's letter describing the latter's Chilean illness (the letter written at Valparaiso on 13 October 1834 reached Shrewsbury about 21 January 1835), he became so disturbed at thinking of his son being "ill & forlorn" that his daughters, for a time, could "hardly" speak about the letter to him.[58] Then Catherine Darwin, on 28 January 1835, wrote her brother a letter which expressed the affection and concern which Darwin's family felt for him.

> I cannot tell you how sorry we were to hear that you have been ill, my dear Charley. It must have been so trying for you being ill when you were on an Expedition, and I am sure you must have suffered very much by forcing yourself to travel on, while so unfit for it. We are in hopes of hearing from you soon again, as we are doubly anxious to hear of you now. Papa charges me to give you a message from him; he wishes to urge you to think of leaving the *Beagle*, and returning home, and to take warning by this one serious illness; Papa says that if once your health begins to fail, you will doubly feel the effect of any unhealthy climate, and he is very uneasy about you, and very much afraid of the fevers you are liable to incur in those Countries. Papa is *very much in earnest*, and desires me to beg you to recollect that it will soon be four years since you left us, which surely is a long portion of your life to give up to Natural History. If you wait till the *Beagle* returns home, it will be as many years again; the time of its voyage goes on lengthening & lengthening every time we hear of it; we are quite in despair about it. —Do think of what Papa says, my dear Charles; his advice is *always* so sensible in the long run, and do be wise in time & come away before your health is ruined; if you once lose that, you will never recover it again entirely. —I wish it was possible that anything we can say may have some effect on you; do not be entirely guided by those you are with, who of course, wish to keep you, & will do their utmost to that end, but do think in earnest of Papa's strong advice & opinion.[59]

Susan and Caroline then each wrote Darwin letters in which they, also, urged him to return home.[60]

Darwin received his sisters' letters in Lima, Peru, in July 1835. In his letter of reply, after informing his sisters that "in a short time we sail for the Galapagos," he wrote: "I am both pleased and grieved at all your affectionate messages, wishing me to return home. —If you think I do not long to see you again, you are indeed spurring a willing horse; but you can enter into my feelings of deep mortification if any cause even ill-health should have compelled me to have left the *Beagle*. I say should have, because you will agree with me, that it is hardly worth while now to think of any such step."[61]

Fifteen months later, on 4 October 1836, he returned to his home in Shrewsbury. His sister Caroline found him "looking very thin but well," and full of "affection and delight" at being reunited with her and his family.[62]

3

The Beginning of Chronic Illness

During the first nine months of his return to England, Darwin moved to lodgings in London, studied his *Beagle* collections, wrote most of his *Beagle* travel narrative, and gave some papers to the Geological and Zoological societies. He announced his theory of coral atoll formation, which seems to have been generally accepted. He told his friend Fox: "I have plenty of work for the next year or two, and till that is finished I will have no holidays."[1] He made no complaints about his health,[2] and he gained almost sixteen pounds in weight.[3]

Over the next twelve months he continued to work at writing up his *Beagle* geological and zoological observations. He also began to secretly write some evolutionary notebooks. During these months he began complaining of illness.

His earliest recorded complaint was in a 20 September 1837 letter to his old Cambridge teacher, Professor Henslow: "I have not been very well of late with an uncomfortable palpitation of the heart, and my doctors urge me *strongly* to knock off all work & go and live in the country for a few weeks."[4] "My doctors" probably refers to two socially and medically prominent London physicians: his previously mentioned relative, Dr. Henry Holland, and Dr. James Clark[5]—who was well regarded by Holland—and who in 1837 had been made physician in ordinary to Queen Victoria. On 14 October, in another letter to Henslow, Darwin gave ill health as one of his reasons for refusing the secretaryship of the Geological Society: "My last objection is that I doubt how far my health will stand the confinement of what I have to do without any additional work. I merely repeat, that you may know that I am not speaking idly, that when I consulted Dr. Clark in town, he at first urged me to give up entirely all writing, and even correcting press for some weeks. Of late, anything which flurries me completely knocks me up afterwards and brings on violent palpitation of the heart. Now the Secretaryship would be a periodical source of more annoying trouble to me, than all the rest of the fortnight put together."[6]

Sometime in May 1838 he wrote his sister Caroline: "I hope I may be able to work on right hard during the next three years, otherwise I shall never have finished.—but I find the noodle & the stomach are antagonistic powers, and that it is a great deal more easy to think too much in a day than to think too little—what thought has to do with disgesting roast beef, I cannot say, but they are brother faculties."[7] On 15 June he informed Fox: "I have not been very well of late, which has suddenly determined me to leave London earlier than I had antici-pated."[8] He then went, for several weeks, on a geological trip to Scotland.

In July 1838 he wrote in one of his evolutionary notebooks: "Now that I have a test of hardness of thought, from weakness of my stomach I observe a long castle in the air, is as hard work (abstracting it being done in open air with exercise etc, [not] no organs of sense being required) as the closest train of geological thought."[9] By "long castle in the air" he meant his imaginings. In the same notebook he recorded how he experienced different disturbed feelings. "Fear must be simple instinctive feeling: I have awakened in the night being slightly unwell & felt so much afraid though my reason was laughing & told me there was nothing, & tried to seize hold of objects to be frightened at—(again diseases of the heart are accompanied by much involuntary fear)   In these cases probably the system is affected, & by *habit* the mind tries to fix upon some object."[10] "Much involuntary fear" may describe his reaction to his cardiac palpitations. His nocturnal "slightly unwell" may refer to an upset stomach. After noting that "confession of error" did not produce mental relief,[11] he noted how angry feelings—which he may have experienced at the time—influenced body actions. "When a man is in a passion he puts himself still, & walks hard. (He cannot avoid sending will of actions to muscles any more than prevent heart beat.) remember how Pincher does just the same. I noticed this by perceiving myself skipping when wanting not to feel angry—Such efforts prevent anger, but observing eyes thus unconsciously discover struggle of feeling. It is as much effort to walk then lightly as to endeavor to stop heart beating: on ceasing, so does other."[12]

In August 1838 he observed how, as he sat in the library at the Athenaeum Club and read a review of Auguste Comte's *Philosophy*, his reading caused him to "remember, & to think deeply," and to become "very much struck with an intense headache." And how, after reading Charles Dickens' *Sketches by Boz*, "my head got well."[13]

This September 1837 to August 1838 year of "I have not been very well"—of disturbed feelings, and physical symptoms of "uncomfortable" and "violent" cardiac palpitations, gastric upsets, and headaches —was the beginning of the illness which would persist for most of Darwin's life. Darwin thought that this onset of illness was caused by mental pressures, especially the pressures of his scientific work: "the noodle & the stomach are antagonistic powers"; a "test of hardness of thought" was felt as "weakness of my stomach"; "My doctors urge me strongly to knock off all work." Darwin, however, does not indicate what work caused him the greatest pressure. Some work did not upset his health. Previously, for five years on the *Beagle* cruise and for nine months afterward, he had performed hard mental work and (except for seasickness and infections) had no serious illness. It seems likely that, during this year of illness, the scientific work which caused Darwin the most pressures—and hence caused most of his illness— was his secret work on evolution.

From July 1837 to September 1838 he had written four evolutionary notebooks: three notebooks on *Transmutation of Species*; and *M Notebook*, which studied the inheritance of mental and physical traits and diseases in humans. In his first *Transmutation Notebook* (written July 1837 to February 1838) he discussed his theory of evolution— what he called "My theory." He had probably first thought of this theory in the spring of 1837; it was based, mainly, on his *Beagle* observations of the relation between fossil and living South American animals, and the geographical distribution of closely related organic species in South America and on the Galapagos Islands. It held that a physically isolated population, left to itself, would gradually evolve new species.[14] In his first *Transmutation Notebook* he noted how "My theory" explained some facts, and could not explain other facts. He was especially troubled by being unable to ascertain the means by which particular species could cross oceans and settle the lands they now occupy.[15] It was important that he ascertain these means of species transport because his theory postulated that certain species had not been created in the lands they now occupy, but had migrated there, after evolving from parent species in other lands. Because of these and other difficulties—while persisting in his belief in evolution— toward the end of his first *Transmutation Notebook* he put "My theory" aside. In his second, and most of his third *Transmutation Notebook* (written February to September 1838), he considered the

variform facts of species life and death, reproduction, extinction, and geographical distribution; and he searched, vainly, for "*causes* of changes"[16]—causes of evolution.

He had, probably, begun his evolutionary speculations not because he wanted to be a revolutionary and overthrow the existing concept that species were immutable (although he would eventually revolutionize thinking), but because of a simple curiosity to know about the "why" of species life and death,[17] and because of an altruistic desire to add to and "give zest to" areas of thought.[18] Very soon, however, he began to find that thinking about the possibilities of evolution caused him to experience several kinds of psychic stresses. There was the strain of the sustained intellectual discipline needed to reason from diverse facts. Early in his second *Transmutation Notebook*, referring to his search for plausible causes of evolution, he wrote: "This multiplication of little means & bringing the mind to grapple with great effect is a most laborious & painful effort of the mind (although this may appear an absurd saying) & will never be conquered by anyone (if he has any kind of prejudices) who just takes up & lays down the subject without long meditation.—His best chance is to have [pondered] profoundly over the enormous difficulty of reproduction of species & certainly of destruction; then he will choose & firmly believe in his new faith of the lesser of the difficulties."[19]

At this time evolutionary ideas were generally regarded as implausible, and were sometimes further regarded as immoral and irreligious. Darwin had read how the French naturalist Buffon had been forced to recant his theory about the history of the earth because it had been judged to contradict Scripture; he had witnessed how a member of the Edinburgh Plinian Society had expressed materialist ideas about the nature of organisms and the mind, and then had these ideas suppressed by the Society.[20] Less than a year after he had begun his evolutionary speculations, in his second *Transmutation Notebook*, Darwin wrote: "Mention persecution of early Astronomers,— then add chief good of individual scientific men is to push their science a few years in advance only of their age, (differently from literary men,) must remember that if they *believe* & do not openly avow their belief they do as much to retard as those whose opinion they believe have endeavoured to advance cause of truth."[21] In the same notebook he went on to write: "I fear great evil from vast opposition in opinion on all subjects of classification, I must work out hypothesis & compare it with results: if I acted otherwise my premises would be disputed."[22] The "vast opposition" included not only prevailing general opinion, but all of his old and new scientific friends and acquaintances: the anatomist Owen; the ornithologist Gould; the zoologists Waterhouse, Jenyns, and Blyth; the botanist Henslow; the amateur naturalist Fox; and the geologist Lyell. He frequently met and corresponded with most of these men; they supplied him with the scientific facts for his evolutionary speculations, and he respected them for their knowledge (he knew that some knew more in their respective fields than he did) and for being honorable men. His father had taught him never to become a friend of a man he did not respect.[23] And yet he knew that all these men disbelieved in evolution, and he felt their disbelief as a "great evil."

In a 30 July 1837 letter to his esteemed friend Lyell, Darwin commented on the relation between South American fossils and living South American animals, and on the different species of Galapagos Island birds.[24] He seems to have wanted to discuss these observations—which had caused him to believe in evolution—with Lyell. He may also, during the winter of 1837–39, have disclosed his evolutionary belief to Lyell.[25] Lyell's books had influenced his thinking in geology and natural history, and he felt that in searching for a cause for evolution he was "following the example of Lyell in Geology."[26] We do not possess Lyell's reply to the 30 July letter, and we do not know what he said to Darwin about evolution. We may, however, surmise that Lyell articulated his disbelief in evolution; and that he warned Darwin that evolutionary ideas would encounter great opposition.

In writing his official *Beagle* narrative, *Journal of Researches* (mostly written in 1837, though not published until 1839), Darwin presented hints and evidences of evolution and then refrained from discussing evolutionary views. And after 1837–38, for years, he seems to have concealed his evolutionary views from all of his friends and acquaintances.

Thus, knowing Darwin's tendency to react to psychic stress by developing psychophysiologic symptoms of cardiac palpitations and gastric upsets, it seems likely that the beginnings of his illness were caused by the psychic stress of his thinking evolutionary thoughts. By the mental "pain" that he experienced when he searched for a plausible cause of evolution, and his "difficulty" in finding this cause. By his "fear" of being criticized by prevailing opinion, and—especially—the "great evil" of being criticized by scientific men whom he respected. His illness, which he first complained of on 20 September 1837—"I have not been very well of late"—may have actually begun in July 1837 when, in his first *Transmutation Notebook*, he first committed his evolutionary ideas to writing. In his *Journal*, where he listed the important events of his life for 1838, his first two references to his illness occur in the context of his work on species: "May 1st Unwell, working at Geolog: as named and 'species'." "June (Beginning). Preparing 1st part of Birds. St Jago Geology some little species theory, & lost very much time by being unwell."[27]

It is not clear how much of his working time was lost by illness. His overall work capacity does not seem to have been seriously impaired. In 1837–38, in some notes in which he speculated on his future prospects of work and marriage, he made two prescient observations about his health: First, "It is very bad for one's health to work too much." Then marriage, although it would mean *"terrible loss"* of working time, would also offer: "Children—(if it please God)—constant companion (friend in old age) who will feel interested in one, object to be beloved and played with—better than a dog anyhow—Home, and someone to take care of house—Charms of music and female chit-chat. *These things good for one's health.*"[28] Soon he would choose a wife who would possess, as one of her virtues, being "good" for his health.

Around the end of September and early October 1838, in the last sections of his third *Transmutation Notebook*, Darwin discovered, in the War of Nature, the creative force for evolution he had been searching for. He saw that, in the course of the war waged between organic forms, "those forms slightly favoured" would get "the upper hand" and form new species.[29] He would, later, call this view his theory of natural selection.

On 11 November 1838, he became engaged to his cousin Emma Wedgwood. Then, for several months, he stayed in London and she in her country home of Maer, and they exchanged letters.

She early wrote him about her concern for his health. "Tell me how you are. I do not like your looking so unwell & being so overtired when *I* come & look after you I shall scold you into health like Lady Cath. de Burgh used to do to the poor people."[30] As the weeks passed he noted that he "wasted some time by being unwell,"[31] and her apprehension about his health grew. She then wrote him less humorously and at greater length:

> You have looked so unwell for some times that I am afraid you will
> be laid up if you fight against it any longer. Do let off to Shrews-
> bury & get some doctoring & then come here & be idle. . . . I am
> sure it must be very disagreeable & painful to you to feel so often
> cut off from the power of doing your work & I want you to cast out

of your mind all anxiety about me on that point & to feel sure that
nothing could make me so happy as to feel that I could be of any
use or comfort to my own dear Charley when he is not well. If you
knew how I long to be with you when you are not well! You must
not think that I expect a holiday husband to be always making himself agreeable to me & if that is all the 'work' that I shall have it will
not be much for me to bear whatever it may be for you. So don't be
ill any more my dear Charley till I can be with you to nurse you &
save you from bothers.[32]

She would never waver in her desire to be his "nurse" and comforter.

Three days before their marriage he wrote her: "My two last days in
London, when I wanted to have most leisure, were rendered very
uncomfortable by a bad headache, which continued two days and two
nights, so that I doubted whether it ever meant to go and allow me to
be married."[33] This was one of his most protracted and severe
headaches.

On 29 January 1839, he and Emma married and moved into a new
London home. In February they gave some dinner parties, visited with
friends—one visitor commented that few couples seemed happier[34]—
and went to the theater and concerts. He began learning German,
worked on geological subjects—a paper on earthquakes and a book
on his theory of coral atoll formation—and did "a little work on
Species."[35]

His illness then worsened, continued worse for over three years,
and altered and dominated his life.

4

Worsening Illness

On Friday, 15 March, Emma wrote one of her sisters, "My Charles[1]
Has been very unwell since Sunday. We went to church at King's
College, and found the church not warmed, and not more than
half-a-dozen people in it, and he was so very cold that I believe it was
that which has made him so unwell."[2]

In April and May 1839 Darwin visited his Wedgwood relatives at
Maer and his father and sisters at Shrewsbury, and was "unwell
almost the whole time."[3] At Shrewsbury he received some "doctoring"
of an undetermined nature from his father which first made him feel
better.[4] In August and September he again visited Maer and Shrewsbury, and then returned to London and wrote in his *Journal*: "During

my visit to Maer, read a little, was much unwell, & scandalously idle.
I have derived this much good that *nothing* is so intolerable as
idleness."[5] In October 1839, in a letter to Fox, he described his past
and present state of health: "I had fully intended, when at Maer to
have paid you the morning visit I talked of, but during my whole visit
in the country I was so languid & uncomfortable that I had but one
wish & that was to remain perfectly quiet & see no one.—I scarcely
even enjoyed my visit to Shrewsbury.—I have been much brisker
since my return to London, & I ["I" written over "am"] am now
getting on steady, though very slowly with my work, & hope in a
couple of months to have a very thin volume 8vo on Coral Formations
published.... We [he and Emma] are living a life of extreme
quietness . . . we have given up all parties, for they agree with neither
of us. . . ." He concluded: "My dear Fox, excuse this letter—I am very
old and stupid."[6]

On 7 February 1840, Emma wrote her aunt that her husband "had
certainly been worse for the last six weeks, and has been pretty
constantly in a state of languor that is very distressing, and his being
obliged to be idle is very painful to him."[7] Darwin consulted Dr.
Henry Holland, and reported that the latter "thinks he has found out
what is the matter with me, and now hopes he shall be able to set me
going again."[8] Dr. Holland's treatments (the nature of which is
unknown) were ineffective, and Darwin seems to have stopped
consulting Holland for many years.[9]

On 10 February Emma again wrote to her aunt: "It is a great
happiness to me when Charles is most unwell that he continues just as
sociable as ever, and is not like the rest of the Darwins, who will not
say how they really are; but he always tells me how he feels and never
wants to be alone, but continues just as warmly affectionate as ever,
so that I feel I am a comfort to him. And to you I may say that he is
the most affectionate person possible."[10] Emma would devotedly
nurse her husband for the rest of his life, and he would find great
comfort in her nursing.

In July 1840 Darwin reported to Fox:

And now for myself, about whom I can now give a very good account.—I have during the last six weeks been gradually, though
very slowly, gaining strength & health, but prior to that time I
["have been" crossed out] was for nearly six months in very indifferent health, so that I felt the smallest exertion most irksome. This
is the reason I have been so long without writing. I had no spirits to
do anything. I have scarcely put pen to paper for the last half year

& everything ["in the publishing line" inserted] is going backwards.
I have been much mortified at this, but there is no help but patience.—My Father, who has certainly in a quite unexpected degree
put me on the course in getting well (having put a stop to periodical
vomiting to which I was subject) feels pretty sure that I shall before
long get quite well.—At present I only want vigour—in ["saying"
crossed out] wanting which, however, one wants almost all which
makes life endurable.

He goes on to write: "I am determined to obey implicitly my Father &
remain absolutely quiet."[11] Whereas Darwin's references to feelings of
depression are frequent, this is his only reference to the symptom of
"periodical vomiting." How his father successfully treated his vomiting
is unknown. From this time on, for almost a decade, he seems to have
relied mainly on his father for medical advice.

   In November 1840 his father directed that he take a prescription
containing logwood, cinnamon, and potassium bicarbonate.[12] All of
these medicines were used in gastrointestinal disorders: logwood for
diarrhea and to improve the tone of the colonic musculature; cinnamon to improve appetite and digestion, and relieve flatulence;
potassium bicarbonate as an alkali to counter the acidity which was
thought to be the cause of some gastrointestinal disease. Darwin may
have taken this prescription for his upset stomach; also for diarrhea,
although there is no definite evidence that he ever had severe lower
bowel disease. It is not known how frequently, or for how long, he
took it. He may have tried other medicines, although there is no
mention of medicines in his extant letters.

   Early in 1841 he told Fox: "My strength is gradually, with a good
many oscillations, increasing; so that I have been able to work an
hour or two several days in the week. . . . I am forced to live,
however, very quietly and am able to see scarcely anybody & cannot
even talk long with my nearest relations. I was at one time in despair
& expected to pass my whole life as a miserable useless, valetudinarian
but I have now better hopes of myself."[13] His "better hopes" then
dimmed, for in June 1841, during a visit to Shrewsbury, he wrote
Lyell: "My father scarcely seems to expect that I shall become strong
for some years; it has been a bitter mortification for me to digest the
conclusion that the 'race is for the strong,' and that I shall probably do
little more but be content to admire the strides others make in
science."[14] Dr. Darwin thus seems to have reversed his July 1840
positive prognosis that his son would "before long get quite well."
Darwin thought that his father could "predict with remarkable skill

the course of any illness":[15] to now hear from his father that he was doomed in his future work efforts was, probably, the greatest despair he could feel.

Darwin next mentioned his health in a September 1841 letter to Fox: "For myself I have steadily been gaining ground & really believe now I shall some day be quite strong—I write daily for a couple of hours on my Coral Volume & take a little walk or ride every day—I grow very tired in the evenings & am not able to go ["Out" inserted] at that time or hardly receive my nearest relatives—but my life ceases to be bothersome, now that I can do something."[16] Several days later, in another letter to Fox, he wrote: "But I am grown a dull old spiritless dog to what I used to be.—One gets stupider as one grows older I think."[17] Thus the man who had once been gregarious with his peers, and omnivorous of life, now withdrew from most people; and denigrated himself as "old," "spiritless," and "stupid."

Early in May 1842 Darwin wrote Emma (then visiting Maer) about finally finishing and publishing his coral book, and about the impact of his illness on his work:

> On Saturday I went in the City and did a deal of printing business. I came back gloomy and tired; the government money has gone much quicker than I thought, and the expenses of the Coral volume are greater, being from £130 to £140. I am be-blue-deviled. I am daily growing very old, very very cold and I daresay very sly.[18] I will give you statistics of time spent on my Coral volume, *not* including all the work on board the *Beagle*. I commenced it 3 years and 7 months ago, and have done scarcely anything besides. I have actually spent 20 months out of this period on it! and nearly all the remainder sickness and visiting!!!.... Yesterday I went at 2 o'clock and [had] an hour's hard talk with Horner on affairs of Geolog. Soc., and it quite knocked me up,[19] and this makes my letter rather blue in its early stages.[20]

In his *Journal* he noted that much of his working time had been "lost by illness."[21] However, publishing his coral book—which, he noted, "was thought highly of by scientific men"[22]—may have also given him the feeling of progressing in his work; this positive feeling may have then stimulated him to write out—in May–June 1842—the first short and rough "pencil sketch" of his evolutionary theory.[23]

In June 1842, feeling physically "stronger than I had been for some time," he made a ten-day trip through North Wales, climbing steep mountains and walking long distances "for the sake of observing the effects of the old glaciers which formerly filled all the larger valleys."

After this trip he again complained of the debilitating effects of his illness.[24] And the man who was only thirty-three years old—and who had once enjoyed vigorous physical activity—became (for most of the time) only able to take small walks.

In his *Autobiography* Darwin summarized the 1839–42 period of his illness as follows: "During the three years and eight months whilst we [he and Emma] resided in London, I did less scientific work, though I worked as hard as I possibly could, than during any other equal length of time in my life. This was owing to frequently recurring unwellness and to one long and serious illness."[25] This "long and serious illness" may refer to his "periodic vomiting," which occurred mainly in the first half of 1840, and which his father assuaged.

What caused his illness to exacerbate? The cause which seems most likely is that he was confronted with anxieties which were deeper and more numerous than his previous anxieties.

He confronted, first of all, certain repercussions from his theory of natural selection. He later commented that in natural selection he "had at last got a theory by which to work."[26] He meant that he had a theory which he believed was plausible—more plausible than previous evolutionary theories—and which through hard work could be proven. For Darwin the future prospects of working on, and proving, his theory held several very positive and personal meanings. He would develop his talents for collecting scientific facts, and for scientific speculation. He would "uphold," "under a different form," the evolutionary ideas of his grandfather.[27] Proving his theory would require a good part of his working life, would become his professional identity and primary claim to fame among scientific men.

Believing in his theory also posed difficulties. Several days after discovering natural selection he observed: "The difficulty of multiplying effects & to conceive the results with that clearness of conviction, absolutely necessary as the basal foundation stone of further inductive reasoning is immense."[28] Despite his theory, and his "immense" mental efforts, there were many important unexplained facts about species. He still could not, for instance, elucidate the means of ocean migration that resulted in the geographical distribution of particular species.

His doubts about the general truth of natural selection were then, probably, accentuated because of his doubts about his geological theory of Glen Roy. In February 1839 he had published an article which held that the parallel roads of Glen Roy (a geological site in Scotland) had been formed by the subsiding ocean.[29] Less than two years later, Louis Agassiz, the Swiss naturalist, came to England and proclaimed that there had been an Ice Age—the existence of an Ice Age was then unknown—in which glacial lakes had formed the parallel roads.[30] Darwin soon came to believe in the reality of an Ice Age, and although he persisted in upholding his Glen Roy ocean theory, he also "to some extent doubted" this.[31] His doubt made him feel exposed to geologists as the originator of a questionable discovery. He then probably reasoned that if a new, hitherto unknown, phenomenon could shake his Glen Roy theory, a similar fate could overtake natural selection.[32]

Although he hoped eventually to convince others to believe in his species ideas, he went on concealing these ideas from everyone. He was not only afraid of being wrong and of being against prevailing thinking; he was especially fearful that natural selection contained aspects which, in the prevailing morality, could and would be regarded as reprehensible. Natural selection relied on secondary, natural causes, rather than on God, for the creation of new species. When he thought of this Darwin did not mean to be antireligious, and he believed in a "Creator" who was distant from species.[33] However, he must have felt that such a belief would not be countenanced by the Church, a large section of the public, and by his religious friends— Henslow, Fox, Adam Sedgwick (all ordained ministers), and FitzRoy. Was he thinking about being attacked for the irreligious nature of his theory on Sunday, 9 March 1839, when he and Emma attended services in the church at King's College, and he felt "so very cold" and "so unwell"?

Emma was deeply religious and "distressed" that her husband did not share her faith.[34] Darwin knew this and it pained him.[35] Religious differences, however, did not alter the feelings of devotion that he and Emma felt for each other: his need to be cared for by her and her selfless desire to give him this care.

A main force of natural selection was the War of Nature. To understand Darwin's attitude toward this war we must first note how, during the *Beagle* cruise, when he was in a tropical forest—where diverse animals and plants lived crowded close together and "where," he wrote, "the powers of life are predominant"—he felt like a blind man who first saw, and he experienced a confusion of uplifting feelings.[36] Sorting these out, he then wrote in his pocket notebook: "Sublime devotion the prevalent feeling."[37] Thinking of a tropical forest he could think about nature simply and happily; he did not have to worry about convincing himself and others of a particular theory. When he returned home he was able to experience similar feelings for an English forest. "In the whole world," he had told Fox in August 1837, "there cannot be anything more delightful than a wooded country in England during the Autumn."[38] Then on 12 March 1839, four months after discovering natural selection, he wrote in his fourth *Transmutation Notebook*: "It is difficult to believe in the dreadful but quiet war of organic beings going on [in] the peaceful woods & smiling fields."[39] What he found "difficult" was to collate his new insight that a forest contained the War of Nature—a "dreadful" war because it caused the massive death of ill-adapted species—with his previous feelings of "sublime devotion" and "delight" for a forest. Most of the time he would manage this difficulty by avoiding thinking about the dreadful side of the war and thinking about its positive side: how it acted as a pressure force which, in selecting out better-adapted species, performed the "exalted object" of producing "higher animals."[40] Sometimes, when looking at beautiful wooded scenery, he was able to put all thoughts of the origin of species out of his mind; he was then able to again feel some of his previous feelings of "delight." Then there were moments—some of these will be described —when he would see the dreadful side of the war: when he suffered from seeing too much, and from thinking of how others would dispute and reprobate him for what he was seeing. It was, perhaps, because of these moments of involvement with evil that his value for many positive things diminished. That he, who had once felt like a blind man first seeing, came to feel "like a man who has become colour-blind."[41] This may refer not only to his diminished feelings for scenery, but to his loss of positive feelings for such different "colours" of life as poetry, the plays of Shakespeare, music, and pictures. He felt these losses as "a loss of happiness," and as, perhaps, "enfeebling the emotional part of our nature."[42]

He also had marital anxieties. Before his marriage, in 1837–39, he had feared that the demands of a wife would mean *"terrible loss of time"*—his working time which he regarded as precious. After his marriage, although he developed affectionate feelings for his wife and children—he had a son in December 1839 and a daughter in March 1841—he may have experienced moments when he felt that the demands of his family were interfering with his scientific work, and especially interfering with the great work demands of natural selection. In letters to his hardworking scientific friends he would later write: "I hope that your marriage will not make you idle: happiness, I fear, is not good for work."[43] "Children are one's greatest happiness, but often & often a still greater misery. A man of science ought to have none,—perhaps not a wife; for then there would be nothing in this wide world worth caring for & a man might (whether he would is another question) work away like a Trojan."[44]

When Emma was pregnant he wrote mainly about her discomfort, and did not express happy anticipatory feelings about having a new child; the process of a birth deeply upset him. In July 1840, seven months after Emma was delivered of her first child, he wrote Fox: "What an awful affair a confinement is; it knocked me up almost as much as it did Emma herself."[45] Early in 1841 he wrote Fox: "Emma expects to be confined in March—a period I most dearly wish over."[46] One reason he may have been upset over Emma's pregnancies and births was because they curtailed her caring for him.

So, in 1839–42, as Darwin began raising a family and entering upon his identity as the discoverer of a new theory of evolution, he developed different anxieties: about his theory; about his family; and about the conflict between his family and his work. Each of these anxieties was deep, painful, and unresolvable (at least in the near future), and the accumulation of all probably exacerbated his illness.

In 1841, in a letter to Fox, he added the following postscript: "If you attend at all to Nat. Hist. I send you this P.S. as a memento, that I continue to collect all kinds of facts about 'Varieties & Species' for my some-day work to be so entitled—the smallest contributions thankfully accepted—descriptions of ["offspring of" inserted] all crosses between all domestic birds & animals ["dogs, cats, &c &c" inserted] very valuable."[47] He was casually, yet firmly, declaring that despite anxieties and physical illness, he was determined to go on collecting facts which would develop his theory of natural selection. He would recollect that, at this time, he could "sometimes" collect "facts bearing on the origin of species . . . when I could do nothing else from illness."[48]

Thus, more and more, his theory became his vocation and an integral part of his everyday life.

5

The Move to Down

In July 1840, Darwin wrote Fox that he and Emma desired to live in the country: "I think we shall never be able to stick all our lives in

London: & our present castle in the air is to live near a station in
Surrey about 20 miles from Town."[1] He regarded London as "a vile
smoky place, where a man loses a great part of the best enjoyments in
life";[2] and as a "great Wen,"[3] full of "dirt, noise vice & misery."[4] He
thought that attending London's social events and scientific meetings,
and being exposed to its air, was bad for his health.[5] In the country
there would be the pleasure of country walks—he had missed these
"very much" in London[6]—and the beneficial effects of social isolation
and "pure air."[7]

His belief in the badness of London and the goodness of the country
had been stimulated by several individuals. Doctors Holland and
Clark, who had previously urged him to live in the country, both held
this belief.[8] Doctor Clark had stated that a change from city to
country ameliorated many diseases, including "dyspepsia and various
nervous disorders";[9] and that London's air was a "destructive malady
. . . justly termed *Cachexia Londinensis* which preys upon the vitals
and stamps its hues upon the countenance of almost every permanent
resident in this large city."[10] (This reflected the prevailing idea that
many diseases were caused by miasmas in the air arising from
decaying organic matter—especially from decaying human excrement
in London's sewers.[11]) Emma, who had an "inclination" for living in
the country,[12] thought that London's air had a "bad effect" on the
development of her son's speech.[13] Dr. Erasmus Darwin had written
that air was "nutritious,"[14] and that "constant immersion in pure air is
now known to contribute much both to the health of the system, and
to the beautiful color of the complexion."[15] Dr. Robert Darwin
probably held similar views, and when he was in his early thirties—
with a wife and a small daughter—he had moved out of Shrewsbury
proper to live in the Mount. The Mount stood on an elevation on the
edge of Shrewsbury, and was exposed to country air. Darwin, also,
was in his early thirties—with his wife and small son—when he first
spoke of moving to a country house near London.

From 1840 into 1842 Darwin and Emma searched in vain for a
suitable country house. Darwin discussed these searches with his
father, and, in July 1841, he wrote Emma from Shrewsbury: "I have
partly talked over the Doctor about my buying a house without living
in the neighborhood half-a-dozen years first."[16] In the summer of 1842
he purchased—for the sum of £2,200, which his father gave him[17]—
Down House and eighteen acres of land near the village of Downe in
Kent. He thought Down House "ugly" and planned to alter it.[18] He
wrote his father and sisters about the advantages of Down's location:

"on a fine day the scenery is absolutely beautiful"; "the country is extraordinarily rural and quiet"; "the charm of the place to me is that almost every field is intersected ... by one or more foot-paths. I never saw so many walks in any other country."[19] "It is really surprising," he wrote, "to think London is only 16 miles off."[20] He would then comment, with a touch of awe, that Down was located "absolutely at extreme verge of world":[21] he wanted to be isolated from the world of London's bad air, noise, and people, and yet to have the world of London's scientific museums, societies, and scientific men close by, so that when the need arose he could contact them.

In September 1842 he and his family moved into Down. Here he would live for the remaining forty years of his life.

He soon made changes in the house and garden, and then created the Sandwalk—a 1 1/2-acre strip of land which he planted with trees and circled with a sandy path. This would become his favorite walking place.[22]

In December 1843 he began to correspond with Joseph Hooker about his *Beagle* plant collections. Hooker, a rising young botanist, was the son of the eminent botanist Sir William Hooker.[23] In a letter of 11 January 1844, Darwin made Hooker his first confidant: he revealed some of the history and content of his evolutionary thoughts.

> I have been now ever since my [*Beagle*] return engaged in a very presumptuous work, and I know no one individual who would not say a very foolish one. I was so struck with the distribution of the Galapagos organisms, etc., and with the character of the American fossil mammifers, etc., that I determined to collect blindly every sort of fact which could bear any way on what are species. . . . At last gleams of light have come, and I am almost convinced (quite contrary to the opinion I started with) that species are not (it is like confessing a murder) immutable. Heaven forfend me from Lamarck nonsense of a 'tendency to progression', 'adaptations from the slow willing of animals,' etc.! But the conclusions I am led to are not widely different from this; though the means of change are wholly so. I think I have found out (here's presumption!) the simple way by which species become exquisitely adapted to various ends. You will now groan, and think to yourself, 'on what a man have I been wasting my time and writing to.' I should, five years ago, have thought so [too]. . . . [24]

The vivid words, "like confessing a murder," are stated suddenly— and parenthetically, like many of Darwin's strong feelings—and are then immediately repressed or suppressed. These words have several meanings. They (along with the rest of the letter) express Darwin's great anxiety and embarrassment at finally (after years of conceal- ment) confiding some of his species thoughts to a man whom he respects, and whose help he wants to gain. They also, probably, express some of his moral feelings about his theory of evolution: evolution operates not by the morally tolerable Lamarckian mechan- ism of "slow willing," but by the morally intolerable mechanism of "murder." "Murder," the massive murder of all unfit, aptly describes and characterizes the War of Nature. Then, in "confessing" to this murder, Darwin is claiming the priority of being a first discoverer: although the War of Nature has been long known, he is the first to have appreciated its true meaning and magnitude. Ernest Jones has made the interpretation that by "murder" Darwin unconsciously meant "parricide," the murder of God the Father.[25] Jones' interpreta- tion may contain some truth. At this time, as has been seen, although Darwin did not mean to be irreligious, he feared that there were some who would see his ideas as an attempt to destroy God.

In 1844 Darwin enlarged his 1842 "sketch" of his evolutionary theory into a longer and more coherent account; he then showed this to Hooker. The latter, however, after studying the details of Darwin's theory, and the distribution of Galapagos species—the Galapagos data had especially influenced Darwin to believe in evolution—did not (for years) believe in evolution or natural selection. Hooker told Darwin that, on the question of the origin of species, "I have formed no opinions of my own.... I argue for immutability, till I see cause to take a fixed post...."[26] Yet he thought the species question "a most fair and profitable subject for discussion";[27] and he became Darwin's scientific helper, intellectual confidant, and intimate friend.

Hooker had trained to be a physician, and had experienced psychophysiologic illness. As a result of giving a public talk he suffered from "violent palpitation,"[28] "physical nausea," and "severe nervous reaction."[29] Doctors had told him that he had "slight disease" of the heart, and that he "need not expect ever to attain a freedom in public delivery."[30] Hooker soon developed a sympathetic interest in Dar- win's illness. Darwin responded to this, and in March 1845 wrote Hooker: "You are very kind in your enquiries about my health; I have nothing to say about it, being always much the same, some days better ["than" crossed out] & some worse.—I believe I have not had one ["whole" inserted] day or rather night, without my stomach having been greatly disordered, during the last three years, & most days great prostration of strength: thank you for your kindness, many of my friends, I believe, think me a hypochondriac."[31] Darwin's night illness would become a chronic part of his illness.[32]

In June 1845 Darwin reported to Hooker that he had been working too hard and had "some unwellness."[33] Hooker replied: "I am sorry to hear that you have been still suffering a little. I would willingly take a little bad health (temporarily only) & let you work a bit in comfort, you do so richly deserve a little peaceful working."[34] Hooker would become, along with Fox, Darwin's medical confidant.

In 1844–47 Hooker made visits of several days' duration to Down. During his visits, Darwin—after breakfast at about 8 A.M.—would "pump" him for about half an hour in his study about topics that he was working on: "questions botanical, geographical, &c."[35] "These morning interviews," Hooker recollected, "were followed by his [Darwin's] taking a complete rest, for they always exhausted him, often producing a buzzing noise in the head, and sometimes what he called 'stars in the eyes', the latter too often the prelude of an attack of violent eczema in the head during which he was hardly recognizable. These attacks were followed by a period of what with him was the nearest approach to health, and always to activity."[36] Darwin was well by noon, and for the rest of the day talked with Hooker— happily, vigorously, and without mishap. The afternoon talks, as remembered by Hooker, "turned naturally on the scenes we had witnessed in faraway regions and anecdotes of our seafaring lives [Hooker had made a voyage to Antarctica], and on discoveries in science."[37]

The exact clinical nature of Darwin's "eczema attacks," and their relation to his previous lip condition, cannot be determined. It seems likely, however, that the particular attacks observed by Hooker— with their sudden beginning, brief duration, and sudden end—were psychophysiologic symptoms, caused by Darwin's discussing with Hooker "questions botanical, geographical, &c." These were "questions" concerning the means by which species of plants and animals had crossed oceans to settle lands and achieve their present geographical distribution. As has been seen, the attempt to elucidate these means of species transport had caused Darwin anxiety. After his morning talks with Hooker his anxiety must have increased, because the information Hooker gave him frequently did not answer his difficulties, and sometimes increased them. (When Hooker began to study some of the plants Darwin had collected during the voyage of the *Beagle*, he reported to Darwin: "The more I see the less I am inclined to take migration as a sufficient agent in effecting the strange similarity between the Alpine Floras of V.D.L. [Van Diemen's Land] N.Z. [New Zealand] & that of Fuegia [Tierra del Fuego]. . . . I fear that they neither belong to transportable species or orders or present any facilities for transport: I promise you an honest investigation."[38]) Darwin was, also, probably ashamed of exposing to Hooker—his friend, yet a nonbeliever in natural selection—the shortcomings of his theory. His feelings of anxiety and shame then caused his "eczema attacks." His "eczema" cleared when he stopped talking about evolutionary topics, and it did not recur when he talked to Hooker about topics not directly concerned with evolution. Because Hooker gave him facts—and his main purpose was to accumulate facts bearing on natural selection—he persisted in his morning talks and braved his "eczema attacks."

After several years of these talks he painfully felt the shortcomings of his evolutionary theory, and he wrote Hooker that when he would publish this theory, "I dare say I shall stand infinitely low in the opinion of all sound Naturalists—so this is my prospect for the future."[39] Largely because of these feelings, after finishing his three volumes on the geology of the voyage of the *Beagle* in 1846, instead of beginning to prepare his theory for publication, he began to work on classifying barnacles.

He was also sensitive to criticisms of his Glen Roy theory. In 1847 David Milne published a paper postulating that the roads of Glen Roy had been formed not by the sea or glacial lakes (as Darwin and Agassiz had, respectively, held), but by lakes formed by dams of "detrital matter."[40] After reading this paper Darwin confided to Hooker: "I have been bad enough for these few ["last" inserted] days, having had to think & write too much about Glen Roy (an audacious son of dog ["Mr. Milne" inserted] having attacked my theory) which made me horribly sick."[41] There was then a discussion on Glen Roy, and Darwin told Hooker that "the confounded subject has made me sick twice."[42] He recognized the validity of the arguments against his Glen Roy theory, yet he persisted in believing in it. One reason for his persistence was that his view of the marine origins of Glen Roy was part of a general tectonic theory of subsidence and elevation of the earth's surface to which he was deeply committed.[43] He then wrote a letter about Glen Roy to the Edinburgh newspaper, *The Scotsman*. This letter is extant and has been described as follows: "Unlike most first drafts written by Darwin this one is filled with corrections: hardly a sentence is completed without being partly or entirely rewritten. Darwin obviously was in a state of considerable anxiety and uncertainty. A nine-page letter, the first four and one-half pages are a support of the glacial theory ... the last part of the letter is a refutation of the Agassiz theory and a defence of his own marine theory."[44] After writing this letter, Darwin did not send it to *The Scotsman*. Over the next fourteen years the subject of Glen Roy would continue to cause him anxiety, and perhaps, also, physical illness.[45]

In the 1840s he became aware of a new threat to his health. After talking to individuals—other than Hooker, Emma, or members of his Down family—he began to "almost always" suffer from episodes of "excitement, violent shivering and vomiting attacks."[46] These were, probably, psychophysiologic episodes which were caused by various factors: his antipathy to the person he was conversing with and/or the subject of conversation; his dislike of being distracted from his scientific work; and his changing the specific fears which he felt about his scientific work into a general fear of revealing himself through conversation, and then of being reproached for what he revealed. In one conversation he could have been upset by one, all, or different combinations of these factors. Because of these postconversation upsets, he went on avoiding most people. When "relations" visited him he would keep them company for "some time after dinner in silence."[47]

At Down he settled into a routine of alternating periods of scientific work—he worked, for 1 to 1½ hours at a time, in the early morning, late morning, afternoon, and early evening—and then periods of different leisure activities. These were a sort of daily mental and physical health regimen which rested him from his work, and assuaged some of his anxieties and some of his psychophysiologic symptoms.

His most frequent leisure activity was to be read to by Emma, three or four times a day, for about an hour each time. They shared similar tastes in nonscientific books, and they read works which were currently popular and advertised by Mudies Library in London;[48] Mudies had come into being about the time they moved to Down, and perhaps along with many wealthy country dwellers they came to have a Mudies subscription which entitled them to regularly receive parcels of newly published books.[49] They read works of history, biography, travels in foreign lands, and novels. Reading a novel caused Darwin to experience what he described as "a wonderful relief and pleasure."[50] He eagerly entered into the novel's unfolding plot, and he was especially concerned about its ending: he insisted that the ending should not be revealed until the reading of the novel was finished, and that it should be a happy ending.[51] He would discuss, with Emma and members of his family, the charms and attributes of the novel's heroine. His daughter recollected that he was "often in love with the heroines of the many novels that were read to him,"[52] and he would imagine that some heroines were more beautiful than they were actually portrayed.[53] Sometimes, during his afternoon reading period, a novel which at first stimulated him would then so relax him that he would briefly fall asleep.[54] Novel reading—as much as, if not more than, any other leisure activity—distracted him from the anxieties and guilt involved in his work.

The one nonscientific reading that he did by himself was *The Times*. Every day he read through *The Times*, informing himself of the main news events[55] and observing movements in the stock market (so he could follow his investments);[56] he was especially interested in the law reports.[57] He became so accustomed to *The Times* that he once would jokingly call it "meat, drink, & air."[58]

At noon and at four in the afternoon he would take walks around the Sandwalk—at noon he would walk around the Sandwalk exactly five times (about one mile)—or on other parts of his estate.[59] He walked alone (in later years he would be accompanied by his dog), or with members of his family and/or friends. When alone he would sometimes stop and observe plants and animals, or else he would be oblivious to his surroundings and think about the everyday problems of his family and Down estate, and his scientific work. He would also indulge in pleasant fantasies. As he had previously written, "Now that I have a test of hardness of thought, from weakness of my stomach I observe a long castle in the air, is as hard work (*abstracting it being done in open air, with exercise etc, [not] no organs of sense being required*) as the closest train of geological thought."[60] Walking rapidly gave him relief when he felt angry.[61] Walking was his only exercise.

In the early evening he would play two games of backgammon with Emma. If he won, he would jokingly proclaim how much his score had exceeded the score of his wife,[62] and he would chaff Emma and tell her that she believed that backgammon was "all luck."[63] If he was losing he would let himself go in bursts of loud complaints to his wife, exclaiming "bang your bones,"[64] and "confound the woman."[65] This humorous boasting (he was usually outwardly modest) and humorous anger (he always had difficulty in expressing serious anger[66]) may have cleared his mind and mentally refreshed him, for after back-gammon he did some German scientific reading by himself—reading which he found especially onerous.[67]

After his scientific reading he would listen to Emma play the piano. He complained that his appreciation of music had waned as he grew older, and that "music generally sets me thinking too energetically on what I have been at work on, instead of giving me pleasure."[68] Yet as he listened to Emma play—as she played both he and she were silent[69]—he was affected by what he heard; he once made a list of the compositions which he especially liked and the impression each made upon him (the list, which probably included compositions from Handel and Beethoven, has since been lost).[70]

During most of his indoor leisure—when reading *The Times* or listening to Emma read or play the piano—he would recline on a sofa or bed, always lying flat on his back, and sometimes putting his hands under his head.[71] Lying in this horizontal position was perhaps a carry-over from the days when he was treating his seasickness aboard the *Beagle*, and this position may have eased his upset stomach. However, in the evening when conversing with his family or friends, he would sit "very erect"[72] in a high chair made still higher by being placed on a footstool; he would then sometimes place his feet on another chair.[73] He told visitors that this peculiar way of sitting was "to guard his weakness,"[74] "to guard against . . . digestive trouble,"[75] and "to keep off giddiness and nausea."[76] Why this way of sitting should so affect him is unknown.[77]

He described his Down life as going on "like clockwork,"[78] and as "uniform"[79] and "the dullest possible" life.[80] By this he meant that every day (including holidays and weekends) he followed the same unvarying routine. With this routine he was able to accomplish a steady amount of work, and in 1845 he reported to Fox: "My stomach continues daily badly, but I think I am decidedly better than one or two years ago."[81]

6

The Death of Dr. Darwin,
Dr. Gully's Hydropathy

During his early years at Down, Darwin corresponded closely with his father and sisters, Catherine and Susan, in Shrewsbury. His letters reveal his dependence on his father for medical care, money, and different kinds of advice.

In September 1842, as he was moving into Down, he wrote

Catherine about a letter which he had enclosed along with his letter to her. "Will you ask my Father to listen to ["the" crossed out] my letter to Mr. Cottrell [Mr. Cockell][1] who is the surgeon of Down. He introduced himself to me. I have been able through Mr. Cresy[2] to hear [a] good character of him from a physician who formerly saw much of him. I do not like his manners but upon deliberation we have determined it will be best [to] employ him. He is only two fields off. I do not much like my own letter and should be much obliged for any suggestions when it is returned. Emma suggested my putting in about increased terms afraid he should think my plan was only for economy." He added: "I ought to have said that Mr. Cottrell [Mr. Cockell] introduced himself to me, so I begin Dear Sir."[3] After this, neither he, nor members of his family, seem to have consulted Mr. Cockell.[4]

In his letter to Catherine he went on to write about Mr. Blunt, a Shrewsbury chemist who was his pharmacist and whom he regarded as "the best chemist in the world."[5] "Mr. Blunt's bill is come and is only £8.18.11!!! I have written to thank him. Will my Father be so kind as to add this to other items and I will ask for no more? I think I shall get through (thanks to *you*) pretty well."[6] This indicates that (at least at this time) Dr. Darwin paid for the medications of his son and the latter's family.[7] After telling Catherine "I feel sure I shall become deeply attached to Down," Darwin ended his letter with a final request: "Mr. Blunt has sent me a classified list of my medicines. I should be very much obliged if it would not be giving too much trouble to my Father if either of you [Catherine or Susan] would sometimes read it over to him and in that case I would send it, and with pen write opposite each ordinary dose for child of 18 months old so that we might give a little less or more according to a child's age. Is there any ordinary rule of proportion in doses between an 18 months old child and grown up person?"[8] "My medicines" meant medicines for himself, his thirty-six-month-old son William, his eighteen-month-old daughter Annie, and Emma, who was in an advanced state of pregnancy. (On 23 September 1842, Emma gave birth to a daughter, Mary Eleanor, who died after three weeks.) This letter may have caused Dr. Darwin to write some prescriptions for children's medications in his prescription book.[9]

In 1844–45 Darwin wrote his sister Susan: "Thank, also, my Father for his medical advice— I have been very well since Friday, nearly as well as during the first fortnight & am in heart again about the non-sugar plan. I am trying the very bitter, weak, but thoroughly

fermented Indian Ale, for luncheon & ["it" inserted] suits me very
well."[10] Indian ale, also called bitter ale, was bitter because it
contained hops: a plant which was "Stomachic and Tonic" and
"slightly Narcotic," and which belonged to a class of vegetable
medicinal substances known as "bitters."[11] Darwin had probably used
it at least once previously in 1836.[12] The "non-sugar plan" may refer to
the prevailing medical notion that "in some constitutions there is a
peculiar tendency to an abnormal oxidation" of sugar into poisonous
oxalic acid, and that because of this some individuals were "sometimes
benefited by an injunction to abstain entirely" from sugar.[13] In the
future Darwin would make frequent "vows" never to eat sweets, and
then he would never be able to keep these.[14]

In September 1845 he wrote Susan (and through her, his father): "I
have taken my Bismuth regularly, I think it has not done me quite so
much good, as before; but I am recovering from too much exertion
with my Journal."[15] He had, evidently, taken bismuth previously.
Bismuth nitrate was used to treat stomach pains and chronic
vomiting. It was held that, since bismuth was apparently not absorbed
by the intestines, it exerted its therapeutic effect "by simply cloaking
some of the delicate or irritable portions of the mucous surface with an
insoluble white covering."[16] Bismuth (presumably) did not benefit
Darwin, for he makes no further reference to it. The "Journal" that he
mentions was the second edition of his *Beagle* narrative, *Journal of Researches*, where he hinted—more strongly than in the first edition—at
the evolutionary implications of some of his *Beagle* observations.

These letters to Susan indicate that his medical regimen tended to be
changed, and that it was largely aimed at treating his upset stomach.

Darwin usually visited with his Shrewsbury family for about two
weeks, once in the spring and again in the fall. He talked to his father
about his finances, his wife—Dr. Darwin praised Emma and her care
of him[17]—the illnesses and care of his children, and his own illness.
In October 1843, while at Shrewsbury, he wrote Emma: "I told him
[Dr. Darwin] of my dreadful numbness in my finger ends, and all the
sympathy I could get was, 'Yes-yes-exactly-tut-tut, neuralgic, exactly,
yes, yes!!' nor will he sympathize about money, 'stuff and nonsense' is
all he says to my fears of ruin and extravagance."[18] Dr. Darwin seems
to have been trying to reassure his son. Darwin regarded his father as
unsympathetic, yet there is no indication that he questioned his
father's judgment or ability. The cause of this "dreadful numbness" of
the "finger ends" is unknown (this is the only time, throughout his
illness, that Darwin mentions this symptom).

As Darwin watched his father age he thought of death "drawing slowly nearer and nearer."[19] He also felt depressed when he saw his father gaining weight, and becoming unable to move around.[20]

In May 1848—as his father was completing his eighty-second year—Darwin made his spring visit to Shrewsbury. He wrote Emma that Dr. Darwin complained of difficulty in breathing and talking, and had an occasional "dying sensation"; but that his father "thought with care he might live a good time longer."[21] He then wrote Emma a succession of notes about himself: 22 May: "Really yesterday I was not able to forget my stomach for 5 minutes all day long."[22] 25 May: "The day here is almost continual anxiety."[23] On Saturday, 27 May, as he thought of leaving Shrewsbury for Down, he wrote Emma: "I am weak enough to-day, but I think I am improving. My attack was very sudden: Susan was very kind to me but I did yearn for you. Without you when sick I feel most desolate. I almost doubt whether I shall be able to travel on Monday; but I can write no more now. I do long to be with you and under your protection for then I feel safe."[24] His "sudden attack" may refer to what he would later describe as a "fit of flatulence."[25] On Thursday, 1 June, he returned to Down.[26]

In July 1848 his illness worsened, and he suffered from symptoms which he described as follows: "Unusually unwell, with swimming of head, depression, trembling—many bad attacks of sickness";[27] "I was almost quite broken down, head swimming, hands trembling & never a week without violent vomiting";[28] "my nervous system began to be affected, so that my hands trembled, and head was often swimming";[29] "my hands were becoming tremulous & head often swimming";[30] "incessant sickness, tremulous hands and swimming head";[31] "involuntary twitching of the muscle . . . fainting feelings &c—black spots before eyes, &c."[32] He also feared that he was "rapidly" dying.[33] As his illness persisted into the fall of 1848, he became progressively less able to work and "too dispirited" to answer the letters of Hooker and other friends.[34]

"Incessant sickness" and "many bad attacks of sickness" refer to frequent episodes of vomiting. Tremor, muscle twitching, visual disturbances, and fear of death seem to have been new complaints in his illness, and were perhaps manifestations of severe anxiety. A probable cause for this exacerbation of illness was the impending death of Dr. Robert Darwin: Darwin was fearful of losing his father, on whom he depended for many things, including medical advice. Emma, because of the birth of a new child in August 1848,[35] may have for a time become less able to care for him; and her incapacity may have further accentuated his feelings of loss and impending loss.

Despite his illness he saw his father in Shrewsbury from 10 to 25 October.[36]

In the fall of 1848 he was visited by his old *Beagle* shipmate Bartholomew J. Sullivan, who found him "very weak" and only able to take "a very short walk." Sullivan then told him of people with stomach illness and "very weak digestion" who had benefited from Dr. Gully's hydropathy treatment.[37]

Dr. James Manby Gully had been born in Kingston, Jamaica, in 1808, had studied medicine at the University of Edinburgh and the École de Médecine at Paris, and then established himself as a physician in London. In 1840 he published a book, *The Simple Treatment of Disease*, which criticized many established medical practices. In 1842, with Dr. James Wilson—who had been impressed with the therapeutic power of hydropathy during a visit to the European continent—Dr. Gully founded the Hydropathic Establishment at Malvern; this soon became famous for its water cure, attracting many eminent Victorians (Tennyson, Carlyle, Bishop Wilberforce) and patients from Europe and America.[38] In 1846 Dr. Gully had published a lucidly written and widely read book (it passed through nine editions) entitled *The Water Cure in Chronic Disease*.[39]

Darwin was at first "very hopeless" about being aided by hydropathy; however, when Sullivan pressed him to try this treatment, he wrote to Shrewsbury asking the opinion of his father. Dr. Darwin, in what may have been his last medical advice, replied that his son should try hydropathy, but should wait to do so until winter had passed and spring had come.[40]

On 13 November 1848, Dr. Robert Darwin died. Darwin visited Shrewsbury on 17–26 November,[41] and said he was too ill to attend his father's funeral, or to act as one of his executors.[42] In the following months he grieved, and remembered his father's "sagacity" and "affectionate ... disposition."[43] Darwin's illness continued to be severe. When his sisters Susan and Catherine visited him at Down he avoided them.[44] He consulted Dr. Henry Holland (whom he had last consulted nine years previously). Dr. Holland told him that his illness was unique, and did not fit any known classification of illness; that it was not "quite" dyspepsia, and "nearer to suppressed gout."[45] Then Fox told him of patients who had been helped by hydropathy, and urged him to try it. Darwin then read Dr. Gully's book, and may have corresponded with Dr. Gully, who impressed him as sensible and cautious.[46]

In *The Water Cure in Chronic Disease* Dr. Gully had divided "dyspepsia" into "nervous dyspepsia" and "mucous dyspepsia."[47] The first was seen as "a chronic inflammation of the nerves of the stomach": treatment consisted of small feedings of nonirritating food, and a hydropathy regimen—sitz baths, foot baths, wet sheet packing, and rubbing with a dripping sheet—which aimed at drawing the blood away from the stomach and establishing "a counteracting irritation process in some organs distant from the stomach." A process "resembling as nearly as possible in its character that which it is intended to remove—namely a nervous irritation." The sitz baths, through irritating the skin of the loins, were seen as making "the patient forget all his sensations about the stomach."[48] "Mucous dyspepsia" referred to a stomach which was underactive and obstructed in its function: treatment consisted of developing a progressively greater tolerance for food and exercise; and a hydropathy regimen consisting of sweating, followed by a "cold shallow bath for three or four minutes after it, so as to produce a vehement revulsion to the skin," and then a douche and a wet packing. The aim of this regimen was to "rouse" the underactive system to "extraordinary efforts."[49] These two kinds of dyspepsia could exist in combination.[50] Dr. Gully wrote that a physician should learn to "vary the application" of the different modalities of a hydropathic regimen, "suspending some and augmenting others, to meet the endless vagaries of a nervously morbid stomach."[51]

This was a regimen which was new, and carefully thought out; and which differed from the other existing treatments for dyspepsia— treatments which Dr. Gully regarded as "effete and inefficient, if not positively harmful."[52] In *The Water Cure* Dr. Gully stated: "I cannot but repeat the strong conviction I have that *medication never did, never will, never can, cure a case of chronic dyspepsia: and that, short of organic change, the hygienic water treatment seldom if ever fails to cure it.*"[53]

After learning about the water cure, Darwin, although not supported by Dr. Holland, determined to try it. On 10 March 1849, with his wife, six children and their governess, and servants, he moved to Malvern.[54] Here he rented a house and grounds for his family.[55] He then went to the Hydropathy Establishment,[56] where he was examined by Dr. Gully. Doctor and patient were only one year apart in age, and had been contemporaries at Edinburgh Medical School.[57] Although Darwin disliked Dr. Gully's belief in homeopathy—Dr. Robert Darwin disliked Dr. Gully's belief in homeopathy—Dr. Robert Darwin had been critical of homeopathy[58]—he quickly developed a strong attraction for him, feeling that (to some degree) he compensated for the loss of his father. He told his sister Susan: "I like Dr.

Gully much—he is certainly an able man: I have been struck with how many remarks he has made similar to those of my Father. He is very kind and attentive."[59] Dr. Gully was first "puzzled"[60] by Darwin's symptoms; then he became confident that he could cure them, and he communicated this confidence to his patient. He does not seem to have made a definite diagnosis. His treatments suggest that he may have regarded Darwin's illness as a combination of "nervous" and "mucous" dyspepsia.

On 19 March, nine days after coming to Malvern, Darwin described his treatments in a letter to Susan:

> A 1/4 before 7 get up, & am scrubbed with rough towel in cold water for 2 or 3 minutes, which after the first few days, made & makes me very like a lobster—I have a Washerman, a very nice person, & he scrubs behind while I scrub in front.—Drink a tumbler of water & get my clothes on as quick as possible & walk for 20 minutes—I cd. walk further, but I find it tires me afterwards—I like all this very much.—At same time I put on a compress which is a broad wet folded linen covered by mackintosh & which is 're-freshed'—i.e. dipt in cold water every 2 hours & I wear it all day except for about 2 hours after midday dinner.—I don't perceive much effect from this of any kind—After my walk, shave & get my breakfast, which was to have been exclusively ["bread" is crossed out] toast with meat or egg, but he has allowed me a little milk to sop the *stale* toast in. At no time must I take any sugar, butter, spices, tea bacon, or anything good.—At 12 o'clock I put my feet for 10 minutes in cold water with a little mustard & they are violently rubbed by my man: this coldness makes my feet ache much, but upon the whole my feet are certainly less cold than formerly.—Walk for 20 minutes & dine at one.—He has relaxed a little about my dinner & says I may try plain pudding, if I am sure it lessens sickness.—After dinner lie down & try to go to sleep for one hour.—At 5 o'clock feet in cold water—drink cold water & walk as before—Supper same as breakfast at 6 o'clock.—I have had much sickness this week, but certainly have felt much stronger & the sickness has depressed me much less.—Tomorrow I am to be packed at 6 o'clock ["A.M." inserted] for 1 & 1/2 hrs. in ["towel" crossed out] Blanket, with hot bottle to my feet & then rubbed with cold dripping sheet; but I do not know anything about this.[61]

Five days later he reported to Fox: "I much like & think highly of Dr. Gully. He has been very cautious in his treatment & has even had the charity to stint me ["to" inserted, then crossed out] only ["to" inserted] six pinches of snuff daily.—Cold scrubbing in morning, 2 cold feet bath & compress on stomach is as yet the only treatment, besides change of diet &c.—I am, however to commence tomorrow a sweating process.—I am already *certainly* stronger & perhaps my stomach somewhat better. . . . I expect fully that the system will greatly benefit me, and certainly the regular Doctors c^d do nothing."

He then told Fox: "The only disagreeable part as yet to me, has been the excessive irritation of skin which comes on every evening over [my] whole body.—So that I cannot sit quiet one minute after six or seven oclock.—This no doubt will before long go off."[62] As Dr. Gully carefully regulated his treatment, Darwin's skin irritation eased. Dr. Gully had written in *The Water Cure* that, in hydropathy, "it is not desired to produce a suppurative congestion of the skin,—such as would generate boils, but that amount of cutaneous irritation which is exhibited in a rash or itchy eruption"; further, that this skin irritation was part of the "counteracting irritative process" which eased the nervous irritation of the stomach, and that "nervous dyspeptics" were "peculiarly grateful in its results."[63] As Darwin felt his stomach becoming better, he, too, came to believed this and—out of a feeling of "gratitude" for hydropathy—he would tell an acquaintance: "Physiologically it is most curious how the violent excitement of the skin produced by simple water, has acted on all my internal organs."[64]

In April he reported to Fox: "I now increase in weight, have escaped sickness for 30 days, which is thrice as long an interval as I have had for last year: & yesterday in 4 walks I managed seven miles! I am turned into a mere walking and eating machine.—Dr. G. however finds he is obliged to treat me cautiously & during last week all my treatment has been much relaxed." Always conscious of money, Darwin then observed: "There are many patients here even already: last summer I hear he had 120!—He must be making an immense fortune."[65]

After almost four months of hydropathy he wrote Fox: "I consider the sickness as absolutely cured. And about 3 weeks since I had ["had" written over "have"] 12 hours without any flatulence, which showed me that it was possible that even that can be cured, as Dr. G. has always said he could. The Water Cure is assuredly a grand discovery & how sorry I am that I did not hear of it, or rather that I was not somehow compelled to try it some five or six years ago. Much I owe to you for your ["large" inserted] share in making me go this spring."[66]

He told Fox that his treatments had "the most extraordinary effect in producing indolence & stagnation of mind; till experiencing it, I could not have believed it possible."[67] Several months previously, at the beginning of his Malvern hydropathy, he had written his sister Susan: "I am become perfectly indolent which I feel the oddest change of all to myself is the greatest mental effort done by me since coming here."[68] His mental "indolence and stagnation" meant that he was able, for a time, to deny the anxieties that had caused his illness to exacerbate.

On 30 June he and his family returned home. He had stayed at Malvern for sixteen weeks—the longest continuous period he ever would be away from Down.

7

Self-Observation
and Self-Treatment

At Down he made two additions to his daily routine. He rose very early and took long walks of three or four miles before breakfast in the Sandwalk, or other woods. Sometimes during these walks, in the dusk of the early morning, he would walk very slowly, "just quietly putting down his foot & then waiting before the next step," a manner of walking which he had learned in the tropical forests of Brazil during the *Beagle* voyage. In this way he was able to observe scenes of animal life in the woods; once he watched, for a long time and at a distance of only a few feet, a vixen playing with her cubs. He soon shortened these morning walks to about two turns around the Sandwalk (less than half a mile).[1] His daily routine thus came to consist of walks in the morning, noon, and four in the afternoon.

He then determined to follow the instructions of Dr. Gully and continue his water treatments for (what he thought would be only) another year.[2] He built what he called the "douche":[3] a small house, "shaped something like a very diminutive church," which stood outside his main Down house and close to a well,[4] and which contained a bathtub (it has been stated that this bathtub was in his study,[5] but there is no evidence for this). Water for the bathtub was drawn from the well, as there was no running water. Here he began taking daily water treatments, which were prepared and administered by his male servant Joseph Parslow.[6] He also began writing, on loose sheets of foolscap, daily entries about his health; what would be called his *Diary of Health*. He would keep this *Diary* for 5 1/2 years—from 1 July 1849 to 16 January 1855—and it would fill sixty-four foolscap sheets.[7]

What follows, based on Darwin's letters and his *Diary*, will first describe his treatments and his illness during these 5 1/2 years and will then comment on his *Diary*.

His *Diary* records that his home hydropathy consisted of five modalities: sweating (effected by exposure to a lamp), a shallow bath, a douche, wrapping himself in several dripping sheets, and then (infrequently) a foot bath. Following Dr. Gully's advice on how to "meet the endless vagaries of nervously morbid stomach," he varied his use of each modality. Ten months after leaving Malvern he wrote Fox: "My treatment varies every 4 or 6 weeks—About 8 weeks since I left off the Lamp for a month: on an average I have had it therefore the last 9 months from 2 to 4 times a week & so with Douche.—For present fortnight I am having Douche daily, which is first time since leaving Malvern. Having gained weight ever since I commenced is a clear sign that I have not overdosed myself."[8] He would sometimes vary the hydropathic modalities daily and weekly, usually using several at once, and never all five together. When he sojourned at the country houses of his sister Caroline and Wedgwood relatives his hydropathy consisted only of his using dripping sheets.[9]

For two years, from July 1849 until June 1851, he took some form of water treatment almost every day; he was determined "to remain slave to treatment."[10] For most of this period he "regularly" wrote medical reports about himself (based on his *Diary*) to Dr. Gully, who then "instructed" him on his treatments.[11] On 11–18 June 1850, he saw Dr. Gully at Malvern.[12] He felt that he should be "under the orders of one Doctor,"[13] and not "blindly" treat himself.[14] In his letters to Fox he discussed his treatments and his doctor. "Your aphorism that 'any remedy will cure any malady' contains, I do believe, profound truth,—whether applicable or not to the wondrous Water Cure I am not very sure.—The Water Cure, however, keeps in high fashion, & I go regularly on with douching &c &c."[15] Although he maintained his confidence in Dr. Gully's clinical experience and therapeutic caution, he criticized him for believing not only in homeopathy, but in mesmerism and clairvoyance. "It is a sad flaw," he told Fox, "I cannot but think in my beloved Dr. Gully that he believes in everything— when his daughter was very ill, he had a clairvoyant girl to report on internal changes, a mesmerist to put her to sleep—an homeopathist, viz Dr. Chapman; & himself as Hydropathist! & the girl recovered."[16]

Several months after writing the above passage, on the insistence of Dr. Gully, Darwin reluctantly agreed to have a consultation with a woman who was reputed to have powers of clairvoyance which enabled her "to see the insides of people & discover the real nature of their ailments." After being introduced to the clairvoyant, Darwin showed her a sealed envelope and said to her: "I have heard a great deal of your powers of reading concealed writings & I should like to have evidence myself; here in this envelope there is a bank note & if you will read the number I shall be happy to present it to you." She answered scornfully: "I have a maid-servant at home who can do that."[17] She then told him that "the mischief" was in his stomach and lungs,[18] and described to him "a most appalling picture of the horrors which she saw in his inside."[19] He then came to believe that she had "followed ... some unconscious hints" from Dr. Gully and his assistant.[20]

In March 1851 Darwin came to Malvern bringing his ten-year-old daughter Annie, who was gravely ill. Despite Dr. Gully's close care, Annie died on 23 April 1851, and was buried in the old Abbey churchyard at Malvern.[21] Following this Darwin disliked thinking about Malvern—associating it with Annie's death and grave—and he seems to have stopped his contact with Dr. Gully. His *Diary of Health* records that he stopped hydropathy in June 1851, then resumed it in August 1851. In March 1852 he told Fox that hydropathy "always" caused him "good effect."[22] However in August 1852 he noted in his *Diary*: "Six weeks treatment: not much good effect, extremely tired in Evening. I do not think last treatment did me much good." On 30 November 1852 he stopped hydropathy for a year; in December 1853 he resumed it for a month; he then ceased all hydropathy for several years. Despite this cessation he went on believing in the beneficial effects of hydropathy.

His *Diary* reveals that he occasionally took medications and substances that he thought were beneficial: 24 December 1850: "Began Tartar Emetic Ointment, & rubbed in for 12 days"; 9 January 1851: "Began Tartar" (this was then crossed out); 27 February 1851: "Tartar Emetic O. in evening." This may mean that he changed the taking of tartar from day to evening. Perhaps he hoped that this time change would benefit his nocturnal symptoms. His indications for using tartar emetic ointment are not known.[23] On 4 March 1851, because of stomach discomfort, he took croton. Croton was a medicinal substance, found in plants, which was used as a tonic and in treating dyspepsia.[24] For several days in December 1853 he noted the effects of coffee and tea: coffee usually caused him to be "wakeful"; with tea the "wakeful" effect was not as pronounced; with both beverages he was usually able to have a "good" night.[25] For several months in 1854, for unknown reasons, he took lemons: 23 January 1854: "1/2 lemon twice"; 24 January: "Whole lemon twice a day"; 8 March: *"Left off Lemon"*; 5 April: "Half-Lemon."[26]

In September 1854, for three successive days, he carefully observed the cathartic effects of decreasing doses of Aloes:

6 September: "30 drops of Cordial Aloes   no work"
7 September: "20 drops of do [ditto]   no work"
8 September: "10 drops purged   5 work"

Alongside the above three entries he then wrote: "10 drops twice a day w^d be enough." On 17 November 1854, he noted: "20 drops of li[quor] Inf[usion] Aloes."[27]

On 16 October 1851, he wrote "(Electric Chains to Waist)," and on 19 October, "(do [ditto] neck)." A hydroelectric chain was composed of alternate brass and zinc wires which, when moistened with vinegar, gave out electric shocks.[28] It was applied to different body parts, for varying lengths of time, and was used to treat "cases of partial paralysis, neuralgic headaches, and many other nervous diseases, and . . . in relaxed conditions of the muscle fibre."[29] Darwin does not state why, or for how long, he used electric chains.

In his *Diary* Darwin summarized his illness for each day and then each night. The day symptoms he noted most frequently were "flatulence" and "fits of flatulence" (abbreviated as "flat," "ft," "fits of ft," or simply as "fits"). These seem to have been almost entirely confined to his stomach (in the *Diary*, complaints about the lower intestine are rare). Flatulence was a medical term, often used during Victorian times. In the 1858 English *A Dictionary of Practical Medicine*, "flatulency" was defined as "an undue formation of air in the stomach or intestines, with frequent rejection of it,"[30] and was then discussed in an article which filled six printed columns. It was held to be mainly caused by diseases of the stomach and intestine, "habits," and "nervous and hypochondriacal temperaments";[31] and was sometimes thought to be a "primary disorder."[32] Stomach flatulence was described as producing "acid, bitter, nidorous, or foetid" odors in the mouth, dry cough, and "fulness of the epigastrium and hypochondria, with a painful sense of distension, or severe gastrodynia, frequent respiration, and heavy pain or oppression in the lower parts of the chest."[33]

Darwin would never fully describe where, or how, he experienced "flatulence." Once he would comment: "I feel nearly sure that the air is generated some where . . . lower down than the stomach & as soon as it regurgitates into the stomach the discomfort comes on."[34] This would suggest that the pain of flatulence was located in the upper part of his abdomen. When he reported "fits of flatulence"—and when he once reported "sudden attack"[35]—these may both describe the same clinical phenomenon: a sensation of abdominal discomfort which came on suddenly, lasted a variable period of time, and then subsided suddenly.

The *Diary* shows that Darwin had flatulence on most days, in varying durations and frequencies (the frequencies of his "fits of flatulence" ranged from one to seven daily), and in greatly varying intensities which he tried to quantitatively describe as follows: "almost," "barely," "very slight," "slightest," "slight," "moderate," "good deal," "considerable," "much," "rather bad," "baddish," "not bad," "bad," "very bad," "sharp," "sharpish," and "excessive." It will be seen that when Darwin wrote "excessive" he was, really, experiencing an excessive amount of pain.[36] He also noted other stomach symptoms: "nausea," "vomiting," and "retching." He noted that he sometimes vomited, and/or retched up, "acid," "acid & slime," and once (on 14 August 1849) "acid & clots of blood." On Sunday, 11 April 1852, he wrote: "Cold, Sundays Stomach[37] not bad." Along with his stomach symptoms he sometimes experienced different kinds of anxiety which he described as "fright," "sinking sensation," "trembling," and "shivering." After much flatulence he would sometimes write "oppressed," "fatigued." Occasionally he wrote "Heavy," which may have described a depressed feeling and/or a sensation in his stomach.

Next to flatulence, his most common complaints were boils. These occurred in varying numbers and sizes. Once a boil began, he often recorded its development and whether it subsided or "broke." Usually he made no mention of how he treated his boils. However, on 13 January 1853, he wrote "got boil not well painful in night." On 15 January, "core extracted." 16 January: "Poorly very excessive flt ["Bad" crossed out] Vomiting." He then became well. Other frequent symptoms were "headaches," which almost always occurred in conjunction with flatulence; "colds," which were mostly afebrile and uncomplicated;[38] and skin conditions which he called "rash," "erythema," and "eruption," and which differed in their durations. Some of his skin symptoms may have been caused by the mechanical irritation of his hydropathy treatments. Sometimes, without mentioning any other symptoms, he wrote "weakish," "languid," "weak and languid."[39]

At night he suffered from such day symptoms as headaches, a "heavy" feeling, flatulence, nausea, retching, and vomiting. On 8 July 1849, he wrote in his *Diary*: "Poorly, much flat; excessive at night with slight trembling & fright"; on the night of 25 December: "Vomit ["not acid" inserted] dazzle, headache excessive ft"; on 18 March 1853: "Well *very* in morning; Poorly in evening: dazzling and headache." He sometimes wrote that at night he was "heazish," or "heazyish," which may have described breathing difficulties and coughing.[40] At night he mainly described himself as either "good," "moderate," "poor," "wakeful," "restless," or "indifferent." During the first week of March 1852 he recorded in his *Diary* that his nights were good; however, on 7 March 1852, he told Fox: "My nights are *always* bad & that stops my becoming vigorous."[41] He probably meant that he was "*always*" tormented by different nocturnal obsessional thoughts: a scientific problem that he had been working on during the day, that he could not dismiss from his mind; a troublesome conversation that he had during the day; his failure to answer a troublesome letter. These nocturnal obsessions would often cause him to lie awake, or sit up in bed, for hours.[42] Sometimes he would get up from his bed at night, seek out an individual whom he had conversed with earlier, and explain to this individual exactly what he had meant to say.[43] When obsessed with thoughts "of a horrid spectacle" he would try to drive these thoughts away by "closing my eyes firmly."[44] He was especially vulnerable to nocturnal obsessional thoughts because when he was lying in his bed he lacked the leisure activities—his book reading, music, and backgammon—which would distract his thoughts.

In each *Diary* entry he summarized his health, usually with the words "well very," and the degree of wellness was emphasized by the "very" being either not underlined, or underlined with one or two dashes. At the end of each month he sometimes made a note of his weight—between July 1849 and December 1853 he gained over thirty-three pounds—and he counted up the number of "double-dash" days. He valued these double-dash days for their feeling of well-being and for the work that he could accomplish, and he sometimes commented on them as follows: December 1851: "19 double-dashes Best since Jan. 1850" (in January 1850 he had twenty-four double dashes); August 1853: "17 Double-Dashes, but I think I am not so strict as I used to be"; April 1854: "Only 3 Double Dashes & two of them not good!"; May 1854: "Eight Double, but night *much* better."

Collating his *Diary* with letters and memoirs, it can be seen how travels affected his health. On 11–12 September 1849, he and Emma went to Birmingham for a meeting of the British Association for the Advancement of Science. During the meeting he thought the meeting place "large & nasty," and the meeting "not very brilliant,"[45] and he had increasing day and night flatulence. After eight days he and Emma started for Warwick and Kenilworth, but he "broke down,"[46] and returned to Down, where he spent a day in bed feeling "Poorly" and with "a good deal of ft."[47] He then told Henslow: "I think I stand any change, even worse than formerly & my stomach has not gotten over the excitement of Birmingham as yet."[48] On 4 September 1850 he wrote Fox that he was "very full of the subject of schools," and thinking of the "awful experiment" of sending his eleven-year-old son William to the Bruce Castle School.[49] This school did not stress Latin and had "much novelty" in its curriculum.[50] In his *Diary* entry for 6 September he noted his visit to the school, which was at Tottenham, in the environs of London, as follows: "London. Well not quite. excessive ft. slight headache." At night: "excessive ft." (On the preceding days he had complained of "much" flatulence.) He then had severe flatulence for several nights, perhaps from worrying about the Bruce Castle School. Eventually William was sent to Rugby. In August 1851 he and his family went to London for three weeks and visited the Crystal Palace and Great Exhibition of 1851 in Hyde Park. This was the first great "World Fair," seen daily by enormous crowds, and remembered "with wonder and admiration by all."[51] Although Darwin "intensely" enjoyed the Exhibition,[52] it may have been too exciting for him, for he had two to three fits of flatulence every day. On 23–27 March 1852, he visited William at Rugby and enjoyed "very well" health, with the "very" underlined. He went on, from 23–27 March, to visit his sisters Catherine and Susan at Shrewsbury; his health then became "Poor" and "not well," and he had fits of flatulence. On 17 November 1852 he went for the day to London and—along with Hooker[53] and crowds estimated at hundreds of thousands—viewed the body of the Duke of Wellington lying in state in the hall of Chelsea Hospital[54] (the date was also the fourth anniversary of the death of his father); he had two fits of flatulence and his night was "poor." In 1853 he twice visited the Crystal Palace— which was being built anew at Sydenham—and each time he suffered some accentuation of his flatulence.[55]

On 13–17 August 1853, he and his family stayed at The Hermitage, home of his brother-in-law Harry Wedgwood. Nearby was Chobham Camp where, since June, a force of about ten to sixteen thousand English soldiers and dragoons had been engaged in mimic warfare (the first protracted large-scale mimic warfare in the history of the peacetime British Army[56]). For three days Darwin watched this "warfare," feeling "intense enjoyment" and "happy excitement";[57] "he was," his son George recollects, "keener than anyone in his interest."[58] On this occasion his "excitement" did not disturb his health. In his *Diary*, he described himself as "Well Very" (the "Very" was twice doubly underlined); his nights, however, were either "goodish" or "indifferent." On 10 June 1854, he, Emma, and Emma's sixty-one-year-old sister, Elizabeth Wedgwood, traveled to Sydenham to watch—along with tens of thousands of spectators—Queen Victoria open the new Crystal Palace.[59] It was an event which Darwin, in a letter to his son William, described as follows: "I did not much care for it: it was so hot that Aunt Elizabeth fainted dead away and it was very frightening and disagreeable; and we had to lay her flat on the ground."[60] In his *Diary* he recorded his health as "Poorly & sickness & bad headache"; his night was "good." On 13–15 July 1854 he sojourned at Hartfield, which was the home of some Wedgwood relations.[61] Here there was a forest which was "wild" and "lonely" and he greatly enjoyed walking in it alone.[62] In his *Diary* he described his health as "well" and "Well very," and his nights as "goodish" and "good."[63]

An overview of his travels, as recorded in his *Diary of Health*, indicates that several times each year he visited London (some of these visits were to attend scientific meetings and study barnacles at the British Museum) and the homes of relatives; and that he sometimes remained well, and sometimes had varying degrees of flatulence.

Although traveling did not always make him sick, thinking about traveling was painful—sometimes merely anticipating a trip may have caused him to become ill[64]—and he came to feel that all travels were hazardous to his health. He excused himself from visiting Fox by writing to his old friend: "Very many thanks for your most kind & large invitation to Delamere, but I fear we can hardly compass it. I dread going anywhere, on account of my stomach so easily failing under any excitement."[65] Several months later he told Fox that because of his "dreadful flatulence" he could "in fact . . . go no-where."[66] One result of avoiding visits to his friends was that he gained more time for his work. In his *Autobiography* he would write that his illness, although it had cost him working time, had also "saved me from the distractions of society and amusements."[67]

Other events, in addition to travels, affected his health. On 22 February 1851, when Lyell visited him at Down, he wrote in his

Diary: "Well barely much ft." During a 22–25 October 1851 visit by
Lyell and Mrs. Lyell he had "3 or 4 fts," "much flat," and "slight
headache." (It is not known what he and Lyell discussed during these
visits.) In October 1852, however, he had two "Dinner Parties"
without any ill effects. On 17 May 1850, he wrote: "1 fit of ft. from
excitement." The nature of the "excitement" is not specified. On
several occasions he became sick from food: 30 August 1859: "*much
ft.* from spice"; 24 June 1850: "2 long fits of ft evening (Salad)"; 27
April 1853: "Poorly sickness from indigestion"; 15 July 1853 (during
the evening while he was staying at Sea House, Eastbourne): "Dreadful vomiting from Crab." In January 1850, a week before and a week
after Emma gave birth to a fourth son, he had a good deal of nocturnal
flatulence. In April 1851 he stopped his *Diary* for twelve days during
the illness and death of his daughter Annie; then for about ten days he
had an increase in his flatulence, and felt "oppressed." In May 1851, a
week before and a week after Emma gave birth to a fifth son, he had a
"slight Eruption." A cold or boil would sometimes not much disturb
him, and at other times it would cause variform symptoms, including
headache, depression, flatulence, and vomiting.[68]

In the first ten days of July 1854 he recorded in his *Diary* the
following small exacerbation, and then remission, of illness: 1 July:
"Well *very*," night "moderate"; 2 July: "Well not quite, 2 Boils," night
"good"; 3 July: "Poorly, *sickness*," night "poorish"; 4 July: "Rather
poorly," night "goodish"; 5–7 July: "Cold, Bad Boil, rather poorly,"
night "goodish"; 8–9 July: "Well 2 or 3 fts," night "goodish" and then
"good"; 10 July: "Well *very* (some occas. ft)," night "goodish." This
exacerbation may have been caused by a combination of psychological and organic factors: by his boil and cold; and then by having
visitors, and his discussing with Hooker the meaning of "highness"
and "lowness" in species—a subject which had a bearing on natural
selection—and by his answering Hooker's criticisms of his evolutionary ideas.[69]

Many times the *Diary* recorded an exacerbation of illness without
any apparent cause.

Let us now consider what the *Diary of Health* reveals about some of
the overall patterns of Darwin's illness, in 1849–54, and then his
attitude toward his illness.

The *Diary* indicates that almost any physical or mental event which
disturbed Darwin's daily routine could cause him some small degree of
illness, and that his illness mainly centered on his stomach. He lived
under the tyranny of gastric flatulence day and night—a tyranny

compounded of pain, apprehension of pain, and apprehension of uncontrolled vomiting. The vomiting, however, never became long uncontrolled as it had previously; Darwin's symptoms were subacute and never seriously interrupted his work schedule. He described the state of his illness, and the relation of his illness to his work, in letters to Fox and his ex-servant Covington: "Not that I am at all worse, perhaps rather better & lead a very comfortable life with my 3 hours of daily work, but it is the life of a hermit";[70] "I am sorry to say that my health keeps indifferent, and I have given up all hopes of ever being a strong man again ... but natural history fills up my time."[71] One reason for his illness remaining subacute was that he confronted events which were only moderately disturbing, and avoided things which were deeply disturbing. Although he went on worrying and thinking about natural selection—and discussed aspects of it with Hooker—he worked mainly on barnacles. This work, although mentally and physically extremely arduous and furnishing some evidence for evolution, was descriptive and did not cause the anxieties that work on natural selection caused.

Why did Darwin keep his *Diary of Health*? There were several reasons: to observe the effects of hydropathy so that first he and Dr. Gully, and then he alone, could regulate these effects. Then to observe how different factors (travels and visitors, medicines proper and substances used as medicines, electric chains, and so on) influenced his illness. And then to obsessively record the details of his symptoms; his *Diary* entries, with their meticulous record of daily and hourly small clinical changes, possess a peculiar and unique color and form. He expressed some of his thoughts about medically observing himself in a May 1854 letter to Hooker: "I am really truly sorry to hear about your stomach. I ["really" crossed out] *entreat* you to write down your own case,—symptoms—& habits of life, & then consider your case as that of a stranger; & I put it to you, whether common sense w^d. not order you to take more regular exercise & work your Brain less. ["N.B. Take a cold bath & walk before breakfast" inserted] I am certain in the long run you would not lose time. Till you have a thoroughly bad stomach, you will not know the really great evil of it, morally physically, & every way. Do reflect & act resolutely. Remember your troubled heart-action formerly plainly told how your constitution was tired. But I will say no more, excepting that a man is mad to risk health, on which everything—including his *childrens inherited health*, depends.— Do not hate me for this lecture." At the end of the letter he wrote: "Adios, my dear Hooker; do be wise & good & be careful of your stomach, within which, as I know full well, lie intellect, conscience, temper & the affections."[72]

In this letter Darwin's message to his friend and fellow invalid is summed up in the words "reflect & act resolutely": through medical self-observation and medical self-treatment be your own doctor.

Darwin became, for a time, his own doctor, not only because of the exigencies of his illness but because of psychological factors: the influences of his dead father. In obsessively recording his symptoms and the effects of treatment, he was putting into practice his father's early medical training and wish that he observe and treat the sick, and his father's last wish that he have hydropathy. Then, in observing himself like a doctor, he was posthumously becoming like his father who had once been his doctor. At this time he also became fat like his father;[73] and he may have begun doing his scientific work on a stool which had belonged to his father.[74]

After writing his last *Diary of Health* entry on 16 January 1855, Darwin went on writing the daily dates until 31 January, and then stopped all writing. He would not renew his *Diary of Health*. Although he would remain deeply concerned about his illness and treatments, the intensity of his desire to medically observe and treat himself would diminish. His memory of his physician father, instead of influencing him to be his own doctor, would become a medical ideal, an ideal to contemplate and speak about, rather than act on. He would tell his family that his father had been "the wisest man I ever knew," and he would then "quote some maxim or hint of his father's on very many cases of sickness and questions of treatment."[75] He had an "unlimited belief in Dr. Darwin's medical instinct and methods of treatment,"[76] and he would talk about his father's medical prowess to his friends.[77] Throughout his life he would go on revering his father as a doctor.

8

Dr. Lane and Moor Park

On 18 January 1855, two days after writing the last entry in his *Diary*, Darwin moved with his whole family from Down to London, into a house on Upper Baker Street. He described his London sojourn, and the reasons for it, in a letter to Fox: "At the end of the year we had two of our little Boys very ill with fever & Bronchitis & all sorts of ailments.

Partly for amusement & partly for change of air we went to London & took a House for a month, but it turned out a great failure, for the dreadful frost just set in when we went, & all our children got unwell & Emma & I had cough, & colds, & rheumatism nearly all the time."[1] His comment about a "change of air" may have expressed a modification of his previous opinion that London air was bad and country air good. However, at one time, he did state that in "old cases" of whooping cough a "change of air" was "often *very* useful."[2] On 15 February 1855, he and his family returned to Down.[3]

In September 1854 he had finished with barnacles. He then began working on natural selection.[4] Trying to demonstrate how plants could cross oceans, he tried soaking seeds in salt water and then feeding them to fish. In his "imagination" the fish would swallow the seeds, fish and seeds would then be swallowed by a heron, the heron would fly to a new land and there void the seeds which would "splendidly" germinate.[5] When he found that the seeds sank in salt water, and that fish ejected the seeds from their mouths, he wrote Fox: "All nature is perverse & will not do as I wish it, & just at present I wish I had the old Barnacles to work at & nothing new."[6] However he persisted in his experiments on possible means of "transportation of all organic beings."[7] He also began sorting his voluminous notes about species.[8] He feared that the number of facts he had to know would "overpower" him,[9] and that when he got together his notes natural selection would turn out to be "an empty puff-ball."[10]

He wrote Hooker: "I should have less scruple in troubling you if I had any confidence what my work would turn out. Sometimes I think it will be good; at other times I really feel so much ashamed of myself as the author of the *Vestiges* ought to be of himself."[11] *Vestiges of Creation*, a book enunciating an amateurish and speculative theory of evolution, had been vilified by theologians and ridiculed by reputable scientific men (including several friends of Darwin's); its anonymous author had been variously denounced as "atheist, shallow smatterer, and credulous dupe."[12] Darwin feared that when he published his work it would encounter a similar reception; he also hoped that his evolutionary theory was more convincing than that of *Vestiges'* and any previous evolutionary theory.

Throughout 1854 and 1855 he held back from beginning to write up his work. On 16 April 1856, he talked with Lyell at Down and disclosed to the latter—probably for the first time—the main tenets of natural selection. Lyell did not become a convert to this theory, yet he was impressed with it and he wanted to understand it in more detail. He promptly and "strongly"—first verbally and then in letters—urged Darwin to publish his views.[13] "Out with the theory," Lyell wrote Darwin on 1 May 1856, "& let it take date & be cited & understood."[14] At this time Charles Bunbury—a botanist who was Lyell's brother-in-law—also urged Darwin to publish his evolutionary thoughts.[15] Darwin then began to write what he hoped would become a comprehensive and very big book on natural selection, and from May 1856 to June 1858 he wrote up about two-thirds of the topics he intended to discuss.[16]

As his writing progressed—"sometimes in triumph, sometimes in despair"[17]—he expressed, to his old friends and new acquaintances, some of his intense anxieties. In June 1856, referring to the evidences he would muster for his theory, he told Fox: "My work will be horridly imperfect & with many mistakes so that I groan & tremble when I think of it."[18] In July 1856, referring to the War of Nature, he suddenly wrote Hooker: "What a book a Devil's Chaplain might write on the clumsy, wasteful, blundering low and horribly cruel works of nature!"[19] Here, because he is proclaiming the importance of the War of Nature, he sees himself as possessing the identity of a book-writing "Devil's Chaplain." This identity is severely negative and masochistic because it fuses two of his most painful feelings: his horror about the War of Nature and his apprehension that his ideas will be considered immoral and irreligious. A week later, in the course of first confiding his evolutionary ideas to a new correspondent, the staunchly Presbyterian American botanist Asa Gray, he wrote Gray: "I know that this will make you despise me."[20] When he found that he had erred in calculating the quantitative relations between genera, species, and varieties he wrote Hooker: "I am the most miserable, bemuddled, stupid Dog in all England, & am ready to cry at vexation at my blindness & presumption."[21]

He continued to suffer anxiety over the "means of transportation of all organic beings." On 3 October 1856, he told Fox: "No subject gives me so much trouble & doubt & difficulty, as the means of dispersal of the same species of terrestrial productions on the oceanic islands. Land mollusca drive me mad, & I cannot anyhow get their eggs to experimentise on their power of floating & resistance to injurious action of salt-water."[22] He told Hooker that the transport of land mollusks "tormented & haunted" him.[23] In a letter to Hooker, in which he discussed species transport, he called himself "Your insane & perverse friend."[24] However his persistent experiments then began to be successful, and in early 1857 he told Hooker: "The distribution of

F. W. Molluscs, has been ["a" inserted] horrid incubus to me, but I think I know way in; when first hatched they are very active, & I have had 30 or 40 crawl on a dead Duck's foot; & they cannot be jerked off, & will live 15 & even 24 hours out of water."[25] Solving this problem made him "feel as if a thousand pound weight was taken off my back."[26] He was also able to demonstrate that fish would "greedily" eat the seeds of aquatic grasses, "& that Millet seed put into Fish & given to Stock & then voided will germinate."[27] The demonstration of these means of transport, and of other facts about the geographical distribution of species, were striking evidences for evolution— evidences which had been presented by no one before Darwin.[28]

As he worked on his big book, Darwin was concerned not only about his evolutionary theory but about the health of his eight living children. In the early 1850s he had written that his "dread"[29] and "bug-bear"[30] was that his children would develop "hereditary ill-health"[31]—would inherit his ill health. He had written that "even death is better" for his children than to have his kind of illness.[32] In the middle and late 1850s he began to feel that his "dread" was becoming a reality. In September 1857 he reported to Hooker: "It is a strange thing, & I am sure you will sympathize with us, that for the last ten days our darling little fellow Lenny's health has failed, *exactly* as three of our children's have before, namely with extremely irregular & feeble pulse; but he is so much better today that I cannot help having hopes that, unlike the former cases, it may be something temporary. But it makes life very bitter."[33] He wrote Fox that his children's illness was "strange & heart-breaking. A man ought to be a bachelor, & care for no human being to be happy! or not to be wretched."[34] About this time he probably began to notice that Charles Waring Darwin—his tenth and last child, born December 1856—was turning out to be mentally retarded.

During the first year of writing his big book he became tired by his work, and felt that he was "a good way from being a strong man."[35] However he noted that his vomiting "never (or almost never)" occurred.[36] Perhaps his ability to express some of his troubled feelings about his work and children to Hooker and others—more people than he had expressed them to previously—eased his anxiety so that it did not cause severe stomach symptoms.

In October 1856 Fox wrote that he was at Malvern, undergoing hydropathy for an affliction of his legs and back, and that he had visited the grave of Annie Darwin. Darwin, in his letter of reply, expressed his strong feelings for his ill friend and dead daughter, and his aversion to going to Malvern:

> I do most sincerely hope that the water-cure will complete the good work which it has begun; the loss of locomotion to a man so active and energetic as yourself would be grievous. No one can wish more truly for your recovery than I do. Thank you for telling me about our poor dear child's grave. The thought of that time is yet most painful to me. Poor dear happy little thing. I will show your letter tonight to Emma.—About a month ago I felt overdone with my work, & had almost made up my mind to go for a fortnight ["to Malvern" inserted]; but I got to feel that old thoughts would revive so vividly that it would not have answered; but I have often wished to see the grave, & I thank you for telling me about it.[37]

He also refrained from going to Malvern because he continued to be deeply critical of Dr. Gully's beliefs in homeopathy, mesmerism, and clairvoyance.[38] He then wrote Fox that he had "no faith whatever in ordinary doctoring," yet "great faith" in hydropathy and that he was considering going to a hydropathy establishment at Moor Park.[39] Over the following months he watched the progress of Fox's Malvern treatments, writing his friend: "Most heartily glad I am that Dr. Gully has done you some good."[40] And he went on working, although Emma warned him against "overwork" and urged him to go to Malvern.[41]

In February 1857 he told Fox: "I do not think I shall have courage for Water Cure again: I am now trying mineral acids, with, I think, good effect."[42] "Mineral acids" probably meant a mixture of muriatic (hydrochloric) acid and nitric acid.[43] It was believed that in some cases of "dyspepsia" the stomach did not secrete acids and that treatment should consist of replacing these missing secretions. Acids were also thought to act as "tonics."[44] It is not known for how long Darwin took "mineral acids"; their "good effect" had apparently ceased by April.

On 22 April 1857, feeling "very much below par at home" and that he had "worked too hard at home on my species book,"[45] he went by himself for two weeks to the hydropathic establishment at Moor Park, Farnham, Surrey (a place once famous as the home of Sir William Temple and his secretary Dean Swift).[46] At Moor Park—after a week of daily shallow baths, douches, and sitz baths[47]—he reported to Hooker that he had "already received an amount of good, which is quite incredible to myself & quite unaccountable. I can walk & eat like a hearty Christian; and even my nights are good." He commented to

Hooker that the hydropathy of Moor Park, like that of Malvern, helped him deny some of his anxieties: "Hydropathy . . . dulls one's brain splendidly, I have not thought about a single species of any kind since leaving home."[48] He returned to Moor Park in June and November 1857, for periods of one to two weeks of hydropathy.[49] He does not seem to have gone on with hydropathy at home, as he had done after Malvern.

He found in Moor Park, besides hydropathy, other benefits and attractions which (he would recollect many years later) caused him to feel "rested and improved and full of enjoyment."[50]

He was, physically at least, sometimes relieved of the pressures of his family (sometimes Emma and/or his sick daughter Etty who also received hydropathy may have been with him at Moor Park).[51] He was also, to some extent, relieved of the severe pressures of writing his big book (he would, as will be seen, go on thinking about some aspects of his evolutionary work). "Moor Park," he wrote Fox, "I like *much* better as a place than Malvern."[52] He found that Moor Park's woods were "very pleasant for walking."[53] He would describe these woods as "very wild and lonely, so just suits me. . . . There is an exquisite mixture of ancient Scotch Firs and very old magnificent Birches."[54]

The physician to Moor Park, Dr. Edward Wickstead Lane, was only thirty-five years old (thirteen years younger than Darwin, and probably the youngest physician Darwin had yet consulted), and lacked the national prominence of Dr. Gully. In 1850 he had studied law at Edinburgh University, and in 1853 he obtained his M.D. degree from Edinburgh University. In 1854 he had come to Moor Park. He was charming and, despite his youth, he had read widely in medical and general literature and had thought deeply about the philosophy and efficacy of different medical treatments.[55] After first meeting Dr. Lane, Darwin's confidence in doctors and medical treatments—which had waned since his contact with Dr. Gully—was renewed, and he reported to Fox: "I like Dr. Lane & his wife & her mother, who are the proprietors of this establishment very much. Dr. L. is too young, but that is his only fault—but he is a gentleman & very well read man. And in one respect I like him better than Dr. Gully, viz that he does not believe in all the rubbish which Dr. G. does; nor does he pretend to explain much which neither he nor any doctor can explain."[56] During his second Moor Park visit he told Hooker: "Dr. Lane & Wife, & mother-in-law Lady Drysdale are some of the nicest people, I have ever met."[57] He read Dr. Lane's just-published small book, *Hydrop-*

athy: Or, The Natural System of Medical Treatment. An Explanatory Essay,[58] and commented that it was "very good & worth reading."[59]

In his book Dr. Lane summarized what he called "the philosophy of hydropathy" as follows:

> Hydropathy ... is based on one ... distinctively characteristic idea ... that nature possesses ... in the original construction of the living organism, her own means of restoration, when that organism is overtaken by disease; that she is constantly endeavoring to work out her own cure; that she frequently succeeds in her efforts ... when her powers are not sufficient the aid of art is to be invoked, that aid must be founded on a consideration of the primary laws of health as unfolded by physiology ... hydropathy is grounded ... on the belief that the mass of chronic diseases are most effectually and most safely cured ... by the identical means ... modified ... according to circumstances, that are requisite for maintaining the animal economy in health.... Its cardinal medicines are the apparently simple medicaments of air, exercise, water, and diet ... along with healthy moral influences.[60]

Dr. Lane later wrote an account of Darwin at Moor Park, which is the only extant recollection of Darwin by a physician who treated him.[61] Lane described his patient's illness as follows:

> Mr. Darwin was ... a great sufferer of dyspepsia of an aggravated character, brought on, as he always supposed, by the extreme seasickness he underwent in H.M.S. 'Beagle.' ... In the course of a long professional experience I have seen many cases of violent indigestion, in its many forms, and with the multiform tortures it entails, but I cannot recall any where the pain was so truly poignant as in his. When the worst attacks were on he seemed almost crushed with agony, the nervous system being severely shaken, and the temporary depression resulting distressingly great. I mention this circumstance because it was then that I first perceived the wonderful sweetness and gentleness of his nature, his patience, and the gratitude with which he received the most ordinary services and tokens of sympathy.... Of course such attacks as I have spoken of were only occasional—for no constitution could have borne up long under them in their acute phase—but he was never to the last wholly well.[62]

Lane's account, although not specifying the exact nature and location of his patient's pain, reveals just how deeply the latter suffered; and knowing this affords further insight into Darwin's previous accounts of his illness. When Darwin wrote that he had a "sudden attack," and "fits of flatulence" which were "very bad," "excessive," and "sharp," he may have been describing brief periods (the exact duration is never specified) of pain which were crushing, torturing, and emotionally overwhelming. And when he wrote that he had lesser degrees of flatulence he may have been describing lesser degrees of pain.[63]

Lane recollected that Darwin—"apart from his feeble health, and constantly in spite of it"—would eagerly socialize with the many different people who were at Moor Park: conversing and joking, "he dearly loved a joke, seeming to enjoy it to his heart's core"; and laughing "with a mock-mischievous expression that took you captive."[64] Darwin told his family how he made friends with Miss Butler, an Irish lady. Both he and she had the same habit of putting salt on the tablecloth to eat with their bread. She charmed and amused him with "bright anecdoty talk" and by claiming to have seen the ghost of her father "when he *didn't* die."[65] In the absence of his family and friends she became his solace and comfort.

Lane's most vivid recollection was of the walks that he and his patient took in Moor Park's woods: Darwin

> was then literally "all eyes." Nothing escaped him. No object in nature, whether Flower, or Bird, or Insect of any kind, could avoid his loving recognition. He knew about them all . . . could give you endless information in his own graphic way about them . . . a question of comparative Botany or Zoology would crop up and carry him back to his great voyage in the 'Beagle', with countless anecdotes of all he saw of nature and of men in the course of it—the whole delivered . . . in a manner so full of point and pith and living interest, and so full of charm, that you could not but be supremely delighted, nor fail to feel . . . that you were enjoying a vast intellectual treat to be never forgotten, and that these were indeed red-letter days in your calendar.[66]

After a sojourn at Moor Park, Darwin would return to Down and, feeling better, recommence work on his species book; soon, he would again feel ill. Attributing his illness to "nothing but the mental work,"[67] he would for a time go on working. In June 1857 he had written Hooker: "It is most provoking that a cold on leaving Moor Park suddenly turned into my old vomiting, & I have been *almost* as bad since my return home as before, notwithstanding the really surprising state of health I was in then. I fear that my head will stand no thought, but I would sooner be the wretched contemptible invalid, which I am, than live the life of an idle squire."[68] Rather work and be a "wretched contemptible invalid" than be well and "idle"! In these self-punitive, rough, and eloquent words Darwin was stating what had become one of his main credos. He was, also, grimly anticipating a future of work and suffering.

In January 1858, in a letter to Hooker in which he mentioned the illness of himself and his family, he let himself go in a sudden burst of feeling: "Oh health, health, you are my daily & nightly bugbear & stop all enjoyment in life." Then he quickly apologized: "But I really beg pardon, it is very foolish & weak to howl this way. Everyone has got his heavy burthen in this world."[69] By mid-April his health had become "very bad from overwork";[70] and so for two weeks—Tuesday, 20 April to Tuesday, 4 May—he sojourned at Moor Park.[71] There he had hydropathy, three times a day, every day.[72] In his extant letters·he gave a detailed account of his various activities and concerns during these two weeks.

After Emma wrote him that she was "headachy," he wrote back suggesting that, after he returned home, she and their daughter Henrietta come to Moor Park for hydropathy.[73] He then added: "I wish you knew how I value you; and what an inexpressible blessing it is to have one whom one can always trust, one always the same, always ready to give comfort, sympathy and the best advice—God bless you, my dear, you are too good for me."[74] He corresponded with his son William—who was then eighteen years old, and whom he called "my dear old fellow"—following William's activities, sending him money, and encouraging him to read and study.[75] In his letters to Emma and William he commented on the trial of Simon Bernard, accused of attempting to assassinate the French Emperor Napoleon III,[76] and on a discovery by the photographer Claudet;[77] and he expressed strong opinions on several novels. He told Emma he was reading a novel which was "feminine, for the author is ignorant about money matters, and not much of a lady—for she makes her men say 'My Lady.' "[78] He had curiously mixed reactions to *Riverston*,[79] by Georgiana Craik:[80] "I like Miss Craik very much, though we have some battles, and differ on every subject."[81] He urged William to read *The Three Chances*,[82] which he described as "very clever, and part very amusing."[83]

Moor Park had a billiard table and he began to play billiards enthusiastically.[84] He journeyed from Moor Park to the military camp at Aldershot, a distance of about four miles, and there watched Queen Victoria review troops.[85] For undetermined reasons[86] he found the review "too much," and it caused him to feel "poorly."[87]

He wrote his ex-servant Covington that he spent his day "doing nothing" and "loitering about" Moor Park's woods.[88] He wrote Emma how he once fell asleep in the Moor Park woods, and then "awoke with a chorus of the birds singing around me, and squirrels running up the trees, and some woodpeckers laughing, and it was as pleasant and rural a scene as I ever saw, and I did not care one penny how any of the beasts or birds had been formed."[89] He experienced these "pleasant" feelings because he was able, for a time, to put thoughts of natural selection and the War of Nature out of his mind, and to recapture some of his early feelings for wooded scenery.

He did not, however, spend all of his day "doing nothing" and not caring about natural selection. There were times when he would closely study the different plants in the Moor Park wood; and he would "reflect with astonishment at the play of forces which determine the presence & relative number of the ... plants which may be counted in it"[90]—the "play of forces" was, of course, the War of Nature. When he was in the wood he would also spend "hours"[91] watching "many thousands" of ants.[92] He was intent on observing the different kinds of work done by each ant, and he thought that he had found "the rare slave-making species."[93] His observations on the division of labor among ants caused him to reflect deeply: at first he saw these observations as a "grave difficulty" to his theory of natural selection;[94] then he came to realize that what he had seen was, really, an example of the "efficiency" of natural selection.[95]

Although he complained that the other patients at Moor Park were a "horrid dull set,"[96] he made the acquaintance of a Hungarian— whom he described as a "thorough gentleman ... with broken health"[97]—who promised to write him about the occurrence of stripes in Hungarian horses.[98] The occurrence of these stripes was evidence for the evolution of different breeds of horses from a common ancestor. He received a visit from Fox, and in his talk with his old friend he obtained information about the occurrence of certain traits in different species of birds[99]—more evidence for the evolution of one animal from another. He corresponded with Hooker, Lyell, and others about different aspects of his evolutionary theory.[100] On one day he wrote "six longish" letters.[101] He seems to have done some writing on his book.[102]

In the last days of his two-week sojourn at Moor Park he began feeling "splendidly well,"[103] was able to make "some splendid strokes" at billiards,[104] and one day walked four miles.[105] "As usual," he told Hooker, "hydropathy has made a man of me for a short time."[106]

It was only a very short time. Nine days after his return to Down he informed his son William: "It is very disheartening for me, that all the wonderful good which Moor Park did me at the time, has gone all away like a flash of lightning now that I am at work again."[107] He planned that Emma and Henrietta would go to Moor Park, and that he would then return there.[108] As he went on writing his big book he commented that he had "to discuss every branch of natural history, and the work is beyond my strength and tries me sorely."[109]

9

Illness and Writing
The Origin of Species

In June 1858 Darwin stopped work on his big book because Alfred Wallace sent him what he described as "an essay containing my exact theory [of natural selection]."[1] He felt "forestalled,"[2] and as if he had lost his "priority of many years";[3] and he turned to Lyell and Hooker for advice. His two friends arranged that his and Wallace's evolutionary writings—Wallace's essay and Darwin's 1844 essay and an 1857 letter to Asa Gray—be publicly read at a 1 July 1858 meeting of the London Linnean Society. This public reading, however, made practically no impact on those who heard it.[4]

At this time Darwin was concerned not only about the priority of his ideas but about a succession of illnesses in his family. First, toward the end of June, his daughter Etty became "seriously ill with an attack very like diptheria,"[5] and one of her nurses contracted this illness. As Etty and her nurse began recovering, his son Charles Waring—who was 1½ years old and severely mentally retarded—fell ill with scarlet fever and died on 28 June. Charles Waring's death saddened Darwin, yet he was also "thankful" that he had been freed from the pressures of caring for his son.[6] Charles Waring's impairment may have been too painful for him to think about: in his letters to Fox and Hooker— where he commented on the illnesses of his different children—he had not mentioned Charles Waring.

After Charles Waring's death one of his nurses contracted scarlet fever, and it was feared that a scarlet fever epidemic might break out in Down House and Downe. On 2 July, following the urging of Fox and others, Darwin moved most of his family out of Down to the home of his sister-in-law, Sara Elizabeth Wedgwood, in Hartfield, Sussex. He wrote Fox that he and Emma would stay at Down "till Etty

can move & I of course stay till nurse is out of all danger whatever."[7]
His fear of an epidemic of scarlet fever made him feel "terribly
anxious";[8] yet in his letters he makes no mention of any stomach
complaints. On 5 July, with Charles Waring's nurse recovering and
Etty becoming stronger, he felt relieved and "more happy."[9] On 9
July, he, Etty, and Emma joined their family at Hartfield. The Darwin
family then spent much of the summer at different country houses.
The feared epidemic of scarlet fever apparently became a reality, for
on 21 July Darwin reported to Fox: "There has been another child die
in village of Down; which makes the fifth; so we rejoice we acted on
your advice & left home."[10] On 13 August the Darwins returned to
Down.[11]

Darwin was relieved that his children were (for the moment) free
from infections; however, he went on worrying over, and feeling
responsible for, their tendency (now present in five children) to have
an "irregular pulse." "This is," he wrote Hooker, "my accursed
constitution showing itself under a new form."[12]

In the summer of 1858 he began to write what he called "an
abstract" of his big book.[13] His usual slow rate of writing now
quickened. For now more than ever—although still beset by doubts
and anxieties—he was driven to publish his theory. Two forces which
especially drove him were his rivalry with Wallace and his ambition
to make an impact on thought. (The 1 July Linnean Society papers,
when published in October 1858, only influenced a very few naturalists.[14]) After about one year of "hard" writing he finished his
"abstract," which, when published, would be *The Origin of Species*.[15]

During this year he was almost always conscious of how the
pressures of writing up his theory affected his stomach. In November
1858 he wrote Fox: "I am working slowly & steadily at my Abstract &
making progress & hope to print in the Spring. My stomach has been
bad enough, & I have lately spent a very pleasant week at Moor Park,
& Hydropathy & idleness did me wonderful good & I walked one day
4 1/2 miles,—quite Herculean feat for me!"[16] "Bad enough," in
Darwin's vocabulary, probably meant that he had much flatulence
but no vomiting. At Moor Park he was never entirely idle, and at this
time he may have continued his observations on ants and worked on
his "abstract."[17]

As his "abstract" neared completion, his stomach symptoms
became more severe, and he went to Moor Park from 5 to 29 February
1859. From there he reported to Fox:

> I have been extra bad of late, with the old severe vomiting rather
> often & much distressing swimming of the head: I have been here a

> week & shall stay another & it has already done me good. I am
> taking Pepsine, i.e. the ["chief" inserted] element of the gastric juice,
> & I think it does me good and at first was charmed with it. My
> abstract is the cause, I believe of the main part of the ills to which
> my flesh is heir to; but I have only two more chapters & to correct
> all, & then I shall be a comparatively free man.[18]

This is the only reference that Darwin makes to pepsin. He probably
took pepsin because it was held that his vomiting was caused by a
failure of his stomach to secrete pepsin (the same reasons that had
caused him to try "mineral acids" two years previously).[19] He
recorded in his *Journal* that the two weeks at Moor Park "did not do
me so much good as usual."[20]

At Moor Park he probably continued to enjoy playing billiards, and
early in 1859 he bought a billiard table for himself—selling a gold
watch which had belonged to his father and some beautiful and
valuable Wedgwood ceramics in order to get the necessary money[21]—
and installed the table in a room in Down House.[22] In March he
reported to Fox that playing billiards at home "does me a deal of good,
and drives the horrid species out of my head."[23] For several years
billiard playing would be a welcome diversion from the pressures of
his work; then he would lose interest in billiards.[24]

In the last stages of the writing of his "abstract" he described his
health, and the relation between his health and work, in a series of
letters to Hooker (Hooker, as always, was his main intellectual
confidant): 7 April 1859: "My god how I long ["for my stomach's
sake" inserted] to wash my hands of it,—for at least one long spell."[25]
"It" was his abstract, which he had completed and was now correcting. 12 April: "Do not, pray, think of giving up coming here: I
shd. extremely regret it. With you I can go away the *moment* my
stomach feels bad, & that is the important point for me."[26]

Five weeks later, when he had finished correcting his "abstract," he
wrote Hooker: "My health has quite failed."[27] He described his
symptoms as "bad vomiting ... & great prostration of mind &
body."[28] On 21 May he went to Moor Park,[29] telling Hooker that his
"object" in going was "to drive the subject [the subject of the origin of
species] out of my head."[30] After six days at Moor Park he reported:
"entire rest & the douche & Adam Bede [George Eliot's recently
published novel *Adam Bede*] have together done me a world of
good."[31]

His health did not remain "good" for long. At the end of May he
began correcting proofs of his book, sent him by his publisher John
Murray, and he found that his corrections—entailing considerable

revision and rewriting—were "terrifically heavy," "most difficult,"[32] and upsetting to his stomach. Emma, putting aside her misgivings about the irreligious nature of the book, aided him in his corrections.[33] On 2 July he wrote Hooker: "I have been bad, having had two days of bad vomiting owing to the accursed Proofs—I shall have to go to Moor Park before long."[34] As his vomiting went on being "bad" he went to Moor Park from 19 to 26 July.[35] On 28 July he wrote Hooker: "Take warning by me & do not work too hard. For god's sake, think of this.—It is dreadfully uphill work with me getting my confounded volume finished."[36] On 1 September he wrote Hooker: "I had a terrible long fit of vomiting yesterday, which makes the world rather extra gloomy today, and I have an insanely strong wish to finish my accursed Book."[37] He then wondered whether, after finishing his book, he would "ever be good for anything again."[38]

He would later tell a friend that, during the year when he was working on his book, he "had seldom been able to write, without interruption from pain, for more than twenty minutes at a time!"[39] He referred to episodes of stomach pain.

On 10 September he finished correcting his last proofs—his book was now entitled *The Origin of Species*—and the next day he wrote Hooker: "Oh good Heavens, the relief to my mind & body to banish the whole subject from my mind."[40]

He now planned, as part of his medical treatment, a long period of "rest & hydropathy."[41] He would first go, for three or four weeks, to a new hydropathic establishment which had opened three years previously at Ilkley House, near Ilkley, in Yorkshire.[42] He would return to Down for a week, and afterward go to Moor Park for three or four weeks.[43] He told Fox: "I intend, if I can keep to my resolution of being idle this winter. But I fear ennui will be as bad as a bad stomach."[44] He thought that, because of the time of year, he would not be able to rent a house for his family in Ilkley. He then feared being alone in Ilkley House, and he wrote Miss Butler—the Irish lady whose conversation had charmed him at Moor Park—the following note: "My object in troubling you . . . a trouble, which I hope & believe you will forgive— is to know whether there is any chance of your being at Ilkley in beginning of October. It would be rather terrible to go into the great place & not know a soul. But if you were there I should feel safe & home-like. You see that all your former kindness makes me confident of receiving more kindness."[45]

He arrived in Ilkley House on 3 October and (presumably) met with Miss Butler, for on 5 October he wrote Fox: "I am in this establish-

Illustrations

Charles Darwin, 1849, the year he
began hydropathy at Malvern, and
then at Down. (Courtesy of Radio
Times Hulton Picture Library.)

Charles Darwin, 1854. (Courtesy of the
Syndics of the University Library,
Cambridge.)

Charles Darwin, probably in his late 50s or early 60s. At this time he was very sick, and worried about the health of his children and attacks on *The Origin*. When he was fifty-five Asa Gray wrote to him: "Your photograph with the venerable beard gives the look of your having suffered, and, perhaps from the beard, of having grown older. I hope there is still much in you—but take it quietly and gently!" (Courtesy of the American Philosophical Society.)

The last photograph of Charles Darwin. "It was at his (Darwin's) home that I saw him, a year and a half before his death. . . . He was one of those men whose character was palpably written on his face. . . . he had a quiet contemplative look, with an occasional slight smile passing over his countenance which made one feel perfectly at ease in his company. . . . His look was both penetrative and meditative. . . . it had . . . the keenness and sensitiveness of the man whom nothing escaped, who saw everything there was to see, whose eyes seemed to pierce beneath the surface of things" (James Bryce, "Personal Reminiscences of Charles Darwin and of the Reception of the 'Origin of Species,' "*Proceedings of the American Philosophical Society,* 1909). (Courtesy of the Syndics of the University Library, Cambridge.)

Emma Darwin, 1840. At this time Emma had been married one year and, in a letter to an aunt, she expressed the following feelings for her sick husband: "It is a great happiness to me when Charles is most unwell that he continues just as sociable as ever, and is not like the rest of the Darwins, who will not say how they really are; but he always tells me how he feels and never wants to be alone, but continues just as warmly affectionate as ever, so that I feel I am a comfort to him. And to you I may say that he is the most affectionate person possible." (Courtesy of the American Museum of Natural History.)

Dr. Robert Waring Darwin. (Courtesy of the Royal College of Surgeons of England.)

TUDOR HOUSE.

Published by Thos Hartley   Stationer, Malvern

Great Malvern.

The "rigors" of the "Cold Water Cure,"
as practiced at Malvern. A comic
sketch. The patient, imprisoned, is tormented by a fly. The engraving is dated
May 1869. There are others in the series.
(From the Gerald Morice Collection.)

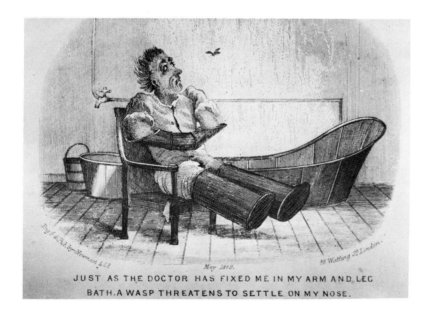

JUST AS THE DOCTOR HAS FIXED ME IN MY ARM AND LEG
BATH. A WASP THREATENS TO SETTLE ON MY NOSE.

Dr. Gully's Hydropathic Establishment,
showing Tudor House and Holyrood
House connected by the "Bridge of
Sighs." (From the Gerald Morice Collection.)

General view of Malvern, Worcester-
shire, as it appeared in the days of the
"Cold Water Cure." In back are the Mal-
vern Hills, called "the mountain" by
Charles Darwin. In the center is the
Priory Church. (From the Gerald
Morice Collection.)

Joseph D. Hooker. (Crown Copyright,
reproduced with the permission of the
Controller of Her Majesty's Stationery
Office, and of the Director, Royal
Botanic Gardens, Kew.)

Dr. Henry Holland. (By courtesy of
the Wellcome Trustees.)

Dr. James M. Gully. (By courtesy of the Wellcome Trustees.)

Dr. William Jenner. (By courtesy of the
Wellcome Trustees.)

Dr. William Brinton. (By courtesy of
the Wellcome Trustees.)

Dr. Henry Bence Jones. (By courtesy of
the Wellcome Trustees.)

Dr. Andrew Clark. (By courtesy of the
Wellcome Trustees.)

ment & have ["a" inserted] sitting room & bedroom. . . . I always hate
everything new & perhaps it is only this that makes me at present
detest the whole place & everything except one kind lady here, whom
I knew at Moor Park."[46] In the same letter he urged Fox to come and
stay with him. Fox did not come, and he makes no further mention of
Miss Butler. He was then able to rent a family house, and on 17
October his family joined him at Ilkley.[47] The Darwins would sojourn
at Ilkley for almost two months (abandoning plans to go to Moor
Park), and Emma and Henrietta would undergo hydropathy.[48]

Soon after coming to Ilkley Darwin suffered what he aptly
described as "a series of calamities":[49] first a sprained ankle; then a
"badly swollen whole leg"[50] resembling "elephantiasis," a swollen face
with "eyes almost closed up," and "much rash"; and "a frightful
succession of boils—four or five at once."[51] The cause of this swelling
and "rash" are obscure. Ilkley's physician, Dr. Edmund Smith,
assured him that this was a "unique crisis" which would do him "much
good."[52] He did not believe this and he could only feel "quite ill,"[53]
and as if he was "living in Hell."[54] Because of his boils and difficulty in
walking he was at first only able to undergo a little hydropathy. After
about six weeks he began improving, and then for ten days he felt
"splendidly well."[55]

In two letters to Fox he gave his impressions of Dr. Smith. "Dr.
Smith, I think, is sensible, but he is a Homeopathist!! & as far as I can
judge does not personally look much after patients or anything else."[56]
"Dr. Smith . . . they all say . . . is very careful in bad illness but he
constantly gives me impression as if he cared very much for the Fee &
very little for the Patient."[57] Dr. Smith was fifty-five years old; he has
been described as "able and conscientious," yet not in good health,
and not vigorous in his hydropathic work.[58]

At Ilkley Darwin received letters from some of those to whom he
had sent prepublication copies of *The Origin*. Hooker (at long last)
and Thomas Huxley wrote of their support for *The Origin*'s ideas, and
their responses—those of men whose opinion he respected—caused
him to feel "cockered up."[59] Adam Sedgwick, his old friend and
geology teacher, wrote him a letter of disapprobation, ridicule, and
"pain,"[60] which caused him to "grieve."[61] On 24 November 1859, *The
Origin* was published, sold out its first edition, and (unlike the
Linnean Society papers) began making an impact on peoples' thinking. When Darwin returned to Down early in December he began
receiving a "Multitude of Letters" expressing different opinions about
him and his book.[62] Some admired him as "the greatest revolutionist

in natural history of this century";[63] others called him "the most dangerous man in England,"[64] and feared and hated him—and he especially disliked being hated.

10

Illness and *The Origin*
Controversy (I)

Toward the end of December 1859, Darwin's stomach began causing him what he described as "incessant discomfort, I may say misery."[1] Because of this, early in 1860, he consulted "a Mr. Headland": probably Dr. Frederick W. Headland, a London physician, author of a prize-winning book, *An Essay on the Action of Medicines in the System*, and editor of *Dr. Royle's Manual of Materia Medica and Therapeutics.*[2] Dr. Headland started him on "a course of nitro-muriatic acid [perhaps different doses of the "mineral acids" he had taken three years ago], eating no sweet things, & drinking some wine."[3] In March he told Fox that "as yet" he felt no relief, "& I shall go to my grave, I suppose, grumbling & growling with daily, almost hourly, discomfort."[4]

Early in March he suffered, very briefly, from a new symptom. On 2 March he told Asa Gray: "I have had very short but sharpish touch of illness,—a slight touch of pleurisy, & am weak."[5] The next day he told Hooker: "I had an attack of fever (with a touch of pleurisy) which came on like a lion, but went off as a lamb, but has shattered me a good bit."[6]

His strength returned, and in May he wrote Fox that, as a result of Dr. Headland's regimen, he felt better.[7] (After this he makes no further mention of Dr. Headland, or the latter's treatment.) He also went on to tell Fox: "I do not know whether you ever see ["various" inserted] Reviews, but the attacks have been falling thick and heavy on my ["now" inserted] case-hardened hide."[8] Two of the bitterest reviews were written by his old friends: the geologist Adam Sedgwick and the anatomist Richard Owen.

He was not as "hardened" to attacks as he had hoped. On 26 June—with *The Origin* about to be publicly debated at the British Association meeting in Oxford—he wrote Hooker that he could not be in Oxford, because "my stomach has utterly failed."[9] From 28 June to 7 July he went for hydropathy to Dr. Lane's new establishment, which had moved from Moor Park to Sudbrook Park, Richmond, Surrey.[10]

From Sudbrook Park he wrote Hooker: "I have been very poorly, with almost continuous bad headache for 48 hours, & I was low enough, & thinking what ["a" inserted] useless burthen I was to myself & all others."[11] He was "cheered"[12] and felt better when he heard that, during the Oxford debate, Hooker and Huxley had defended *The Origin* against the attacks of Richard Owen, Robert FitzRoy, and Bishop Samuel Wilberforce. "I am glad I was not at Oxford," he wrote Hooker, "for I should have been overwhelmed, with my stomach in its present state."[13] He then wrote Huxley: "I honour your pluck; I would as soon have died as tried to answer the Bishop in such an assembly."[14]

After July 1860 he seems to have had no further professional contact with Dr. Lane. The reasons for the cessation of this warm doctor-patient relationship are obscure. Perhaps Darwin disliked Dr. Lane's new hydropathy establishment (his letters from Sudbrook Park, compared with those from Moor Park, are strikingly devoid of comments on his surroundings). He may, also, have been reluctant to leave his sick daughter Etty. He continued to have pleasant memories for his sojourns at Moor Park, and for Dr. Lane and Dr. Lane's family.[15]

Etty was ill from the spring of 1860 until the summer of 1861:[16] her symptoms were described first as "odd fever—partly remittent partly typhoid,"[17] and then as "indigestion and weakness."[18] During the year of her illness Darwin moved with her to different places of convalescence, closely observed the course of her illness (asking Hooker for advice on her medications[19]), aided in nursing her (during her previous illness he had played backgammon with her regularly every day[20]), and because of her condition suffered "incessant anxiety."[21] Etty would recollect that his "tender sympathy and emotion" was "almost too keen" for her.[22] He twice consulted Dr. (now Sir) Henry Holland about Etty (although he seems to have no longer consulted Holland about his own health), and he was somewhat reassured when Holland prognosticated (correctly) that Etty, in time, would recover.[23] He then worried about the decaying teeth of his son George, and told Hooker: "It is strange how immediately any mental excitment upsets & utterly prostrates; seeing George chloroformed for his teeth brought on my stomach illness."[24]

When his son Leonard was recovering from a dangerous fever he twice wrote that he and his family, and "all Darwins," "ought to be exterminated."[25] This referred to his strongly held opinion that the Darwins were predisposed to illness and that this predisposition was evil and hereditary.[26]

In the winter of 1860–61 he wrote Hooker that he had insomnia and "my heart is almost always palpitating,"[27] and "my stomach now keeps bad nearly all day and night."[28] He thought of traveling to Malvern to "try a little water-cure."[29] Emma, as in past years, urged him to do this. He then kept putting off the actual trip. He was reluctant to revive memories of Annie, move his whole family, stop work on the book which would be the sequel to *The Origin—The Variation of Animals and Plants under Domestication*—and stop experiments on the fertilization of orchids and other botanical experiments. So he went on working, sometimes fearing that he would "soon entirely fail."[30] He tried to regulate the length of his work periods by the sensation he felt in his stomach: "I know well that my head would have failed years ago," he wrote Hooker, "had not my stomach always saved ["safed" crossed out] me from a minute's over-work."[31]

Emma, because of her unwavering concern over his illness, felt anxiety over his religious disbelief and wrote him in a letter: "I cannot tell you the compassion I have felt for all your suffering. . . . Nor the gratitude I have felt for the cheerful and affectionate looks you have given me when I know you have been miserably uncomfortable. . . . I mind your suffering nearly as much as I should my own and I find the only relief to my own mind is to take it as from God's hand and to try to believe that all suffering and illness is meant to help us exalt our minds and to look forward with hope to a future state." She then begged him to pray "to Heaven for the sake of your daily happiness. . . . I feel in my inmost heart your admirable qualities and feelings and all I would hope is that you would direct them upwards, as well as to one who values them above everything in the world. . . . I shall keep this by me till I feel cheerful and comfortable again about you. . . . I thought I would write it partly to relieve my own mind." She, after writing such a letter, did gain some mental relief and was better able to nurse him. He, after reading her letter, remained unaffected by her plea for prayer and Christian belief. Yet, touched by her concern for him, he preserved her letter, and wrote on it: "God bless you. C.D. 1861."[32]

In March 1861 Hooker informed him that Professor Henslow—who had greatly aided him in his early career, and been a constant friend[33]—was slowly dying from disease of the heart and lungs.[34] Darwin promptly expressed his feelings of affection and respect for Henslow as a man.[35] He then wrote Hooker that he was "not equal" to visiting Henslow, because "any mental excitment" would "upset" his health.[36] He did not explain what would be upsetting about such a visit. He may have wanted to avoid seeing a dying friend who was

deeply religious and who held traditional views on species (although
Henslow did not actively oppose *The Origin*).[37] He worried about not
visiting Henslow, and how Hooker would regard this (Hooker was
Henslow's son-in-law, and was nursing Henslow)—at this time he
seems to have been unable to discuss with Hooker the differences of
opinion between himself and Henslow—and he wrote Hooker a letter
reaffirming his affection for Henslow and grimly pictured the precarious state of his physical health:

> I am much pained to think of poor dear Henslow's state. . . . I write
> now only to say that if Henslow, you thought, would really like to
> see me, I would of course start at once. The thought had once oc-
> curred to me to offer, & the sole reason why I did not was that the
> going with the agitation would cause me probably to arrive utterly
> prostrated, I shd. be certain to have severe vomiting afterwards,
> but that would not much signify, but I doubt whether I could stand
> the agitation at the time. I never felt my weakness greater evil. I
> have just had specimen for I spoke a few minutes at Linn. Soc.[38] on
> Monday & though extra well, it brought on 24 hours vomiting. I
> suppose there is some Inn at which I could stay, for I shd. not like
> to be in the House (even if you could hold me) as my retching is apt
> to be extremely loud.—I shd. never forgive myself, if I did not in-
> stantly come, if Henslow's wish to see me was more than a passing
> thought.

At the end of the letter he repeated: "I Shd. *never* forgive myself, if I
disappointed the most fleeting wish of my master & friend to whom I
owe so much."[39]

Darwin did not journey to Henslow's home in Hitcham, Suffolk,[40]
and he thus spared himself the pain and humiliation of vomiting when
he was in the company of his friends. Several weeks later Henslow
died, and Darwin then wrote Hooker: "I fully believe a better man
never walked this earth."[41]

During the following year his illness does not seem to have been
severe. In June 1862 he wrote Hooker that he had "violent skin
inflammation" and "hands burning as if dipped in hell fire."[42] He then
reported that his skin was better, and "the Doctors told me it was
Eczema that I have had."[43] His "Doctors" have not been identified. He
does not seem to have had a regular doctor.

In late 1862 Hooker, in a letter to a friend, depicted Darwin as
follows:

> Darwin still works away at his experiments and his theory and
> startles us by the surprising discoveries he now makes in botany;

his work on the fertilisation of orchids is quite unique—there is nothing in the whole range of Botanical Literature to compare with it, and this, with his other works, 'Journal,' 'Coral Reefs,' 'Volcanic Islands,' 'Geology of Beagle,' 'Anatomy, etc., of Cirripedes' and 'Origin,' raise him without doubt to the position of the first Naturalist in Europe, indeed I question if he will not be regarded as great as any that ever lived; his powers of observation, memory and judgement seem prodigious, his industry indefatigable and his sagacity in planning experiments, fertility of resources and care in conducting them are unrivalled, and all this with health so detestable that his life is a curse to him and more than half his days and weeks are spent in inaction—in forced idleness of mind and body.[44]

In November 1862 Darwin wrote Hooker about a new medication for his stomach: "Did you ever hear of 'Condy's Ozonised Water'? I have been trying it with I think, *extraordinary* advantage—to comfort at least, a tea-spoon in water 3 or 4 times a day.—If you meet any poor dyspeptic like me, suggest it."[45]

He could not have used "Condy's Ozonised Water" for long, for in 1863–64 and 1865 he suffered two exacerbations of his illness which were as severe as his 1839–42 and 1848–49 exacerbations.

11

Illness and *The Origin*
Controversy (II)

Months after publishing *The Origin* Darwin became "painfully" aware that he was "hated" by Richard Owen,[1] and that Owen's "power of hatred was certainly unsurpassed."[2] By 1862 he had come to regard Owen as *The Origin*'s "chief" and most "annoying" foe.[3] (Owen was England's leading anatomist, and had once been Darwin's friend and scientific helper.) Early in January 1863 Darwin read an article by his old and close friend, Hugh Falconer, which showed that Owen had made unauthorized use of some of Falconer's scientific work.[4] He then wrote Hooker: "I am burning with indignation & must exhale ... read the first part of Falconer's paper ... & mark Owen's conduct. I could not get to sleep till past 3 last night for indignation."[5] When he said that he was "burning with indignation" he was, literally, reporting that thinking of Owen made him feel excessively hot. At this moment he may have had a flush over parts of his body. (His son would observe that "often a mental cause would make him too hot, so that he would take off his coat if anything went wrong in the course of his work."[6]) Two days later Darwin wrote Falconer: "You would laugh if you would have seen how indignant all Owen's mean conduct . . . made me. . . . The case is come to such a pass, that I think every man of science is bound to show his feelings by some overt act, and I shall watch for a fitting opportunity."[7] On the same day he also wrote Thomas Huxley: "I cannot say how indignant Owen's conduct . . . has made me. I believe I hate him more than you ["do" inserted] even perhaps more than good old Falconer does. But I have bubbled over to one or two correspondents on this head, & will say no more."[8] His two letters are both dated "Dec. 10th," instead of 10 January. He probably made this mistake because he wished it was still December, when he would not have to confront Owen's conduct.

He would "say" no more, but his disturbed feelings about Owen may have persisted, and then caused his health to become "bad enough" (he does not specify his symptoms).[9] At the end of January he told Hooker: "We are going to London on Tuesday evening for a week, chiefly to see if change will do me good."[10] A change in locale (the new locale being the home of a Darwin relation) was Darwin's new way of treating his illness. (This was a reversal of his previous opinion that a move from home was upsetting to his health.) For ten days, 4 to 14 February, he and his family stayed in the London home of his brother Erasmus. From there he happily wrote Fox: "I . . . came here to see if a change w^d. do me some good & it has succeeded."[11] Back in Down he remained "wonderfully improved" for several weeks.[12]

Two months after his "hate" and "indignation" at Owen, he experienced feelings about Lyell which—although quite different from those about Owen—may also have upset his health.

These feelings were caused by his reading, at the end of February 1863, Lyell's just-published book, *The Antiquity of Man*. For years he had implored Lyell—his old friend and mentor—to unequivocally support natural selection. Soon after *The Origin* was published he had written Lyell that the latter's support for natural selection would "do far more to convince the world than mine."[13] Lyell had then withheld full support. However, Darwin continued to hope for this support. Now, on reading *The Antiquity of Man*, Darwin realized that Lyell retained his doubts about the truth of natural selection, and that his unequivocal support would not be forthcoming. Darwin then sent Lyell a letter containing the following passages: "I will first get out what I hate saying, viz. that I have been greatly disappointed . . ."; "I

hope to Heaven I am wrong . . . but I cannot see how your chapters
can do more good than an extraordinarily able review";[14] "forgive me
for writing with perfect freedom, for you must know how deeply I
respect you as my old honoured guide and master."[15] He told
Huxley: "I am fearfully disappointed at Lyell's excessive caution in
expressing any judgment on Species or origin of Man."[16] He wrote
Hooker that Lyell's position made him "deeply disappointed (I do not
mean personally)";[17] and "put me in despair."[18] Because of his
"respect" for Lyell (he knew that Hooker also held this respect) he
could not fully express all of his negative feelings. When he told
Hooker that he was "not personally" disappointed by Lyell he was,
probably, trying to deny that he really was "personally" disappointed.
He may have felt anger at Lyell, and an inability to express this.
Whatever his full feelings about Lyell were, the feelings that he did
express—his "disappointment" and "despair"—were intense and disturbing, and these feelings may have then caused his "improved"
health to relapse.

On 5 March—ten days after reading *The Antiquity of Man* and
with Lyell due to visit him at Down—he told Hooker: "I have been
having very bad 10 days with much sickness & weakness, & have been
obliged to stop ["the" inserted] Lyells. It breaks my heart, but Emma
says, I believe truly, that we must all go for two months to Malvern. It is
very pricking after London doing me so much good. . . . A good severe
fit of Eczema would do me good, & I have a touch this morning &
consequently feel a little alive. This might save me from Malvern."[19]
"Much sickness" presumably meant frequent episodes of vomiting. He
wrote Asa Gray, who had become one of his intimate friends and
confidants, that he was fearful that six or eight weeks at Malvern
would interrupt work on *The Variation of Animals and Plants under
Domestication*.[20] Gray replied: "Now please, do not think of being ill
this spring and passing all your valuable time—wasting it—at water-
cure."[21]

On 13 March he reported to Hooker: "I have been very busy & not
a little uncomfortable, for frequent uneasy of fullness, slight pain &
tickling about the heart. But as I have no other symptoms of Heart
complaint, I do not suppose it is afflicted. Were you not similarly
plagued before you went to India?"[22] Hooker then described his heart
symptoms and Darwin commented that these seemed "very like mine:
but thank God I have not yet come to have 'worms crawling over my
heart.' "[23] Darwin makes no further reference to his heart. Because of
his persisting eczema, he held off going to Malvern, and then

consulted a medical practitioner whom he jokingly called "the great Mr. Startin,"[24] Mr. James Startin, a surgeon who had become a noted skin specialist.[25] Mr. Startin prescribed a locally applied medication (its chemical composition is unidentified) which Darwin described as follows: "*certainly* to me very soothing. The muddy stuff must be shaken, a little poured out & smeared on part with broad camel brush & then mopped nearly dry with a bit of rag."[26] It is not known how long Darwin used this. He sent Startin's prescription to Hooker,[27] presumably for the latter to use on his "eczema."[28]

As Darwin continued "sick" (his symptoms undescribed)[29] into April he twice consulted "Dr. Jenner,"[30] probably Dr. (later Sir) William Jenner, a very prominent London physician.[31] At the end of April and beginning of May—hoping that a change in locale would again help him—he visited the country homes of the Reverend Charles Langton (married to his cousin Charlotte Wedgwood) at Hartfield, Sussex, and his sister, Mrs. Caroline Wedgwood, at Leith Hill Place.[32] He stated that "the change did me no good."[33] About this time his eczema stopped, and soon he would again complain that without it he felt "languid & bedeviled."[34]

At the end of May he was in bed with what he called "everlasting sickness" and "my old enemy sickness" (probably vomiting)[35] and "devilish headaches."[36] He was thinking of going to Malvern when he heard from Fox that Dr. Gully was severely ill.[37] He then wrote Fox: "Gully will be a great loss & I hardly know whom to consult there. I must be under some experienced man, for I could not stand much hard treatment. All this Everlasting illness has stopped my work much. I am glad you told me about Dr. Gully for I had heard only a rumor."[38]

Little is known about his illness from June into August. Beginning the middle of August, he began vomiting every morning. After a fortnight of this, on 2 September 1863, he and his family moved to Malvern.[39] There he rented a house, and—"feeling very sorry not to be under Dr. Gully"[40]—he put himself under the care of Dr. James Ayerst, a hydropathist, hygienist, and homeopathic practitioner, who at this time was an associate of Dr. Gully's.[41] He began a regimen of "2 or 3 wet rubbings in the day & small walks in the garden."[42] Dr. Gully, recovering from his illness, saw him twice and approved of his treatment.[43] Emma visited Annie's churchyard grave;[44] her husband thought about Annie, and seems to have avoided her grave.[45] After a month, on 6 October, Darwin wrote Hooker: "I am very weak & can write little. My nervous system has failed & I am kept going only by repeated doses of brandy; but I am certainly better, much, & sickness stopped."[46] By "failure" of "nervous system" he might have meant a transient episode of loss of memory.[47] Dr. Gully then declared that Darwin was "not strong enough" to bear the water treatment,[48] and on 14 October he returned to Down.[49]

On the urging of Hooker[50] he turned for medical advice to Mr. George Busk, an ex-naval surgeon with many scientific interests, who was a friend of himself and Hooker.[51] Busk recommended that he consult Dr. William Brinton, of Saint Thomas's Hospital, who had published books on diseases of the stomach and food and its digestion.[52] On 10 November 1863, after Brinton had visited him at Down, Darwin informed Hooker: "Dr. Brinton ... does not believe my brain or heart are primarily affected; but I have been so steadily going down hill, I cannot help doubting whether I can ever crawl a little up hill again. Unless I can, enough to work a little, I hope my life may be very short; for to lie on sofa all day & do nothing, but give trouble to the best and kindest of wives & dear good children is dreadful."[53] He still maintained contact with Dr. Gully, and on 13 November he wrote Hooker: "Dr. Brinton tells me that a little head-work not bad.[54] Dr. Gully writes again this morning to do nothing for 6 months. I presume I must observe & judge for self."[55] This may have been his last contact with Dr. Gully.[56]

His health reports to Hooker then varied. On 16 November: "I have now been six days with no vomiting! ! ! & my head feels more solid."[57] 23 November: "Since writing I have had much sickness & am weak...."[58] 5 December: "I have had a bad spell, vomiting every day for eleven days, & some days many times after every meal."[59]

On 8 December Emma reported to Fox on the condition of her husband: "He is wonderfully cheerful when not positively uncomfortable. He does not feel the least temptation to disobey orders about working for he feels quite incapable of doing anything. His good symptoms are losing *no* flesh & having a good appetite so that I fully hope that in time he will regain his usual standard of health which is not saying much for him."[60] From this we learn that at this time Darwin's vomiting—although it sometimes occurred "after every meal"—did not interfere with his intake and digestion of food, or with his general nutrition.

Dr. Brinton treated his patient with "mineral acid"[61]—this was the third time, within a period of seven years, that the latter had taken "mineral acid"[62]—and visited him in December assuring him that he would regain his "former degree of health."[63]

In January 1864 Darwin wrote Hooker: "I have had some fearful

sickness; but what a strange mechanism one's body is; yesterday
suddenly I had a slight attack of rheumatism in my back & I instantly
became almost well & so wonderfully strong that I walked to the
Hothouse,[64] which must be more than 100 yards."[65]

Early in 1864 he terminated with Dr. Brinton. He then saw no
doctors, avoided seeing his friends, and was only in contact with
members of his Down household. He wrote Hooker: "It pleases me
much that you wish to come here to see me but ['I' crossed out, 'at'
inserted] present my health is so doubtful that it really w^d not be
worth while ... for on many days I c^d only shake hands with you, &
on my better days, c^d only talk ten minutes—you may be sure I will
let you know when I get really at all better."[66]. About this time
Hooker, who had visited a friend living near Down House, wrote him
with great feeling: "I yearned to go over and see Mrs. Darwin, but it
would have been too great a punishment to both of us (you and me). I
cannot tell which I crave for most, another little girl or for you to get
well."[67] One of Hooker's little daughters had died four months
previously.

For months Darwin vomited "almost daily." "I sh^d suppose," he
wrote Hooker, "few human beings had vomited so often during the last
5 months."[68] In February 1864, he described to Hooker the relation
between his vomiting and his eating, and the frequency of his
vomiting episodes: "You ask about my sickness—it rarely comes on
till 2-3 hours after eating, so that I seldom throw up food, only acid &
morbid secretion; otherwise I sh^d have been dead, for during more
than a month I vomited after every meal & several times most nights.
On my well days I am certainly stronger."[69] He also had some mild
eczema which—because of its mentally stimulating effects—he wished
would be stronger.[70]

He was nursed by Emma—both he and she feared that his vomiting
would never stop—and by his servant Parslow, who previously had
aided him in his home hydropathy. With Parslow he had a special
patient-nurse relationship, the exact nature of which largely defies
definition. For a brief period he stopped reading *The Times*. Emma,
and his daughter Henrietta, read him many nonscientific books—he
found these "amusing," "less tiring" than *The Times*, and "trashy."[71]
Because of his illness he stopped working on *The Variation of Animals
and Plants under Domestication*. On the days when he felt "well" and
"stronger" he got up from his sickbed and walked to his garden and
new hothouse and did some experiments on plants.[72] Emma had
observed that his botanical work was a "great blessing," because it

eased his anxiety.[73] Despite his illness he was able to write two botanical papers.[74]

For an unusually long time he delayed writing to Asa Gray. Then Gray—who corresponded with Hooker—wrote him: "Here we are past mid winter, and not being stimulated as of old by your exciting letters, I have not written you a line since Christmas. . . . I write now to say how *very sorry* I am that the word or two I get about you from Hooker, gives me the idea that you are having an uncomfortable and suffering time, as well as entirely broken off from scientific work. I feel very sorry about it, and do long for better news of you." Gray, who had graduated from Fairfield Medical School (College of Physicians and Surgeons of the Western District of the State of New York), went on to comment on his friend's illness:

> We can sympathise with you all the more from what my wife has undergone, with a most detestable stomach. Soon after Christmas it got complicated with a bad liver, and what not, and laid her up for a month or two, most of the time in bed, and a sad time we have had of it. She is now convalescent, however, tho' still feeble. This trouble, which certainly was all buried in the digestive organs, upset her head completely, with giddiness and pain and manifold discomfort upon any exertion, even simple listening to reading, let alone reading herself. I have a notion you suffer much in the same way. And as she is slowly throwing it off, so I trust will you, please Providence, and that soon.[75]

We do not know how Darwin felt when he read that some of his symptoms were strikingly similar to those of Mrs. Gray. About the middle of March he again turned to the prominent Dr. William Jenner, whom he had consulted one year previously. Dr. Jenner (like Dr. Brinton) first assured him that there was "no organic mischief" and that he would "some day get over this sickness."[76] Then Dr. Jenner, probably reasoning that his patient's vomiting was caused by excess of gastric acid, prescribed a regimen of drinking very little and taking several different alkaline medicines[77]—what Darwin described as "enormous quantities of chalk, magnesia & carb[onate] of ammonia."[78] Darwin took these in "very frequent doses,"[79] and Fox advised him on a "way of taking chalk."[80]

Darwin, in letters to Hooker, happily reported how this regimen at last decisively checked his vomiting. 27 March: "Hurrah! I have been 52 hours without vomiting!!"[81] 13 April: "Dr. Jenner has done me much good & is, I am sure, a most able doctor." He wrote that his vomiting remained "checked" and that he was "gaining vigour."[82]

25 April: "I keep going on very well, though weak."[83] 15 May: "I have been ["more than" inserted] a month without sickness, but I do not at all rapidly grow strong, & have to go to bed 2 or 3 times per day."[84] He worked for a few hours daily on plant experiments, and commented that this "little" work "makes a wonderful difference in my life."[85] On 28 May he wrote Asa Gray: "Your kindness will make you glad to hear that I am nearly as well as I have been of late years, though a good deal weaker." Disagreeing with Gray's belief that a divine intelligence guided natural selection, he concluded his letter by teasing his American friend as follows: "I send a Photograph of myself with my Beard. Do I not look reverent—."[86]

A month later he wrote Hooker: "I keep on improving & am now much as usual, except that anything which is hard to understand or which hurries me, knocks me up."[87] The words *knocks me up* describe an anxiety state, which had taken the place of his previous upset stomach. He worried that Hooker was "greatly overworked" and might "break down," yet he urged his friend to visit him. Then both probably worried that, as a result of their conversation, he would become sick. After Hooker's visit, in which they discussed his plant experiments, he reassured his friend: "Your visit did me no harm: on the contrary it did me good & has interested me in my work.—In fact you have cockered me up to that degree that I want to observe all I can."[88]

As he recovered, his friends sent him letters of rejoicing. Hooker told him: "I am so glad that Jenner has done you good. I shall certainly vote for him for F.R.S. this year."[89] Huxley (who was frequently ill, and who had received some medical training) warned him: "The news you give of yourself is most encouraging; but pray don't think of doing any work again yet. Careful as I have been during this last winter not to burn the candle at both ends, I have found myself, since the pressure of my lectures ceased, in considerable need of quiet, and I have been lazy accordingly."[90] Asa Gray sent him an affectionate letter which, while replying to his letter of 28 May, pointedly did not refer to his "reverent" tease:

> I can do little more than . . . tell you how *heartily rejoiced* I am to hear from you that you are *nearly as well as ever.* I am most thankful to hear it! Your photograph with the venerable ["head" crossed out] beard, gives the look of your having suffered, and, perhaps from the beard, of having grown older. I hope there is still much work in you—but take it quietly and gently! You will be glad to hear that Mrs. Gray, with whom you sympathise so kindly, is get-

ting to have a very reasonable stomach again, and is gaining strength apace, in spite of very sultry weather. She takes the greatest interest in you and in your letters, and desires to be particularly remembered as well as to congratulate you upon your restored health.[91]

After a month's delay Darwin replied to Gray: "I have taken a long time to thank you for your pleasant & most friendly note. . . . I am not ungrateful, but I have less strength (though still gaining same & now at least living down stairs) than formerly & after my two hours ["work" inserted] glad to be quite idle. I have little to say; for my soul has been absorbed with climbing plants, now finished & tomorrow I begin again, after 13 months interruption on 'Variation under Domestication.' "[92]

The next day, 14 September 1864, he did begin work on *The Variation of Animals and Plants under Domestication.*[93] He found this work "a good deal harder" than work on plants.[94]

In October he wrote Hooker: "The Lyells have been here & were extremely pleasant, but I saw them only occasionally for 10 minutes & when they went I had an awful day of vomiting; but I am slowly getting up to my former standard.—I shall soon be confined to a living grave & fearful evil it is."[95] Although he and Lyell felt warmly toward each other, he also still resented Lyell's failure to support his evolutionary ideas, and this latter feeling probably caused his illness to exacerbate. This exacerbation lasted only one day—he was, perhaps, becoming resigned to Lyell's nonsupport.

A week later he wrote Asa Gray that he was back to his "uniform life" and "liv[ing] on endless foolish novels which are read aloud to me by my dear womenkind"; and that "Phosphate of iron, which I hear is often used with you, has done me good. Lady Lyell[96] was giving me a wonderful account of the benefit a dyspeptic lady had received from a Philadelphia medicine, which is imported into England & is called 'Syrup of Phosphates'. Did you ever hear of it? I am tempted to try it, if I knew of what it was composed."[97] At this moment "phosphate of iron"[98] seems to have replaced his previous medications of chalk, magnesia, and carbonate of ammonia. He then makes no further mention of phosphates and, presumably, he soon stopped taking them.

In November 1864 he was awarded the greatest honor an English scientific man could receive—the Copley Medal of the Royal Society. He had been proposed for the Copley by George Busk. In a letter to Busk, in which he expressed "cordial thanks" for Busk's Copley support, Darwin also wrote: "You will remember that you were so

kind as to advise me a year & a half ago about my incessant sickness. I
have got over this, but still keep very weak & fear I shall ever remain
so."[99]

About this time he described his health grimly, yet not despairingly,
to Fox: "As for myself, I fear I have reached my sticking point. I am
very weak & continually knocked up, but able most days, to do from
2 to 3 hours work, & all my Doctors tell me this is good for me; &
whether or no, it is the only thing which makes life endurable to
me."[100] For most of the rest of 1864 he remained at this "sticking
point."

12

Illness and *The Origin*
Controversy (III)

"You ask how I am," Darwin wrote Hooker early in January 1865; "I
have now had five pretty good days, but before that I spent fully a
third of my time in bed, but had no actual vomiting."[1] He may have
been describing a period of depression which—for the moment—was
better. He went on to despair about doctors: "Dr. Jenner is exhausted
as to doing me any good. All Doctors seem to think that I am a case of
suppressed gout: do you know of any good man hereafter to consult? I
did think of trying Bence Jones; but I know it is folly & nonsense to try
anyone."[2] At this time, although the diagnosis of suppressed gout was
sometimes made[3] (it had been suggested fifteen years previously as a
diagnosis for Darwin's illness), it was not always accepted, as is
shown by Hooker's reply to Darwin's letter: "What the devil is this
'suppressed gout' upon which doctors fasten every ill they cannot
name? If it is *suppressed* how do they know it is gout? If it is apparent,
why the devil do they call it suppressed? I hate the use of cant terms to
cloak ignorance."[4] After reading this Darwin must have had increased
misgivings about doctors.

On 2 February Darwin complained, vaguely, about having had "an
extra bad time."[5] On 3 February Hooker told him that he had some
eczema for which he consulted Mr. Startin.[6] Darwin then despon-
dently wrote Hooker about his health and doctors, and commented on
the energizing effect of his eczema: "I have been having 5 or 6
wretched days, miserable from morning to night & unable to do
anything ["but am much better today" inserted]. How I wish I could

beg borrow or steal your eczema, intensified a dozen fold; for this alone would do me good. I hope Startin has done you good. I wish I knew whether it was any earthly use consulting any Doctor, for I can get nothing out of Dr. Jenner."[7] In another letter to Hooker, written two months later, he was again despondent about himself and doctors: "I work a little every day with groans & sighs & am as dull as a fig.—It is hopeless & useless but, *when you meet* Busk, ask him whether any man is better than Jenner for giving life to a worn out poor Devil."[8] In both of the above letters he makes no mention of stomach or other symptoms, and he may have—again—been suffering mainly from a depression. Although Hooker again contacted Busk, Darwin did not (at this time) consult a new doctor.[9]

On 22 April he "Fell ill."[10] In a 2 May letter to Hooker he refers to having "sickness,"[11] a word which, as has been seen, usually denotes vomiting. On 4 May he happily wrote Hooker of a remission: "You will be glad to hear, I know my dear old friend, that my ten or 12 days of weakness has suddenly ceased, & has left me not much the worse: I feared it was the beginning of another six or nine months miserable attack & feared it much: Jenner has been here, & is evidently perplexed at my case; he struck me as a more able & sensible man, than he did before, for then I could not talk with him: I shall consult no one else."[12]

In the same 4 May letter he wrote his reactions to hearing that his ex-*Beagle* captain, Robert FitzRoy, had committed suicide: "I never knew in my life so mixed a character. Always much to love & I once loved him sincerely; but so bad a temper & so given to take offence, that I gradually quite lost my love & wished only to keep out of contact with him. Twice he quarreled bitterly with me, without any just provocation on my part. But certainly there was much noble & exalted in his character."[13] The subject of one of these quarrels may have been *The Origin*, which had offended the deeply religious FitzRoy.[14] Darwin's feelings about FitzRoy's suicide, which were certainly conflicting and strong, may have caused his illness to exacerbate. After 4 May his episodes of daily vomiting returned and showed no signs of abating.

He then recalled that, several months previously, Dr. John Chapman—a physician who (presumably) was unknown to him—had sent him a book describing a new ice treatment for seasickness.[15]

Dr. Chapman was a man of variform parts: editor and publisher of the prestigious literary periodical *Westminster Review*, and friend of George Eliot and other literary notables; author of insightful articles on medical education and medical reform; and a practicing physician who had developed a new treatment for several different diseases (including epilepsy, neuralgia, paralysis, cholera, menstrual disorders, and dyspepsia and seasickness) which consisted in the application of ice, placed in a specially designed ice bag, on the spine.[16] This treatment was based on the idea that since most diseases were of nervous origin they could be influenced by applications of heat and cold to the spine. In his book, entitled *Sea-Sickness: Its Nature and Treatment*, Dr. Chapman had written: "Ice is a direct sedative to the spinal cord, if appllied immediately over it: by lessening the amount of blood in it, ice lessens its functional and especially its automatic or excito-motor power. The therapeutical applications of this fact are numerous and immensely important."[17] The book contained the case histories of a number of persons who described how their seasickness had been greatly alleviated by the ice treatment.

Darwin read Dr. Chapman's book, pondered over it for about one week, and then determined to leave Dr. Jenner and try the ice treatment. He wrote Dr. Chapman a letter requesting him to come to Down, and raising some questions: "My sickness is not from mere irritability of stomach but is always caused by acid & morbid secretions. I am anxious not to try any new treatment unless you have had experience in some similar cases leading you to think it advisable."[18]

Dr. Chapman agreed to come. Darwin then sent him a page of notes in which he first, starkly and unsparingly, depicted the mixture of nervous and psychophysiologic symptoms which made up his invalid condition:

Age 56–57.—For 25 years extreme spasmodic daily & nightly flatulence: occasional vomiting, on two occasions prolonged during months. Vomiting preceded by shivering, ["hysterical crying" inserted] dying sensations ["or half-faint" inserted]. & copious very palid urine. Now vomiting & every passage of flatulence preceded by ringing of ears, treading on air & vision. ["focus & black dots" "Air fatigues, specially risky, brings on the Head symptoms" "(nervousness when E.[19] leaves me.—" inserted] (What I vomit intensely acid, slimy (sometimes bitter) consider teeth.) Doctors ["puzzled" inserted] say suppressed gout—No organic mischief, Jenner & Brinton.—Family gouty.—

[Alongside the above passage is written "Extreme secretion of saliva with flatulence."]

Tongue crimson in morning ulcerated—stomach constricted drag-
ging. ["Feet coldish" inserted] Pulse 58 to 62—or slower & like
thread. Appetite good—not thin. Evacuation regular & good. Urine
scanty (because do not drink) often much pinkish sediment when
cold—seldom headache or nausea.—Cannot walk abv ½ mile—
always tired—conversation or excitement tires me much.—Heavy
sleep—bad day. Eczema—["(now without)" inserted] lumbago—
fiendish-rash.—Always been temperate—now wines comfort me
much—could not take any formerly. Physic no good—Chalk &
Magnesia.—Water cure & Douche—Last time at Malvern could
not stand it—

There are then two passages which seem to have been written at
another time and which, instead of merely describing a symptom,
reflect on the pathological genesis and nature of Darwin's stomach
discomfort:

I fancy that when much sickness my stomach is cold—at least water
is very little warmed. I feel nearly sure that the air is generated some
where ["under" crossed out] lower down than the stomach & as soon
as it regurgitates into the stomach the discomfort comes on—Does
not throw up the food. [This last passage is in Emma's writing.]

At the bottom of these notes, separated from the other writing,
there were queries to Dr. Chapman about his ice treatment:

Instruction—How soon any effect? How long continue treatment?[20]

On some day toward the end of May Dr. Chapman came to Down.
There he liked, and was liked by, Darwin and Emma;[21] and he may
have felt honored to be treating the author of *The Origin of Species*.[22]
He started Darwin on the following regimen: a bag (or bags) of ice
applied to the spine three times a day, for 1½ hours each time.[23] On 1
June Darwin told Hooker that he was trying the ice "at first with
strong hope, now with weak hope."[24] On 7 June he reported as
follows to Dr. Chapman: "It is certain that the ice does not stop either
flatulence or sickness"; he thought the ice caused his pulse to
accelerate; he "liked" the ice for an hour, then he became "weary of
it."[25] By July he had stopped the ice treatment, commenting that "the
ice to spine did nothing,"[26] and he had stopped his contact with Dr.
Chapman as well.

Emma wrote: "We liked Dr. Chapman so very much we were quite
sorry the ice failed for his sake as well as ours."[27] Dr. Chapman would,
years later, send Darwin an inscribed copy of his book *Neuralgia and
Kindred Diseases of the Nervous System*.[28]

After the failure of the ice treatment, Darwin went on suffering from "incessant vomiting."[29] He avoided seeing his friends, and he wrote Hooker that he could do no work.[30] However in May, despite his illness, he had written a forty-one-page essay entitled "Hypothesis of Pangenesis."[31] This was a theory of heredity, which he had begun to think about during his first severe period of illness twenty-five or twenty-six years ago,[32] now committed to writing for the first time. It was closely reasoned and based on numerous observations. At the end of May he had sent a copy of "Pangenesis" to Huxley, asking for comments, and telling Huxley that he hoped to "publish" his hypothesis in his "next book"[33] (*The Variation of Animals and Plants under Domestication*). After receiving this essay Huxley told the German evolutionist Ernst Haeckel: "Darwin has been very ill for most than a year past, so ill, in fact, that his recovery was at one time doubtful. But he contrives to work in spite of fate, and I hope that before long we shall have a new book from him."[34]

On 18 July Darwin reported to Hooker: "I keep very weak & had much sickness yesterday, but am stronger this morning."[35] Along with this letter Emma wrote a letter of her own to Hooker:

> I do hope Charles is making a little progress in spite of frequent returns of the sickness but there is a degree of vigour about him on the well days which make me hope that his constitution is making a struggle. If he conquers this sickness I do hope you will be able to come & see him before long & I am sure there is nobody in the world he cares so much to see. He had one terribly bad week.[36]

Here we have a glimpse of Emma's faith in her husband's capacity to get over the worst of his illness, and her altruistic concern that he keep in contact with his best friend. Emma's devotion to her husband made a deep impresison on her aunt Fanny Allen, who spoke of Emma as "a chosen one of Heaven," and "an exception to every wife."[37] In the 1850s Emma had suffered "much" from headaches;[38] by the 1860s her headaches had become "repeated."[39] She sometimes treated herself by staying for hours in a darkened room.[40] Her headaches—although they worried and concerned her husband[41]—did not interfere with her care for him.

For Darwin the summer and fall of 1865 resembled the winter of 1864: he vomited almost daily, was without a regular doctor, did little or no work (he had some correspondence with Huxley about pangenesis), and only saw his Down household. He was not, however, totally isolated from world events. On 16 August he read in *The*

Times of the death of Hooker's father, and then he immediately sent his "best of old Friends" a condolence note in which—after commenting on the "happy" and "active" life of Hooker Sr.—he wrote: "As I had not heard for some time from you, I have been continually thinking of you & had a presentiment of some ill news; but did not fear your Father." He closed his note with "I am bad, so no more."[42]

His next extant letter to Hooker, written on 27 September, contained news of a new doctor who had effected a positive change in his health: "Did I ever tell you that I have put myself under Bence Jones, & I am sure he has done me good by rigorous diet. I have been half starved to death & am 15 lb lighter, but I have gained in walking power & my vomiting is immensely reduced. I have my hopes of again some day resuming scientific work, which is my sole enjoyment in life."[43] Dr. Henry Bence Jones—whom several months previously Darwin had thought it would be "folly and nonsense" to consult—was, like Dr. Jenner, a prominent London physician with a large and remunerative practice. He was also a chemist and physiologist, who had made discoveries in physiology and pathology (he had first described the protein in the urine since known as the Bence Jones protein); and he was a friend of several noted scientific men (he would write a two-volume biography of Michael Faraday).[44] Under Dr. Bence Jones' diet, which consisted of "scanty" amounts of "toast & meat,"[45] Darwin went on "slowly getting better."[46] In November he went to London, where he probably saw Dr. Bence Jones, and where he "fell ill again with cold,"[47] which he said "threw me back a whole month."[48] However, by the end of December he returned to work on the manuscript of *The Variation of Animals and Plants.*[49]

In April 1866 he attended a London soirée of the Royal Society where he was presented to the Prince of Wales and saw the leading scientific men of London. Because of his years of withdrawal, and his beard, almost all of his old friends did not recognize him. "His Dr. Bence Jones was there," Emma reported, "and received him with triumph, as well he might, it being his own doing. . . . Dr. B. J. is to do me some good too. I am to drive everyday, and Charles to ride."[50] Darwin would then ride daily for about three years—"much" enjoying riding and believing that it "improved" his health[51]—until one day his horse fell and rolled on him, bruising him seriously, and he then gave up riding.[52]

In 1866 Dr. Bence Jones detected fluid in one side of his own chest, and he became seriously ill through the winter of 1866–67. He then began to recover.[53] In February 1867, Darwin reported to Fox: "Poor

Bence Jones has been for months at death' door, & he was quite given
up; but has rallied in surprising manner from inflammation of Lungs
& heart-disease."[54] Although Bence Jones slowly recovered, his ener-
gies never fully returned, and his health continued poor until early in
1873 when he was forced to retire from medical practice altogether. He
died in April 1873.[55] Darwin may have stopped seeing Bence Jones in
1866. Then, for several years, Darwin had no regular doctor.

From 1866 to 1872 he produced three sequels to *The Origin*: *The
Variation of Animals and Plants under Domestication, The Descent of
Man,* and *The Expression of Emotions in Man and Animals*; and he
prepared fourth, fifth, and sixth editions of *The Origin.* Although he
daily suffered from what he called "much energetic discomfort,"[56]
which was probably mainly an upset stomach, his daily work
schedule was only once seriously interrupted. From 23 June to 16 July
1868, he had an illness whose causes are obscure and whose symptoms
he only described as "so bad that I could do nothing"[57] and "I broke
down."[58] He treated himself by moving with Emma, and his daughter
Henrietta, to Dumbola Lodge, Freshwater, on the Isle of Wight. Soon
after arriving at the lodge he commented that "even two days from
home" had made him feel better.[59] He soon recovered his capacity for
daily work. During his stay at the lodge he was seen by William
Allingham, an Irish poet,[60] who in his diary perceptively described
Darwin's invalidism and its advantages:

> August 11.—To Freshwater; engage bedroom over little shop,
> and to the Darwins. Dr. Hooker in lower room writing away at his
> Address;[61] going to put 'Peter Bell's' primrose into it and wants
> the exact words. Upstairs Mrs. Darwin, Miss D. and Mr. Charles
> Darwin himself—, yellow, sickly, very quiet. He has his meals at
> his own times, sees people or not as he chooses, has invalid's privi-
> liges in full, a great help to a studious man.[62]

In 1871–72 natural selection was severely criticized—in articles and
a book, *The Genesis of Species*—by the biologist St. George Mivart.
This criticism caused Darwin to feel anxious and discouraged,[63] yet his
stomach did not become severely upset. He closely studied *The
Genesis of Species*—his copy of this book has an annotation on nearly
every second page[64]—and then, in his sixth, and last, edition of *The
Origin,* he wrote: "After reading with care Mr. Mivart's book, and
comparing each section with what I have said on the same head, I
never before felt so strongly convinced of the general truth of the
conclusions here arrived at, subject, of course, in so intricate a

subject, to much partial error."[65] He answered Mivart, and went on believing in his theory;[66] and he seems to have reached a stage where he was able to confront criticism without becoming severely ill.

At this time he became better able to bear some of his antipathies. Referring to his enemy Richard Owen, he told Hooker: "I used to be ashamed of hating him so much, but now I will carefully cherish my hatred & contempt to the last day of my life."[67]

13

Improved Health, Old Age

During the last decade of his life (1872–82) Darwin was still regarded as an invalid by himself and others, and he went on living the constricted, rigid, and "perfectly uniform"[1] life of a valetudinarian. Any effort outside his daily routine was a "severe exertion" and caused "subsequent suffering."[2] Because he was afraid of upsetting his health, he would limit his conversation with visitors.[3] When he anticipated leaving Down for a holiday, he would suffer from a "miserable sinking feeling."[4] In the fall of 1872 he wrote Fox: "How I wish I could accept your invitation & pay you a visit at Sandown; but I have long found it impossible to visit anywhere: the novelty & excitement would annihilate me."[5]

He experienced several episodes of acute illness. In the fall of 1872, when he was working on the sundew plant, *Drosera*, he wrote that "my head . . . failed,"[6] and that he "broke down."[7] Emma told a relative: "I have persuaded Charles to leave home for a few weeks. The microscopic work he has been doing with sundew has proved fatiguing and unwholesome, and he owns that he must have rest."[8] After three weeks of sojourning at Sevenoaks Common, and enforced idleness, Darwin recovered. Then, from 17 to 23 December, he visited his brother Erasmus in London, and reported that he was "unwell all time."[9]

In the summer of 1873 he had a new kind of illness: what he described as an episode of "much loss of memory & severe shock continually passing through my brain"[10]—perhaps an episode of cerebral anoxia. He consulted Dr. Andrew Clark, a London doctor who at this time, like Jenner and Bence Jones before him, held a leading medical position and a large and prestigious medical practice.[11] Patients valued Dr. Clark for his sympathy, attentiveness, practicality, and common sense; and also criticized him for his rigid insistence that a treatment—especially a diet—be carried out in a "minute" manner.[12]

After first examining Darwin, Dr. Clark told him that he would be able to do him "some good and that there was a good deal of work in him yet," and that he would prescribe treatments.[13] "Dr. Clark," Emma wrote a few days later, "has not sent the dietary yet and we are rather trembling as to how strict he will be."[14] After the diet was sent, in September 1873, Darwin wrote Hooker: "Dr. Clark is convinced that the brain was affected only secondarily for which thank God, as I would far sooner die than lose my mind. Clark is doing me good by an abominable diet."[15] However in December he wrote Huxley (a year earlier Huxley had benefited from a "special diet" prescribed by Dr. Clark[16]) that he was beginning "to fear that diet will do only a little for me. The great benefit at first was, I believe, merely due to a change, & changes of all kinds are at first highly beneficial to me."[17] Darwin seems to have then stopped his diet for a while. In the first three months of 1874 he made some medical notes in a "Private Diary."[18] 20 January 1874: "Began Dr. Clark's Physic. Strychnine & Iodine."[19] 24 January: "Like all Dr. Clarks Physic did me harm." 22 February: "Began Dr. Clarks Diet." This refers either to Dr. Clark's first diet, or to a new diet prescribed by Dr. Clark. 17 March: "Began strict diet again after 1 week of lax diet." 29 March: "Lax Diet." Then, for this period of treatments, there are no further "Diary" notes. Presumably he again, and finally, stopped his diet, for on 4 March 1874, he had written Hooker: "All the good from Dr. Clark's diet has vanished: I fear that it was only the good of any change; but it is a great advantage to have a beneficial change to turn to."[20] From this time on he became a regular patient of Dr. Clark.

In April–May 1875 he wrote up his observations on insectivorous plants. In June–July he went for a holiday to Abinger Hall.[21] He then described this period of work and holiday as follows: "I was quite knocked up & worried with the subject, so that I had to take a month's complete rest away from home."[22] He does not seem to have consulted Dr. Clark.

On 4 July 1876, he saw Dr. Clark at Down, for an unspecified reason, and then told his son George: "Dr. Clark was very nice when here, and enquired much about you."[23] In September 1876 he wrote a correspondent: "I am at present much overworked & out of health."[24] Then, for about two years, he seems to have made no complaints of illness.

From 27 February to 5 March 1878, he went to London to see Dr. Clark "on account of Giddiness."[25] On 2 March he noted in his "Private Diary": "Began dry treatment," presumably a treatment prescribed by Dr. Clark. Several days later he wrote Hooker about his symptoms and treatment: "I have been suffering from constant attacks of swimming of the head which makes life an intolerable bother & stops all work—Dr. Clark has put me on a dry diet & I would have given a guinea yesterday for ["a" inserted] wine-glass of water."[26] After this, he makes no further reference to his head symptom or a diet.

Darwin's feelings about Dr. Clark were mixed. He followed (at least for a while) Dr. Clark's treatments, and respected the latter's medical opinions—Emma would say that Bence Jones and Clark were the two doctors that did him "good" and that Clark did him "great good."[27] He was also angry that Clark would not accept a fee for his services—Clark did this, perhaps, because of his feelings about treating such a famous patient—and he does not seem to have ventilated this anger to his doctor.[28] His comments about Clark lack the warmth that he had expressed for Gully and Lane.

It is evident that, during the last decade of his life, Darwin continued to have chronic and acute illness. However, the two individuals who knew most about his health and who were his two main nurses—Emma[29] and his servant Parslow[30]—both observed that, during this last decade, his overall health had significantly improved. And in 1880 he wrote his old friend Herbert: "My health is better than it used to be, but I live in a perpetually half knocked-up condition."[31] By this sentence he meant that, although he still suffered from moderate to severe anxiety, his stomach was "better" than previously. He suffered no serious exacerbation of vomiting, and in his letters he complains much less of daily stomach distress; and because of his better stomach he was able to work more steadily. (Whether his skin and heart symptoms also improved cannot be determined.)

What caused this amelioration of a thirty-five-year-old illness? It may be that, as Darwin grew older, his stomach became less irritable because it secreted less acid. A more apparent cause, however, is that Darwin felt better in his stomach because some of the psychological factors which had upset his stomach waned and changed.

After 1872 he gave up writing on theoretical and controversial issues. Even when he thought about controversial points he seems to have avoided an emotional involvement. In 1874 he told Fox that he felt "as old as Methusaleh; but not so much in mind, except that I think one takes everything more quietly, as not signifying so much."[32]

As has been seen, during the years of *The Origin* controversy, he had learned that when ill, or convalescing from illness, he frequently could only work on plants; this work kept him in better health than other scientific work. After 1872 he worked mainly on plants. This botanical work enabled him to develop some of his evolutionary ideas, and gave him more happiness than any other kind of scientific work. He found that plants were doubly lovable: as objects for scientific investigation and simply as objects to look at and to touch. Frank Darwin has vividly described his father's attitude toward plants: "He had great delight in the beauty of flowers. . . . I think he sometimes fused together his admiration of the structure of a flower and its intrinsic beauty. . . . He had an affection, half artistic, half botanical, for the little blue Lobelia . . . I used to like to hear him admire the beauty of a flower; it was a kind of gratitude to the flower itself, and a personal love for its delicate form and color."[33] Sometimes his botanical work caused him extreme mental stress: moments when, as has been seen, he "broke down,"[34] or suffered great mental anguish.[35] However, he was always able to recover from this stress and bring each of his botanical investigations to a successful fruition.

Sometimes when he took a holiday after a period of overwork "it seemed as through the absence of the customary strain allowed him to fall into a peculiar condition of miserable health."[36] He needed work for his state of mental well-being; and in his 1880 letter to Herbert he observed: "I . . . am never happy except when at work."[37] When one of his sons once urged him to "take some rest away from home in order to regain his strength," Darwin replied "that the truth was that he was *never* quite comfortable except when utterly absorbed in his writing."[38]

Other causes for Darwin's improved health were the occurrence of several quite different events, each of which caused him much happiness. Natural selection came to be accepted by many of those whom he respected, including (in 1868) by Charles Lyell. His income from his property, investments, and books steadily increased, and in 1876 he wrote: "I never imagined that I should be so rich a man as I am."[39] The "inherited" ill health of his children remained the "greatest drawback" in his life;[40] yet his children, also, came to give him much happiness. He rejoiced first in the marriage of his daughter Etty,[41] and then in the marriages of three of his sons, one of whom he had feared to be an "inveterate bachelor."[42] In 1876, noting that all his five sons (including three with ill health) were having successful careers, he exclaimed: "Oh Lord, what a set of sons I have, all doing wonders."[43] When his children moved from his home the conflicts between his work and his family lessened; at the same time he delighted in keeping in frequent contact with his children, and in loving and being loved by them.[44] He was especially happy when his son Frank became his secretary, and then aided him in his botanical work.

During this last decade, without the distraction of caring for children, Emma was able to be especially attentive to the needs of her husband. She never left him for a night,[45] and "her whole day was planned out to suit him, to be ready for reading aloud to him, to go his walks with him, and to be constantly at hand to alleviate his daily discomforts."[46] Only Emma knew the "full amount of suffering" that her husband experienced,[47] and she daily watched over his health. When he would talk to a scientific friend, Emma would note the time the talk began and after about forty-five minutes she would enter the room—"smilingly" and without saying a word—and Darwin would then cease his conversation.[48] When Emma observed that Darwin was becoming overworked she would persuade him to take a short holiday. He would then "bargain" with her, "stipulating, for instance, that he should come home in five days instead of six."[49] In his 1876 *Autobiography* he expressed his gratitude to his wife for her care of him: "She has been my greatest blessing. . . . She has never failed in the kindest sympathy towards me, and has borne with the utmost patience my frequent complaints from ill-health and discomfort. . . . She has been my wise adviser and cheerful comforter throughout life, which without her would have been during a very long period a miserable one from ill-health."[50]

14

The Final Illness

From 2 June to 4 July 1881, Darwin (then 72 1/2 years old) and his family took a holiday at Lake Ullswater and lived at Glenrhydding House, Patterdale.[1] One Sunday at Patterdale Emma wrote that her husband, after climbing some rocks by the side of Lake Ullswater, had "a fit of his dazzling . . . and came down."[2] In the middle of June, Darwin wrote Hooker that he was depressed and preoccupied with death: "I am rather despondent about myself . . . idleness is down-right misery to me, as I find here, as I cannot forget my discomfort for an hour. I have not the heart ["or strength" inserted] at my age to begin any investigation, lasting years, which is the only thing which I enjoy, & I have no little jobs which I can do.—So I must look forward to Down grave-yard as the sweetest place on this Earth."[3] He told Wallace that "I cannot walk and everything tires me, even seeing scenery."[4] During his stay at Patterdale he consulted Dr. F. C. MacNalty, who thought that Darwin had angina pectoris. "My father," Dr. MacNalty's son wrote, "later told me that he found symptoms of myocardial degeneration in Darwin and considered that his health was precarious."[5]

In the fall of 1881, however, Darwin did not complain of any symptoms and was able to work on the action of carbonate of ammonia on roots and leaves.[6] Then in December 1881, when he was in London visiting his daughter, Henrietta Litchfield, he experienced giddiness and an irregular pulse.[7] At first he did not see Dr. Clark, and Emma visited the latter and reported her husband's symptoms. "Dr. Clark," Emma wrote, "said that shewed that there was some derangement of the heart, but he did not take a serious view of it."[8] Dr. Clark then saw Darwin and reassured him that his cardiac condition was not serious. Darwin may not have believed this for, at this time, he told his friend, the geologist John Judd, that he had "received his warning." "And he intimated to me," Judd later recollected, "that he knew his heart was seriously affected."[9]

Darwin returned to Down and for about two months was free of cardiac symptoms. Early in 1882 he suffered from a cough and Emma insisted that he take some quinine. "Though I have very little faith in medicine," he wrote a friend, "this, I think, has done me much good."[10]

On 3 March 1882, Henrietta Litchfield arrived at Down. Several days after her arrival she was told by her mother that her father was experiencing "some pain in the heart" during and after his afternoon walks. From then on Henrietta closely observed her father's condition. On 7 March Darwin had a "sharp fit of pain" in the Sandwalk and got home with difficulty—he then stopped his daily turns around the Sandwalk.[11]

Emma then wrote Dr. Clark a letter, asking him to come to Down, and telling him that he would be paid a fee. Clark came on 10 March.[12] He arrived very late, and his visit was described by Henrietta as follows: "Dr. Clark arrived in a very excited & hurried state & after saying he w^d never come again if they offered him his fee & that he only had half an hour went in to my Father. He there let him quite see that he had angina pectoris."[13] At this time the diagnosis of "angina pectoris" meant coronary thrombosis and organic disease of the heart.[14]

Following this visit Darwin became, in the words of Henrietta, "excessively depressed."[15] He withdrew to his bed and room and had his meals in his room. He experienced a fit of precordial pain at least every day, exhaustion, insomnia, "half fainting feelings"—which he had termed "dying sensations" and which may have been similar to the "dying sensations" of his father.[16] He was depressed because of several medical and psychiatric causes: he was experiencing—with his pain and "fainting sensations"—the actual effects of heart disease and heart insufficiency; Dr. Clark's diagnosis of "angina pectoris" had convinced him (as he told Emma) that he would not be able to work again;[17] and then he was angry at Dr. Clark—because of the latter's hurried visit, frank diagnosis, and insistence on not being paid—and yet he was unable to openly express his anger,[18] and he may have turned this anger against himself (as is the case with some depressed people) and thus increased his depression.

His anger at Clark must have increased when the latter waited some days before sending him instructions for a diet and medicines.[19] The medicines included amyl nitrite, which had recently come into use as an "antispasmodic" for treating the spasm of the coronary vessels which were held to be a cause of angina pectoris.[20]

Several days after Dr. Clark's visit Darwin was seen by Dr. Norman Moore—a young and rising London physician[21]—who had told him that he did not have angina, "but only weakness."[22] Dr. Moore, however, altered nothing in Dr. Clark's treatments. Darwin was cheered by Dr. Moore's opinions and began to have meals with his family again, walk a little in his orchard, and play backgammon with Emma.[23]

On 4 April he noted in his "Private Diary" that he was having "much pain." Emma persuaded him not to try and see Dr. Clark but to consult with Dr. Moore, and also Mr. Charles Allfrey, a surgeon.[24] Since he was determined not to affront Dr. Clark, it was arranged that these consultations be in *"nominal conjunction* with Dr. Clark."[25] On 5 April Dr. Moore and Mr. Allfrey examined him, then continued Dr. Clark's treatment (which greatly reassured him), and also tried a little nux vomica,[26] which he found did him no good.[27]

He then went on making medical entries in his "Private Diary." 6 April: "Very tired Pain in evening—2 doses." This last may have meant two amyl nitrite pills. 8 April: "No dose only trace of pain." He had "no bad pain" on 9 April, and "very slight attack Pain" on 10 April, and on neither day took any antispasmodics. 11 April: "Some pain at [illegible word] night & discomfort 2 doses of tr anti-spasmodics." On 12 April he noted that his son George had returned to England from a trip to the West Indies, and then wrote: "Bad pain at night—2 doses." 13 April: "Stomach excessively bad—went to bed at 2° but no pain & no dose." 14 April: "1 attack slight pain 1 dose." 15 April: "no pain & no dose at Dinner—dropped down." On this occasion he was seized with giddiness while sitting at dinner in the evening, and fainted in an attempt to reach the sofa. Within minutes he recovered consciousness, drank some brandy, was helped to his study by his son George, and seemed relatively well. Henrietta wanted to send for Mr. Allfrey; Emma thought that his last medical examination had made him ill, and so no doctor was sent for.[28]

He made two more "Diary" entries. 16 April: "Very slight pain several times before [illegible writing[29]]—no dose." 17 April: "Only traces of pain no dose." These were his final medical notations about himself. The persistence of pain indicated that his coronary arteries were becoming progressively more impaired.

On the night of 18–19 April he experienced more pain, and awoke Emma and sent her to his study for a capsule of amyl nitrite. When she returned, he was deeply unconscious. She gave him brandy and he slowly recovered. He thought that he was dying and after some special words to her he said, "and be sure to tell all my children to remember how good they have always been to me"; and "I am not the least afraid to die."[30]

At about 2 A.M. on 19 April Mr. Allfrey arrived (having been sent for by Emma) and was "the greatest possible comfort." He spent the night with Darwin, and left Down at 8 A.M. when his patient was asleep.[31]

After Mr. Allfrey left, Darwin began to have nausea and violent vomiting and retching. Emma said she never saw anyone suffer as he did: "He was longing to die."[32]

These symptoms continued through the morning and early after-noon: Mr. Allfrey and Dr. Walter Moxon[33] were sent for; and (as Emma retired to rest) Darwin was attended by Henrietta and his son Francis—"you two dears," he told them, "are the best of nurses."[34] As he went on suffering from "overpowering nausea interrupted by retching,"[35] Henrietta said, "this terrible nausea still goes on." He answered: "It is not terrible. But it is nausea."[36] He several times said "if I could but die";[37] and "oh god, oh god," which was his way of expressing distress.[38] His children gave him sips of beef tea with brandy in it, and then some pure whiskey which Mr. Allfrey had advised him to try.[39]

Francis Darwin, who had studied medicine, noted that as the afternoon progressed he became "more and more pulseless."[40]

At about twenty-five minutes past three he said "I feel as if I should faint"; he then became unconscious. Mr. Allfrey and Dr. Moxon arrived at Down House and rushed to his room. "As soon as they came in," Henrietta recollected, "they saw it was hopeless but the instinct of doctoring prevailed & they ordered a mustard poultice which I rushed off to get—But it was never put on—He was unconscious & there was the heavy stertorous breathing which precedes Death—It was all over before four o'clock-"[41]

At the time of his death Darwin was seventy-three years and two months old. The physicians who treated him diagnosed his final illness as "anginal attacks," with "heart-failure" and signs that his "heart and greater blood vessels were degenerating."[42]

15

Symptoms, Treatments, Habits

Although Darwin's illness consisted of symptoms which were variform and changing, and which involved different parts of his body, the most frequent symptoms, and those which most impaired his capacity to work, involved his stomach. When he spoke of his "sickness," this almost always referred to his stomach; when he spoke of his "illness," this usually referred to his stomach. When he complained of weakness and unusual head sensations, he was probably mainly describing sequels of his upset stomach. When he complained about what he thought was heart pain—"fullness, slight pain & tickling about the heart"[1]—he may have been describing pain which originated in his stomach.

When he was a youth he knew that he had a vulnerable stomach, and that several quite different psychic stresses upset his stomach. Yet these stresses did not involve his studies and/or his choice of a vocation, and his stomach illness was not serious. It was only when he was twenty-seven, and beginning to do the hard thinking which was part of his beginning scientific vocation, that he observed: "I find the noodle & the stomach are antagonistic powers." For most of his adult life he then experienced this "antagonism," and it caused him pain and vomiting. Pain and vomiting may be conceptualized as psycho-physiologic disorders of the stomach, that is, they were the physical concomitants of a negative emotional arousal. The pain varied in frequency, duration, and intensity—much of Darwin's daily life was lived on a rack which consisted of fluctuating degrees of pain—and when the pain was severe there ensued (what Dr. Lane had called) a "temporary depression" which was "distressingly great." Yet this pain and depression did not become protracted, and Darwin was soon able to go on with his work.

With his vomiting it was different. When his vomiting became recurrent and fixed in different patterns—"periodic" (1839–41), once a week (1848–49), and daily (1863–64 and 1865)—he was affected not by the physiologic effects of the vomiting (his nutrition and physical health remained stable) but by the psychological symptoms which were associated with the vomiting. These symptoms were variform—"ringing in ears," "treading on air," seeing "black dots," "trembling," "swimming head," "shivering," "hysterical crying," and "faint sensa-tions" which he called "dying sensations"—and behind these symp-toms there was always a core of anxiety and depression.[2] The overall effect of these symptoms was that he became physically and mentally weak, and was only able to work a little or not at all. His inability to work then accentuated his depression and caused him to hate himself: "*nothing* is so intolerable as idleness"; "unless I can . . . work a little, I hope my life may be very short."[3] Once, during a period of vomiting, he wrote Hooker: "I am languid & bedeviled & have writing & hate everybody. No, that is not true for in my worst states I do not hate you."[4] He was able to curb some irrational hates, maintain a daily contact with Emma (perhaps also with his servant Parslow), and he never seems to have been suicidal. Yet during these "worst states"— when he seems to have spent his waking hours reclining in silence on a bed or sofa—he experienced an intellectual and emotional nadir and his value of life was low.

Once the pattern of vomiting was broken (this usually meant that the frequency of the episodes of vomiting was diminished) his depression and "worst state" eased and he was able to do some work and start a cycle of recovery. After recovery he must have, very frequently, had the fear that his vomiting and "worst states" would recur.

His sensations of "black dots," "swimming head," and faintness may have sometimes been caused not just by anxiety but by the effects of overbreathing, which is a frequent manifestation of anxiety. However, he never seems to have recorded the frequency of his respirations.

Little is known about the causation and nature of his many skin symptoms. He never defined, or named, the afflictions of his hands and lips that he suffered from as a youth (his friend Herbert, half a century later, recollected that Darwin had "an eruption about the mouth"). In his 1849–55 *Diary* he wrote that he had skin symptoms which he called either "eruption," "rash," or "erythema." He does not describe what he meant by these terms, each of which may have denoted several quite different skin disorders. Nothing is known about the cause of his 1862 episode of "burning" and "violent skin inflammations" of his hands, which doctors called "eczema."[5] It seems evident that in the 1840s, as a result of anxieties about natural selection, he had (what Hooker later called) "attack[s] of violent eczema."[6] It may be that, after the 1840s, he continued to have similar anxiety-induced eczema attacks—and that these included the (what he called) "fits of eczema" which he had in the 1860s.[7] Sometimes hydropathy would cause "an excessive irritation" of the skin of his whole body.[8] He may have had allergic skin reactions from medicines, house furnishings, clothing, or from the various organic objects to which he was exposed: the vegetation on his grounds; the plants he grew in his house, garden, and hothouse; the dogs and cats in his house; the horses, cows, and pigs on his farm.[9] For about eight years he handled and dissected thousands of barnacles and he may have had allergies to some of these, and to other animals that he sometimes dissected. None of his skin reactions, however, can be correlated with taking a particular medicine, or with exposure to a particular inorganic or organic object.[10]

He probably had been taught by his father to differentiate an abnormal from a normal pulse. Then, at different times in his life, he diagnosed himself as having episodes of abnormal pulsations which he called "palpitations." He did not state the frequency and duration of these episodes, or whether "palpitations" meant a disorder of heart rate, or rhythm, or a combination of both. When his pulse was apparently normal, he worried that it was "like [a] thread."[11] Certainly some of his "palpitations" were caused by anxieties. He also may have had "palpitations" from smoking, inhaling snuff, drinking alcohol, coffee, and tea, or taking certain medicines; however, he did not record what substances he was taking when he had "palpitations." Some of his palpitations may have been episodes of idiopathic paroxysmal tachycardia, which can be exacerbated by both psychological and organic causes.[12]

Thus, although his illness mainly originated in psychological causes, the possibility cannot be excluded that he also, sometimes, had organically caused skin disease and heartbeat disease.

In his *Autobiography* he wrote that, because of episodes of illness after conversations, he had "lost the power of becoming deeply attached to anyone, not even so deeply to my good and dear friends Hooker and Huxley, as I should formerly have been."[13] However, in his correspondence with Fox, Hooker, and Huxley, he revealed that his capacity for friendship with men—although perhaps diminished— was still considerable.

In 1851 he wrote Fox: "Long continued ill health has much changed me, & I very often think with pain how cold & indifferent I must appear to my few old friends to what I was formerly: but I internally know that the inner part of my mind remains the same with my old affections. Believe me, my dear Fox, I am & shall ever be your affectionate friend."[14]

In his correspondence with Hooker he expressed a variety of affectionate feelings. In the fall of 1863, when he was very sick, he sent Hooker the following letter:

> My dear old friend
>   I must just have pleasure of saying this.
>   your affect.
>   C. Darwin[15]

Several weeks later he told Hooker: "I shall be glad to hear sometimes about your boy whom you love so.—Much love much trial, but what an utter desert is life without love."[16] When he was almost sixty-four, and Hooker fifty-five, he wrote the latter: "You have sometimes spoken to me as if you felt growing old: I have never seen any signs of this, & I am certain that in the affections, which form incomparably the noblest part of a man's nature, you are one of the youngest men that I know."[17]

In 1872–73 Huxley was ill, depressed, and burdened with financial worries. Lady Lyell suggested to Emma Darwin that Huxley's friends should join together and make him a gift so that he could take a holiday. Darwin "eagerly" took to this scheme, "and became its active promoter, whilst carefully avoiding publicity."[18] He consulted with Huxley's doctor, then contacted eighteen scientific friends of Huxley[19] and raised £2,100 which was deposited in Huxley's bank account.

"We have done this," he wrote Huxley, "to enable you to get such complete rest as you may require for the reestablishment of your health.... We are all your warm personal friends ... there is not a stranger or mere acquaintance amongst us.... We all feel towards you, as we should to an honoured & much loved brother. I am sure that you will return this feeling, & will therefore be glad to give us the opportunity of aiding you in some degree, as this will be a happiness to us to the last day of our lives."[20] In another letter to Huxley he then commented: "To my mind any mark of ["this" crossed out] friendship from such men would be a thousand times more valuable than all the medals & such like honours which can be thought."[21] After Huxley had taken a holiday Darwin, for a while, continued to worry about his friend's health.[22]

Sometimes Darwin's illness would interfere with his feelings for his children. His son Leonard has this recollection: "As a young lad I went up to my father when strolling about the lawn, and he, after, as I believe, a kindly word or two, turned away as if quite incapable of carrying on any conversaton. Then there suddenly shot through my mind the conviction that he wished he was no longer alive. Must there not have been a strained and weary expression in his face to have produced in these circumstances such an effect on a boy's mind?"[23] Episodes such as this must have been short and infrequent. William Darwin recollects that when his father was ill "it threw a certain air of sadness over the life at Down," but that as soon as he "was a trifle better his natural joyousness and gaiety flowed out, and what we very vividly remember is the delightful playmate he made for us as children."[24] Francis Darwin has described his father's dominant attitude toward his children as follows: "He kept up his delightful, affectionate manner toward us all his life. I sometimes wonder that he could do so, with such an undemonstrative race as we are; but I hope he knew how much we delighted in his loving words and manner."[25]

Let us now consider some aspects of Darwin's medications. As an impressionable youth of seventeen he treated patients with tartar emetic, reported on the effects of this to his father, and felt a never-to-be-forgotten "pride" when some patients got better. This experience gave him faith in the therapeutic effects of medicines and taught him that the effects of all medicines must be rigorously evaluated. As he settled into a life of illness he sometimes despaired of medicines. In September 1850 (when he was under the care of Dr. Gully, who was against most medicines) he told Fox: "How true is a remark I saw the other day by Quetelet,[26] in respect to evidence of curative processes, viz that no one knows in disease what is the simple result of nothing being done."[27] However, for most of his life he believed that there existed, or would exist, medicines that would help him; and he was willing, sometimes on what seems to have been hearsay, to try practically any medicine. We possess only a partial record of the medicines that he took. For his stomach alone he tried logwood, bitters and different tonics, bismuth, mineral acids, alkalies, pepsin, "Condy's Ozonised Water," and phosphate of iron and other iron compounds. For his skin he tried arsenic, tartar emetic ointment, Mr. Startin's "muddy stuff," and probably many other medicines. "At one time," his son Leonard recollects, "perhaps for a short time, he used to keep a stinging lotion of some kind on the chimney-piece [in his study], so that he could reach out for it at any moment, and by dabbing it on to his forehead help himself to carry on [with his scientific work] in spite of his aching head."[28] He had a tendency to be, at first, enthusiastic about the effects of a new medicine. He then carefully studied (over varying periods of time) exactly how the medicine affected him, noting its dosage and the time of day he used it. He tried bismuth twice and mineral acids three times. He then would, invariably, conclude that the medicine did not help him. (His attitude toward medicines was analogous to some of his other attitudes. In his *Autobiography* he wrote: "I am . . . a poor critic: a paper or book, when first read, generally excites my admiration, and it is only after considerable reflection that I perceive the weak points."[29]) At the end of his life he came to have "very little faith" in the steady use of medicines, and he came to believe only in the momentary effectiveness of different changes—new locales, new diets, and new medicines.

One substance that he used for most of his life was that powdered preparation of tobacco known as snuff. He began taking snuff when he was an eighteen- or nineteen-year-old student at Edinburgh, and was given snuffboxes—which he valued greatly—by his friend Squire Owen and by his maternal aunt Mrs. Wedgwood.[30] During the *Beagle* cruise he made notes to purchase "Snuff" and a "Snuff box."[31] At different times he then tried to curb his taking of snuff. On 30 December 1838, a month before his marriage, Emma wrote him: "Don't you wish you could be married like a royal Prince without being at your wedding? You may be allowed to carry a few pinches of snuff in your pocket for that morning only."[32] In 1846, at the insistence of Emma, he stopped taking snuff for about one month.[33] In 1849, at the insistence of Dr. Gully, he first limited his snuff to six pinches daily;[34] then he resolved to do without it[35] —and he placed his snuffbox in his cellar and the key to the box in his garret.[36] Soon he began breaking his resolve when he visited the Downe home of his friend, the Reverend J. Brodie Innes.[37] He would tenderly recollect how his little daughter Annie got him snuff: "Her dear face now rises before me, as she used sometimes to come running downstairs with a stolen pinch of snuff for me her whole form radiant with the pleasure of giving pleasure."[38] Perhaps after Annie died in 1851 he was able to keep his resolve when he was at home, for his account books contain no mention of snuff from 1851 until 1856[39] —when he again began regularly taking snuff. In the first part of 1858, during his sojourn at Moor Park, he stopped taking snuff for an undetermined period.[40] He then seems to have taken snuff for the rest of his life. He would take a pinch, with "clocklike regularity," at 10:30 every night as he undressed before going to sleep.[41] The amounts of snuff that he took during the rest of the day varied; he tried to limit these amounts by keeping his snuff in a jar in the hall, where he would have to walk to get it. In his later years he took two kinds of snuff: a heavy, damp, dark brand, which he greatly liked, and a light, powdery, "Irish black guard," which he only took because it was weaker.[42]

He may have thought that taking snuff prevented his having "a cold in his head."[43] He called snuff "my chief comfort"[44] and "that chief solace of life";[45] when he was without it he said he felt "most lethargic, stupid and melancholy."[46] His son Francis wrote that "snuff stirred him up & kept him going."[47] Sniffing snuff may have aided him in his scientific thinking. His geologist friend Judd, who visited him in his Down study when he was in the last years of his life and working on earthworms, recollected: "At the side of the little study stood flower-pots containing earth with worms, and without interrupting our conversation, Darwin would from time to time lift the glass plate covering a pot to watch what was going on. Occasionally, with a humourous smile, he would murmur something about a book in another room, and slip away; returning shortly, without the book but with unmistakable signs of having visited the snuff-jar outside."[48]

Some brands of snuff—adulterated by red and yellow ocher, red lead, chromate of lead, and bichromate of potash—were thought to cause flatulence, vomiting, and severe gastritis, if taken in large quantities.[49] It is not known if Darwin ever used any of these adulterated brands. Snuff, because it contained nicotine, may have caused some of his episodes of palpitations.[50] His son Francis thought that snuff may have injured his sense of smell.[51] Since he took snuff for about ten years before he became seriously ill, and then for ten years after his illness had become better, it is unlikely that snuff toxicity was a cause of his illness. (The possibility that he changed brands of snuff, and that a new brand may have caused some of his episodes of illness, cannot be excluded.)

In addition to snuff he sometimes took other preparations of tobacco. During the *Beagle* cruise, when he was with the Gauchos of Argentina, he smoked what he called "cigar[s]"[52] and "little cigaritos."[53] He then did not smoke until his late years when he took a little Turkish cigarette at three o'clock and another at six o'clock.[54] At these times he lay on the sofa listening to a novel, and smoking—in contrast to the stimulation of snuff—relaxed and rested him.[55]

His drinking of alcohol, and his attitudes toward drinking, had a long history. In his *Autobiography* he wrote that, when he was a student at Cambridge, "I got into a sporting set, including some dissipated low-minded young men. We often used to dine together in the evening . . . and we sometimes drank too much, with jolly singing and playing at cards afterwards."[56] He told his son Francis that "he had once drunk too much at Cambridge."[57] He told Hooker "that he had got drunk three times in early life, and thought intoxication the greatest of all pleasures."[58] During his middle age he sometimes curtailed his drinking, and at other times, enjoyed what he drank. In 1854 he wrote Hooker: "My London visits have just lately taken to suit my stomach admirably; I begin to think that dissipation, high-living, with lots of claret, is what I want, & what I had during the last visit."[59] The next year he wrote Hooker: "N.B. If you want to enjoy perfect health as I do this morning eat turtle soup on two successive days, & drink quantum suffi of wines of all kinds."[60] A few years later he told a friend: " 'Floreat Entomologia'!—to which toast at Cambridge I have drunk many a glass of wine. So again, 'Floreat Entomologia.' N.B. I have *not* now been drinking any glasses full of wine."[61]

In 1860 Dr. Headland prescribed "drinking some wine" as part of his medical regimen.[62] Over the following years wine comforted Darwin when ill. In 1863, when his "nervous system failed," he was for a time "kept going only by repeated doses of brandy."[63] In 1865, when he was very ill, he wrote about himself: "Always been temperate—now wines comfort me much—could not take any formerly."[64] In his old age he drank a glass of sherry at lunch and supper, and abstained from other liquor.[65] His son Francis observed that he "enjoyed and was revived by the little he did drink."[66]

He also had a "great horror" that "any one might be led into drinking too much."[67] He once, "very gravely," told his son Francis that he was "ashamed" that he had been drunk at Cambridge. After hearing this Francis wrote: "it made me feel ["solemnly" crossed out] strongly how much ashamed one ought to be of being ["tipsy" crossed out] drunk; and it added to my respect for my father."[68] Darwin's "horror" of drunknenness had several origins: he, perhaps, feared his tendency to be stimulated by small drinks; a paternal great-grand-father and grandmother had both died from alcoholism,[69] and he may have thought that alcoholism was inherited; and then he was in-fluenced by the anti-alcoholic opinions of his grandfather and father. Dr. Erasmus Darwin had drunk as a student, curtailed his drinking after an attack of gout, and then publicly spoken about the toxic effects of alcohol.[70] Dr. Robert Darwin "was vehement against drinking, and was convinced of both the direct and inherited evil effects of alcohol."[71] In 1876—in a letter to Dr. Benjamin Richardson, then president of a Temperance Banquet—Darwin summarized the anti-alcoholic views of himself and his forebears: "I have been brought to the conviction, from the very large experience of my father and my grandfather, which has extended over a century, that no cause has led to so much suffering and inherited ill-health as the consumption of alcohol."[72]

In the first period of his illness, after brief consultations with Drs. Holland and James Clark, Darwin became a patient of his father. The details of the medical interactions between the physician father and his sick son are only a little known. Dr. Darwin's treatments were sometimes ineffective; on at least one occasion Darwin felt that his father was unsympathetic to his complaints. Yet he became de-pendent upon his father for medications, diets, and diverse kinds of medical advice; his father checked his "periodic vomiting" and saw him through his 1839–42 years of illness. He was his father's patient for about ten years—the longest he was ever with any one doctor—and while his father lived he never tried to put himself under the long-term medical care of another doctor.

After his father's death, in the years when his illness was severe, he consulted many physicians: he developed warm personal feelings for Drs. Gully and Lane (like Dr. Darwin, both were professionally successful outside the world of London medicine) and he came to respect Dr. Jenner; but he did not stay with any doctor for a long time—and he regarded all doctors as inferior to his father.[73] Yet on three occasions—1848–49, 1863–64, and 1865—when he had severe vomiting, he was only able to stop this when a physician prescribed a treatment. On each occasion it was a different physician with a different medical regimen: Gully with hydropathy; Jenner with chalk, magnesia, and carbonate of ammonia; Bence Jones with starvation.

He derived some gains from his illness. He observed that his "eczema" sometimes "energised" him, and that being ill "saved me from the distractions of society and amusement."[74] His son Leonard thought that his illness enabled him to avoid "extraneous duties" and taught him never to waste a minute of his short working day.[75] The poet Allingham was impressed by how Darwin's invalid regimen suited his studious ways.[76] Sir George Pickering has recently asserted that Darwin's illness—primarily because it enabled him to avoid social distractions and concentrate on collecting evidence for his evolutionary theory—was essential for the successful development of his work, and was a "creative illness."[77] "Without that illness," Sir George writes, "the great work would not have been done, or done in such a splendid style."[78]

This last assertion seems only partially true. In the years 1837–39—when his illness was only moderate and not yet a force which shaped his life—Darwin originated his evolutionary theory, did more work than at any other time of his life, and socialized a great deal.[79] If his health had not worsened he may have continued this regimen; his socialization with some individuals would have given him evidence for his theory; and he may have found excuses for avoiding socialization which did not aid his work. We have seen how, when his illness did worsen—as in 1839–42, 1848–49, 1863–64, and 1865—it could impair and/or destroy his working capacity. He estimated that illness "annihilated several years of my life"[80]—not the years of his old age but several of his best working years. Instead of saying that his illness was "creative," it seems truer to say that he usually struggled against the destructive effects of his illness, and that sometimes (when not severely ill) he could use his illness to avoid situations which would distract him from his work.

His struggle to work despite his illness made his life—the life which was outwardly dull and "uniform"—an inner drama which underwent tense fluctuations: declines into his "worst states" when he was unable or unwilling to work, and then ascents into states of work. He always managed to regain his desire to work, and he expressed this desire—after twenty years of illness and work and two periods of "worst states"—in his previously quoted statement: "I would sooner be the wretched contemptible invalid, which I am, than live the life of an idle squire."[81] With the money he inherited from his father he could have lived as an idle squire and spared himself much illness. He never attempted to do this. After twenty-seven years of illness and work, and three periods of "worst states," he spoke of his work as "the only thing which makes life endurable to me."[82] In the last years of his life Emma came to believe "that she did not wish him to live without working."[83]

He called his work "my passion":[84] it was, simply, a passion to comprehend more and more of the world of nature.

His struggle to work despite illness impressed not only his family and friends but those who knew him only slightly. The English journalist Frederic Harrison has the following, 1860s or 1870s, recollection: "Professor Tyndall, Dr. Carpenter, Charles Darwin I have met; but my intercourse with them gave me no opportunity of colouring in any way the impression left by the reading of their works. To witness in private the extraordinary nervous delicacy under which Darwin passed his life, gave a striking proof of the genius which in spite of physique so slight, enabled him to achieve his immense triumphs of thought."[85]

By rigidly adhering to his daily routine of work and leisure, by thinking about his work in some of his periods of leisure, and by working intensely in his brief work periods, Darwin was able to do a prodigious amount of work—perhaps more work than most of his illustrious contemporaries.[86] And, as a noted psychoanalyst has observed, despite his very great anxieties he was able to keep the content of his work free from neurotic inroads.[87]

2

Theories of the Origins of the Illness

1

The Theories of Darwin and His Doctors

Most of Darwin's doctors were "puzzled" about the cause of his illness;[1] only a few seem to have made a diagnosis. Some called the illness, simply, "dyspepsia of an aggravated character,"[2] or "catarrhal dyspepsia."[3] Others saw it as a form of gout: "suppressed gout,"[4] "nearest to suppressed gout,"[5] and "various irregular manifestations of a gouty constitution, such as eczema, vaso-motor nerve storms, vertigo, and other disorders of sensation."[6]

Darwin's disease was thought to be related to gout for the following reasons: It had been observed that when a gouty inflammation of a joint subsided, this was sometimes followed by a disturbance of some other body organ or function. This later disturbance was thought to be caused by a spread of the gout, and was called "retrocedent gout."[7] Victorian doctors further believed that some illnesses of the nervous, circulatory, and digestive systems—in which gouty inflammation of the joint was absent—were caused by gout, and should be diagnosed as "suppressed gout."[8] Dr. Henry Holland—who had said that Darwin's 1848–49 illness was "nearest to suppressed gout"—believed that gout was "dependent on a *specific material agent*, capable of showing itself in various ways; and of affecting, directly or indirectly, almost every part or function of the body."[9]

It was thought that there was a close relation between gout and disorders of the stomach. Dr. Holland wrote that there was an "undoubted connexion between dyspeptic disorders and the irregular forms of the gouty constitution; a connection sufficiently close and familiar to observation to justify the belief of relation to some common cause; acting under different modifications from age, sex, and other temperament of body; as well as from variations, it may be, in the quality or proportion of the morbid matter itself."[10] Some physicians held that "flatulency . . . generally ushers in an attack of

109

gout."[11] Dr. Alfred Garrod, a leading authority on gout,[12] propounded that: "those varieties of dyspepsia which lead to the excessive formation of uric acid in the system, tend powerfully to the production of gout";[13] "that in gouty cases ... an excess of uric acid circulating in the blood may itself give rise to a secondary form of dyspepsia, and cause many of the premonitory symptoms referable to the digestive organs, so commonly met with in gouty subjects";[14] and that severe and prolonged study and mental anxiety could cause gout.[15]

Dr. Garrod had shown that in gout the blood uric acid level is elevated, and in 1854 he introduced the following "thread test" for uric acid. Blood was drawn from the patient—since there was a "natural repugnance" to drawing blood,[16] it was sometimes possible to make a blister and draw off its serum—and the blood or serum was acidified, and then evaporated; if uric acid was present crystals formed which adhered to a fine thread. Garrod held that if these crystals did not form, and the results of the "thread test" were negative, the diagnosis of gout was excluded.[17] This "thread test"—one of the earliest of bedside diagnosic tests[18]—soon became widely used. It is not known whether Darwin ever had this test.

Since gout was regarded as a "hereditary disorder,"[19] Darwin's doctors may have postulated that he had inherited his form of gout from some of his ancestors. It seems likely that his paternal grandfather, Dr. Erasmus Darwin, had acute attacks of gout in his joints;[20] and his father,[21] and a great-grandfather,[22] may have had gout.

The concept of "suppressed gout" explained Darwin's illness to some of his doctors. Today, however, this concept is no longer held. Darwin's symptoms—especially his upset stomach and his episodes of facial "eczema"—are not part of the present clinical picture of gout. Although he sometimes complained of "rheumatism,"[23] he does not seem to have had the attacks of severe joint pains and swelling which Dr. Erasmus Darwin had and which are characteristic of gout.

Darwin came to believe that there were three causes for his illness: heredity; some of the ill effects of the *Beagle* cruise; and the pressures of scientific work.

In 1838 (in the course of searching for the causes of heritable variation) he recorded in one of his evolutionary notebooks what his father had told him about the inheritance of diseases and mental and physical traits. Dr. Robert Darwin had observed that when attending one patient "he could not help thinking he was prescribing to his [the patient's] father."[24] In 1839 Darwin read Dr. Henry Holland's just-published *Medical Notes and Reflections*, and made numerous annotations in the chapter "On Hereditary Disease." At the end of the book he wrote: "Strong sentence on Hereditariness."[25] The sentence he had marked read: "Seeking then for the most general expression of facts, we may affirm that no organ or texture of the body is exempt from the chance of being the subject of hereditary disease."[26] In his fourth *Transmutation Notebook* he made a note to "ask" Dr. Holland for more details about the inheritance of certain traits.[27] Over the years, in the course of developing his theory of evolution, he read widely about inheritance. In 1868, in his book *The Variation of Animals and Plants under Domestication*, he published examples of the inheritance of illness, including gout: "With gout, fifty percent of the cases observed in hospital practice are, according to Dr. Garrod, inherited, and a greater percentage in private practice."[28] In *The Variation* he also published his theory of pangenesis: this held that the body cells gave off gemmules which became part of the reproductive cells, and that "man carries in his constitution the seeds of an inherited disease."[29]

He then applied his ideas about the inheritance of illness to himself in two ways. He thought that his family was "gouty,"[30] and that his illness was caused by his inheritance of this "gouty" tendency.[31] He may have regarded gout, "suppressed gout," and "gouty constitution" as the same entity. He then held that some of his children had "inherited from me feeble health."[32] He may also have thought that a further cause for his children's inherited ill health was his marriage to his cousin.[33]

Darwin's opinions about the aftereffects of his *Beagle* seasickness changed. In 1857–59 he told Dr. Lane that he "supposed" his seasickness caused his subsequent dyspepsia.[34] In 1864 he told his brother Erasmus that he did "not believe" his seasickness "was the cause of my subsequent ill health."[35] In 1871 he said to a visitor that "some of his friends" thought that his illness "might be attributed to long-continued seasickness on his voyages years ago": he then did not express an opinion on this subject, and abruptly changed the conversation.[36] Several years later he read a biography of himself by an American physician, Titus Munson Coan,[37] which contained the following passage: "Mr. Darwin returned from this five years' [*Beagle*] voyage with health permanently impaired; and this was due, as I learn from private sources of information, to a quite extraordinary cause,— to his almost continuous sea sickness, namely during the whole time, amounting to months or years, during which the 'Beagle' was at sea. From this strain Mr. Darwin's constitution never quite rallied; since 1836 he has been an invalid."[38] Darwin did not comment on this passage.[39] He was silent about the seasickness theory of his illness, probably because he had come to steadily disbelieve in this theory.[40]

In 1870 he read a biography of himself by a German physician-scientist, Wilhelm Preyer;[41] this stated that, during the *Beagle* cruise, his "health was permanently shattered by the meager ship's food, and also from the unusual strain of the land trips."[42] In a letter to Preyer, in which he expressed his appreciation of the biography, Darwin said nothing about his *Beagle* illnesses.[43] He never seems to have complained about the *Beagle* food. He was, however, "sometimes inclined to think that the breaking up of his health was to some extent due" to his September–November 1834 episode of Chilean fever.[44]

(The hereditary nature of Darwin's illness, and the aftereffects of his *Beagle* seasickness, will be discussed in the next section.)

Darwin came to know that sustained thinking on one idea (a mode of thinking which was especially necesssary for his evolutionary work),[45] scientific controversy, and horrible ideas[46] could all make him sick. He did not, however, try to analyze his mental attributes and the deeper psychological forces which caused him to have an upset stomach. He came to rely on the sensations of his stomach— rather than his thoughts and feelings—to inform him when he had overworked.[47] When he was an old man he wrote: "I have never tried looking into my own mind."[48]

Yet, although he kept much of his mental life secret, he was determined to preserve all of his books and papers. And in his various medical notes and diaries, his personal and scientific writings, his letters, and the annotations to his books, he left a medical-psychological record of himself (perhaps more intimate than he realized), which those who came after him could study and interpret.

2

Several Different Theories, and a Comparison of Darwin's Illness with the Illnesses of His Relations and Children

On or soon after Darwin's death in 1882, a number of different accounts of Darwin the man, which contained passing references to his illness, were published. An anonymously written obituary in the *British Medical Journal* stated that "during all his life" Darwin suffered from "a condition of the nervous system reacting upon the digestive organs which necessitated the greatest care."[1] This was not further elaborated, and it is not clear what was meant by "a condition of the nervous system," or how this "condition" then "reacts" on the body.

Most of the accounts—obituaries in *Lancet*[2] and *The Times*,[3] short biographies by G. W. Bacon[4] and Professor L. C. Miall,[5] and memoirs by Darwin's *Beagle* companion John Lort Stokes,[6] his physician Dr. Lane,[7] and his biologist friend George J. Romanes[8]—all postulated that Darwin's illness was the result of his *Beagle* seasickness. Exactly how seasickness exerted its impact—whether it acted on the stomach or nervous system or both—was not specified. Asa Gray wrote that Darwin had been ill "from the time of the voyage of the *Beagle*," and that his illness was "not unlike seasickness."[9] Then Thomas Huxley, in a Royal Society obituary on Darwin, commented that the 1834 episode of Chilean fever "seems to have left its mark" on Darwin's "constitution."[10] Huxley's son Leonard, in a short biography of Darwin, later agreed with this view of his father.[11] Many years later the surgeon, Sir Buckston Browne, would say that Darwin became "the victim of chronic indigestion, induced by five years of hardship at sea, with scant accommodation on a small ship and with roughly prepared food."[12]

There are three objections to the above views. First, Darwin had a tendency to suffer from a psychically upset stomach years before the *Beagle* cruise (and before he went on the cross-channel voyage to France). Second, although he complained of some increase in stomach discomfort (while at sea) for about four months after his Chilean fever, he did not complain about his stomach (aside from seasickness) for the last 1 1/2 years of the *Beagle* voyage. After his return home he made no complaints about his stomach for about 1 1/2 years—until May 1838, when he was deep in evolutionary speculations. Third, there is no hard evidence that seasickness can cause permanent organic damage to the stomach. It is possible that years of seasickness made some lasting psychological impact on Darwin: that the experience of seasickness accentuated his tendency to react to negative emotions by having an upset stomach.

Darwin's son Leonard then came to believe that his father's illness had been "pyorrhoea, or some other form of auto-poisoning, and that any excitement made the poison flow more freely."[13] Darwin did have some unspecified trouble with his teeth (this will be discussed in another section); there is, however, no evidence that "pyorrhoea" causes the symptoms that made up his illness. Leonard Darwin does not specify what he means by "other form of auto-poisoning."

Five years after Darwin's death, in 1887, Francis Darwin published a three-volume edition of his father's *Life and Letters*. This book stated, without comment, Darwin's thoughts about the causes of his illness, and touched on the course and nature of most of his symptoms; it was stressed that he suffered from chronic indigestion, and that his life was "one long struggle against the weariness and strain of sickness."[14] Although *Life and Letters* became the main published source for information about Darwin's illness, it possessed several shortcomings: it omitted many facts about treatments, doctors, and symptoms; and when Darwin, in the course of describing his illness, had written "vomiting," Francis Darwin had sometimes either deleted this word or substituted the word "sickness." ("Sickness" was a word which had sometimes been used by Dr. Robert Darwin and Charles Darwin to denote vomiting.) Because of this editing, the severity of some of Darwin's gastric symptoms and the exact nature of some of the exacerbations of his illness were obscured.

Since the publication of *Life and Letters,* theories about the cause of Darwin's illness have proliferated. The proponents of these theories have been mostly English or American doctors who have followed— frequently with great distinction—different careers as medical researchers, general medical practitioners, medical internists, parasitologists, ophthalmologists, and psychiatrists and psychoanalysts. They have studied Darwin's illness because of their admiration for his work and their professional interest in understanding the nature of illness. Their theories of his illness have varied widely, reflecting different degrees of knowledge about Darwin, different periods of medical thought and knowledge, and different interests, predilections, and points of reference for viewing and studying illness. What follows will summarize and evaluate these theories and, where indicated, further information about Darwin's health and life will be presented.

The first article devoted solely to discussing the origins of Darwin's illness was by Dr. William W. Johnston, a well-known American practitioner of medicine, and teacher of the theory and practice of medicine in Columbian University, Washington, D.C.[15] It was entitled "The Ill Health of Charles Darwin: Its Nature and Its Relation to His Work," and was published in 1901 in the *American Anthropologist*. Dr. Johnston presented all of the *Life and Letters* evidences of illness, stressed the relation between Darwin's performance of mental work and his illness, and then stated that Darwin was "suffering from chronic neurasthenia of a severe grade."[16] The term *neurasthenia*—first used in 1868 and then increasingly used—described

a clinical condition characterized by overwhelming weakness, weariness, and exhaustion; insomnia and diffuse anxiety; and a variety of
somatic disturbances including cardiac arrythmias, gastric and colonic
upsets, and vasomotor instability so that the skin was sometimes
flushed and sometimes sweating and cold. Neurasthenia was thought to
be caused by a loss of nervous energy: it was thought that the nervous
system had undergone an actual loss of energy, the way a partially
discharged battery undergoes a loss of voltage.[17] As Dr. Johnston
pictured it, Darwin, because of his "intense and sustained" mental
work, suffered from a "continued overstrain of exhausted nerve cells.
They never, however, rendered the cerebrum incapable of the highest
intellectual work, although making the accomplishment of this work
both painful and difficult. . . . The chronic indigestion and disturbance
in the action of the heart were the usual well-recognised accompani-
ments of loss of the normal nerve supply to the digestive organs and
the heart."[18]

Today the term *neurasthenia* is used only to describe a state of
weakness, fatigue, and exhaustion; and it is used infrequently.
Whether the nervous system undergoes a loss of energy remains
unproved.[19] Dr. Johnston was correct in pointing out the relation
between Darwin's illness and work. Yet, because he does not recognize that it was only certain kinds of work which made his subject ill,
he makes several errors and omissions. He, quite wrongly, has
Darwin's illness beginning during the *Beagle* voyage (the period when
Darwin, aside from seasickness and infections, was in excellent
health); and he does not mention that there were periods when
Darwin worked hard and was not ill.

In 1903 Dr. George M. Gould—an American physician who was a
prolific writer on medical subjects, and who specialized in correcting
errors of refraction of the eye[20]—published a small book entitled
*Biographic Clinics: The Origin of the Ill-Health of De Quincy,
Carlyle, Darwin, Huxley, and Browning.* Dr. Gould, respectfully
disagreeing with Dr. Johnston, postulated the following: Darwin (as
well as the other subjects of *Biographic Clinics*) had a "refractive
anomaly of the eyes," a failure to successfully adapt to near vision,
which caused him to excessively strain his eyes when he read and (to a
lesser extent) when he used a microscope. This excessive eye strain
caused his stomach upsets, headaches, apathy and exhaustion, and
cardiac pain and palpitations; Dr. Gould asserts that these symptoms
"are precisely those which the best American oculists find are the most
common symptoms of this refractive anomaly of the eyes."[21] Dr.

Gould further believes that Darwin's *Beagle* "sea-sickness" was not due to the sea but to his eyestrain when working with his microscope in his *Beagle* cabin;[22] and that Darwin felt better during his last ten years because he became presbyopic, and did not have to try to adapt to near vision.[23]

There are several serious objections to Dr. Gould's theory. It is questionable whether uncorrected errors of refraction could produce such symptoms as Darwin's episodes of gastric pain and vomiting and his episodes of facial "eczema."[24] Darwin frequently became ill from events which put no strain on his eyes, such as a conversation, or thinking troubled thoughts at night. During the 1850s, after almost twenty years of illness, there are several indications that his vision was acute. For about five years, from 1849 to 1854, he studied the minute anatomy of barnacles, work which involved him in hours of sustained and concentrated looking into a microscope. Yet during these years his illness did not become severe. (In his *Diary of Health* he notes that he had a "sty" in his eye on 3 February 1853 and 8 December 1854.) Dr. Lane has described how at Moor Park, from 1857 to 1859, Darwin was "all eyes" so that: "Nothing escaped him. No object in nature, whether Flower, or bird, or Insect of any kind could avoid his loving recognition."[25] In 1859 he helped his sons identify the beetles they caught.[26] Only in his "later years" did Darwin require some visual aids.[27] When he was fifty-three, in April 1862, his son William gave him a pince-nez,[28] which he then used "only for reading" and in carrying out some of his experiments.[29] Then, when he wanted to closely examine an object, he used a set of sectional glasses which he carried in a little portmanteau.[30]

After the publication of Dr. Gould's eyestrain theory, two physicians suggested psychiatric theories.

Sir Arthur Keith, the eminent English physician, anatomist, physical anthropologist, champion of Darwinism, and student of Darwin's life,[31] believed that Darwin became ill because of mental overwork. This resembled Dr. Johnston's neurasthenic theory, without being called neurasthenia and without postulating a loss of nervous energy. In his book *Darwin Revalued*—written in 1954 and published in 1955, the year its author died—Sir Arthur writes:"Darwin was familiar with the fact that when he overworked his stomach suffered. The puzzling aspect of his case, so it seems to me, is that notwithstanding he still continued to overwork his brain. . . . As we trace the development of Darwin's ill health, we find that when he gives up overworking his brain, his digestive organs at once assume their normal silent function."[32] Sir Arthur perceives Darwin's determination to work in spite of his illness, yet he does not indicate that some kinds of work did not greatly disturb Darwin's health, and that stresses other than work made him ill.

Dr. Walter C. Alvarez, a noted American physician and medical writer[33] who specializes in treating patients with gastroenterologic and psychoneurotic problems, has commented upon Darwin's illness for nearly three decades in sections of his medical books and in articles and letters in medical journals[34]—at the age of ninety Dr. Alvarez kept a set of Charles Darwin's published works in his office.[35] Dr. Alvarez makes two assertions. First, that Darwin's illness may be diagnosed as "a mild form of depression"[36]—also called "a minor 'equivalent' of the depressive psychosis"[37]—and that his symptoms were "the *manifestations* of a depression."[38] Second, that he inherited this depression from his Darwin and Wedgwood relations.[39]

Dr. Alvarez never precisely defines what he means by a depression which is "a minor 'equivalent' of the depressive psychosis." (After reading Dr. Alvarez's account of Darwin's illness one physician thought that Darwin may have had a form of schizophrenia.[40]) Darwin was not so much a depressed personality—although he could become severely depressed—as a personality who was exquisitely sensitive to different events, and who reacted to these events with a range of different feelings which included anger, guilt, depression, and excitement. His periods of illness were caused by a variety of feelings. Dr. Alvarez does not differentiate between times when Darwin was primarily depressed, and when his depression was secondary—a psychic reaction to vomiting and physical suffering. The diagnosis of "mild depression" does not explain why Darwin became ill at certain times and remained relatively well at other times.

Dr. Alvarez thinks that the illnesses of Darwin's relations— uncles Erasmus Darwin, Jr., and Tom Wedgwood, cousin Francis Galton, brother Erasmus Alvey Darwin, and others—resembled Darwin's illness, and that because of this resemblance the illness of the latter was inherited. But were these illnesses similar? What follows will summarize what is known about the major illnesses of six of Darwin's relations, including the four mentioned by Dr. Alvarez.[41] We shall not try to survey personality traits or neurotic traits of Darwin's relations, as these cannot be accurately assessed.

1. A paternal grandmother, Mrs. Mary Darwin, had episodes of severe pains in her head and right upper quadrant, which were followed in about an hour by "violent convulsions." She sometimes,

also, had episodes which her physician-husband described as "temporary delirium, or what by some might be termed insanity" which lasted about half an hour and then cleared. These symptoms began when Mrs. Darwin was in her twenties and continued for four to six years. To relieve her pain she began drinking, and then concealed this from her husband—her father had been "a drunkard both in public and private" and died a drunkard. Her drinking led to signs of liver failure—ascites, bleeding—and then a gradual sinking into coma, and at the age of thirty-one she died.[42] The diagnosis of her illness will be discussed later.[43]

2. Maternal uncle, Tom Wedgwood, had the following illness: "A grave constitutional disease which . . . made the last ten years of his life utterly miserable. . . . The doctors seem to have agreed that it had to do with the digestive system. Some called it a paralysis or semiparalysis of the colon. One considered it to be the sequel of an attack of dysentery which he had when a student at Edinburgh. Others would only call it 'hypochondria'. Whatever the physical cause was, a main feature of the disease was a continual recurrence of fits of depression, sometimes lasting for weeks together. His mental misery at these times, especially towards the close of his life, made his condition hardly distinguishable from one of insanity."[44] During his illness he was unable to accomplish any work, and he died mysteriously at the age of thirty-four.[45]

3. Paternal uncle, Erasmus Darwin, Jr., was a successful and respected lawyer, who was "gentle, ingenious, and affectionate"; yet shy and "without any known or suspected attachment of the impassioned kind."[46] When he was forty he withdrew from his law practice and friends, bought a small country estate, and then drowned himself.[47]

4. Paternal half-cousin, Francis Galton, had a nervous breakdown when he was twenty-one and a student at Cambridge, which he described as follows: "I suffered from intermittent pulse and a variety of brain symptoms of an alarming kind. A mill seemed to be working inside my head; I could not banish obsessing ideas; at times I could hardly read a book, and found it painful even to look at a printed page. Fortunately, I did not suffer from sleeplessness, and my digestion failed but little . . . a brief interval of complete mental rest did me good . . . I had been much too zealous, had worked too irregularly and in too many directions, and had done myself serious harm." After several months of mental rest Galton recovered completely.[48] From thirty-one up to about fifty-four Galton had "giddiness and other maladies prejudicial to mental effort," and treated himself by changing his habits, traveling, and outdoor exercise. When he was forty-four he had "a more serious break-

down than had happened . . . before," and treated himself by
changing his "mode of life."[49] When he was fifty-four he had an
episode of "irregular gout and influenza."[50]

5. Darwin wrote that his older brother, Erasmus Alvey Darwin,
had "weak health" as a boy and that "as a consequence he failed in
energy." He added that Erasmus' "spirits were not high, sometimes
low, more especially during early and middle manhood."[51] Erasmus was unable to work, never married, and lived to the age of
seventy-seven. The nature of Erasmus' inertia and "low spirits" is
obscure. When Erasmus was fifty-three, Darwin reported to Fox:
"but Eras. not so well with more frequent fever fits and a good deal
debilitated."[52] Two years later Erasmus wrote his brother: "My
ague[53] has left me in such a state of torpidity that I wish I had gone
through the process of natural selection."[54] When Erasmus was
fifty-six Darwin told Fox: "Erasmus, I grieve to say, has not quite
lost his ague."[55] This suggests that Erasmus suffered from a febrile
illness, and it has been postulated that he had "tubercular damage
to one lung."[56]

6. Darwin's older sister, Caroline, married her cousin Josiah Wedgwood, had four children, seemed to be in relatively good health, and
when she was seventy-four Darwin reported to Fox: "You ask about
Caroline: she is aged in her body & infirm, but very brisk in mind."[57]
Then two years later, Darwin wrote Fox: "You enquire about poor
Caroline. She is in a piteous state & has now been confined to her bed
for 20 months—She is a little better & we have been scheming whether she shd. return to Leith Hill in a special train & bed carriages, but
it is decided she is yet too weak, & God knows whether she will
ever return."[58] One and a half years later Darwin told Fox: "Caroline is better in general health & comes down stairs every day but I
fear will never leave Leith Hill Place."[59] Caroline then seems to
have remained in relatively stable health, able to move about her
Leith Hill house, until her death at eighty-eight in 1888.[60]

Comparing the illnesses of the above six individuals one is impressed
by how each illness—including the depressions of Tom Wedgwood,
Erasmus Darwin, Jr., and Erasmus Alvey Darwin—differed from
the other in its history and major symptoms, and how the causes
of each illness were obscure and perhaps different. None of the above
illnesses resembled Darwin's illness in its history, or manifested
Darwin's stomach or skin symptoms (Tom Wedgwood's gastrointestinal symptoms were confined to the lower part of the intestinal
tract; Darwin's symptoms were confined to the upper part of the
intestinal tract). From the available evidence (admittedly incomplete)

one may conclude that when the youthful Darwin manifested a psychic vulnerability of his stomach, and an undetermined affliction of his skin, he was manifesting two new Darwin-Wedgwood traits.

Dr. Alvarez further postulates that Darwin passed on his "inherited mild depression" to some of his children.[61] Let us summarize what is known about the childhood and adult illnesses of Darwin's ten children, and then determine how these relate to Darwin's illness.

Mary Eleanor Darwin died as an infant from unknown causes. Charles Waring Darwin never talked or walked, and died at the age of 1½ from scarlet fever.[62] When Annie Darwin was ten her father wrote: "She inherits I fear with grief, my wretched digestion."[63] Several weeks later Annie died from unknown causes.[64] The seven surviving Darwin children had many of the infectious diseases of childhood;[65] these were recorded, along with vaccinations, in the Down family Bible.[66] Francis Darwin and Leonard Darwin were "ill" (symptoms not described) when they were, respectively, six and four.[67] When Leonard Darwin was twelve he had recurrent scarlet fever[68] and developed severe complications[69]—eventually he completely recovered. Henrietta Darwin, during her adolescence, had a succession of sicknesses. When she was fourteen she became "out of health" and was treated with hydropathy.[70] At fifteen she had an illness "like diptheria," from which she only very slowly recovered.[71] From seventeen to eighteen, for a period of about one year, she was severely ill with fluctuating fever, weakness, "indigestion,"[72] and may have had "some fluid accumulated" in the abdomen.[73] She then slowly recovered, remaining for a while "a sad invalid."[74] Darwin called her illness "odd fever—partly remittent, partly typhoid":[75] Henrietta thought that she had typhoid fever.[76] When Horace Darwin was eleven Darwin reported that he was "strangely ill, with singular involuntary movements, for two months; but at last he is decidedly better. We feared much that there was mischief in the Brain, but it now seems clear that it was all sympathetic with irritation of stomach."[77] A year later Darwin described Horace as "a regular invalid with severe indigestion, clearly inherited from me."[78]

In the late 1850s and early 1860s five of the Darwin children— including Elizabeth, Leonard, and Horace—experienced a disorder of the pulse, which Darwin successively described as "feeble & often very irregular,"[79] "irregular,"[80] "intermittent (but only symptomatically so),"[81] and "intermittent weak."[82] Darwin commented that this pulse disorder of his children was "a curious form of inheritance from my poor constitution, though I never failed in exactly that way."[83] (He

does not specify the differences between his pulse disorder and those
of his children. And, as has been seen, he described his disorder
mainly as "palpitations."[84])

All of the seven surviving Darwin children then lived long lives.
Henrietta, George, Francis, Leonard, and Horace developed hypochondriacal concerns about their health, and this was most pronounced with Henrietta. It was said of Henrietta that "ill health
became her profession and absorbing interest."[85] This hypochondriasis of the Darwin children was caused by several factors: by some
children experiencing prolonged bouts of childhood illnesses (this was
especially true of Henrietta); by all children being aware of childhood
illnesses in their Down home; by all children being aware of the illness
of their father, and their mother's nursing of him and worry about
him; and by all children being confronted with their father's great
concern about his illness and their states of health—his feeling that his
children had inherited his illness, his close observation of them and his
frequent checking of their pulse, and his conviction that Darwins
were doomed to be sick. How much of the adult illnesses of Henrietta,
Francis, Leonard, and Horace was imagined and how much real
cannot be determined—little is known about the clinical manifestations of their illnesses.[86]

Some things are known about the illness of Darwin's fifth child and
second son George. George "fell ill" when he was twenty-four, and
then became very ill when he was twenty-seven and twenty-eight and
continued to be ill for years. He suffered from "digestive troubles,
sickness and general discomfort and weakness."[87] "Sickness" probably
means vomiting. Sir Clifford Allbutt, Regius Professor of Physic at
Cambridge, diagnosed George's case as "gastric neurosis," and treated
him by emptying his stomach through a tube.[88] Although George
expected to die from some of his "attacks" of illness,[89] his health
gradually improved, and when he was forty-nine he underwent a
"rest-cure" which produced a "permanent improvement, although
his health remained a serious handicap throughout his life,"[90] and "his
nerves [were] always as taut as fiddle strings."[91] Despite his illness he
accomplished much scientific work, and he died at the age of
sixty-seven.[92] Thus much of George's illness—its onset, physical
symptoms, and course—seems to resemble the illness of his father.
Exactly how George's illness related to that of his father—inheritance
of an organic predisposition, being psychologically conditioned by
seeing his father ill (and seeing his father become ill because of him[93]),
or a combination of both of these—cannot be determined.

Thus Dr. Alvarez's postulation that Darwin's illness was inherited lacks evidence, and his postulation that this illness was then (in some unspecified manner) passed on to the Darwin children requires much qualification.

3

Psychoanalytic Theories

For a period of about fifty years, all of the psychiatric theories of Darwin's illness—except for those of Johnston, Keith, and Alvarez—explained this illness by psychoanalytic concepts of psychic conflicts.

The first psychoanalytic theory was presented by Dr. Edward J. Kempf, an American psychiatrist who was an early member of the American Psychoanalytic Association;[1] it was entitled "Charles Darwin—The Affective Sources of His Inspiration and Anxiety Neurosis," and was published in 1918 in the *Psychoanalytic Review*.[2] In 1927 the Hungarian psychoanalyst, Dr. Imre Hermann, published a psychoanalytic study of Darwin's life in *Imago*, the German-language Austrian periodical devoted to the nonmedical applications of psychoanalysis.[3] In the 1940s and 1950s Dr. Douglas Hubble and Dr. Rankine Good—two psychoanalytically oriented English psychiatrists—published articles and letters on Darwin's illness in English literary and scientific journals.[4] In 1956 Dr. Erasmus Darwin Barlow, Darwin's great-grandson and then a research fellow in psychological medicine, published in *The Listener* a popularly written summary of the illnesses of members of the Darwin family entitled "The Dangers of Health."[5] In 1963 Dr. Phyllis Greenacre, a leading American psychoanalyst, published as a Freud anniversary lecture: *The Quest for the Father: A Study of the Darwin-Butler Controversy, as a Contribution to the Understanding of the Creative Individual.*[6]

These studies differ in their depiction of Darwin's clinical symptoms, and offer different psychological explanations for the causes of some of these symptoms. Dr. Kempf diagnosed Darwin's September 1831 hand complaints as "neurotic hands," which "would lead one strongly to suspect an auto-erotic difficulty that had not been completely mastered."[7] Dr. Hermann believed that Darwin's November–December 1831 Plymouth illness was caused by the reactivations of an old "birth trauma" and an old "fear of death," the latter "provoked by ... old guilt feelings due to killing of animals [the father]...."[8]

These explanations may be valid, yet they should be supported by more evidence, other possible explanations should be mentioned, and even as conjectures they do not enhance our view of Darwin the man. They reflect an early period of psychoanalysis, when theoretical concepts were applied to biography in a simplistic and reductionist manner. Some of the later psychoanalytic views of Darwin, reflecting the growth of psychoanalysis, are more tempered. In 1954 Dr. Hubble, after commenting that it was "plain" that Darwin's illness was "neurotic," added, "I admit that we have yet much to learn of the constitutional and environmental causes of neurosis."[9] In 1963 Dr. Greenacre gave this cautious overview: "His [Darwin's] symptoms were those which fifty years ago would have been called neurasthenia. Probably now we would think of them as a severe anxiety neurosis in an obsessional character, certainly much complicated by genius. Perhaps we would not even venture a diagnosis in a condition with such polymorphous symptomatology."[10]

All of the above studies postulate that Darwin had hostility for his father which he repressed; it is then further postulated—in somewhat different ways by different authors—that this repressed hostility contributed to Darwin's illness.

Dr. Rankine Good pictures a direct—although unconscious—struggle of a son revolting from his father:

There is a wealth of evidence that unmistakably points to . . . [Darwin's] symptoms as a distorted expression of the aggression, hate, and resentment felt at an unconscious level by Darwin towards his tyrannical father, although, at a conscious level, we find the reaction-formation of the reverence for his father which was boundless and most touching. At the same time, the symptoms represent, in part, the punishment Darwin suffered for harbouring such thoughts about his father. For Darwin *did* revolt against his father. He did so in a typical obsessional way (and like most revolutionaries) by transposing the unconscious emotional conflict to a conscious intellectual one—concerning evolution. Thus, if Darwin did not slay his father in the flesh, then in his *The Origin of Species, The Descent of Man,* &c., he certainly slew the Heavenly Father in the realm of natural history. (There is good evidence that Robert Waring, Darwin's father, was inimicably disposed to Erasmus, his father and Darwin's grandfather, as a man and to his heterodox scientific views, including evolution.)[11]

Dr. Douglas Hubble thinks that Darwin needed to deny his father's rebuke that he was idle,[12] and that this need then caused an obsession.

"Charles Darwin's illness, then, arose from the suppression and non-recognition of a painful emotion. Such an emotion is always compounded of fear, guilt, or hate—and it is painful because it conflicts with the inner image of himself which each person carries. In the case of Charles Darwin this emotion arose from his relationship with his father—the adored god who had unjustly condemned him for idleness—and thereby created the obsessional urge for work and for achievement."[13] Dr. Phyllis Greenacre thinks that Darwin had an "unusual capacity for neurotic denial,"[14] and that it was his need to deny his paternal aggression which contributed to his illness. "Nor did he [Darwin] really seem aware of his hostility to his personal father, which was betrayed, however, by the unfailingly exaggerated and superlative terms in which he spoke of Dr. Robert Darwin, except for a few timid complaints of the possible injustice of his father's derogation of him.... The massive aggression which had to be repressed contributed to the obsessional neurosis and the associated imposing array of somatic symptoms which so innocently incapacitated him, dominating his life and that of his whole household."[15]

Before evaluating the above views let us summarize what is known about the history of Darwin's attitudes toward, and relations with, his father.

Darwin's recollections in old age of his youthful relations with his father (written about three decades after his father's death) infer that he was angry when his father rebuked him for being idle, and that he feared to openly oppose his father's opinions.[16] One cause for his November–December 1831 episode of illness was that he had opposed his father's initial wish that he not sail on the *Beagle*; yet there were also other causes, among them the varied and very real dangers (to life and to health) of the *Beagle* voyage.[17] In the years when he was becoming ill and developing his evolutionary ideas he seemed to draw closer to his father: the latter gave him an annual income,[18] making him financially independent, and left him free to do as he pleased in his scientific work. It is not known whether he disclosed his evolutionary speculations to his father (there is no evidence for Dr. Good's assertion that his father was opposed to evolution), but his father gave him information about human behavior, illness, and heredity, which he used in his evolutionary thinking and wrote down in the first fifty-five pages of his *M Notebook*. In these first *M Notebook* pages he writes *father* in three different ways: "my Father," "my F.," and, most frequently, "my father."[19] In his previous letters "Father" has been written out and capitalized.[20] It may be that "father" indicates that he feels more intimate toward, and less in awe of, his father. He then became dependent on his father for medical care, and when his father died his feelings of loss were a cause for his 1848–49 illness.[21]

He frequently spoke to his children about his memories of his father. His daughter Henrietta recollects him saying: "I think my father was a little unjust to me when I was young, but afterwards I am thankful to think I became a prime favourite with him."[22] Henrietta further recollects that when he said these words he had an "expression of happy reverie . . . as if he were reviewing the whole relation, and the remembrance left a deep sense of peace and gratitude."[23]

Now let us consider the different psychiatric views of Darwin's feelings about his father. It seems likely that, as Dr. Hubble postulated, his father's rebuke of him was a force in creating his obsession to work. All of the psychiatric views hold that his youthful fear of opposing his father—the fear which was one cause for his 1831 illness—persisted throughout his mature years. However all of the evidence indicates that, during these years, father benefited son in various ways, and son appreciated this and felt much warmer toward father than earlier. When son praised his father he may have expressed a deep and sincere feeling—and not a "reaction-formation" or "neurotic denial" of paternal antipathy. How much Darwin's youthful fear of opposing his father influenced—and was displaced onto—his mature fears of opposing individuals and institutions cannot be determined. What is apparent is his realistic appreciation of the manifold dangers of his theory of natural selection—these included the danger of being attacked and rejected by scientific institutions and individuals whom he cared about.[24]

In 1965 Dr. John Bowlby—the distinguished English child psychoanalyst, who had investigated the impact on children of the early loss of a parent—wrote a short letter to the British Medical Journal suggesting that Darwin's illness may have been a bereavement reaction to the illness and death of his mother, Mrs. Susannah Darwin.[25] Dr. Bowlby wrote that his bereavement hypothesis could be tested, "to a limited degree," in the following ways:

> First, it presupposes that Darwin's mother suffered from an illness . . . similar to his own. Secondly . . . that Darwin's symptoms would have become exacerbated at certain times, the so-called anniversary' reactions. Those would occur (a) around 15 July each year (the date of his mother's death), (b) in the year 1861 when Darwin himself reached the age that his mother had been at the time of her death, and perhaps also (c) when one or the other of his

own children reached the age of 8—namely, his own age at the time of his mother's death.

Let us apply these tests.

Nothing is known about the history or nature of Susannah Darwin's last illness.[26] It is only known that she died on 15 July 1817,[27] when she was 52 1/2, and when her son Charles was eight years and five months. The latter's illness did first begin in July 1837, the twentieth anniversary of his mother's death, and it may be that the disturbing memories of his mother made it harder for him to bear the pressures of his evolutionary thoughts. However, his illness did not seriously worsen until March 1839. His second big exacerbation of illness began in July 1848, and it may be that the anniversary of his mother's death made it harder for him to bear the impending death of his father. It was his father's death, however, that then caused his illness to worsen. His *Diary of Health* shows that his stomach complaints were unremarkable in July of 1850, 1851, 1852, and 1854; his stomach became somewhat worse around 15 July 1849, and on the night of 15 July 1853 (at this time, however, he ascribed his illness to eating a crab). He was ill very briefly (it is questionable just how ill he really was) in July 1860, but then he was under the great pressures of the British Association Oxford meeting. His long and severe illnesses of 1863–64 and 1865 did not begin in July. Two of his eight children died before the age of eight. Eight of his children reached the age at the death of his mother—eight years and five months—on the following dates: May 1848, August 1849, February 1852, December 1853, December 1855, January 1857, June 1858, and August 1859. His illness does not seem to have become especially worse on any of these dates. He attained the final age of his mother—52 1/2 years—in August 1861, at which time he was in relatively good health.

If Darwin's memories of his mother did cause his illness to exacerbate, this occurred infrequently, and was only one of several psychological causes.

4

The Possibility of Chagas' Disease, Other Possible Medical Causes

After many psychological causes for Darwin's illness had been enunciated, infectious causes were considered.

In August 1958, Professor George Gaylord Simpson—an eminent American paleontologist, evolutionist, and Darwin scholar—wrote a review of Darwin's *Autobiography* in which he suggested that, instead of a psychophysiologic illness, Darwin may have had chronic brucellosis,[1] an infection undiagnosed in Victorian times, endemic in some areas (such as Argentina) visited by the *Beagle*, and capable of producing Darwin's symptoms. Professor Simpson may have been influenced to think of brucellosis because he had suffered from this infection. He did not, however, press his suggestion or offer definite proof for brucellosis.

In September 1959 a medical writer stated that Darwin may have contracted amebiasis during his *Beagle* travels.[2] Dr. Phyllis Greenacre, the psychoanalyst, later wrote that Darwin had "severe attacks of malaria while on the voyage of the *Beagle*."[3] There is no evidence for these assertions.

Then in October 1959, Professor Saul Adler, an Israeli parasitologist of world renown,[4] published an article on "Darwin's Illness" in *Nature*:[5] here, after saying that brucellosis infection could neither be proved nor disproved, he cited a previously unnoticed passage in the *Beagle* narrative, *Journal of Researches*, where Darwin described how on 25 March 1835, while in the village of Luxan, in the province of Mendoza, Argentina, he had been bitten by "the great black bug of the Pampas." Professor Adler identified this "black bug" as "*Triatoma infestans*"—a frequent carrier of the protozoan *Trypanosoma cruzi*, which causes Chagas' disease. He reported that, according to South American physicians and scientists, in Mendoza province about 60 percent of the population gave a positive complement test for Chagas' disease and about 70 percent of *T. infestans* were infected with *T. cruzi*; and that in Chagas' disease the *Trypanosoma* frequently invade the heart muscle and destroy the nerves of the intestine, causing cardiac and intestinal disorders. In Chagas' disease there are also periods of latency. Professor Adler concluded that Darwin's symptoms could be "fitted into the framework of Chagas disease at least as well as into any psychogenic theory for their origin." Since Chagas' disease would not be known until 1909, this would explain why no Victorian doctor was able to diagnose it.

For several years Professor Adler's theory of Chagas' disease dominated the thinking about Darwin's illness, and was accepted and elaborated upon by men with different training and viewpoints. Dr. Lawrence A. Kohn, American medical internist and emeritus professor of clinical medicine at Rochester Medical School, New York (in a

1963 essay "Charles Darwin's Chronic Ill Health"[6]), and Sir Gavin de
Beer, English biologist and director of the British Museum, Natural
History (in his 1964 biography, *Charles Darwin*[7]), both independently
reviewed Darwin's symptoms and then stated that Chagas' disease
could account for these. In 1964 Sir Peter Medawar, director of the
National Institute for Medical Research (in Great Britain) and winner
of the Nobel Prize for medicine in 1960, wrote, in an article entitled
"Darwin's Illness":

> I believe that Darwin was organically ill (the case for his having
> had Chagas' disease is clearly a strong one) but was also the victim
> of neurosis; and that the neurotic element in his illness may have
> been caused by the very obscurity of its origins, by his being
> "genuinely" ill, that is to say, and having nothing to show for it—
> surely a great embarrassment for a man whose whole intellectual
> life was a marshalling and assay of hard evidence . . . ill people
> suspected of hypochondria or malingering have to pretend to be
> iller than they really are and may then get taken in by their own
> deception. They do this to convince others, but Darwin had also to
> convince himself, for he had no privileged insight into what was
> wrong with him.[8]

In 1966 Dr. James A. Brussel, an American psychiatrist, published an
essay, "The Nature of the Naturalist's Unnatural Illness: A Study of
Charles Robert Darwin," in which he concurred with Sir Peter:
"Charles Darwin was organically ill [Chagas' disease] and, secondarily, functionally ill. . . . This interpretation is not offered as a
compromise or as an acceptable means of negotiation for peace
between the warring factions of psychiatry and internal medicine. It is
submitted as the answer."[9] Others also held that Darwin suffered from
both an infection and a neurosis.[10]

That Darwin was anxious and neurotic because he did not know the
cause of his illness is an insightful observation. That he had Chagas'
disease was, however, seriously challenged: first by the psychiatrist
Dr. Douglas Hubble and then by Dr. A. W. Woodruff, professor of
clinical tropical medicine at the London School of Hygiene and
Tropical Medicine.

In 1964 Dr. Hubble wrote a short letter to the *New Statesman* in
which, after reaffirming his belief in the psychiatric origin of Darwin's
illness, he pointed out that Darwin was bitten by *Triatoma infestans*
on 25 March 1835 and "that during the subsequent 18 months of the
Beagle's voyage he lived a life of hard physical activity without any
hint of illness. In fact Darwin displayed the symptoms of neurosis

before he set sail on the *Beagle*, and his illness did not become disabling until after his marriage in 1839—four years after the Benchuca bite."[11] As I have shown, from a reading of Darwin's extant letters, it can be seen that he had no complaints of illness for the first nine months (October 1836 to July 1837) after his return from the *Beagle*. In 1965 and 1968 Professor Woodruff published two articles[12] in which he marshaled the following detailed evidence against Darwin ever having had Chagas' disease. Chilean public health statistics revealed that, in the regions of Chile which border Mendoza province (precise figures for Mendoza could not be obtained), the incidence of *T. cruzi* in men and in *T. infestans* was only about 15 percent and 24 percent, respectively, much lower than the 60 percent and 70 percent cited by Professor Adler. Moreover, the majority of persons with Chagas' had been exposed not just for a few weeks but for several years—*T. infestans* produce infection not by biting but by contaminating their bite with their excreta, hence a person can be bitten and yet not infected.[13] The health records of the *Beagle* crew were examined and no evidence for Chagas' disease was found. "The epidemiological evidence," writes Professor Woodruff, "indicates that although there was the possibility of exposure to infection there is no strong possibility that he [Darwin] was infected."[14]

Professor Woodruff then stressed (along with Dr. Hubble) that Darwin had symptoms of his illness before the *Beagle* voyage; and that if he had *T. cruzi* organic heart disease it would have been unlikely for him to exercise daily, have no physical signs of heart failure,[15] and improve in health in his later years.[16] I may add that Chagas' disease does not explain his "fits" of facial "eczema"; and if he had *T. cruzi* organic disease of the bowel it would have been unlikely for him to recover as quickly and effectively as he did from his severe spells of vomiting.

"Darwin," Professor Woodruff concluded, "may have been infected with *Trypanosoma cruzi*, but the essential point is that this is no more than a parasitological possibility; it does not provide a diagnosis which explains any significant proportion of the symptoms or course of the illness."[17] Dr. Woodruff's diagnosis (concurring with that of Dr. Greenacre) was that Darwin had "an anxiety state with obsessive features and psychosomatic manifestations."[18] Professor Adler, after the publication of Professor Woodruff's first article, published a letter affirming his belief that in March 1835 "Darwin was exposed to ideal conditions for infection with *T. cruzi*."[19] He planned to write a paper showing that "Darwin's symptoms fit Chagas' disease like a glove,"[20] but he died in January 1966. Since his death several biographers of Darwin have stated that their subject had Chagas' disease; yet none of these biographers, or anyone else, have tried to answer the criticisms of the Chagas' disease theory which were enunciated by Dr. Hubble and Professor Woodruff.[21]

Other medical (as opposed to psychiatric) diseases were then held to be the cause of Darwin's illness. Since Darwin had severe episodes of vomiting and abdominal pains, several physicians have suggested that he may have had appendicitis, duodenal ulcer,[22] chronic cholecystitis, or "smouldering hepatitis."[23] He gave no history of jaundice, which would be expected in the last two conditions, and the course and pattern of his vomiting and abdominal pains are not characteristic of any of these diseases.[24] However the possibility cannot be excluded that at times—in addition to his psychically upset stomach—Darwin may have had one or several of these abdominal diseases. In 1963 Dr. Lawrence Kohn suggested that Darwin may have had a diaphragmatic hernia: "He [Darwin] had to eat simply. . . . He apparently improved when . . . put . . . on strict diets . . . a plan of small meals. . . Repeatedly he is described as having to sit up at night in bed or in a chair because of indigestion, and this is characteristic of a hiatus hernia. Flatulence accompanied these nights, and this is usually associated with large bowel distension, but the term has been used to include belching."[25] There are several evidences against this diagnosis. Darwin did get better when Dr. Bence Jones put him on small feedings, and when Dr. Andrew Clark put him on a strict diet which may have consisted of small feedings. However, during the later part of his sojourn at Malvern, his eating increased with no ill effects to his stomach. He seems to have eaten well at Moor Park when he was recovering from his illness. Every day, immediately after lunch, he lay on the sofa reading *The Times*, and seemed to suffer no illness from this reclining[26]—when he had severe vomiting he sometimes was relieved by reclining. His flatulence does not seem to have become appreciably worse at night when he was lying in his bed. He seems to have sat erect in a high chair mainly (if not only) in the evening, several hours after a small supper; and his erect sitting seems to have been more of a compulsion than a way of aiding the emptying of his stomach.[27]

Several metabolic diseases were considered as possible causes for Darwin's illness. In 1959 Dr. DeWitt Stetten, Jr., then associated with the National Institute of Metabolic Diseases (American), stated that Darwin had gout[28] (not to be confused with the Victorian diagnosis of "suppressed gout"). No evidence was offered for this, and as has been noted Darwin did not give the history of acute joint pains characteristic of gout.

In 1966 and 1967 Dr. Hyman J. Roberts, an American medical internist, suggested that Darwin may have had an illness which Roberts had described and called the "syndrome of narcolepsy and diabetogenic ('functional') hyperinsulinism."[29] This syndrome consists of narcolepsy—meaning episodes of "irresistible drowsiness and actual sleep" in a subject who is well rested and not physically fatigued—and a variety of symptoms—headache, abdominal pain, cardiac arrythmias, peripheral neuropathies—all occurring several hours after meals and believed to be, largely, caused by hypoglycemia.[30]

Let us see how this syndrome applies to Darwin. When he was not doing his scientific work he spent most of his time in other kinds of mental activity: reading or having read to him a wide variety of books; writing and reading letters; examining his plants; reading the daily newspapers; making financial investments; playing backgammon with his wife. Sometimes around three in the afternoon, while his wife was reading to him, he would fall asleep, presumably put to sleep by the sound of her reading. He would then always wake up a few minutes before four. Aside from this afternoon nap he does not seem to have had any other daily episodes of sleep or drowsiness.[31] Certainly this is not the picture of narcolepsy. The symptoms and exacerbations of his illness cannot be definitely related to his diet; although, as has been seen, he would sometimes become better for a time on a new diet. He had a craving for sweets which, for years, he tried to control by going on sugar-free diets. Toward the end of his life he partly gave in to this craving and would have fruits (apples and bananas were favored) and sugar at breakfast, and sherry and sweet pudding at lunch and supper.[32] Whether his craving was due to hypoglycemia cannot be ascertained. He was very punctual about eating his meals, and if he had to wait he would eat something. However, if he knew several hours beforehand that his meal would be late, "he could manage to wait much more easily."[33] This last suggests that his meal punctuality was due to psychological compulsion, rather than to a low blood sugar level.

In the 1960s Dr. Torben K. With, a Danish physician who specialized in studying the metabolic disease of porphyria,[34] read—in Desmond King-Hele's recently published biography of Dr. Erasmus Darwin—an account of Mrs. Mary Darwin's episodes of convulsions, insanity, and pains in the abdomen and head.[35] Dr. With thought that these episodes might have been caused by acute intermittent porphyria; since porphyria was hereditary, the possibility was raised that some of Mary Darwin's descendants may have had porphyria in a manifest or latent form.[36] It is possible that Mrs. Caroline Wedgwood's old-age episode of physical incapacity and then recovery[37] could have been caused by acute porphyria, which is not uncommon in old age. However Caroline's incapacity could have been due to many causes— vascular, neurologic, psychic (depression or hysteria). Charles Darwin suffered from severe abdominal pains, but his other symptoms do not resemble porphyria or the symptoms of his grandmother. He had frequent headaches, but these were rarely severe and never seem to have been "violent." Although there were times when he was severely anxious and/or depressed, he was never delirious or insane. He never seems to have had a convulsion, although one was feared in 1863. In porphyria there are skin lesions after exposure to light, and a dark urine—although this is not always present. There is no evidence that Darwin's skin complaints were related to light. In May 1865, when he was very ill and drinking little, Darwin reported that his urine was "scanty," with "pinkish sediment when cold"[38]—the cause of this sediment is obscure. He also observed that his urine was, usually, "very palid."[39] Had he had episodes of dark urine it would be expected that he, or some of his physicians, would have commented on it. As far as can be determined, none of Mary Darwin's descendants manifested her symptoms. In the present Darwins, the presence of porphyria could be determined by biochemical tests.

5

The Possibility of Arsenic Poisoning

In October 1971 John H. Winslow, Ph.D., from the department of geography-anthropology, California State College, published (as one of the Memoirs of the American Philosophical Society) a ninety-four-page brochure entitled *Darwin's Victorian Malady: Evidence for its Medically Induced Origin.*[1] This was the first book and the longest work on Darwin's illness. Dr. Winslow rejected all previous theories of his subject's illness—he was especially critical of psychiatric theories; he held that Darwin became ill from chronic arsenic poisoning (a cause which had previously been thought of and then dis-counted[2]). Dr. Winslow presented two main arguments: that twenty-one manifestations of Darwin's illness and of arsenic poisoning form "a very close match";[3] and that Darwin took arsenic, probably internally in the form of Fowler's solution, beginning in his teens and continuing throughout his life; or that he possibly "either ceased to take arsenic or significantly lessened the amount he was taking sometime during his late middle age."[4]

Let us consider these arguments. The illness of Darwin and the illness of chronic arsenic poisoning both manifested erythema, ec-zema, paresthesias, and headaches; also cardiac palpitations, weak-ness, and depression. These manifestations, however, lack specificity, and may be similar only in name. There is no evidence that Darwin's erythema (which was never described), his fluctuating episodes of facial "eczema," his paresthesias (once described as numbness at the end of his fingers), and his headaches (very variable in character and duration) were similar to the erythema, eczema, paresthesias, and headaches of arsenic poisoning. Cardiac "palpitations" vary greatly in nature and intensity, and are present in many illnesses. Depression and weakness are, of course, tendencies which are part of most illnesses.

There are definite differences between Darwin's gastrointestinal upsets and those of arsenic poisoning. Darwin's acute nausea and vomiting would sometimes abruptly cease, and his stomach would return to normal, or near-normal, function. In the acute gastroenter-itis of arsenic poisoning, where there was "intense irritation, conges-tion, intestinal capillary hemorrhage, and a swollen and thickened appearance of the gastrointestinal tract,"[5] such abrupt reversals are unusual. The gastrointestinal upsets of arsenic poisoning are usually characterized by nausea and vomiting, disturbances of the lower part of the bowel, and anorexia followed by weight loss. Darwin never complained of serious lower bowel disease. In May 1865, when he was vomiting every day, he wrote: "Evacuation regular & good."[6] How much he suffered from anorexia is uncertain. In 1849 he wrote that he had been "oppressed" by his food;[7] in 1857 he commented that (because his illness had improved) he could "eat like a hearty Christian"[8]—this comment may refer to a previous anorexia. In 1863 and 1865, despite severe vomiting, he ate regularly and his appetite remained good,[9] and throughout each of his four major periods of vomiting he did not complain of weight loss. It was when he was recovering from his vomiting, and under the care of a physician, that he had large changes in weight: in 1849–50 he gained weight;[10] in 1865 he lost weight.[11]

Dr. Winslow contends that Darwin had two physical signs which were especially indicative of arsenic poisoning: horny keratoses and "a brown or coppery complexion." The evidence for the first is a photograph of Darwin at the age of fifty-one (reproduced in Lady Barlow's edition of Darwin's *Autobiography*), which is said to reveal *"multiple corn-like elevations"* on Darwin's hands, and a photograph of Darwin as an old man showing a "wart-like feature on his right cheek."[12] After studying both photographs I could not ascertain the "corn-like elevations" on the hands.[13] I could confirm the "wart" on the cheek (the "wart" is also apparent in the 1881 painting of Darwin by John Collier); however, the "wart" is not specific for any particular skin condition. As for Darwin's complexion, different observers described it as follows: "brown out-of-door looking complexion";[14] "ruddy";[15] "very ruddy";[16] "yellow."[17] Darwin described himself as "ruddy" in 1849;[18] in 1873 he described his complexion as "Rather sallow," and the complexion of his father as "Ruddy."[19] His facial coloring, thus, may have varied; at times, it may not have been prominent. Descriptions of Darwin's features by John Fiske,[20] Ernst Haeckel,[21] and Ferdinand Cohn[22] omit any mention of his facial colors. Sir William Osler, in a 1915 recollection of an 1874 meeting with Darwin, wrote: "A most kindly old man, of large frame, with great bushy beard and eyebrows."[23] One would expect that Osler, a sharp observer of physical signs, would have remarked on Darwin's complexion if it had been unusually colored. Dr. W. D. Foster, after studying an oil painting of Darwin at Down House, thought that Darwin's complexion was "within normal limits."[24] In view of the above, one cannot make a definite statement about the color of Darwin's complexion.

In the course of trying to demonstrate a similarity between Darwin's illness and arsenic poisoning Dr. Winslow makes a series of statements about Darwin's health that are either untrue or only partially true.

Darwin is said to have had "catarrhal dyspepsia," and "a bout of pleurisy, and pleurisy and fever": this is then compared with "a catarrhal state of the exposed mucous membranes of the nose, larynx, pharynx, trachea, and bronchi . . . quite common in cases of chronic arsenic poisoning."[25] This comparison is not valid. The diagnosis "catarrhal dyspepsia" (applied to Darwin by the *British Medical Journal*[26]) was a Victorian medical non sequitur because it was not supported by any direct examination of Darwin's stomach—Darwin did not have stomach roentgenograms, gastroscopy, or a postmortem examination of his stomach. As far as can be determined, Darwin only once had what he called a "very short but sharpish touch ... of slight ... pleurisy,"[27] that "came on like a lion, but went off as a lamb."[28] He complained of many "colds" but he does not describe what he meant by a cold. He only occasionally complained seriously of coughing, which is a pathognomonic symptom of catarrhal states of the larynx, trachea, and bronchi.

It is said that Darwin "mentioned growing bald at the age of twenty-eight"; that he was "predominantly bald at thirty-three"; and "very bald except for the side of his head and perhaps a fringe in back a few years later."[29] It is then further stated: "There is a tendency for hair to fall out in cases of arsenic poisoning.... Alternatively, Darwin may have inherited the trait."[30] Darwin never mentioned growing bald at twenty-eight.[31] A portrait of him at thirty-one shows that he had a full head of hair.[32] He was certainly not "predominantly bald at thirty-three," though at this time his hair had probably begun to recede. His hair can be seen steadily receding in pictures of him at forty,[33] forty-three,[34] and forty-four,[35] and by fifty-one he was entirely bald on the upper parts of his head.

It is asserted that Darwin had "*tooth and gum problems*; five molars out at once at the age of forty-three; fairly early loss of all teeth; pyorrhea; sore gums"; and that "gums are sometimes sore and swollen in cases of chronic arsenic poisoning."[36] Let us summarize what is known about Darwin's teeth. During the *Beagle* voyage, in his pocket notebook, in which he kept different memoranda, he once reminded himself three times of his need for a dentist; about a month later he then wrote "great teeth."[37] In his *Diary of Health* he recorded that on 16 June 1852 he began to have "toothache," and that on 24 June he had "teeth out & chloroform"—his extracted teeth, he told Fox, consisted of five molars.[38] In March 1861 he wrote Hooker about the dental problems of his son George: "Poor George has literally every tooth in his head, except for a few lower incisors decayed: they have all gone suddenly together ["& has been stopped & drawn by Mr. Woodhouse" inserted] & I fear this points to some deep flaw in his constitution, which was formerly indicated by his intermittent pulse."[39] Darwin does *not* say whether he thinks George has inherited his tooth decay. In May 1865, after describing the taste of his vomit in his mouth, he wrote: "consider teeth."[40] This may mean that he thinks the taste of his vomit was influenced by the state of his teeth. Forty-five years after Darwin's death, his son Leonard recollected that his father had "pyorrhea," but gave no further details.[41] Francis Darwin writes that his father "sometimes thought meat uneatably tough which was not really so,"[42] but he does not indicate that Darwin had chewing difficulties, or that he was edentulous. It is nowhere mentioned that Darwin was edentulous. Considering the above evidence, one cannot make any conclusion about the nature or severity of Darwin's tooth and gum problems except to say that he rarely mentions his teeth (in contrast to his other medical complaints) and does not complain of sore gums.

Since Dr. Winslow has, apparently, not directly studied Darwin's *Diary of Health*, he has relied on the opinions of those who have written on the *Diary*. Influenced by Sir Buckston Browne—who has reported that in the *Diary* Darwin "mentions lumbago and arthritis"[43] —Dr. Winslow states that Darwin had *"arthritis; lumbago; gout; suppressed gout; gouty constitution."* This is then compared to the arthralgia—"usually located around the knee, ankle or foot, and less frequently in the wrist or hand"—of those who have chronic arsenic poisoning.[44] Darwin's 1849–55 *Diary of Health* contains only the following mentions of "rheumatism" and "lumbago": 14 August 1851: "rheumatism"; 15 August 1851: "little rheumatism"; 6–10 August 1854: "Bad boil. Lumbago: very poorly." In March 1855 Darwin reported to Fox that he and Emma had a month of "coughs & colds & rheumatism."[45] In October 1856 he told Fox that he had recently experienced "just a touch" of "my back feeling locked & rigid! I never felt such a thing before."[46] In January 1864 he told Hooker of a "slight attack of rheumatism in my back," which stimulated him to walk.[47] In May 1865 he said that he had "lumbago" (at this time, because he felt "tired," he could only walk half a mile).[48] We do not know what he meant by "rheumatism" and "lumbago": it seems evident, however, that these occurred less frequently than his stomach and skin symptoms, and that they were not incapacitating. He did not, as mentioned previously, complain of pains in his extremities, such as occur in arsenic poisoning (and in gout).

Dr. W. D. Foster, in his study of Darwin's *Diary of Health*, has written that it is "not clear" what Darwin meant by the "fits" which he frequently records in the *Diary*. Dr. Foster then suggests that these "fits" were, probably, "of psychogenic origin."[49] Dr. Winslow, after quoting this opinion of Dr. Foster, states that these "fits" may be related to the "epilepsy-like seizures" of Darwin's maternal grandmother, Mrs. Mary Darwin; or that the "fits" may have been caused by arsenical neuritis. The symptoms of arsenical neuritis are described as "motor and sensory sensations (sometimes pains) which may be violent in character. They are usually located initially in the hands and feet, and they then soon rise slowly up the trunk."[50] Since (as has been previously indicated) the *Diary of Health* "fits" were most likely episodes of gastric flatulence,[51] they certainly do not resemble the symptoms of Mrs. Mary Darwin or of arsenical neuritis. Nor is there any evidence that Darwin ever had "epilepsy-like seizures,"[52] or symptoms which resembled the motor and sensory sensations of arsenical neuritis.

Having now compared Darwin's symptoms with the symptoms of arsenic poisoning, it can only be concluded that there is not "a very close match" between the two groups of symptoms. Let us now review what is known about Darwin's taking of arsenic. Darwin, according to the memoirs of J. M. Herbert, took "small doses" of arsenic in 1828–31, and was (presumably) benefited by this, and also impressed by his father's warning about arsenic's toxicity.[53] In September 1831 he was tempted to take arsenic for his hands,[54] but then desisted.[55] After this, for the remaining fifty-one years of his life, he makes no mention of taking arsenic in his different medical writings, where he frequently mentions his medications; these include his many letters to Fox and Hooker, his letters to other friends and his sisters, his *"Receipts" and "Memoranda" Book, Diary of Health*, and his "Private Diary."

Dr. Winslow raises the possibility that, since some Victorian doctors prescribed arsenic, some of Darwin's doctors may have prescribed arsenic for him. The attitudes toward arsenic of five of Darwin's doctors—Henry Holland, James Clark, Edmund Smith, William Jenner, Henry Bence Jones—are unknown. Three doctors were critical of arsenic: Robert Darwin feared its toxic effects; James Gully regarded it as very injurious when used to treat "indigestion";[56] William Brinton, after twenty years of clinical experience, felt it was largely ineffective in dyspepsia.[57] Edward Lane, against using medications in treating dyspepsia, may have been against arsenic.[58] John Chapman, believing in the efficacy of his ice treatment, may not have used arsenic. Three doctors were partial toward arsenic. Dr. Frederick Headland regarded Fowler's solution as of "great use" in gastrodynia;[59] the medication that Headland gave Darwin, however, was a course of Nitro-muriatic Acid.[60] Mr. James Startin prescribed internally taken arsenic, along with other drugs, for a variety of skin conditions, and internally taken and/or locally applied arsenic for lupus.[61] If the unidentified "muddy stuff" that Mr. Startin prescribed for local application contained arsenic, its effects could not have been too toxic, for Darwin mopped it "nearly dry" and seems to have only used it from March to May 1863.[62] Dr. Andrew Clark wrote that arsenic, strychnine, and opium in "certain small doses" were useful in "special circumstances";[63] the medications that he prescribed for Darwin were strychnine and iodine, and Darwin seems to have stopped taking these after a month.[64] Thus there is no evidence that the three doctors who did prescribe arsenic ever prescribed it for Darwin.

It may be that Darwin abstained from taking arsenic after 1831 because of warnings about arsenic's toxicity from his father—whose medical opinions he respected and remembered—and from *Zoonomia* and *The Edinburgh New Dispensatory*. It was, perhaps, because of his fear of arsenic poisoning that his *"Receipts" and "Memoranda" Book* contained the two October 1862 *Times* clippings on chemical tests for detecting arsenic.[65]

Dr. Winslow also states that Darwin may have become sick from medically prescribed calomel, taken alone or with arsenic.

During the *Beagle* cruise in 1833, Darwin made a note to "Buy knife, Prometheans, medicine, Calomel";[66] in 1834 he was treated with calomel for his episode of Chilean fever.[67] After his return home he was first in contact with Drs. Holland,[68] James Clark,[69] and his father, all of whom used calomel. The *"Receipts" and "Memoranda" Book* shows that Dr. Darwin prescribed calomel in soap pills, and for different illnesses in children, but that he was cautious in his prescribing and sometimes advised against giving calomel.[70] In his letters to his father and sisters, while mentioning his different diets and medications, Darwin makes no mention of calomel. In the early nineteenth century there was a controversy about calomel's efficacy and safety, and in the decades after Dr. Robert Darwin died, this controversy burgeoned.[71] During these decades Darwin consulted some practitioners who used calomel—Mr. Startin[72] and Dr. F. W. Headland[73]— and some who were against its use—Drs. Gully,[74] Brinton,[75] and Lane.[76] What he thought about calomel, and whether he used it—his daughter Etty used calomel on at least one occasion[77]—is unknown.

It is, of course, possible that Darwin suffered toxic reactions from some of the many medications that he took. However, his taking of a particular medication cannot be correlated with any of the large or small exacerbations of his illness. Since he was cautious, and a careful observer of the effects of medications, he probably was alert to note the toxic reactions of a new medicine. His tendency to eventually stop a medication (with the exception of snuff) would have limited any toxic reactions that he did suffer.

In summary it may be said that the evidence given in *Darwin's Victorian Malady*, and all of the presently available evidence, do not prove that chronic arsenic or calomel poisoning were the cause of Darwin's illness. In order to establish this proof new evidence must be presented.

6

Recent Theories

In 1974 four books were published which suggested different causes for Darwin's illness.

Dr. Howard Gruber, professor of psychology at Rutgers University, and Dr. Paul H. Barrett, professor of natural science at Michigan State University, published *Darwin on Man*, a transcription of Darwin's 1838–39 evolutionary notebooks M and N, along with a brilliant study of the growth of Darwin's evolutionary thought. In a footnote in this book it was suggested that Darwin may have become ill because of "a severe allergy, possibly to pigeons, with which Darwin associated much."[1] It is possible that Darwin was allergic to some of the objects he lived with and worked with.[2] There is, however, no evidence that he was allergic to pigeons. When he was a small boy, growing up at the Mount, his mother was breeding pigeons;[3] yet, as far as can be ascertained, he was not ill. In the early 1850s he began examining and dissecting dead pigeons; he then built a large aviary (near where his hydropathy douche was located) and here he experimented in crossing and breeding different strains of pigeons. Every day, from 1856 to 1859, he would go to the aviary and closely examine the pigeons[4]—yet during these years his illness was subacute and did not become especially severe. He does not seem to have been exposed to pigeons during the very severe exacerbations of his illness in 1839–42, 1848–49, 1863–64, and 1865. The main symptoms of his illness were not similar to the symptoms of pigeon allergy.[5]

Mr. James Bunting published *Charles Darwin*, one of a new English series of short, popularly written, biographies of famous individuals. Mr. Bunting warns his reader that his book is not "intended to be accurate in every detail," and that he has "spiced" some facts "with a little imagination." Yet he has long thought about his subject—his relations knew the Darwins and Wedgwoods[6]—and has studied manuscript as well as printed sources. His main aim is to portray Darwin "as he really was."[7] In his chapter "Was Darwin Really Ill?" he suggests that Darwin was really a hypochondriac. He then makes the following (presumably serious) assertion: "Perhaps the whole crux of the matter lies with Emma Darwin herself. We know, from all we have read and heard about her, that she made a positive fetish of the health of her husband and children. In her letters she dwells at great length on her husband's illness, whereas he makes so little mention of it. And we must remember that there is no record of Charles suffering from his mysterious malady until after his marriage. Perhaps it existed more in Emma's imagination than in his own."[8] Mr. Bunting, in addition to his misinformation about Darwin's illness, does Emma a grave injustice. Emma worried about her husband's illness; she did not exaggerate it. When her husband was ill she was always quite realistic about his needs for treatment, and for periods of rest; and she was, also, realistic in her optimism that he would recover.

Then there were books by two prominent English doctors. Sir Hedley Atkins, former president of the Royal College of Surgeons of England, published *Down: The Home of the Darwins*;[9] Sir George Pickering, former professor of medicine in the University of London and Regius Professor in the University of Oxford, published *Creative Malady*.[10] Each of these books contained a chapter on the symptoms and causation of Darwin's illness. Sir Hedley and Sir George— although skeptical of psychoanalytic concepts—believed that Darwin's illness was a psychoneurosis caused by his evolutionary theory.

Sir Hedley depicted Darwin's interaction with his theory as follows:

> Poor Darwin! He had so many real worries—the opprobrium which he incurred when his views on evolution were made known in *The Origin* and particularly in the *Descent of Man*, the knowledge that his wife, whom he loved dearly, could not but disapprove of the consequences of the revelation of his ideas and the fact that he had so few friends and allies in the battle for what he believed to be the truth. These worries playing upon a naturally reserved and sensitive nature would be likely to affect far more insensitive men than he.[11]

Sir George believed that Darwin was afraid of putting forward a hypothesis which lacked scientific proof.[12] He postulated that "the cause of Darwin's psychoneurosis" was "the conflict between his [Darwin's] passionate desire to collect convincing evidence for his hypothesis and the threat imposed on his work by social intercourse."[13]

I believe that the evidence shows that Darwin's feelings about his evolutionary theory were a major cause for his illness. These feelings, however, were much more complex than Sir Hedley or Sir George indicate. Darwin suffered because he had "so few friends": he also suffered because old friends (like Owen and FitzRoy) opposed his theory, and because the few friends that he did have (Lyell and Hooker) had reservations about his theory. He had a conflict between his desire to collect facts and the threat imposed on his work by social intercourse; and he was relieved when he obtained evidence which supported his theory, and when his theory answered questions about the origin of species. He also suffered illness when some evidence—such as the facts Hooker brought him about the geographical distribution of plants—did not uphold his theory. The more he collected evidence and explored the multitudinous ramifications of natural selection, the more he encountered—along with problems solved—new problems which could not be solved. The unsolved new and old problems caused him to be tortured with obsessional thoughts, and to become (in his words) "tired" in his thoughts and physical actions.

Sir Hedley and Professor C. D. Darlington[14] think that a cause of his illness was Emma's disapproval of the religious consequences of natural selection. Early in his marriage Darwin knew that Emma's religious belief represented some of the opposition that his ideas would encounter, and this must have increased his anxiety about expressing these ideas. It is not evident that he experienced Emma's disapproval as a chronic pressure. Over the years, as he became dependent on Emma for caring for him, he may have accustomed himself to become unaffected by her religious views.

7

The Evidence for Psychological Causation

Since Darwin's illness consisted of several nonspecific symptoms, a conclusive diagnosis of this illness would require different laboratory examinations: an electrocardiogram and gastrointestinal roentgenograms; tests for allergens, bacteria, and protozoa; liver function tests; blood and urine tests for sugar, proteins, poryphria, and uric acid levels; tests for toxic drugs Darwin may have taken. If these examinations did not reveal an organic cause, or causes, the likelihood of psychiatric causes would be strong.

Since the above examinations did not exist during Darwin's life, it may be impossible to ever be certain about the causation of his illness. At present the best that can be done is to evaluate which cause—among many possible causes—best accords with the known facts.

Let us now recapitulate some of the evidence which suggest that psychological stresses were the most probable cause for Darwin's symptoms. There was Darwin's youthful tendency to suffer stomach and nervous upsets from psychic stimuli; his frequent adult complaints that thinking and mental work upset his stomach and caused him to become ill. Although his stomach, heart, skin, and cerebral symptoms were nonspecific, the characteristics of these symptoms to fluctuate in intensity, to undergo sudden exacerbations and remissions, and to run an overall course which was essentially non-deteriorative are indicative of psychic (as opposed to organic) causes. Then there was the simultaneous occurrence of his beginning to think evolutionary thoughts and the beginning of his illness, and the cessation of his evolutionary thoughts and the lessening of his illness. Also the correlation of exacerbations of his illness with psychologically disturbing events, such as the death of his father, the suicide of FitzRoy, the attacks of Owen, and the equivocation of Lyell.

It should again be said that, in addition to his psychic illness, he may have had periods when he suffered from medical illnesses—from allergies, or from toxic reactions to some of the drugs he was taking. At times his vomiting and very severe abdominal pain may have been caused by a gastrointestinal ulcer or inflammations of his appendix or gallbladder.

Dr. Winslow, in the course of objecting to psychological theories of Darwin's illness, states that "Darwin revealed the kind of emotional maturity which does not fit the pattern of the neurotic."[1] Maturity and neurosis can coexist in the same person. Darwin revealed great maturity in managing the everyday affairs of his household, and in his relations with his family and some of his friends—he also showed good judgment in his financial investments. When he became ill, after realizing the consequences of his evolutionary thoughts, this illness indicated that he was emotionally and physically sensitive to the difficulties of his theory and to being hated and rejected; it did not indicate that he was neurotic. To recognize the dangers and difficulties and still go ahead with his work—to steadily peer at the facts of life and death and see how these conformed to his theory—all of this required extraordinary strength of will, great faith in the powers of human reason, courage of no mean order, and a touch of defiance. He did have a neurotic side. For most of his life he seems to have been severely anxious—what he described as "a perpetually half knocked-up condition."[2] In his old age (when his evolutionary thoughts were behind him) he would experience a "miserable sinking feeling" before leaving his home for a holiday—a holiday which he knew he would enjoy.[3] This was, certainly, an excessive and inappropriate anxiety reaction. When, after meeting a new individual, he suffered "violent shivering and vomiting," this may (as has been suggested) have been a displacement onto the individual of his anxieties about his evolutionary theory,[4] or it may have been a neurotic reaction to the individual. He was tortured by obsessional thoughts, some of which may have been unrelated to his work.

Assuming that his symptoms were mostly due to psychological causes, there are then questions and problems which, given our present state of knowledge, cannot be answered. Why in June 1858, when Darwin suddenly had to confront many stresses—rivalry with Wallace and the publication of his theory of natural selection, and family death and illness, and the possibility of more death and illness—why, at this time, did Darwin only become "terribly anxious" and not suffer upsets of his stomach, heart, or skin? We cannot explain Darwin's "choice" of different somatic symptoms: why, for example, a stress should at one time cause him "eczema," at another time cardiac palpitations, and at still another time an upset stomach. We do not know why his stomach symptoms should vary so greatly in degrees of pain and vomiting, and the time of day in which they occurred.

In the 1860s he frequently observed that his "fits" of "eczema" energized him. The reasons for this are obscure. There are no skin diseases which are known to regularly cause feelings of energy and well-being. Perhaps (to offer a speculation) his eczema, which (at least on some occasions) was caused by his anxiety, then became an anxiety-reducing device: a substitute object of secondary concern onto which he could shift anxiety from objects of primary concern. In the 1860s the situations which caused him primary concern were the savage attacks on *The Origin*, the equivocation of Lyell and some of his other friends, the illnesses of his children, and his fear of having prolonged vomiting. He knew that these were situations which could become worse, and which he could not control. His fits of eczema were always transient and never seem to have become prolonged; and when his eczema caused him pain or much discomfort (this does not seem to have been too frequent) he seems to have been able to ease this by the application of some lotion. Thus, perhaps, his anxiety over his eczema—by enabling him to avoid his deeper anxieties—gave him a feeling of relief, and then of energy and wanting to work.

There is much about the effects of his treatments that we do not understand. Why some medications (such as "Condy's Ozonised Water") first helped and then had no effect; why other medications— such as mineral acids and alkaline compounds—were effective at one time and ineffective at another. I have suggested why hydropathy worked in 1849; I do not know why it did not work in 1863. Then there were occasions when Darwin's illness exacerbated and/or got better without any apparent cause.

Perhaps as more is learned about the mind-body interaction, and about Darwin the man—and much is still being learned about him— some of these questions will be answered.

Appendixes

A

The "Receipts" and "Memoranda"
Book

In the Royal College of Surgeons, London, there is a manuscript book
which was compiled and used by Charles Darwin and his family. It is
bound in brown leather covers, 6 1/2 inches long and 4 inches wide,
with a metal clasp. On the front cover is written "Receipts," on the
back cover "Memoranda." The book consists of eight "sections" or
"gatherings," totaling 182 pages: of these 128 are blank and 54 contain
written entries—varying in length, format, and handwriting—and/or
pasted-in newspaper clippings. An undetermined number of pages
have been excised.[1]

The history of this book, inferred from its contents, is as follows. It
was at first, during the early 1840s, a medical prescription book of Dr.
Robert Waring Darwin, of Shrewsbury: it contained (among different
entries) Dr. Darwin's prescriptions for Charles Darwin and the latter's
son William. On at least one occasion it was probably sent from Dr.
Darwin at Shrewsbury to the Darwins at Down. At some unknown
time—perhaps before, certainly after, Dr. Darwin's death—Charles
Darwin came to possess the book. Henrietta Darwin, in her memories
of life at Down in the 1850s, writes: "There was a well-stored 'physic
cupboard', and an old red book of prescriptions, chiefly by my grandfather, Dr. Robert Darwin."[2] Darwin and Emma added to the book
clippings, notes about household objects, and many additional medical
prescriptions and notes. The book may have become the Darwin
family's main source of medical information, and it was also used by
Darwin relatives and Downe acquaintances. The book's "red" cover,
noted in the 1850s by Henrietta Darwin, may have been changed to its
present brown covers with their titles of "Receipts" and "Memoranda." Following the death of Darwin the book may have been used
by Emma until her death at Down in 1896. After 1896 the book does

not seem to have had any further use. It became a document which was only rarely mentioned by Darwin scholars, and which has never been transcribed or seriously studied. Yet it gives glimpses of Darwin family life and medical attitudes and practices. It does not, perhaps because of its excised pages, cite some of the medicines (bismuth, pepsin, "Condy's Ozonised Water," phosphate of iron) mentioned in Darwin's letters. It makes no mention of enemas, which Darwin used in his later years.[3]

What follows is a transcription of *"Receipts" and "Memoranda."* The work of preparing this transcription involved deciphering written words and identifying handwritings. From studying the handwriting of members of the Darwin family it became possible to identify the authors of almost all the different entries of *"Receipts" and "Memoranda."*[4] Then there was the problem of how to arrange these entries. To present them in the order in which they were written—they are usually undated and not written in any sequence—would have made for disconcerting reading. It seemed that it would make for a more readable and intelligible transcript if the entries were grouped under their particular author. The following transcription has, thus, been divided into four parts: part 1, prescriptions which come from Dr. Robert Darwin; part 2, entries by Charles Darwin; part 3, entries by Emma Darwin (prescriptions of Dr. Darwin which were written by Emma Darwin and Charles Darwin, and the latter's additions to some prescriptions of Dr. Darwin, have been placed in part 1); and part 4, entries whose authors have not been identified. The contents of each part have then been subdivided according to subject matter. Opposite each transcribed entry there has been indicated the number of the page on which it is written. The subjects mentioned in each entry have, as much as possible, been identified and discussed in collateral notes.

Dr. Robert Darwin's Prescriptions

Although Dr. Darwin held many opinions and was a great talker, he wrote only rarely and disliked writing. "The doctor," an acquaintance recollected, "wrote a bad hand; he used to say if he could not get a pen he could use his thumb—he meant the writing would be as good."[1] This may explain why none of Dr. Darwin's *"Receipts" and "Memoranda"* prescriptions are in his handwriting. Most of these prescriptions are in the handwriting of his daughter Susan. As a young girl, Susan was her father's "favourite";[2] she never married, and during her father's later years she became his companion, nurse, and amanuensis. She could write medical terms and medical measurements, and she signed her father's initials to medical prescriptions. The different Dr. Darwin-Susan Darwin prescriptions follow one another closely on successive pages, and occupy most of pages 6 to 32 of *"Receipts" and "Memoranda."*

A large group of these prescriptions were for unspecified children. Dr. Darwin was interested in observing and speaking to children, and he and his daughters had established the first infant school in Shrewsbury.[3] Because of the actions of his father, Dr. Erasmus Darwin, he had suffered severely from measles as a child.[4] In medicating children he employed commonly used medications, and showed a preference for antimonial wine.

Measles (6)

Not to be kept hot, or to be exposed to strong drafts of cold air— but merely kept rather cool than otherwise—To drink as much water as they like, & to abstain from animal food as far as may be —better take a dose of Calomel[5]—the real danger in Measles which however seldom occurs when properly managed, is the breathing becoming oppressed, and the irruption subsiding suddenly, in which case the only remedy are Leeches and loss of blood[6]—as all sorts of Cordials given to bring back the irruption are highly injurious—A child of 3 after the Measles when a bad cough* *(7) remains—should take 10 drops of Antimonial Wine[7] & Henbane[8] in equal quantities three times a day—This is a very useful Medicine after the Measles as they often have mischief in the Chest—This Medicine however loses its effects when kept *mixed.*—[Charles Darwin, deeply concerned about the transmission of contagious diseases among his children,[9] then wrote the following addition.] Measles come on 14 days after infection—a 3^d person will probably bring it—requires like scarlet fever contact for infection—a bed will be contagious for a month. Time of coming on doubtful in measles & scarlet fever.—In latter put child in separate rooms.— [Darwin's son William had measles twice, the second time in 1855 or 1856 when he was sixteen or seventeen years old.[10]]

Hooping Cough (8)

An Emetic, and afterwards, potash, with sugar & water sweetened to the taste—Quarter of an ounce of Carbonate of Potash[11] in a Pint of water well sweetened with sugar (or an oz of Syrup of

Tolu[12] instead of sugar) It sh^d be renewed daily, and a table spoonful taken a dozen times a day for a child of 8 years old, a teaspoonful for one of 3 & younger—[There was again, in the handwriting
of Charles Darwin, an addition.] To infections before the*   *(9)
Hoop—doubt a third person carrying it—infection as long as Hoop
continues—change of air in old cases often *very* useful. [The Darwin family at Down suffered from whooping cough in 1855.[13]]

Inflamatory Complaints   (11)

Let it drink water freely, and breathe steam, in cases of Croup[14] do
by putting a basin of hot water under its mouth so that the steam
may ascend—In all inflammatory ailments of very young Children,
three drops of Antimonial wine repeated twice a day, is usually
sufficient, but in decided fever, a grain of Calomel with a little
chalk[15] may be safely given. 1 g^r. of Calomel 2 g^r. of Rhubarb[16] &
1 grain of Compound Chalk.[17]

Emetics   (12)

It is not safe to give an emetic to young Babies, or Children of a year
old, as they often will not act:—All Emetics acting in virtue of
their poisonous properties should not remain in the Stomach—
Antimonial Wine answers all the purposes, and if it induces sickness it is all very well—A drop of Salvolatile[18] will sometimes
compose an infant to sleep ["again" crossed out], given at night.—

Cough Drops   (13)

For a child of 5 y.^{rs} old—a Teaspoonful of Antimonial Wine, & 20
drops in 7 tea spoonfuls of water—The Child to take a teaspoonful every 3 hours For a Child of 8 months old 1 teaspoonful of
Antimonial Wine, half a teaspoonful of Henbane, [19] & 8 teaspoon-
fuls of Water—or it had better take the Antimonial wine *alone* 4 or
5 times a day.—5 drops at a time.—

The Thrush[20] (*vulgarly so*   (14)
called)

For a baby of two months old with a constant cough, & *soreness in
the mouth*, one grain of chalk with Opium, [21] with 3 drops of Antimonial wine, to be dropped on brown sugar, *on writing paper*
(that it may not stick to the paper) and the powder to be given
twice a day. morg [morning] & eveg [evening]. N.B. Never give
Calomel, when there is anything the matter with the mouth or
throat.——

Bowel Complaints   (16)

Child about 6 years old. 5 grains of comp.^{d} Chalk *with* Opium, or 8
g.^{rs} of Comp.^{d} Chalk *without* opium: and 2 g.^{rs} of Rhubarb, in
each powder. to be taken twice a day in treacle.[22] —

Dr. Darwin, who was "almost sickened" by "the thought of an
operation" and who "could scarcely endure to see a person bled,"[23]
was very cautious in his use of the commonly accepted procedures of
bleeding[24] and blistering.[25]

Bleeding   (9)

Never put a Leech on a baby *under* 3 months old, if it can be
avoided, as it is very dangerous—When a Leech has been applied,
remember to wet or rub the Leech bite for several days afterwards,
especially if the child seems distressed, as the itching sometimes
produces convulsions, without the cause being suspected—

Bleeding   (10)

Never to lose more than 10 ounces of blood *at a time* and 8 ounces
would be preferable. —

Blister   (10)

My father says blisters are bad to use in early stages of inflammation, and when used to infants to put Cambric handkerchief[26]
between the skin and the blister.—Never allow a young child to be
blistered keep its chest constantly wet, in inflammatory cases, &
put it into a warm bath, & take it out *not* wiping, so that it may
continue moistened.

A Dr. Darwin-Susan Darwin *Prescription for Willy*, written in 1843,
which fills three pages (the longest single entry in *"Receipts" and
"Memoranda"*), seems to be addressed to Charles Darwin, gives the
details of a medical regimen which Darwin should apply to his
four-year-old son Willy—who had fever and enlargement of his neck
glands—and reveals how closely and anxiously Susan and her father
were involved in the treatment of Willy. The prescription frequently
reads like a family letter: Susan refers to Dr. Darwin as "He" and "my
father"; and she is intent on directing her younger brother—"you had
better," "you had better *not*," and "be very careful"—so that he can
exactly follow the recommendations of their father. (In 1841, when
Dr. Darwin and Susan had seen Darwin and Willy at the Mount,

the doctor and his daughter had shown excessive concern over different aspects of Willy's health and well-being.[27]) After writing this Susan probably sent it, in its book, to Darwin at Down.

The prescription reads as follows:

Prescription for Willy: 1843   (20)

"He thinks the Senna[28] is a gentler medicine for Children than Scammony,[29] the latter medicine, is more adapted to adult people. Compound Senna[30] does contain some Scammony.—he quite approves of your trying half an ounce or a Table spoonful of Port Wine, mixed with 3 table spoonfuls of Water to be given once a day, in the middle of the day, when you are sure that he is not feverish, & if it agrees you might give it rather less diluted after the few first days. To be very careful the Wine does not intoxicate or greatly affect Willy, & if you doubt its agreeing you had better give it up, or stop for a few days. & then repeat it after a few days.[31]— my father *very much* urges, the Rust of Iron Chalk & Rhubarb being tried again; he does not quite know how* much Iron he takes,   *(21) but he might take as much as 2 or 3 g.^{rs} of Iron, a day,[32] perhaps the dose he now takes may require to be increased—my Father thinks it possible he may eat too much fruit—My father advises you *not* to consult M^r. Cochell[33] about his Neck—but to keep it warm with a Silk handkerchief—and to bathe it every day with an ounce of bay salt, in a pint of soft water: that will be a strong solution, but my father means it to be rather strong—only if it makes it look inflamed, you must lower the solution. Better keep his   (22) bowels open with Rhubarb & Chalk—Chalk especially would be *very useful* to him[34]—you had better mind that you yourselves do not meddle or press his neck as that often does a gt deal of mischief—The Pint will last several days, as it is only to be sprayed every day. The Chalk may gradually be increased to 8 or 10 g.^{rs} of the *compound* chalk which is a medicine my father has more faith in than anything for Glandular enlargements—you had better *not* give Calomel.————

There was a Latin prescription for Charles Darwin which was first written as:

Tinct Cinamm: comp: ℥ i   (30)
Potassae bicarbon ℥ ii
misce copiat at antea sign Decoctum of Logwood
    C. Darwin Esq. RWD
        14 Nov 1840

("1 ounce of tincture cinnamon compound
2 drachma of potassium bicarbonate
Mix well as previously with decoction of Logwood"
The letters "RWD" are the initials of Dr. Robert Waring Darwin.)

This prescription was then crossed out, and on another page rewritten
as follows:

> Ligni campechensis   (32)
>   Cort Cinnam: à ʒ vi
> coque es aq: font ʒ xvi
> ad colat: ʒ Xl cui adde
>   Tinct: cinnam: comp: ʒ i
>   potassa bi carbon ʒ ii
> take as before

("To a mixture of 6 drachma each of Logwood[35] and cinnamon bark,
add 16 ounces of fountain water. Reduce this to 11 ounces. To this
then add
    1 ounce of tincture of cinnamon compound[36]
    2 drachma of potassium bicarbonate"[37])

There was a note on Henbane.

Henbane Pills   (24)

Henbane is one of the most innocent of all the tribe of Narcotics,[38]
& Tincture perhaps agrees better, than the extract, in form of
pills—you can have it made into pills of 2 g.[rs] of Extract of Henbane in each pill with as much compound Chalk Powder.[39]—

The following liquid mixture was intended to be used as a liniment.

Ward's Essence   (18)

2 Ounces of Camphor
2 Ounces of the strong Liquor Ammonia
A pint of rectified Spirits of Wine
1/2 an oz of Essence of Lemon, or if preferred an oz of the last,—
all mixed & kept close from the air.[40]—

The following prescriptions gave no information on the age or identity
of the recipient, or the indication for use.

8 oz treacle[41] & Vinegar[42]   (23)
24 drops Laudanum[43]

1 dram ipecacuanha wine or 8 g.^{rs} of powder[44]
1 dram tincture benzoin[45]

(On the first line of the above an unknown writer had changed "8"
ounces to "4" ounces, crossed out "& Vinegar" and inserted "4 oz
vinegar"; at the end of the line, "mixed together" had been written
and then crossed out. Beneath this prescription there was added, in the
handwriting of Charles Darwin, "Double all this for Pint.")

    2 drs. [drams] Laud [Laudanum]   (23)
    4 dr [drams] Ipec [Ipecacuanha] for quart
    4 d. [drams] Benz [Benzoin]
    10 ounces and a 1/2 of Decoction of Peruvian Bark   (25)
    1 oz and 1/2 Compound Tincture of Peruvian Bark[46]
    a dram of Sub Carbonate of Ammonia[47]-
    (2 Table spoonfuls twice a day

    Cinnamon Tea   (26)

1 oz of Coarse powdered Cinnamon boiled for ten minutes, or
quarter of an hour, in a pint & a half of water—Then poured off with
the Cinnamon in a jug to stand 12 hours & a Tea cup full warmed
up when wanted A cup taken early in the morg [morning] & again
at 4 oclock in the afternoon with cream.[48]—

    R   (28)
        Tinct. Cort. aurant ℨ [drachma] xiv[49]
        Acidi Sulfur dilut: ℨ [drachma] ii[50]
        Sulph: quinine g.^{r} xvi[51]
    misce [mix] a teaspoonful once or twice a day.
              RWD [Dr. Robert Waring Darwin]
              27 December 1843

(To one side of this prescription there was written, perhaps by
Henrietta Darwin, the word "change," and then an English version of
the prescription: "Tincture of Orange Peel Quinine & Sulph. Acid.")

Three of Dr. Darwin's prescriptions were in the handwriting of
Charles Darwin. Some of these may have been written after Dr.
Darwin's death. For, as has been seen, Charles Darwin remembered,
long and "clearly," many of his father's medical opinions.[52]

    Recipe from Dr. Darwin for an   (34)
    old spare man, in good health,
    but with bad rheumatism at
    night

viz
Every night 10 gr of compound Ipecacuanha Powder
(wh. contains 1 gr. of opium[53])
      8 or 10 ot Rhubarb
   1/2 tea-spoon of Cream of Tartar.[54]
Afterwards to take 1 gr. pill of opium every night, keeping bowels
open with rhubarb. —to wear flannel, night & day, next to skin.[55]

Recipt from Dr. Darwin &   (38)
Mr. Fr. Blunt[56] for sore nipples

2 drachma Borax[57]
2 oz Oil of Almonds[58]
2 oz. Water. (Well mixed)

Dr. Darwin's Soap Pill   (49)

2 g.[rs] Calomel, 2 g.[rs] Antim. Pow. 1 Soap Pill
(i.e. 1/5 of Opium)[59]

One of Dr. Darwin's prescriptions was in the handwriting of Emma
Darwin.

Gin Cordial[60] Dr. Darwin   (15)

1/2 pint of Gin
4 drops oil of Peppermint[61] well mixed
1 dr. laudanum
1 or 2 dr. muriated Tinct. Iron[62]
   Sugar (omitted).
1 1/2 pint water or quassia to make 1 qt[63]
1/2 wine glass for a dose
Poor women weak after lying or with pains in the back.

Charles Darwin's Entries

These were never dated, show a great variability in his handwriting—
caused perhaps by changes in his health, moods, and age—and were
mainly for medications for Darwin, his family, and acquaintances.
They reveal how Darwin exactly recorded the composition and
dosage of a medicine, and how he closely observed the therapeutic
effects of changing the dosage of a medicine. He seems to have,
mainly, learned about new medicines from the oral reports of diverse
individuals (men and women, relations and acquaintances, individuals with varying degrees of medical and scientific education). Some

of the reports were secondhand. Sometimes, after hearing about a new
medicine from one person, Darwin would query another person for
more information about this medicine.[1] Darwin only rarely refers to a
book or article as informing him about a medicine. Although he kept
in his library the two pharmacology works he had studied as a
youth—the 1825 edition of Paris' *Pharmacologia* and the 1826 edition
of Duncan's *The Edinburgh New Dispensatory*—he does not seem to
have studied or acquired pharmacology books after these. He read
some of the medical books of Gully, Lane, and Chapman.[2] There is,
however, no evidence that (except, perhaps, for reading about the
inheritance of different illnesses[3]) he read other medical writings
pertaining to his illness. Among books which are today preserved in
his Down House library there is *Domestic Medicine, A Hand-
book ... popularly arranged. By an eminent Physician* (*London,
1872*). This book has no flyleaf inscription, no markings of any kind,
and its pages are mostly uncut.

Darwin's medical entries may be divided into several categories.
There were three prescriptions for "colds." (Darwin was concerned
about "colds" because these could upset him generally and exacerbate
his vomiting.[4]) These were derived from a "Mr. Williams," Darwin's
sister Susan, and the Downe village doctor, Mr. Engleheart.

Feverish cold & cough.—   (40)
Mr. Williams[5]

Antimonial Wine	1 drachma
Tincture of Squill[6]	do [ditto]
Sweet Spirit of Nitre[7]	2 drachma
Soft Water	6 oz.

Two table-spoonfuls every four hours.

*Susans admirable Cough &
bad Cold mixture—probatum est.*[8]
        grown up person

Sweet Spirits of Nitre	24 drops
Antimonial Wine	12
Sal Volatile	12
Every 3 or 4 hours.	48

Mr. Engleheart[9] for a cold   (50)

5 gr. of nitre[10] with 1 gr. of Ipecacuanha 3 or 2 times a day.—

(Beneath this Darwin wrote, then crossed out, "Made Emma reach[11] 2d
dose did.")

Aperient for do [ditto]   (50)

5 gr. Rhubarb
5 gr. of Jalap
5 gr. of Sulph. of Potash[12]

Two entries were about the treatment of skin conditions.

Mr. Edwards[13]   (29)

Ceratum Resinae. London; best ointment for all purposes see
Duncan's Pharmacopea p. 831[14]

Mr. E. recommends for Chaps ["2" crossed out, "one" inserted]
gr. of Corrosive Sublimate to 1 oz of water.[15]

Erysipelas is made instantly easy by Collodion, which makes   (47)
artificial skin[16]

The following prescriptions may have been used by Darwin to treat
his stomach.

Diluted Muriatic Acid 15 drops   (39)
—   Nitric   —   15 —
Water   2 oz[17]
    Dr. Trout [?Or Prout?][18]—twice a day one hour before meals.

(Alongside this mineral acid prescription, the dosage-conscious
Darwin had written "I think 10 drops enough.")

Effervescing mixture[19]   (40)

Carbonate of Soda[20] 25 gr[s.] in one oz.
  of water
Citric Acid[21]   25 gr[s.]—in do [ditto]

(Beneath this Darwin had written: "for stomach add 20 drops of Sal.
Volatile.")

Carb. of Soda 1/2 oz. Sal Volatile 1/2 oz   (42)
Water 12 oz.

Citric Acid 3 ["2" crossed out] drach. Water 9   (42)
["9" written over "6"] oz.

1 1/2 oz. of alkaline 1 oz of Acid.   (42)

4 drops of Prussic acid[22] twice a day, to be added to the acid—or (42)
3 drops every four hours for 24 hours—for one day—

(In the last year of his life Darwin would request W. and J. Burrow
Ltd., of Malvern, "to send me as usual a case of your Soda
Water—."[23] It is not known for how long or how frequently he took
this soda water.)

There were four entries, each about the treatment of a different illness.

First alleviate suffering   (page 1, inside front cover)
Hemp for Hydrophobia & Tetanus in Journal of
    Soc of Bengal Vol. 8: ["p. 8112" inserted]
    Pt. 2 1839[24]

Cholera[25]   (43)

With Diarrhoea at once give 3 gr. of calomel & 1/2 of opium.—
in 2 hours rhubarb & magnesia[26] & peppermint Water.—

Mr. Atkins[27] *receipt against*   (45)
continued sickness,[28] *used by*
his children.—

15 g[r.] magnesia[29]
4 oz Lime Water[30]
1 drop of essential of Cinnamon or Cassia[31]
a table-spoon-full to be repeated in 1/2 an hour, if needful.—

Prescription of Sir B. Brodie[32]   (48)
for Sophy,[33] *which Susan*[34]
has fd very good for dull
headaches

Quinae disulph.[35]   gr. xvi
Acid Nit. dilut[36]   ℥ Ss [one-half drachma]
Tinct. Aurantii[37]   ℥ xvSs [fifteen and one-half drachmas]
    1 drach per diem (or 2, *I sh[d]* think might be taken)

(A prescription very similar to the above had been published, and
ascribed to a "Mr. Morgan."[38])

One prescription, occupying a whole page, was identified as a "tonic,"
and was specified by Darwin to be for his own use. (It may be that

Darwin regarded some of the previous prescriptions of his father as tonics, and as medicines for his dyspepsia.[39])

Tonic for C. Darwin   (36)

Citrate of iron 1 drachma[40]
Cinnamon Water 1 &1/2 oz.
   Tak[e] a drachma daily.
Cinnamon water to contain one drop of cinnamon oil to 1 & 1/2 oz
of water[41] with a little spirits of Vine.[42]

The following prescriptions do not specify a recipient or conditions for use.

Madder[43]   (27)

Madder   1. oz ⎤
                      ⎬ powder
Cinnamon   1. oz ⎦
["Boil" crossed out] Water 1 & 1/2 pint, to be boiled to one pint
   add soda carb. 1 drach.
brandy half a glass or spirits of wine ["2 oz." crossed out].
Take 2 or 3 Table spoons twice a day.

Camphor[44] *Julep*[45]   (41)

Tinct. of Myrh[46] 1 drach   ⎫
                                   ⎬ 4 drach to 2 parts
Tinct of Camphor 3 drach   ⎭ of water.

Arnic[47] *gargle*   (43)

Alum[48] 2 drachma to pint of water

(When Darwin's Downe friend, Reverend J. Brodie Innes, had a toothache Darwin sent Innes several bottles of medicines along with the following letter: "You must not put, I think more than *one* drop of Chloroform on the tooth.—I send Tincture of Arnica which smarts the skin (*deadly Poison*) to put *outside* . . . I have found two or three drops of Alum and [illegible] Spirits of Nitre (in bottle with a label) *sometimes* do my teeth great good."[49])

Six of Darwin's entries were about nonmedical concerns: the measurements, utility, and costs of different objects which were used in his Down house.

Receipt to kill Bugs   (4)

One oz of *strongest* mercurial ointment with a drach[ma] of
corrosive Sublimate, when used to be mixed with little turpentine.
Mr. Blunt[50]

Two entries were about materials used on constructing a house.

Estimates   (176)

Lead for roof Lewis[51] says is about 23S to 112 lb.—
thickest sheet about 7 lb to square foot.

50S to 100 square feet of one
Lewis says so on guess
inch thick planking

Hurdles 23S per dozen, each six foot long[52]   (176)

Quick lime just slacked,[53] mixed with white of   (181)
Egg, a white good cement for glass. E. Cresy Jun.[54]

There was a pasted-in newspaper clipping about one kind of glue.

Liquid Glue   (page 1, inside front cover)

The following receipt is given by the *New York Tribune* for making
liquid glue, now so popular in America: In a wide-mouthed bottle
dissolve eight ounces of best glue in a half-pint of water, by setting
it in a vessel of water, and heating it until dissolved. Then add
slowly, constantly stirring, two and a half ounces of strong aqua-
fortis (nitric acid). Keep it well corked and it will be ready for use.
It is a handy and valuable composition, as it does not gelatinise, or
undergo putrefaction and fermentation or become offensive, and is
always ready for use.

[Darwin had crossed out the dosage of "two and a half ounces" of
nitric acid, and written instead "5 d[rs.]"]

Then there was a notation about another kind of glue, which like the
first could be made at home.

Receipt to fix thills[55] & boards   (2)

2 oz Sugar
4 oz gum
Table spoonful of ox gall,[56] water quart liquid

dissolve & strain:
add table spoonful of Starch
1/2 drach of Corrosive Sublimate
[illegible word] had better weigh

One entry differed in its contents from all the other writings in *"Receipts" and "Memoranda."*

Two Engravings in Henslow's   (179)
Possession

Foret du Bresil. Dep. [Depeindre] par M. Rugendas
    publie par Rittner[57]

Foret vierge du Bresil par Le Compte de Clarac.
Fortier Sandpret[58]

[Darwin had been deeply impressed by the above two engravings when he had explored the Brazilian forest in 1832.[59]]

Emma Darwin's Entries

As a young unmarried woman Emma first learned about illness through nursing her sick mother.[1] After she married Charles Darwin she then learned about pain, illness, and medical treatments through experiencing difficult pregnancies and labors, from suffering from headaches and toothaches,[2] and through nursing her sick children and invalid husband. She developed a concern about "saving suffering" in others,[3] and came to know enough about medicines so that she could give "medical comforts and simple medicines" to sick people, especially women, in Downe village.[4] She formed opinions about what medical treatments helped her husband,[5] and were effective in certain conditions. Darwin wrote his friend the Reverend J. Brodie Innes that, in a case of toothache, "Mrs. Darwin finds hot fomentations are best."[6] Emma's writings in *"Receipts" and "Memoranda"* were mainly medical and reveal her medical knowledge and interests, and her ability (like Susan Darwin's) to write a medical prescription. Whether some of her entries were dictated by her husband (who frequently dictated letters and scientific notes to her) cannot be ascertained.

Emma's medical entries were as follows.

Citric acid alleviates   (page 1, inside front cover)
the pain of cancer[7]

Quassia[8]   (16)

1/2 oz Quassia chips
    pint
1 1/2 pt boiling water
stand 4 or 5 hours

Antimonie Wine   (44)

2 gr. to Tartar Emetic to 2 oz of Water

Soothing Ointment   (51)

1 oz Oxide ["Lard" crossed out] Zinc[9]
6 oz Lard[10]
1 oz Glycerine[11] mix thoroughly

There were cough prescriptions for Emma's brother-in-law Erasmus,[12] and then for her son Frank.[13]

Cough Mixture   Eras D   (44)

Comp.[ound] Tinc.[ture] ["Comp" crossed out]
Benz.[oin][14]   1 oz
Syrup Poppies alb[us]:[15]   1 oz
Oxymel Squills[16] a̅a̅   ℨ iSs [one and one-half drachma]
    1 tea spoonful 3 times a day

Cough Mixture F. Darwin   (53)

Tinct Benzoin[17]   2 oz
Tinct Myrrh[18]   1 oz
Oxymel Squills[19]   1 oz
Laudanum[20]   1 1/2 dram
    dose 1 dram

There were the opinions of two doctors.

Dr. Willey[21] *on Diptheria*[22]   (52)

equal parts of Tinct Steel[23] & Glycerine[24] & paint the throat

Dr. Moore[25] *on Croupe*[26]   (54)

There is often a spurious sort which sounds just like the real.
Try the temperature: If raised it is the real disorder & give at once
10 g. Ipecac:[27] If not raised it is the spurious & is not dangerous.

In transcribing Dr. Darwin's "Gin Cordial" Emma had noted that it was for "Poor women weak after lying or with pains in the back." In another entry she wrote:

> For weakly girls of 15 or 16. Tea spoonful & 1/2 of   (41)
> muriated Iron[28] in a quart bottle of soft water 1/2 a tea cup full
> every morning before breakfast.

Two of her prescriptions were derived from (or, perhaps, intended for) married women.

> Mrs. Seymour Hill.[29] Bunions[30] Laudanum[31] & goulard[32] in   (46)
> equal quantities weakened with a little water.
> kept on the joint with lint[33] & oilskin

> Acetate Morphia ["10" crossed out] 12 g—   (52)
>   a few drops of acetic acid
>   6 oz water
> 1 or 2 tea spoonfuls[34]
>   Mrs. Brooks[35]

Emma may have worried about lead contamination of the Down House drinking water. On one page she had written "Test for Lead," and beneath this pasted in the following newspaper clipping:

> "There is an easily applied test for lead in water. Take two   (181)
> tumblers; fill one with water which is known not to have been in
> contact with lead; fill the other with the suspected water. Dissolve
> in each about as much bichromate of potash as will stand on a
> groat. By daylight the water in each tumbler will be of the colour of
> pale sherry and water. Cover the tumblers so as to keep out dust,
> and let them stand in a warm place in a room with a fire in it for
> 24 hours. If the suspected water be free from lead it will still
> have the same colour as the other; but if there be lead in the water
> it will have a more or less opalescent tint, as if a drop or more
> milk had been put into it. If there be a great quantity of lead in
> the water a very slight film of lead will be deposited on the glass.
>   Bichromate of potash can be got of good druggists, and a few
> drachma will be enough to test many samples of water."

One entry was about laundering.

> To wash printed dresses—Take about a pint bran,[36] tie it in a
> muslin[37] bag boil it in a pail full of ["soft" inserted] water and (177)
> when the dresses have been washed in this liquor—, which should
> not be used scalding hot—very little if any soap will be found

necessary. yellow soap should not on any account be used nor soda.[38]

On one page Emma, who experienced "constant enjoyment in country sights and sounds" and in her Down garden,[39] had written "To kill wasps," and pasted in another newspaper clipping.

The following remedy, first invented by a near neighbor and   (5)
friend, the late Rev. W. Kirby,[40] will be found efficient:—A hand
glass, commonly used by gardeners (a square one is the best), is the
instrument to be used. This has to be tightly covered at the bottom
with thick white paper varnished to resist the wet. A circular hole,
6 1/2 inches in diameter, is then cut in the centre of the paper, and
the glass is placed on three bricks over a plate filled with beer,
sugar, and a little rum, a moderate distance from the infested spot.
The effect is magical; in a few hours the glass is crammed with
wasps, hornets, and flies (bees will seldom enter), which having
tasted the sweets, fly upwards to the light. A common sulphur
match, made by dipping brown paper into melted brimstone
will destroy thousands. The constant hum of insect life inside will
attract all the marauders from the fruit trees to the glass; and the
scent of the rum is sure to induce the most fastidious wasp to enter,
as no insect can resist its powerful attractions. With two or three of
these machines in my garden I never have a peach or a grape
touched by insects.

Entries Whose Authors Are Unidentified

The following passage is in the handwriting of a small child.

If you boil Castor Oil with an equal quantity of milk,   (46)
sweeten with a little sugar, and stir it well and give it when cold,
children will never suspect it to be medecine, but will like it
almost as well as custard.[1]

On separate pages there were pasted in two small, consecutively published articles from *The Times*; both were about ways of avoiding arsenic poisoning by detecting the presence of arsenic in cloths and household objects (neither article had any handwritten comments). The first article, which appeared in *The Times*, 20 October 1862, stated:

A Test for Arsenic   (page 1 inside front cover)

Dr. Letheby[2] recommends the following method of detecting
the presence of arsenic in wreaths and dresses:— "Put a drop
of strong liquid ammonia (liquor ammonia, the druggist calls it)
upon the green leaf, or dress, or paper, and if it turns blue, copper
is present; and copper is rarely, if ever present in these tissues and
fabrics without arsenic being also present—the green compound
being arsenite of copper. I have tested papers and dresses in this
manner more than a hundred times, and have never failed to discover arsenic when the ammonia changes the green into blue. It is,
therefore, indirectly a very reliable test; and if every lady would
carry with her, when she is shopping, a small phial of liquid
ammonia, instead of the usual scent bottle, the mere touch of the
wet stopper on the suspicious green would betray the arsenic poison
and settle the business quickly."

Two pages after the above there was pasted in a second article from
The Times, 23 October 1862.

Arsenicated Articles of Dress,   (3)
Paper, Confectionary, & c.

To the Editor of The Times. Sir,—In reference to the case of
poisoning by arsenic reported in yesterday's *Times*, I do not wish to
disparage the ammonia test recommended by Dr Letheby, which is
only conclusive of the reaction for copper; but as it is quite possible
to make greens without arsenic (Brunswick green, for instance), it
would be desirable in all cases to establish its presence, which is
easily accomplished by steeping the article for a minute or so in a
mixture of about a teaspoonful each of water and liquid ammonia.
Next invert a wine-glass and place on it one or two drops of the
deep blue liquid; then introduce a fragment, about the size of a
mustard seed, of nitrate of silver, when, if arsenic is present, a
yellow spot will be obtained, which is arsenite of silver.

                                              I am yours, &c.
Cheltenham, Oct. 21   John Horsley, F.C.S.[3]

Beginning in November 1867, and continuing into 1868, there was an
epidemic of typhoid fever in the village of Terling.[4] This epidemic was
thought to have been mainly caused by well water being polluted by
sewage. Terling was about fifty-three miles by road from Downe
(about thirty miles as the crow flies), and the Darwin family may have
become concerned about the possible pollution of their drinking

water—the water for Down House was drawn by a bucket from a well which descended 325 feet into the ground.[5] The following long letter, appearing in *The Times*, 18 June 1868, was then pasted (without any written comments) onto a page of *"Receipts" and "Memoranda."*

Country Wells (178)

Sir,—The fearful epidemic now raging at the village of Terling, near Witham, in Essex, seems to have resulted mainly from well water poisoned by sewage. By the latest accounts the fever has struck down 180 persons out of 900, the fatal cases being 16. These figures should awaken in the mind of every country householder an interest in the situation and condition of his wells. The water supply of London and the large provincial towns has received much attention, and commissioners are looking after our rivers as sources of potable water; but wells, on which the majority of us depend for daily drink, have never obtained effective public notice, and as a consequence, are still generally sunk where most liable to contamination, still often receive the contributions of sewers, &c., carelessly laid within a few feet or inches of the well wall. Every well is but a reservoir for rainfall, an underground cistern into which rain naturally drains after having run a longer or shorter journey through the ground; how important, then, that it should be sunk where nothing but rain can enter, and where the soil in its vicinity can be jealously guarded from intrusion of anything coming under the denomination of sewage. Yet what is the fact? A builder reflects that the time and labour of servants will be economized if the pump be placed within or close to the house, that waste of pipe will be avoided if the well be close to the pump; under the pump-spout he must necessarily have a sink and drain, and down the drain will all sorts of refuse be thrown. Sooner or later the drain leaks, and fouling of the well follows. Let the pump drain and kitchen keep company by all means, but sink the well far from the house, far from any drain, cesspool, pigsty, or other possible source of pollution. Mineral matter dissolved from the soil is comparatively harmless; animal and vegetable matter may be harmless, but may be poisonous, and must, therefore, be kept out by every precaution. Good soil is here our best friend, Nature's own purifier, entirely destroying the substances last mentioned, if only allowed to have fair play; but its power for good is limited, its power for harm terrible, when saturated by drainage from adjacent accumulations of filth.

Polluted water does not generally betray its condition till pos-

sessed of a strong odour; earlier intimation may, however, be
obtained by the following tests:—Half fill a common water-bottle,
cover its mouth with the hand, violently shake for a minute, and
quickly apply the nose. If nothing unpleasant is detected, tightly
cork the bottle, set it aside in a warm place at about the temperature of one's body for a couple or three days, and repeat the
shaking, &c. Water of very bad quality may thus be recognised
without the trouble and expense of analysis.

  I am, Sir, your obedient servant,
  John Attfield, Professor of Practical
  Chymistry to the Pharmaceutical Society.
  17, Bloomsbury-square.[6]

B

Darwin and the Early Use of
Chloroform Anesthesia

On 20 August 1848, at the end of a letter to the London physician Dr.
Francis Boott,[1] Darwin wrote: "my true thanks for all your sympathy
& assistance about Chloriform.[2]"[3] It is not known what Dr. Boott had
done for Darwin. It is, however, clear that the latter was interested in
chloroform; and it may be conjectured that this interest was due to
several factors.

  On 15 November 1847, Dr. James Young Simpson, of Edinburgh
University, had published a *Notice of a New Anaesthetic Agent.* This
described how chloroform, when given to a mother in obstetrical
labor, had put her to sleep and caused her to have a painless birth.[4]
These beneficial effects were quickly reported in medical and lay
publications, and by the end of November chloroform was being used
in obstetrical and surgical cases throughout Britain.[5] Soon some
physicians began saying that the use of chloroform was "unnatural,"
against the teachings of the Bible, and that "chloroform in childbirth
would increase the incidence of bleeding, paralysis, pneumonia, and
so on."[6] Simpson vigorously answered these objections, stressing the
analgesic attributes of chloroform and pointing out that there was no
hard evidence that it caused medical complications.[7] Then, for
several years, the use of chloroform became the subject of an intense
public controversy.[8]

  About the time that Simpson had published his *Notice* Emma

Darwin had become pregnant for the seventh time. By April 1848 Darwin had heard about the "practical use" of chloroform;[9] he then may have discussed with Dr. Boott the pros and cons of giving Emma chloroform. Since he was exquisitely sensitive to pain in himself and others, and since Emma's births had always deeply disturbed him,[10] he must have welcomed the opportunity to anesthetize his wife. But being a cautious man he may have been fearful of chloroform's alleged complications. On 16 August 1848, four days before Darwin wrote to Dr. Boott, Emma had given birth to a son, Francis; at this time she probably did not use chloroform.

Darwin then seems to have thought of chloroform as a local anesthetic, for when his friend, the Reverend J. Brodie Innes, had a toothache, he told Innes: "You must not put, I think more than *one* drop of Chloroform on the tooth."[11]

In 1849 Emma again became pregnant. On 15 January 1850, while she was giving birth to a son, Leonard, Darwin gave her chloroform. He described his action in a letter to Fox: "The day before yesterday Emma was confined of a little Boy. Her pains came on so rapidly & severe, that I c^d not withstand her entreaties for Chloroform & administered it myself which was nervous work not knowing ["from eye-sight" inserted] anything about it or of midwifery. The Doctor got here only 10 minutes before the Birth.—I thought at the time I was only soothing the pains—but, it seems, she remembers nothing from the first pain till she heard that the child was born.—Is this not grand?"[12] Emma had remained unconscious for 1 1/2 hours. (Darwin had never administered chloroform to a human, yet he may have possessed some knowledge of midwifery; in November 1826, during his second year at the University of Edinburgh, he had enrolled in the classes of "Practice of Physic" and "Midwifery." At this time he had decided not to be a doctor, and these were the only clinical courses he took.[13])

Darwin then wrote Henslow[14] and Hooker[15] that he had been "bold" and "very bold" in giving Emma chloroform. He would later tell Hooker that he had been "perfectly convinced that the chloroform was very comforting to oneself as well as ["to" inserted] the patient."[16] Although giving the chloroform had comforted him, he still felt anxiety over Emma's labor, and the prospect of her future labors.

From this time on he regarded chloroform as "the greatest & most blessed of discoveries,"[17] and he zealously advocated its use and minimized its shortcomings. When Fox mentioned some of the objections to chloroform, Darwin replied: "I am sorry to hear about Chloroform; from what Dr. Simpson says I believe in such cases as you mention, the frightened & generally prejudiced doctors do not give enough."[18]

In May 1851 Emma gave birth to a son, Horace; she probably took chloroform, although this cannot be definitely ascertained. In June 1852 Darwin had some teeth extracted and he reported that, because he had taken "wonderful" chloroform, he "felt hardly anything."[19] (Nine years later, however, when he saw his son George chloroformed for teeth extraction, he suffered "stomach sickness."[20]) In October 1852 he told Fox that, because of the "blessed discovery" of chloroform, he could think more happily about his children.[21]

In April 1853 Queen Victoria gave birth to a fourth son and eighth child, Prince Leopold. The Queen "dreaded child-bearing and resented it,"[22] and during the birth of Leopold she used chloroform for the first time. She reported that the effect of the new drug "was soothing, quieting and delightful beyond measure."[23] Her experience "silenced all opposition" to chloroform, and made its use noncontroversial and respectable.[24]

In December 1856 Emma Darwin gave birth to Charles Waring Darwin, her tenth and last child. Darwin reported this to Fox as follows: "Emma produced under blessed Chloroform our sixth boy."[25] It is not known who gave Emma her chloroform.

Throughout his life Darwin continued to feel deeply about chloroform's anesthetic powers. In his *Autobiography* he recollected the "two very bad operations" he had seen when he was a medical student at Edinburgh, and how he had "rushed away" before the operations were completed. He then, retrospectively, commented that these operations took place "long before the blessed days of chloroform."[26]

Some of his last thoughts about chloroform concerned its use, along with other anesthetics, in animal experiments. In January 1875 he told his daughter: "It is certain that physiology can progress only by experiments on living animals. . . . I would gladly punish severely any one who operated on an animal not rendered insensible, if the experiment made this possible. . . ."[27] He did not further comment on his feelings about animal experiments which necessitated the use of no anesthesia. In November 1875 he gave evidence before "the First Royal Commission on Vivisection." The chairman of the commission asked him: "Now with regard to trying a painful experiment without anaesthetics, when the same experiment can be made with anaesthetics, or, in short, inflicting any pain that was not absolutely necessary upon any animal, what would be your view on that subject?"

To this Darwin replied with an unusually strong burst of feeling: "It deserves detestation and abhorrence."[28]

Abbreviations

Manuscripts

CCDL   Christ College Collection of Charles Darwin's Letters to William Darwin Fox

DPL   Charles Darwin Papers and Letters in the University Library, Cambridge; box numbers given correspond to those listed in the *Handlist of Darwin Papers at the University Library* (Cambridge: Cambridge University Press, 1960)

RDC   Robin Darwin Collection of Charles Darwin's papers and letters, on deposit in the Cambridge University Library

Books

Autobiography   Nora Barlow, ed., *The Autobiography of Charles Darwin, 1809–1882. With original omissions restored* (London: Collins, 1958)

"Beagle" Diary   Nora Barlow, ed., *Charles Darwin's Diary of the Voyage of H.M.S. "Beagle"* (Cambridge: Cambridge University Press, 1833)

Calender of the Letters of Darwin to Gray   Bert James Loewenberg, ed., *Calender of the Letters of Charles Robert Darwin to Asa Gray* (Boston: Historical Records Survey, 1939; reprinted by Scholarly Resources, Inc., 1973)

CFL   Henrietta Litchfield, ed., *Emma Darwin: A Century of Family Letters, 1792–1896*, 2 vols. (London: John Murray, 1915)

Darwin and the "Beagle"	Nora Barlow, ed., *Charles Darwin and Voyage of the "Beagle"* (New York: Philosophical Library, 1946)
Darwin and Henslow	Nora Barlow, ed., *Darwin and Henslow: The Growth of an Idea* (London: John Murray, 1967)
Darwin's Journal	Sir Gavin de Beer, ed., *Darwin's Journal, Bulletin of the British Museum (Natural History) Historical Series* 2 (1959):1–21
Gruber and Barrett, *Darwin on Man*	Howard E. Gruber and Paul H. Barrett, *Darwin on Man* (New York: E. P. Dutton & Co., Inc., 1974)
Down: The Home of the Darwins	Sir Hedley Atkins, *Down: The Home of the Darwins. The Story of a House and the People Who Lived There* (London: Royal College of Surgeons of England, 1974)
Journal of Researches, 1839	Charles Darwin, *Journal of Researches into the Geology and Natural History of the Various Countries Visited by H.M.S. Beagle, under the Command of Captain FitzRoy, R.N. from 1832 to 1836* (London: Henry Colburn, 1839)
Journal of Researches, 1845	Charles Darwin, *Journal of Researches into the Natural History and Geology of the Countries Visited during the Voyage of H.M.S. Beagle Round the World,* 2d ed. (London: John Murray, 1845)
LL	Francis Darwin, ed., *Life and Letters of Charles Darwin,* 2 vols. (New York: D. Appleton & Co., n.d.)
ML	Francis Darwin and A. C. Seward, eds., *More Letters of Charles Darwin. A Record of his Work in a Series of Hitherto Unpublished Letters,* 2 vols. (New York: D. Appleton & Co., 1903)
The Rise and Progress of Hydropathy	Richard Metcalfe, *The Rise and Progress of Hydropathy in England and Scotland* (London: Simpkin, Marshall, Hamilton, Kent & Co., Ltd., 1912)
TN	"Darwin's Notebooks on Transmutation of Species," parts I–IV, edited,

with introduction and notes, by Sir
Gavin de Beer; addenda and corrigenda, edited by Sir Gavin de Beer
and M. J. Rowlands; part VI (excised
pages), edited by Sir Gavin de Beer,
M. J. Rowlands, and B. M. Skramov-
sky, *Bulletin of the British Museum
(Natural History) Historical Series* 2
(1960–67):23–200; 3 (1960–67):129–
76. References to the notebooks cite
the part and Darwin's pagination.
Unless otherwise stated this refers to
parts I to IV, edited by Sir Gavin
de Beer. If the page is published in
addenda and corrigenda, or part VI,
this is further noted. Example: TN,
4:5, part VI.

Notes and References

The Manuscript Letters of Darwin,
Hooker, and Asa Gray

Whenever possible the original manuscript version of a letter has been transcribed and quoted from. In my transcriptions I have tried to exactly reproduce the contents of each letter, indicating crossed-out words, original spelling and punctuation, and raised letters. I think this manner of transcription conveys a certain period atmosphere, and aids in understanding Darwin's thought and feeling about his health. When the manuscript source and the published source of the same letter are cited, it is always the manuscript which has been quoted from. Although there are frequent differences between published and manuscript versions, these differences have, usually, not been indicated. I have, however, sometimes indicated the differences when these touch on Darwin's medical symptoms.

To make for smoother reading I have written out addresses which have been abreviated. Thus, when Darwin wrote "Grt. Marlb." and "I. of W.," this has been transcribed as "Great Marlborough Street" and "Isle of Wight." To several addresses at which Darwin resided for short periods—"The Lodge, Malvern," "Moor Park, Farnham, Surrey," "Wells Terrace, Ilkley, Otley, Yorkshire," "Dumbola Lodge, Freshwater, Isle of Wight," I have added commas. I think that this additional punctuation clarifies the address. Two home addresses which Darwin used for years—"Down Bromley Kent" and "Down Farnborough Kent"—I have presented, without additional punctuation, exactly as they were written. Other addresses have, also, been given as originally written.

Throughout this book I have given dates in the order of day-month-year, with no punctuation separating the three items. This policy has necessitated the following changes in dating Darwin's letters. Where Darwin has abbreviated a month, or placed the day after the month—"Feby" or "Dec. 15"—I have written out "February" and "15 December." I have done this to facilitate reading, to avoid different ways of giving dates, and to avoid sprinkling the page with brackets and parentheses; and because doing this does not, really, make any assumptions for Darwin. Weekdays have been given as Darwin wrote them. When a date (day, month, or year) is given which has not been written on the original letter, this date has been placed in parentheses.

In dating Darwin's letters to T. H. Huxley I have usually given the dates that are cited in Warren R. Dawson, *The Huxley Papers, Descriptive Catalogue of the Correspondence, Manuscripts and Miscellaneous Papers of the Rt. Hon. Thomas Henry Huxley, preserved in the Imperial College of Science and Technology, London* (London: Macmillan Co., 1946), pp. 25–32.

I have suggested new dates for several Darwin letters.

Francis Darwin's "Reminiscences of
my Father's Everyday Life"

These "Reminiscences" exist in two versions. The original manuscript, in the handwriting of Francis Darwin, which is in the Cambridge University Library, DPL, Box 140 (3), pp. 1–159. A published version, comprising a part of the manuscript, which is contained in *LL*, 1:87–136. I have used the published version whenever possible, citing it in the order of author, title, *LL*, 1, and page numbers. I have used the manuscript when it contains information omitted from the published version, and I have cited it in the order of author, title, DPL, Box 140 (3), and page.

Introduction

1. For the different theories about the causes of Darwin's illness, see part 2.

2. Ernst Mayr, "Open Problems of Darwin Research," *Studies in History and Philosophy of Science* 2, no. 3 (1971):273–80.

1

The Illness

1 A Family of Doctors

1. Dr. Erasmus Darwin, 1731–1802.

2. Charles Darwin, 1758–78. This uncle had no middle name; Darwin's full name was Charles Robert Darwin.

3. Dr. Robert Waring Darwin, 1766–1848.

4. Erasmus Alvey Darwin, 1804–81. For an account of Erasmus' illness see part 2, §2.

5. *Autobiography*, p. 49.

6. Erasmus Darwin, *Zoonomia; or, The Laws of Organic Life*, vol. 1 (London: Printed for J. Johnston, in Saint Paul's Church-Yard, 1794). Volume 2 was published in 1796. (The two volumes of *Zoonomia* which were read by Darwin are today kept in the Cambridge University Library.)

7. *Autobiography*, p. 47, n. 2. Tartar emetic—antimony potassium tartrate—was, at this time, described as "the most manageable and the least

uncertain of all the antimonial preparations." Depending on its dosage, it was widely used as a cathartic, to induce vomiting or sweating, in fevers, and as a sedative (J. A. Paris, *Pharmacologia*, 3d American ed., 6th English ed. [New York, 1825], 2:53; see appendix A, *Dr. Robert Darwin's Prescriptions*, n. 7).

8.   Francis Darwin, "Reminiscences of my Father's Everyday Life," DPL, Box 140 (3), p. 42.

9.   Darwin's library contains J. A. Paris, *Pharmacologia*, 2 vols., 6th ed. (London, 1825). The front flyleaf of each volume has the signature "Charles Darwin." Neither volume contains any of the markings which Darwin customarily made in books he read. (These two volumes are today kept in Down House.)

10.   J. H. Ashworth, "Charles Darwin as a Student in Edinburgh, 1825–1827," *Proceedings of the Royal Society of Edinburgh* 55 (1934–35):98.

11.   Darwin's library contains Andrew Duncan, Jr., *The Edinburgh New Dispensatory*, 11th ed. (Edinburgh, 1826). On the front flyleaf is the signature "Charles Darwin 1826." There are marginal marks and comments by Darwin in the section on "Weights and Measures" (pp. 106, 107, 110, 111). There are marginal marks in part 2, *Materia Medica*: "Catechu Extractum," from a tree in Hindostan (p. 185); "Ammoniac, a Gum-Resin," from a plant in the north of Morocco (p. 209); "Angelicae Archangelicae Radix," a plant growing wild in England (p. 223); "Radix Recens Ari," a plant from England (pp. 254, 255). Pages 185, 209, 223, and 254 were again noted in the back flyleaf. In part 3, *Preparations and Compositions* (p. 671), it was stated that, for a solution of sulphate of zinc, 16 grains of sulphate of zinc should be dissolved in 8 ounces of water. Opposite this Darwin had written "2 gr to 1 oz *for Eyes.*" On the same page it was also stated that sulphate of zinc, "in doses from ten grains to half a drachma," could be used as an emetic in cases of poisoning. Opposite this Darwin had written "30 grains." And on the back flyleaf, after noting "Zi 671," he wrote "Metric for Poison." Darwin also marked the references (pp. 731, 733) to infusions of rhubarb roots and senna leaves, both of which were used as purgatives. None of Darwin's marks or comments can be dated. (This volume of *The Edinburgh New Dispensatory* is today kept in Down House.)

12.   These notes are kept in "Lecture Notes on Medicine etc. Edinburgh [1825–7]," DPL, Box 5.

13.   The word *empresma* appears to be a creation of the early nineteenth-century popular medical writer, John Mason Good, author of *The Study of Medicine* (1822) and many other medical works. He used it to apply to any kind of inflammation of the viscera of the thorax and abdominal cavity. The word comes from "empresis," used by Galen and other ancient Greek medical writers, for inflammation in general. *Empresma* got a temporary currency with the popularity of Good's writings, and the Edinburgh medical school had fastened onto it in the 1820–30 period. (I wish to thank David D. Murison, editor of *The Scottish National Dictionary*, for informing me about the meaning of *empresma*.)

14. These medical notes are kept in "Lecture Notes on Medicine etc. Edinburgh [1825–7]," DPL, Box 5.

15. Charles Darwin, *"The Life of Erasmus Darwin," together with an Essay on his Scientific Works by Ernst Krause* (New York: D. Appleton & Co., 1880), p. 82.

16. *Autobiography*, p. 48.

17. T. P. Bythell, "Dr. Darwin (March 26th, 1884)," *Salopian Shreds and Patches*, 9 April 1884, p. 27.

18. J. H. Ashworth, "Charles Darwin as a Student in Edinburgh, 1825–1827," *Proceedings of the Royal Society of Edinburgh* 55 (1934–35): 98–101.

19. *Autobiography*, p. 50.

20. Ibid., pp. 56–59.

21. Ibid., p. 48.

22. "I shall ever hate the name of the Materia Medica, since hearing Duncan's lectures at eight o'clock on a winter's morning—a whole, cold, breakfastless hour on the properties of rhubarb!" (Darwin to Hooker, Down, Sunday [18 April 1847], *LL*, 1:323). "Dr. Duncan's lectures on Materia Medica at 8 o'clock on a winter's morning are something fearful to remember" (*Autobriography*, p. 47).

23. Ibid., p. 60.

24. Ibid., p. 68.

25. Erasmus A. Darwin to Charles Darwin, Dr. Butlers, Shrewsbury (postmark 24 February 1825), RDC.

26. Overton was the home of Mrs. Marianne Parker, Darwin's oldest sister, and her husband, Dr. Henry Parker.

27. Catherine Darwin to Charles Darwin, Shrewsbury, Sunday morning, 4 December (postmark 5 December 1825), RDC.

28. Fox attended Christ's College from 1824 to 1829.

29. Fox to Darwin, Upperstone near Nottingham, 30 June 1832, RDC.

30. Darwin to Fox (Shrewsbury, 2 January 1829), CCDL.

31. Darwin to Fox, Christ's College (Cambridge), 1 April (1829), CCDL, *LL*, 1:152.

32. Darwin to Fox, Shrewsbury, Friday (4 July 1829), CCDL, *LL*, 1:154.

33. Charles Darwin to Susan Darwin, 17 Spring Gardens (London), Tuesday (6 September 1831), *Darwin and the "Beagle,"* p. 45.

34. J. M. Herbert to Francis Darwin, 12 June 1882, DPL, Box 112.

35. Darwin to Fox, Cambridge, Thursday (26 February 1829), CCDL, *LL*, 1:150.

36. Sir Henry Holland, 1788–1873 (*Dictionary of National Biography*). Holland was also the physician to Darwin's older brother Erasmus.

37. *CFL*, 1:43, n. 1.

38. These two possibilities are mentioned in John H. Winslow, *Darwin's Victorian Malady* (Philadelphia: American Philosophical Society, 1971), p. 44, n. 12. For a further discussion of this book see part 2, §5.

39. Andrew Duncan, Jr., *The Edinburgh New Dispensatory*, 11th ed. (Edinburgh, 1826), p. 251.

40. In the copies of these books which are in Darwin's library there are no marks in the sections on arsenic.

41. J. A. Paris, *Pharmacologia* (New York, 1825), 2:221.

42. Andrew Duncan, Jr., *The Edinburgh New Dispensatory* (Edinburgh, 1826), pp. 246, 248; J. A. Paris, *Pharmacologia* (New York, 1825), 2:71–74; Erasmus Darwin, *Zoonomia* (London, 1796), 2:727.

43. J. A. Paris, *Pharmacologia* (New York, 1825), 2:71.

44. Andrew Duncan, Jr., *The Edinburgh New Dispensatory* (Edinburgh, 1826), pp. 251–52.

2   The *Beagle* Illnesses

1. Charles Darwin to Catherine Darwin, East Falkland Island, 6 April 1834, *Darwin and the "Beagle,"* p. 99.

2. Darwin to Henslow, Shrewsbury, 30 August 1831, *Darwin and Henslow*, p. 33.

3. Charles Darwin to Susan Darwin, 17 Spring Gardens (London, 6 September 1831), *Darwin and the "Beagle,"* pp. 45–46.

4. Charles Darwin to Susan Darwin (London, 9 September 1831), *Darwin and the "Beagle,"* p. 48.

5. *Darwin's Journal*, p. 7.

6. *Autobiography*, p. 79.

7. Darwin to Henslow, Devenport, 15 November 1831, *Darwin and Henslow*, pp. 48–49.

8. Ibid., pp. 46, 49.

9. *Autobiography*, p. 79.

10. *"Beagle" Diary*, 19 November 1831, p. 8.

11. Ibid., 10–12 December 1831, pp. 12–13. On 15 November 1831, Darwin wrote Henslow: "I have only now to pray for the sickness to moderate its fierceness, & I shall do very well" (*Darwin and Henslow*, p. 48). It is not clear what "sickness" refers to, and it has been suggested that Darwin meant his lip and hand condition (John H. Winslow, *Darwin's Victorian Malady* [Philadelphia, 1971], p. 49). It is more likely that this refers to Darwin's upset stomach and/or his fear of seasickness (which he had expressed to his sister Susan). It will be seen that when Darwin used the word "sick" or "sickness" about himself this usually meant vomiting. (Darwin's father, and his son Francis, also used "sick" to denote vomiting.) A sickness "moderat[ing] its fierceness" could apply to seasickness, which at times was severe and incapacitated him, and at

other times was moderate and permitted him to work. Darwin greatly feared future seasickness, and two days after writing Henslow he wrote Fox: "When I think that I, an unfortunate landsman, am going to undertake such a voyage—I long for the times when sea sickness will drown all such feelings & that ["time" inserted] I do suppose will be the 5th of next month" (Darwin to Fox, 4 Clarence Baths, Devenport [17 November 1831], CCDL).

12. *Autobiography*, p. 79.

13. *"Beagle" Diary*, 11–12 December 1831, pp. 13–14.

14. *Autobiography*, pp. 79–80.

15. On 5 January 1832, Darwin wrote in his diary: "The day has been beautiful & I am so much better that I am able to enjoy it" (*"Beagle" Diary*, p. 20).

16. *LL*, 1:193.

17. *"Beagle" Diary*, 28 December 1831, p. 19.

18. *LL*, 1:197; *"Beagle" Diary*, p. 426.

19. Charles Darwin to Dr. Robert Darwin, Bahia or St. Salvador (8 February–1 March 1832), *Darwin and the "Beagle,"* p. 52.

20. Sago was a starch preparation used medically as a nutrient and a demulcent.

21. *"Beagle" Diary*, 29 December 1831, p. 19.

22. *Darwin and the "Beagle,"* p. 252.

23. *"Beagle" Diary*, 29 December 1831, p. 19.

24. *LL*, 1:197–98.

25. *"Beagle" Diary*, 29 December 1831, p. 19.

26. *"Beagle" Diary*, 6–12 March, 11–13 May 1832, pp. 42, 61.

27. Ibid., p. 61.

28. *Darwin and the "Beagle,"* 11 April 1832, p. 160.

29. *"Beagle" Diary*, 11 April 1832, pp. 52–53.

30. *"Beagle" Diary*, 12 April 1832, p. 53.

31. *Darwin and the "Beagle,"* 12 April 1832, p. 160.

32. See appendix A, *The "Receipts" and "Memoranda" Book*.

33. *"Beagle" Diary*, 27 May 1832, p. 64.

34. Charles Musters, volunteer first class on the *Beagle*, had been a friend and companion of Darwin.

35. Charles Darwin to Catherine Darwin, Rio de Janeiro, May–June (1832), *Darwin and the "Beagle,"* p. 68.

36. *"Beagle" Diary*, 9 May 1832, p. 60.

37. *Darwin and the "Beagle,"* 2 October 1833, p. 208.

38. *"Beagle" Diary*, 2 October 1833, p. 186.

39. "Like most delicate people he [Darwin] suffered from heat as well as from chilliness; it was as if he could not hit the balance between too hot and

too cold" (Francis Darwin, "Reminiscences of my Father's Everyday Life," *LL*, 1:90). This sensitivity to changes in temperature may have made Darwin especially prone to have a heat stroke. See, also, part 1, §11. n. 5–6.

40. *Darwin and the "Beagle,"* 3 October 1833, p. 208.

41. *Journal of Researches*, 1839, p. 148.

42. Ibid.

43. *Journal of Researches*, 1845, p. 128.

44. *"Beagle" Diary*, 5 October 1833, p. 186.

45. Charles Darwin to Caroline Darwin, Buenos Ayres, 23 October 1833, *Darwin and the "Beagle,"* p. 92.

46. *"Beagle" Diary*, 16 November 1833, p. 192.

47. *Darwin and the "Beagle,"* 16 November 1833, p. 213.

48. *"Beagle" Diary*, 11 January 1834, p. 205. Robert FitzRoy, *Narrative of the Surveying Voyages of his Majesty's Ships "Adventure" and "Beagle,"* between the years 1826 and 1836 (London: Henry Colburn, 1839), 2:319–20.

49. *"Beagle" Diary*, 14 January 1834, p. 206.

50. Charles Darwin to Caroline Darwin, 13 October 1834, *Darwin and the "Beagle,"* pp. 106–7. Although Darwin addressed each of his letters to one member of his Shrewsbury family, his letters were read by all his Shrewsbury family.

51. *"Beagle" Diary*, 26 September 1834, p. 249.

52. Charles Darwin to Caroline Darwin, 13 October 1834, *Darwin and the "Beagle,"* p. 107.

53. See appendix A, *Dr. Robert Darwin's Prescriptions*, pp. 11–12, 22.

54. *Darwin and the "Beagle,"* p. 184.

55. *LL*, 1:198. Sir Arthur Keith thought that this illness may have been typhoid fever (Sir Arthur Keith, *Darwin Revalued* [London, 1955], p. 212). However, in 1834, the prevailing fever of Chile was typhus, not typhoid (Lawrence A. Kohn, "Charles Darwin's Chronic Ill Health," *Bulletin of the History of Medicine*, May–June 1963, p. 253).

56. *"Beagle" Diary*, 26 September 1834, p. 249.

57. Charles Darwin to Caroline Darwin (off Valparaiso), 10 March 1835, *Darwin and the "Beagle,"* p. 115.

58. Caroline Darwin to Charles Darwin, Shrewsbury (30 March 1835), DPL, Box 97.

59. Catherine Darwin to Charles Darwin, Shrewsbury, 28 January (1835), DPL, Box 97.

60. Susan Darwin to Charles Darwin, 16 February 1835, DPL, Box 97; Caroline Darwin to Charles Darwin, Shrewsbury (30 March) 1835, DPL, Box 97.

61. Charles Darwin to Caroline Darwin, Lima (Peru), July 1835, *Darwin and the "Beagle,"* p. 125.

62. Caroline Darwin to Elizabeth Wedgwood (Shrewsbury, 5 October 1836), *CFL*, 1:262.

3   **The Beginning of Chronic Illness**

1. Darwin to Fox, Sunday evening (43 Great Marlborough Street, March 1837), CCDL, *LL*, 1:250.

2. Dr. Frederick Burkhardt, editor of the projected edition of *The Collected Letters of Charles Robert Darwin*, informs me that he has read all of Darwin's extant letters for the nine-month period of October 1836 to July 1837, and that these letters contain no complaints of illness.

3. On 7 October 1836, three days after returning home from the *Beagle*, Darwin weighed 10 stone 8 1/4 pounds [his height was recorded as 5 feet 11 3/8 inches]; on 1 December 1836 he weighed 11 stone 12 pounds on the same scale; and on 29 June 1837, again on the same scale, he weighed 12 stone ½ ounce, a gain of almost 16 pounds in 9 months. (The source for this is a transcript of "Weighing Account Book kept by Dr. Darwin." The transcript is unsigned. I thank Dr. Frederick Burkhardt for informing me of this.)

4. Darwin to Henslow, 36 Great Marlborough Street, Wednesday, 20 September 1837, *Darwin and Henslow*, p. 136.

5. Sir James Clark, 1788–1870. Dr. Clark was well "acquainted with the wealthy part of English society . . . and was especially trusted at the [English] court." He also had critics, and in 1861, when he and Dr. Holland were treating Prince Consort Albert, Lord Clarendon remarked that he "would not trust Sir James Clark and Sir Henry Holland to look after a sick cat." In 1829 Dr. Clark published *The Influence of Climate in the Prevention and Cure of Chronic Disease*. He made no real additions to medical knowledge (*Dictionary of National Biography*; Cecil Woodham-Smith, *Queen Victoria* [New York: Alfred A. Knopf, 1972], p. 426). For more on Clark's book, and the influence of air on disease, see part 1, §5, n. 2–15. The relations between Dr. Clark and Dr. Holland are discussed in John H. Winslow, *Darwin's Victorian Malady* (Philadelphia, 1971), pp. 1–2.

6. Darwin to Henslow, 14 October 1837, *Darwin and Henslow*, p. 140. Four months later Darwin did accept the secretaryship of the Geological Society. He held this position from 16 February 1838 until 19 February 1841 (*Darwin and Henslow*, p. 140, n. 2).

7. Charles Darwin to Mrs. Caroline Wedgwood (London, May ? 1838), DPL.

8. Darwin to Fox, 36 Great Marlborough Street (15 June 1838), CCDL, *LL*, 1:260.

9. Charles Darwin, " 'M' Notebook," published in Gruber and Barrett, *Darwin on Man*, p. 272.

10. Ibid., p. 275.

11. Ibid., p. 276.

12. Ibid., p. 278.

13. Ibid., p. 280.

14. Dr. Sydney Smith, "The Origin of the 'Origin,' " *Impulse*, November 1959, pp. 2–4.

15. The different possible ways of species transport are noted in TN, 1:11–12, 82, 192–93, 220, 248.

16. TN, 1:227.

17. In his first *Transmutation Notebook* he wrote: "Why is life short, why such high object—generation" (TN, 1: 2); "The grand question which every naturalist ought to have before him when dissecting a whale, or classifying a mite, a grampus or an insect is What are the Laws of Life?" (TN, 1: 229).

18. Ibid., p. 228: "My theory would give zest to recent and fossil Comparative Anatomy; it would lead to study of instincts, heredity and mind heredity, whole [of] metaphysics."

19. TN, 2:75.

20. Gruber and Barrett, *Darwin on Man*, pp. 37–42, 479.

21. TN, 2:123.

22. Ibid., p. 202.

23. In his *Autobiography* Darwin wrote as follows about his father: "I do not think that I gained much from him intellectually; but his example ought to have been of much moral service to all his children. One of his golden rules (a hard one to follow) was, 'Never become the friend of any one whom you cannot respect' " (*Autobiography*, p. 42).

24. Leonard G. Wilson, *Charles Lyell: The Years to 1841* (New Haven: Yale University Press, 1972), p. 445. Lyell transcribed a passage from Darwin's letter into one of his notebooks, and it is this transcription which has survived.

25. Ibid., pp. 445–46.

26. *Autobiography*, p. 119.

27. *Darwin's Journal*, p. 8.

28. These notes were hurriedly scrawled in pencil on a piece of paper; they are headed "This is the Question," and are published in Darwin's *Autobiography*, pp. 232–34.

29. TN, 3:175.

30. Emma Wedgwood to Charles Darwin, Maer, Sunday (23 December 1838, postmark Monday, 24 December 1838), RDC.

31. *Darwin's Journal*, p. 9.

32. Emma Wedgwood to Charles Darwin, Maer, Sunday (30 December 1838), RDC.

33. Charles Darwin to Emma Wedgwood, Saturday, Shrewsbury (26 January 1839), CFL, 2:24.

34.   Mrs. Hensleigh Wedgwood to Mrs. Marsh, 4 Clifton Terrace, Notting
Hill, 13 February (1839), *CFL*, 2:34.

35.   *Darwin's Journal*, p. 9.

4   Worsening Illness

1.   Emma was writing to her sister, Mrs. Charlotte Langton, who was
married to Charles Langton.

2.   Emma Darwin to Charlotte Langton, Gower Street, Friday (15 March
1839), *CFL*, 2:38.

3.   Elizabeth Wedgwood (sister of Emma Darwin) to her aunt Madame
Sismondi, Maer, Wednesday, 5 June (1839), *CFL*, 2:42.

4.   Ibid.

5.   *Darwin's Journal*, p. 9.

6.   Darwin to Fox, 12 Upper Gower Street, 24 October (1839), CCDL, *LL*,
1:269–70. Although Darwin would on one occasion move briefly from Down
to London to get a "change of air" (part 1, §8, n. 1–2), he seems to have gone
on believing in the good effects of country air. When he was sixty-eight he
said that a sick relative should come to Down, because "I should think
country air must be better for convalescence" (Charles Darwin to his daughter
Henrietta Litchfield, Down, 4 October [1877], *CFL*, 2:228).

7.   Emma Darwin to her aunt Madame Sismondi, 12 Upper Gower Street, 7
February (1840), *CFL*, 2:51.

8.   Darwin to Lyell, Wednesday morning (February 1840), *LL*, 1:271.

9.   Darwin's library contains the 1839 and 1855 editions of Dr. Holland's
collection of medical essays entitled *Medical Notes and Reflections*. The front
flyleaf of the 1839 volume has the signature, "Charles Darwin 1839." In this
volume the essay "On Hereditary Disease" is heavily marked and annotated
(see part 2, §1, n. 25–27, for a further discussion of these annotations), and
the essay "Effects of Mental Attention on Bodily Organs" is occasionally
marked without comments. There are no marks in the essay "On Diet, and
Disorders of Digestion." In this essay Dr. Holland states that, among the
"tonic medicines" used to treat dyspepsia, iron compounds are "the most
generally beneficial," and he then writes: "The ammoniated iron with an
aloetic medicine, or the sulphate of iron in solution with the sulphate of
magnesia or soda will be found among the most beneficial of these forms; and
applicable in numerous cases, without other difficulty than what may arise
from the patient himself. For the imagination of the dyspeptic, as before
mentioned, is ever awake to discover sensations and draw inferences; the
latter often as much diseased as the feelings which prompt them. His
prejudices, easily excited against any remedies, obtain a sort of countenance,
in the case of steel medicines, from the phrases vaguely applied to them by the
ignorant; and it often needs discretion and firmness in the practitioner to
ensure the persistence in their use which alone can render them of avail"

(Henry Holland, *Medical Notes and Reflections* [London, 1839], pp. 360–61). It is possible that, in February 1840, Dr. Holland tried Darwin on these iron medications. (For more on "Tonics" and iron medications see appendix A: *Dr. Robert Darwin's Prescriptions*, n. 32; and *Charles Darwin's Entries*, n. 39, 40.) Darwin's two editions of Holland's *Medical Notes and Reflections* are kept in the Cambridge University Library.

Darwin's library also has the following books by Holland: *Chapters on Mental Physiology* (London, 1852), also the 1858 edition; *Essays on Scientific and Other Subjects* (London, 1862); and *Recollections of Past Life* (London, 1868).

10.   Emma Darwin to her aunt Madame Sismondi, 12 Upper Gower Street, 10 February (1840), *CFL*, 2:51.

11.   Darwin to Fox (7 July 1840), CCDL.

12.   For the details of this prescription, and for further details on the medical uses of logwood, cinnamon. and potassium bicarbonate, see appendix A, *Dr. Robert Darwin's Prescriptions*, pp. 30, 32, n. 35–37.

13.   Darwin to Fox, 12 Upper Gower Street, Monday (January 1841), CCDL.

14.   *LL*, 1:243.

15.   *Autobiography*, pp. 35–36.

16.   Darwin to Fox, Monday (12 Upper Gower Street, September 1841), CCDL.

17.   Darwin to Fox, 12 Upper Gower Street, Tuesday (28 September 1841), CCDL.

18.   This was an allusion to one of Harry Wedgwood's verses—an epitaph on Darwin's sister Susan Darwin.

Here the bones of Susan lie
She was old and cold and sly.

(*CFL*, 2:70, n.1)

19.   "Knocked up" was Darwin's expression for feelings of anxiety.

20.   Charles Darwin to Emma Darwin (Maer), Monday morning (May 1842).

21.   *Darwin's Journal*, p. 11.

22.   *Autobiography*, p. 98.

23.   *Darwin's Journal*, p. 10.

24.   *Autobiography*, p. 99.

25.   Ibid., p. 98.

26.   Ibid., p. 120.

27.   Ibid., p. 49.

28.   TN, 4:5, part VI.

29.   Charles Darwin, "Observations on the Parallel Roads of Glen Roy, and of other parts of Lochaber in Scotland, with an attempt to prove that they are of marine origin," *Philosophical Transactions* 129 (1839):39–81.

30.   Professor Agassiz, "Discovery of the Former Existence of Glaciers in Scotland, Especially in the Highlands," *The Scotsman*, 7 October 1840.

31.   Thomas F. Jamieson, "On the Parallel Roads of Glen Roy, and their Place in the History of the Glacial Period," *Journal of the Geological Society of London* 19 (1863):240.

32.   In his *Autobiography*, referring to his theory of Glen Roy, Darwin wrote: "My error has been a good lesson to me never to trust in science to the the principle of exclusion" (*Autobiography*, p. 84). See, also, part 1, §4, n. 40–45.

33.   Darwin advanced the idea of a distant creator before his discovery of natural selection, in August 1838 (TN, 3:36–37), and then in 1842, in his first "sketch" of natural selection (Darwin and Wallace, *Evolution by Natural Selection* [Cambridge: Cambridge University Press, 1958], p. 86).

34.   *CFL*, 2:173–74.

35.   Soon after their marriage, Emma wrote her husband a letter expressing her religious belief and her concern over his lack of religious belief. At the end of this letter Darwin wrote: "When I am dead, know that many times, I have kissed and cryed over this. C.D." (*Autobiography*, p. 237).

36.   *"Beagle" Diary*, pp. 24–25, 39–40, 427.

37.   *Darwin and the "Beagle*," p. 163.

38.   Darwin to Fox, 36 Great Marlborough Street, 28 August (1837), The Pearce Collection, Woodward Biomedical Library, University of British Columbia, Vancouver, Canada.

39.   TN, 4:114.

40.   Charles Darwin, *On the Origin of Species* (London: John Murray, 1859), p. 490.

41.   *Autobiography*, p. 91.

42.   Ibid., pp. 138–39.

43.   Darwin to Huxley, Down Farnborough Kent, 29 (October 1854), Huxley Papers, Imperial College of Science and Technology, London; Leonard Huxley, *Life and Letters of Thomas H. Huxley* (New York, 1913), 1:140. In dating this letter I have been guided by Warren R. Dawson, *The Huxley Papers, Descriptive Catalogue of the Correspondence, Manuscripts and Miscellaneous Papers of the Rt. Hon. Thomas Henry Huxley, preserved in the Imperial College of Science and Technology, London* (London: Macmillan Co., 1946), p. 26.

44.   Darwin to Asa Gray, Down Bromley Kent, 23 July (1862), Gray Herbarium of Harvard University, Cambridge; *ML*, 1:202; *Calender of the Letters of Darwin to Gray*, p. 44.

45.   Darwin to Fox (7 July 1840), CCDL.

46.   Darwin to Fox, 12 Upper Gower Street, Monday (January 1841), CCDL.

47.   Ibid., *LL*, 1:271–72.

48. *Autobiography*, p. 99.

5 The Move to Down

1.   Darwin to Fox (7 July 1840), CCDL.

2.   Darwin to Leonard Jenyns, 36 Great Marlborough Street, 10 April 1837, *LL*, 1:253.

3.   Darwin here referred to the words of the English author and journalist William Cobbett (1763–1835): "But what is to be the fate of the great wen of all? The monster, called ... 'the metropolis of the Empire'?"

4.   Darwin to Fox, Tuesday, 12 Upper Gower Street (28 September 1841), CCDL.

5.   *Autobiography*, p. 114.

6.   Darwin to Leonard Jenyns, 36 Great Marlborough Street, 10 April 1837, *LL*, 1:253.

7.   Darwin to Fox, 12 Upper Gower Street, Tuesday (28 September 1841), CCDL.

8.   John H. Winslow, *Darwin's Victorian Malady* (Philadelphia, 1971), p. 2.

9.   Sir James Clark, 4th ed. *The Sanative Influence of Climate* (London: John Murray, 1846), p. 2.

10. Ibid., pp. 3–4.

11. Royston Lambert, *Sir John Simon 1816-1904, and English Social Administration* (London: MacGibbon & Kee, 1963), pp. 61, 125; E. Royston Pike, *Human Documents of the Victorian Golden Age (1850-1875)* (London: George Allen & Unwin, 1974), pp. 297–98; Francis H. W. Sheppard, *London 1808-1870: The Infernal Wen* (London: Martin Secker & Warburg, 1971), p. 16.

12. Emma Darwin to her aunt Madame Sismondi, 12 Upper Gower Street, 2 April (1842), *CFL*, 2:69.

13. Emma Darwin to her aunt Madame Sismondi, 12 Upper Gower Street, 8 February (1842), *CFL*, 2:67.

14. Dr. Erasmus Darwin, *Zoonomia* (London, 1796), 2:674.

15. Dr. Erasmus Darwin, *A Plan for the Conduct of Female Education in Boarding Schools* (Dublin, 1798), p. 98.

16. Charles Darwin to Emma Darwin, at Maer Hall (Shrewsbury, 3 July 1841), *CFL*, 2:60.

17. *CFL*, 2:75.

18. Charles Darwin to his sister Catherine Darwin, Sunday (July 1842), *ML*, 1:33.

19. Ibid., p. 32.

20. Ibid.

21.   Darwin to Fox, Down Bromley Kent, Saturday (28 March 1843), CCDL, *LL*, 1:290.

22.   *Down: The Home of the Darwins*, pp. 25–26.

23.   Sir Joseph Dalton Hooker, 1817–1911.

24.   Darwin to Hooker, Down, Thursday (11 January 1844), *ML*, 1:40–41.

25.   Ernest Jones, *Free Associations: Memoirs of a Psychoanalyst* (New York: Basic Books, 1959), p. 204.

26.   Hooker to Darwin, West Park Kew, 14 September 1845, DPL, Box 100.

27.   Ibid.

28.   Leonard Huxley, *Life and Letters of Sir Joseph Dalton Hooker* (London: John Murray, 1918), 1:194.

29.   Ibid., pp. 29–30.

30.   Ibid., pp. 194–95.

31.   Darwin to Hooker, Down Bromley Kent, 31 March (1845), DPL, Box 114, *LL*, 1:318.

32.   See part 1, §6, n. 41. This seems to be the first time that Darwin definitely mentions that he has stomach illness during the night.

33.   Darwin to Hooker, Friday (29 June 1845), *ML*, 1:408.

34.   Hooker to Darwin, 20 Abercrombie Place (Edinburgh), 3 July 1845, DPL, Box 100.

35.   *LL*, 1:387.

36.   Sir Joseph Hooker, "Reminiscences of Darwin," *Nature*, 22 June 1899, p. 188. (These "Reminiscences" were also published in *The Times*, 15 June 1899.)

37.   Ibid.

38.   Hooker to Darwin, Kew, 26 June 1847, DPL, Box 100.

39.   Darwin to Hooker, Down (October 1846), *LL*, 1:319.

40.   David Milne, "On the Parallel Roads of Lochaber, with Remarks on the Change of Relative Levels of Sea and Land in Scotland, and on the Detrital Deposits in that Country," *Edinburgh Royal Society Transactions* 16 (1849): 395–418.

41.   Darwin to Hooker, Down Farnborough Kent, Sunday (12 September 1847), DPL, Box 114, *LL*, 1:329.

42.   Darwin to Hooker, Down Farnborough Kent, Tuesday evening (6 October 1847), DPL, Box 114.

43.   Martin Rudwick, "Darwin and Glen Roy: A 'Great Failure' in Scientific Method?" *Studies in History and Philosophy of Science* 5 (1974):97–185.

44.   Paul H. Barrett, "Darwin's 'Gigantic Blunder,'" *Journal of Geological Education*, January 1973, pp. 19–28.

45.   Darwin persisted in believing in his marine theory until 1861. In that year Thomas Francis Jamieson went to Glen Roy and then wrote a paper

presenting new evidence that Glen Roy had been formed by Ice Age lakes. He sent his paper to Darwin. After reading this Darwin wrote to Jamieson: "Your arguments seem to me conclusive. I give up the ghost. My paper is one long gigantic blunder.... How rash it is in science to argue because any case is not one thing, it must be some second thing which happens to be known to the writer" (Darwin to Thomas Francis Jamieson, Down Bromley Kent, S.E., 6 September [1861]; *Notes and Records of the Royal Society of London* 14 [June 1959]: 38). Darwin then sent Jamieson's letter to Lyell, along with the following note: "I think the enclosed is worth your reading. I am smashed to atoms about GlenRoy. My paper was one long gigantic blunder from beginning to end. Eheu. Eheu" (Darwin to Lyell, Down Bromley Kent, 6 September [1861], Library American Philosophical Society, Philadelphia; *ML*, 2:188).

46. *Autobiography*, p. 115. Darwin may have exaggerated the severity and frequency of these post-dinner-party vomiting attacks. In his "Diary of Health" he recorded that he gave several "Dinner Parties" without any ill effects.

47. Darwin to Fox, Down Bromley Kent, Saturday (28 March 1843), CCDL, *LL*, 1:291.

48. Francis Darwin, "Reminiscences of my Father's Everyday Life," DPL, Box 140 (3), p. 94.

49. Mudies Library began sending out parcels of books to subscribers in the country in the 1850s. A country subscription cost about five guineas (Amy Cruse, *The Victorians and Their Reading* [Boston: Houghton Mifflin Co., 1962], p. 316).

50. *Autobiography*, p. 138.

51. Francis Darwin, "Reminiscences of my Father's Everyday Life," *LL*, 1:102; *Autobiography*, p. 138.

52. *CFL*, 2:118–19.

53. Francis Darwin, "Reminiscences of my Father's Everyday Life," DPL, Box 140 (3), p. 94.

54. Francis Darwin, "Reminiscences of my Father's Everyday Life," *LL*, 1:100.

55. Ibid., pp. 96–97.

56. This is suggested by Sir Arthur Keith, *Darwin Revalued* (London: Watts & Co., 1955), pp. 231–32.

57. Francis Darwin, "Reminiscences of my Father's Everyday Life," DPL, Box 140 (3), p. 23.

58. Darwin to Asa Gray, Down Bromley Kent, 23 February (1863), Gray Herbarium of Harvard University, Cambridge; *LL*, 2:196. *Calender of the Letters of Darwin to Gray*, pp. 49–50.

59. Francis Darwin, "Reminiscences of my Father's Everyday Life," *LL*,

1:90–91, 93–94, 100; George H. Darwin, "Recollections of my Father," DPL, Box 112, p. 12.

60. Gruber and Barrett, *Darwin on Man*, p. 272. My italics.

61. "Perceiving myself skipping when wanting not to feel angry—Such efforts prevent anger, but observing eyes thus unconsciously discover struggle of feeling. It is as much effort to walk then lightly as to endeavour to stop heart beating: on ceasing so does other" (Gruber and Barrett, *Darwin on Man*, p. 278).

62. Darwin to Asa Gray, Down Beckenham Kent, 28 January 1876, Gray Herbarium of Harvard University, Cambridge; *CFL*, 2:221; *Calender of the Letters of Darwin to Gray*, p. 63.

63. Francis Darwin, "Reminiscences of my Father's Everyday Life," DPL, Box 140 (3), p. 32.

64. *CFL*, 2:221.

65. George H. Darwin, "Recollections of my Father," DPL, Box 112, p. 33; Francis Darwin, "Reminiscences of my Father's Everyday Life," DPL, Box 140 (3), p. 32.

66. Francis Darwin, "Reminiscences of my Father's Everyday Life," *LL*, 1:115.

67. Ibid., pp. 103–4.

68. *Autobiography*, p. 138.

69. Leonard Darwin, "Memories of Down House," *The Nineteenth Century and After* 106 (July–December 1929): 120.

70. Francis Darwin, "Reminiscences of my Father's Everyday Life," *LL*, 1:101.

71. Francis Darwin, "Reminiscences of my Father's Everyday Life," DPL, Box 140 (3), pp. 30, 37.

72. Emma Brace, ed., *The Life of Charles Loring Brace, Chiefly Told in His Own Letters* (New York: Charles Scribner's Sons, 1894), p. 320.

73. Francis Darwin, "Reminiscences of my Father's Everyday Life," *LL*, 1:89.

74. Emma Brace, ed., *The Life of Charles Loring Brace, Chiefly Told in His Own Letters* (New York: Charles Scribner's Sons, 1894), p. 320.

75. Thomas W. Higginson, *Cheerful Yesterdays* (New York: Houghton Mifflin, 1901), p. 284.

76. Mrs. Jane Loring Gray to her sister Mrs. Susan Loring Jackson, Down, 28 October 1868; Gray Herbarium of Harvard University, Cambridge.

77. Darwin began sitting in a "high chair . . . supported on a high stool" in the 1840s and kept this up for the rest of his life (*LL*, 1:388).

78. Darwin to J. M. Herbert, Down (1844 or 1845), *LL*, 1:303.

79. Darwin to Mrs. Haliburton, Down, 1 November (1872), *LL*, 2:352.

80. Darwin to J. M. Herbert, Down (1844 or 1845), *LL*, 1:303.

81. Darwin to Fox, Down Bromley Kent, Thursday (14 February 1845), CCDL.

6 The Death of Dr. Darwin, Dr. Gully's Hydropathy

1. "Mr. Cottrell" is probably an error (perhaps made by Darwin, who sometimes misspelled the name of a new person, or by the copyist of this letter, who sometimes had difficulty in transcribing Darwin's handwriting) for Mr. Edgar Cockell. Mr. Cockell became a member of the Royal College of Surgeons in 1808, and moved from London to Downe in 1840.

2. Mr. Edward Cresy (1792–1858) was an architect and civil engineer who became Darwin's friend when the latter settled at Down (*ML*, 1:58, n. 1; Edward Cresy in *Dictionary of National Biography*).

3. Charles Darwin to Catherine Darwin, Friday (16 September 1842), DPL, Box 153–54. This letter begins as follows: "Everything has gone on prosperously. Emma seems to like the place, and Doddy [Darwin's son William] was in ecstasies for two whole days. Weather has been very good and I have stood work perfectly. Tomorrow I go." The contents of the letter indicate that Darwin was just settling at Down. Since *Darwin's Journal* states that Emma moved to Down on (Wednesday) 14 September 1842, and that Darwin moved three days later on (Saturday) 17 September, and since the letter is dated "Friday," it seems likely that this letter was written on Friday, 16 September 1842. This letter exists in the form of a copy.

4. In 1843, when Darwin's son William was ill, Dr. Robert Darwin advised that Mr. Cockell should *"not"* be consulted (appendix A, *Dr. Robert Darwin's Prescriptions*, p. 21).

5. *CFL*, 2:118, n. 2.

6. Charles Darwin to Catherine Darwin, Friday (16 September 1842).

7. At this time Darwin had no paying job, and received no money from his publications; his sources of income were money and stocks given him by his father—in 1837 his father had assured him an annual income of almost £400—and (perhaps) money and stocks given him by his uncle and father-in-law Josiah Wedgwood of Maer (Sir Arthur Keith, *Darwin Revalued* [London: Watts & Co., 1955], pp. 221–32). Darwin was anxious about spending money and paying bills, and he seems to have informed his father of most of his expenditures.

8. Charles Darwin to Catherine Darwin, Friday (16 September 1842).

9. See appendix A, *Dr. Robert Darwin's Prescriptions*, pp. 6–16, 20–22.

10. Charles Darwin to Susan Darwin, Wednesday (1844–45), DPL, Box 153–54. In this letter Darwin writes: "I believe I had better come into the Lincolnshire plan.—I keep quite of opinion that it is very advisable to have

part of one's property in land." In a February 1845 letter to Fox, Darwin writes: "The one other piece of news about myself is that I have turned into ["a" inserted] Lincolnshire Squire! My Father having invested for me in a Farm of 324 acres of good land near Alford" (Darwin to Fox, Down Bromley Kent, Thursday [(14 February 1845), CCDL]). Hence it seems likely that Darwin's letter to Susan was written just before the purchase of the Lincolnshire farm, in late 1844 or early 1845.

11.   J. F. Royle and F. W. Headland, *A Manual of Materia Medica and Therapeutics*, 4th ed. (London: John Churchill, 1865), p. 602. "Bitters" were substances which were bitter to the taste—this was held to be due to an inherent "bitter principle"—and which were thought to act as "tonics" (appendix A, *Charles Darwin's Entries*, n. 39) by giving a "salutary" stimulation to the stomach and system in general (J. A. Paris, *Pharmacologia* [New York, 1825], 1:106–9). There was a variance of medical opinion about the use of bitters in dyspepsia. Dr. Holland held that their use had been "too large and indiscriminate," and that "there are various states of stomach in which the ordinary doses and strength of bitter infusions are injurious; while obvious good is got from a more moderate employment of the same means... the best mode of using bitters is in direct combination with the aperient which may be necessary. Thereby a smaller quantity of the latter is usually rendered effectual; and the noxious effects of repetition materially abated" (Henry Holland, *Medical Notes and Reflections* [London, 1840], pp. 378–79). Dr. Brinton would write that "the various vegetable bitters claim peculiar notice ... because their effects [in dyspepsia] are more uniform and beneficial than those of most other medicines ... most of them increase the appetite ... their prolonged use produces such invigorating effects on the constitution, as to almost suggest some definite chemical purpose being subserved by their addition to the constituents of the organism, beyond any merely alternative effect" (William Brinton, *The Diseases of the Stomach* [London: John Churchill, 1859], pp. 385–86).

12.   *Darwin and the "Beagle,"* p. 252.

13.   F. W. Headland, *The Action of Medicines in the System* (London: John Churchill, 1852), p. 107.

14.   Francis Darwin, "Reminiscences of my Father's Everyday Life," *LL*, 1:96.

15.   Charles Darwin to Susan Darwin, Down, Wednesday, 3 September (1845), DPL, Box 153–54. (This letter exists in the form of a copy. It is published in part, with omission of the medical passage quoted here, in *CFL*, 2:96–97.)

16.   J. F. Royle and F. W. Headland, *A Manual of Materia Medica and Therapeutics*, 4th ed. (London: John Churchill, 1865), p. 186. "Bismuth, some of the effects of which may perhaps be regarded as tonic, is still more useful as a remedy against that form of dyspepsia which constitutes the 'morbid sensibility of the stomach' specified by older writers. Here its effects in allaying flatulence and nausea, and in preventing vomiting, and (still more) in

checking the pain produced by food, are so marked, that we may fairly accept the term of sedative often applied to it" (William Brinton, *The Diseases of the Stomach* [London: John Churchill, 1859], p. 388).

17.   "My father says that Susan . . . was enthusiastic in her admiration of you, in which you know how my father joins. I did not require to be reminded how well, my own dear wife, you have borne your dull life with your poor old sickly complaining husband" (Charles Darwin to Emma Darwin, Sunday [Shrewsbury, October 1844], *CFL*, 2:92).

18.   Charles Darwin to Emma Darwin in London, Wednesday (Shrewsbury, probably October 1843), *CFL*, 2:87.

19.   Darwin to Hooker, Down, Thursday, 27 (September 1865), *LL*, 2:224.

20.   "My visit to Shrewsbury was rather a melancholy one, for though I found my Father better, he is much changed bodily during the last six months" (Darwin to Lyell, Down Farnborough Kent, Sunday [7 March 1847], Library American Philosophical Society, Philadelphia; published in part, with omission of the sentence about Dr. Robert Darwin, in *LL*, 1:329–30).

21.   Charles Darwin to Emma Darwin, Saturday (Shrewsbury, probably 20 May 1848), *CFL*, 2:116–17.

22.   Charles Darwin to Emma Darwin, Monday (Shrewsbury, 22 May 1848), *CFL*, 2:117.

23.   Charles Darwin to Emma Darwin, Thursday (Shrewsbury, probably 25 May 1848), *CFL*, 2:118.

24.   Charles Darwin to Emma Darwin, Saturday (postmark 27 May 1848), *CFL*, 2:119.

25.   See part 1, §15.

26.   *Darwin's Journal*, p. 12.

27.   This passage has been transcribed from the manuscript of *Darwin's Journal*, kept in RDC.

28.   Darwin to Sir John Herschel, The Lodge, Malvern, 13 June (1849), *Notes and Records of the Royal Society of London* 14 (June 1959):34.

29.   Darwin to Hooker, Down Farnborough Kent, The Lodge, Malvern, 28 March 1849, DPL, Box 114, *LL*, 1:340.

30.   Darwin to Fox, 24 (March 1849), The Lodge, Malvern, CCDL.

31.   Darwin to Henslow, The Lodge, Malvern, 6 May 1849, *Darwin and Henslow*, p. 163.

32.   Darwin to Hooker, Down Farnborough Kent, 12 October 1849, DPL, Box 114, *LL*, 1:347.

33.   Darwin to Hooker, Down Farnborough Kent, The Lodge, Malvern, 28 March 1849, DPL, Box 114, *LL*, 1:340.

34.   Ibid.

35.   Francis Darwin was born 16 August 1848.

36. *Darwin's Journal*, p. 12.

37. B. J. Sullivan to J. D. Hooker, n.d. (probably, from internal evidence, written in 1882 soon after the death of Charles Darwin), DPL, Box 106/7.

38. *The Rise and Progress of Hydropathy*, chap. 5; "Dr. James Gully," in *Dictionary of National Biography*.

39. James Manby Gully, *The Water Cure in Chronic Disease: An Exposition of the Causes, Progress and Terminations of Various Chronic Diseases of the Digestive Organs, Lungs, Nerves, Limbs, and Skin; and of Their Treatment by Water and Other Hygienic Means* (New York: Wiley & Putnam, 1847), hereafter cited as *The Water Cure*.

40. B. J. Sullivan to J. D. Hooker, n.d., DPL, Box 106/7.

41. *Darwin's Journal*, p. 12.

42. *Autobiography*, p. 117.

43. Darwin to Hooker, Down Farnborough Kent, The Lodge, Malvern, 28 March 1849, DPL, Box 114, *LL*, 1:340.

44. Charles Darwin to Susan Darwin, Malvern, Monday, 19 March 1849, DPL.

45. Darwin to Fox, Down Farnborough Kent, 6 February (1849), CCDL.

46. Darwin's library does not contain *The Water Cure*; however, in the above letter to Fox he writes: "I must get Gully's Book." About a month later Emma wrote Fox: "Dr. Gully writes like a sensible man & does not speak very confidently" (Emma Darwin to Fox, Down Bromley Kent, Tuesday [March 1849], CCDL). Darwin then wrote Hooker: "I got Dr. Gully's book & made further enqueries" (Darwin to Hooker, Down Farnborough Kent, The Lodge, Malvern, 28 March 1849, DPL, Box 114, *LL*, 1:340).

47. *The Water Cure*, part 11, "Of Particular Chronic Diseases, and Their Treatment"; chap. 1, "Diseases of the Primary Nutritive Organs"; §1, "Mucous and Nervous Indigestion," pp. 68–88.

48. Ibid., pp. 84–86.

49. Ibid., pp. 93–94.

50. Ibid., pp. 99–109.

51. Ibid., p. 87.

52. From the biography of Dr. Gully in *Dictionary of National Biography*.

53. *The Water Cure*, p. 109.

54. *Darwin's Journal*, p. 12.

55. Two weeks after settling at Malvern, Darwin wrote Fox: "We came here this day fortnight & have got a very comfortable house, with a little field & wood opening on to the mountain, capital for the children to play in." At the end of the letter he added: "Have you ever been here? It is a curious & nice place & in summer must be very pretty; we have had half our time foggy or hazy, but most fortunate in not having had any rain" (Darwin to Fox,

The Lodge, Malvern, 24 [March 1849], CCDL).

56. The Hydropathy Establishment at Malvern consisted of two embattled buildings, the Tudor House and the Holyrood House, connected by a "Bridge of Sighs." Men and women patients may have been treated in different houses. I thank Mr. Gerald Morice, journalist and historian of Malvern, for informing me of the history of hydropathy in Malvern.

57. Dr. Gully was at the University of Edinburgh, as an undergraduate in medicine, from 1825 to 1828; Darwin was at the University of Edinburgh, as an undergraduate in medicine, from October 1825 until the spring of 1827. Neither man seems to have commented on this coincidence.

58. Charles Darwin to Emma Darwin in London, Wednesday (Shrewsbury, probably October 1843), *CFL*, 2:87.

59. Charles Darwin to Susan Darwin, Malvern, Monday, 19 March 1849, DPL. It has been said of Dr. Gully by one who knew him: "As a doctor, no one ever consulted Dr. Gully without feeling himself in the grasp of a master mind. His profoundness, penetration, and resources were remarkable, and such as none could forget who ever consulted him. His was a deeply philosophical as well as a medical mind, and it was the innate feeling of his profoundness and might that gave Dr. Gully such power of fascination over patients. At the sick bed his presence always gave relief and assurance. None could ever look into his ruddy face, mostly lighted up with a smile, and not debit the consciousness that he was equal to the emergency, however great it might be" (*The Rise and Progress of Hydropathy*, pp. 73–74).

60. Charles Darwin to Susan Darwin, Malvern, Monday, 19 March 1849, DPL.

61. Ibid.

62. Darwin to Fox, The Lodge, Malvern, 24 (March 1849), CCDL.

63. *The Water Cure*, p. 86.

64. Darwin to Sir John Herschel, The Lodge, Malvern, 13 June (1849), *Notes and Records of the Royal Society of London* 14 (June 1959):34.

65. Darwin to Fox, The Lodge, Malvern, 18 April (1849), CCDL.

66. Darwin to Fox, Down Farnborough Kent, Saturday, 7 July 1849, CCDL.

67. Ibid.

68. Charles Darwin to Susan Darwin, Malvern, Monday, 19 March 1849, DPL.

7 Self-Observation and Self-Treatment

1. George H. Darwin, "Recollections of my Father," DPL, Box 112, pp. 13–14, 30; Francis Darwin, "Reminiscences of my Father's Everyday Life," *LL*, 1:90–91.

2. Darwin to Fox, Down Farnborough Kent, Saturday, 7 July 1849, CCDL.

3. Ibid.

4. George H. Darwin, "Recollections of my Father," DPL, Box 112, p. 12.

5. Sir Buckston Browne writes that "in a curtained corner of his study at Down House he [Darwin] kept a large shallow tin bath, and in the diary 'douches' and 'double douches' are mentioned" (Sir Buckston Browne, "Darwin's Health," *Nature*, 2 January 1943, p. 14). The present-day visitor to Down House is shown, in Darwin's study, this curtained-off corner and bath, where (it is said) Darwin took his douches.

6. Francis Darwin, "Reminiscences of my Father's Everyday Life," *LL*, 1:108.

7. The *Diary of Health* has been partly described, first very briefly by Sir Buckston Browne, "Darwin's Health," *Nature*, 2 January 1943, pp. 14–15, and then in more detail by W. D. Foster, "A Contribution to the Problem of Darwin's Ill-Health," *Bulletin of the History of Medicine* 39 (1965):476–78. Dr. Foster also quotes from the *Diary* in *Isis* 63 (1972): 592. I wish to thank Miss Jessie Dobson, former curator of the Hunterian Museum, Royal College of Surgeons of England, London, for sending me a copy of the *Diary*. I also thank the Royal College of Surgeons of England, and Sir Hedley Atkins, for giving me permission to quote from the *Diary*.

8. Darwin to Fox, Down Farnborough Kent, Thursday (May 1850), CCDL.

9. Shown by the entries in his *Diary of Health*.

10. Darwin to Fox, Down Farnborough Kent, Saturday, 7 July 1849, CCDL.

11. Darwin to Fox, Down Farnborough Kent, Thursday (May 1850), CCDL.

12. *Diary of Health*.

13. Darwin to Fox, Down Farnborough Kent, Thursday (May 1850), CCDL.

14. Ibid.

15. Darwin to Fox, Down Farnborough Kent, 4 September (1850), CCDL.

16. Ibid., printed with some omissions in *LL*, 1:341.

17. George H. Darwin, "Recollections of my Father," DPL, Box 112, p. 49. Darwin's consultation with the clairvoyant took place at Malvern, March–April 1851.

18. Francis Darwin, "Reminiscences of my Father's Everyday Life," DPL, Box 140 (3), p. 85.

19. George H. Darwin, "Recollections of my Father," DPL, Box 112, p. 49.

20. Francis Darwin, "Reminiscences of my Father's Everyday Life," DPL, Box 140 (3), p. 85.

21. *CFL*, 2:132–40.

22. Darwin to Fox, Down Farnborough Kent, 7 March (1852), CCDL, *LL*, 1:349.

23. Tartar emetic ointment, when applied locally, was an irritant which produced vesicles and pustules. It was used as a "counterirritant" in chronic

diseases of the chest and joints (J. F. Royle and F. W. Headland, *A Manual of Materia Medica and Therapeutics* [London: John Churchill, 1865], p. 195; J. A. Paris, *Pharmacologia* [New York, 1825], 2:53–54).

24.   J. F. Royle and F. W. Headland, *A Manual of Materia Medica and Therapeutics* (London: John Churchill, 1865), pp. 586–87.

25.   Tea and coffee were both held to be cerebral stimulants and anti-soporifics. It was also held that they were "sedatives" and that they relieved the "stupor" caused by stimulants or the "drowsiness of fatigue," by counter-acting the plethoric state of the brain, and thus restoring the brain to its normal state (J. F. Royle and F. W. Headland, *A Manual of Materia Medica and Therapeutics* [London: John Churchill, 1865], pp. 321, 460).

26.   Lemon juice was used as a refrigerant, antalkaline, antiscorbutic, and was recommended in rheumatism (J. F. Royle and F. W. Headland, *A Manual of Materia Medica and Therapeutics* [London: John Churchill, 1865], p. 326).

27.   Aloes was the inspissated juice from the leaves of different species of the *Aloe* plant. This juice in small doses was a tonic, in larger doses a cathartic (J. F. Royle and F. W. Headland, *A Manual of Materia Medica and Therapeutics* [London: John Churchill, 1865], pp. 630–34).

28.   *Medical Times & Gazette*, 10 May 1856, p. 464; *The Medical List, or English Medical Directory, for 1857*, pp. 488–89.

29.   *Association Medical Journal*, 15 March 1856, p. 214. The electric chain was used in England in the 1850s and 1860s. In 1866 it was recommended by a group of distinguished London medical authorities, including Sir Henry Holland. In 1867, however, Dr. Julius Althaus stated that the current generated by the chains was "liable to great and sudden variations within a short time," that the chains caused sloughs and cicatrices, and that they "may aggravate the disorder for the relief of which they were brought into play" (Hector A. Colwell, *An Essay on the History of Electrotherapy and Diagnosis* [London, 1922], pp. 104–5).

In 1871 Darwin read an account by a man which claimed beneficial actions for electric chains. In a letter to an acquaintance Darwin then commented on these claims as follows: "Have you heard any credible account of good being derived in dyspeptic & nervous weakness from 'Pulver [Maclers?] Volta-Electric Chain bands': I see he quotes Sir C. Locock, H. Holland, Ferguson &c. &c.—Are all the statements quackery & lies, or c^d it be worth my trying as an experiment?" (Darwin to an unidentified individual, Down, 2 June [1871], Library American Philosophical Society, Philadelphia; mentioned in P. Thomas Carroll, *An Annotated Calender of the Letters of Charles Darwin in the Library of the American Philosophical Society* [Wilmington, Del.: Scholarly Resources Inc., 1976], letter 398, pp. 145–46). It is not known whether Darwin again tried using electric chains.

30.   James Copeland, *A Dictionary of Practical Medicine* (London, 1858), 1:1043.

31. Ibid., p. 1044.

32. Ibid., p. 1043.

33. Ibid., p. 1044.

34. "Darwin's Medical Notes, 1865 May 20," part 1, §12, n. 20.

35. Darwin's 27 May 1848 letter to Emma, part 1, §6.

36. See the observations of Dr. Edward Lane, part 1, §8, n. 61.

37. This probably refers to the type of gastric discomfort which was felt after excessive drinking.

38. On 20 April 1853, however, Darwin wrote in his *Diary of Health* that he had a cold with mild fever and "chest-pain." This only lasted one day.

39. Darwin noted these three conditions in his *Diary of Health* on three different days in July 1853.

40. *The English Dialect Dictionary* (London, 1902) has the following definitions of "Heaze": "To breathe thickly and with difficulty, to wheeze; to cough or 'hawk.' " "As cattle when they clear the windpipe, or force up phlegm." "*Heazy*, adj. hoarse breathing with difficulty, wheezing; *fig.* creaking."

41. Darwin to Fox, Down Farnborough Kent, 7 March (1852), CCDL, *LL*, 1:349.

42. Francis Darwin, "Reminiscences of my Father's Everyday Life," *LL*, 1:102.

43. *LL*, 2:236–38. This contains the recollections of Darwin's son William, and his friends George John Romanes and the Reverend J. Brodie Innes, of how Darwin could not sleep because of conversations he had with them during the day or evening. The recollection of Innes—who was the vicar of Downe—was as follows: "On one occasion, when a parish meeting had been held on some disputed point of no great importance, I was surprised by a visit from Mr. Darwin at night. He came to say that, thinking over the debate, though what he had said was quite accurate, he thought I might have drawn an erroneous conclusion, and he would not sleep till he had explained it." The subject that Darwin was worried about is unknown (*LL*, 2: 237).

44. Charles Darwin, *The Expression of the Emotions in Man and Animals* (New York: Philosophical Library, 1955), p. 33.

45. Darwin to Henslow, Down Farnborough Kent, Wednesday (after 21 September 1849, when Darwin returned from Birmingham), *Darwin and Henslow*, p. 165.

46. Ibid.

47. *Diary of Health*, 23 September 1949.

48. Darwin to Henslow, Down Farnborough Kent, Wednesday (after 21 September 1849, when Darwin returned from Birmingham), *Darwin and Henslow*, p. 165.

49. Darwin to Fox, Down Farnborough Kent, 4 September (1850).

50. Ibid. The Bruce Castle School followed the liberal utilitarian philosophy of Jeremy Bentham and James Mill, and had its students learn science, do much reading on their own, and apply what they had learned to the conduct of their life (J. L. Dobson, "The Hill Family and Educational Change in the Early Nineteenth Century: III. The Bruce Castle School at Tottenham and the Hill's Part in the Work of the Society for the Diffusion of Useful Knowledge," *Durham Research Review* 3 [September 1961]:74–84).

51. Cecil Woodham-Smith, *Queen Victoria* (New York, 1972), p. 317.

52. *CFL*, 2:142.

53. In a May 1854 letter to Hooker, Darwin wrote: "The last grand thing we were at together answered, I am sure, very well, & that was the Duke's Funeral" (Darwin to Hooker, Down Farnborough Kent, 29 [May 1854], DPL, Box 114, *ML*, 1:78).

54. "Everyone from the Queen to the costermonger, went to Chelsea. They assembled in vast crowds before the Hospital was open. On the privileged day thousands failed to gain admission; on the first public day there was a stampede in which two people were killed and dozens injured. The rain fell in torrents, and the crowds went dripping through the glittering darkness to the catafalque they had waited so long to see" (Jan K. Fletcher, *Splendid Occasions in English History 1520–1947* [London, 1951], p. 92).

55. The *Diary of Health* has the following entries for 1853: 4 June: "Well very got much ft. Crystal Palace"; 22 September: "Well very several fits & headache from Crystal Palace."

56. John Fortescue, *History of the British Army* (London: Macmillan Co., 1930), 13:30.

57. *CFL*, 2:154.

58. George H. Darwin, "Recollections of my Father," DPL, Box 112, p. 13.

59. On 29 May Darwin wrote Hooker that he and Emma "in a very profligate manner have just taken a pair of season-tickets to see the Queen open the Crystal Palace" (Darwin to Hooker, Down Farnborough Kent, 29 [May 1854], DPL, Box 114, *ML*, 1:78). Sydenham was about ten miles north of Down and had a special railway station. It is not known how—whether by train or coach—the Darwins traveled to Sydenham.

60. Charles Darwin to his son William Darwin, Down, Wednesday (1854), DPL, Box 153.

61. There were two houses at Hartfield, Sussex, which were about a quarter of a mile apart, and which the Darwins visited: Hartfield Grove, home of Charles Langton and his wife Charlotte Wedgwood, who was Darwin's sister-in-law; and The Ridge, home of Sarah Elizabeth Wedgwood, Darwin's maternal cousin (*CFL*, 2:106).

62. *CFL*, 2:155. George H. Darwin, "Recollections of my Father," DPL, Box 112, p. 13.

63. The *Diary of Health* shows that when Darwin visited Hartfield in October 1850 he had "excessive" flatulence.

64. This was especially so in Darwin's later years (see part 2, §7, n. 3).

65. Darwin to Fox, Down Farnborough Kent, 7 March (1852), CCDL, *LL*, 1:349.

66. Darwin to Fox, Down Farnborough Kent, 24 (October 1852), CCDL.

67. *Autobiography*, p. 144.

68. In the *Diary of Health* there are the following entries: 15 May 1853: "Well *very* yet poorly with small Boil"; night "heazish goodish." 30 March 1854: "Very Poorly much vomiting Bad Boil"; night "bad." On 31 March 1854 the "boil broke," but for several days he continued to feel "poorly" and to be "sick."

69. On 2 July 1854 Darwin wrote Hooker: "I have had the house full of visitors, & when I talk I can do absolutely nothing else; & since then I have been poorly enough, otherwise I sh^d. have answered your letter long before this, for I enjoy extremely discussing such points, as those in your last note. But what a villain you are to heap gratuitous insults on my *elastic* theory; you might as well call the virtue of a lady *elastic*, as the virtue of a theory accomodating in its favours. Whatever you may say, I feel that my theory does give me some advantages in discussing these points." He then discusses his ideas of "highness" and "lowness" in species—he had, apparently, exchanged several letters with Hooker on this subject—and he answered some criticisms of Hooker, and then he wrote: "This note is even feebler than my last, for I feel deadly sick" (Darwin to Hooker, Down, 2 July [1854], DPL, Box 114, published in part in *ML*, 1: 76–77).

70. Darwin to Fox, Down Farnborough Kent, 7 March (1852), CCDL, *LL*, 1:349.

71. Darwin to Syms Covington, Down Farnborough Kent, 23 November 1850, *Notes and Records of the Royal Society of London* (June 1959):20.

72. Darwin to Hooker, Down Farnborough Kent, 29 (May 1854), DPL, Box 114, *ML*, 1:78–79.

73. He did not, however, become as extremely obese as his father.

74. Francis Darwin, "Reminiscences of my Father's Everyday Life," *LL*, 1:122–23.

75. Francis Darwin, "Reminiscences of my Father's Everyday Life," DPL, Box 140 (3), p. 41, *LL*, 1:10.

76. *LL*, 1:10.

77. In the 1850s Syms Covington, Darwin's ex-*Beagle* servant who was then living in Australia, wrote Darwin that he was deaf and considering treatment by an aurist. In his letter of reply Darwin wrote: "As to the Aurist, you may rely on it that the man is advertising humbug. I know plenty of people and have one relation, very deaf, and every one in London would know about this

man's power of curing if true. You may depend on it that besides syringing in certain cases there is little or nothing to be done. My father, who was a very wise man, said he had known numbers who had been much injured by Aurists, and none who had been benefited. A common good surgeon can do all that these humbugs can do. I am very sorry to hear about your deafness increasing, it is a very great misfortune for you, but I fear you must look at it as incurable" (Darwin to Syms Covington, Down Bromley Kent, 16 January 1859, *Notes and Records of the Royal Society of London* 14 [June 1959]:27). George John Romanes, who knew Darwin during the last seven years of the latter's life, recollected that Darwin told him the following "little anecdote" about Dr. Robert Darwin: "For the benefit of the district in which he lived Dr. Darwin offered to dispense medicines *gratis* to any one who applied and was not able to pay. He was surprised to find that very few of the sick poor availed themselves of his offer, and guessing that the reason must have been a dislike to becoming the recipients of charity, he devised a plan to neutralise this feeling. Whenever any poor persons applied for medical aid, he told them that he would supply the medicine, but that they must pay for the bottles. This little distinction made all the difference, and ever afterwards the poor used to flock to the doctor's house for relief as a matter of right" (*Charles Darwin: Memorial Notices Reprinted from "Nature"* [London: Macmillan and Co., 1882], pp. 10–11).

8   Dr. Lane and Moor Park

1.   Darwin to Fox, Down Farnborough Kent, 19 March (1855), CCDL, *LL*, 1: 407.

2.   Appendix A, *Dr. Robert Darwin's Prescriptions*, p. 9.

3.   *Darwin's Journal*, p. 14.

4.   Ibid., pp. 13–14.

5.   Darwin to Hooker, Down, 15 (1855), DPL, Box 114, *LL*, 1:415–16.

6.   Darwin to Fox, Down Farnborough Kent, 7 May (1855), CCDL, *LL*, 1:416, n.

7.   Darwin to Fox, Down Farnborough Kent, 17 May, *LL*, 1:413.

8.   *Darwin's Journal*, p. 13.

9.   Darwin to Fox, Down Farnborough Kent, 27 March (1855), CCDL, *LL*, 1:409.

10.   Darwin to Hooker, Down Farnborough Kent, 26 March (1854), DPL, Box 114, *LL*, 1:404.

11.   Darwin to Hooker, Down (1855), *ML*, 1:85.

12.   Milton Millhauser, *Just before Darwin: Robert Chambers and "Vestiges"* (Middletown, Conn.: Wesleyan University Press, 1959), p. 4.

13.   Darwin to Fox, Down Bromley Kent, 8 (June 1856), The Pearce Collection, Woodward Biomedical Library, the University of British Co-

lumbia, Vancouver, Canada. Published in Leonard G. Wilson, *Sir Charles Lyell's Scientific Journals on the Species Question* (New Haven: Yale University Press, 1970), p. xlviii. See also, *Darwin's Journal*, p. 14.

14.   Leonard G. Wilson, *Sir Charles Lyell's Scientific Journals on the Species Question* (New Haven: Yale University Press, 1970), p. xlvii.

15.   Robert C. Stauffer, ed., *Charles Darwin's Natural Selection: Being the Second Part of His Big Species Book Written from 1856 to 1858* (Cambridge: Cambridge University Press, 1975), p. 8.

16.   Ibid., p. 10.

17.   Ibid., pp. 8–9. This is a quotation from a letter of Darwin to Lyell, written 8 July 1856.

18.   Darwin to Fox, Down Bromley Kent, 8 (June 1856), The Pearce Collection, Woodward Biomedical Library, the University of British Columbia, Vancouver, Canada. Published in Leonard G. Wilson, *Sir Charles Lyell's Scientific Journals on the Species Question* (New Haven: Yale University Press, 1970), p. xlviii.

19.   Darwin to Hooker, Down, 13 July (1856), DPL, Box 114, *ML*, 1:94.

20.   Darwin to Asa Gray, Down, 20 July (1856), *LL*, 1:437; *Calender of the Letters of Darwin to Gray*, pp. 6–8.

21.   Darwin to Hooker, Down Bromley Kent, 14 July (1857?), DPL, Box 114, *LL*, 1:461.

22.   Darwin to Fox, Down Bromley Kent, 3 October (1856), CCDL, *LL*, 1:443.

23.   Darwin to Hooker, Down Bromley Kent, 10 December (1856), DPL, Box 114, *ML*, 1:441.

24.   Darwin to Hooker, Down Bromley Kent, Sunday (October 1856), DPL, Box 114, *LL*, 1:444.

25.   Darwin to Hooker, Moor Park, Farnham, Surrey, Wednesday (29 April 1857), DPL, Box 114, *LL*, 1:450. In *"Life and Letters"* this letter is dated "April (?)" In the letter Darwin infers that this is his first visit to Moor Park, and he states that he has been at Moor Park "for a week." *Darwin's Journal* records that he left Down for Moor Park on 22 April, and returned to Down on 6 May 1857. The letter is clearly dated "Wednesday," and in 1857 Wednesday was on 22 and 29 April. Hence it seems likely that this letter was written on Wednesday, 29 April 1857.

26.   Darwin to Hooker, Down Bromley Kent, 10 December (1856), DPL, Box 114, *ML*, 1:441.

27.   Darwin to Hooker, Down Bromley Kent, 20 January (1857), DPL, Box 114, *LL*, 1:416, n.

28.   Michael T. Ghiselin has evaluated Darwin's work on the geographical distribution of species as follows: "Darwin, in seeing the connection between dispersal mechanism, barriers, and patterns of distribution, had discovered

the definitive evidence for evolution. Nobody had done this before.... Those who seek to deny Darwin credit as the founder of the theory of evolution, on the grounds that others had previously thought of evolution or argued for it, misconstrue the nature of scientific innovation. Before Darwin, evolution was a mere speculation, one which could be invoked to explain some facts but which was unsupported by any truly critical tests. With Darwin's bio-geographical synthesis, evolution became an integral part of a compelling system of explanatory theory" (Michael T. Ghiselin, *The Triumph of the Darwinian Method* [Berkeley and Los Angeles: University of California Press, 1969], p. 38).

29.   Darwin to Fox, Down Farnborough Kent, 7 March (1852), CCDL, *LL*, 1: 350.

30.   Darwin to Fox, 13 Sea House, Eastbourne, 15? or 16? 17? or ? July (1853), CCDL, *LL*, 1:354. "Bugbear" was "a sort of hobgoblin (? in the shape of a bear) supposed to devour naughty children." Also "an object of (needless) dread; an imaginary terror" (*Shorter Oxford English Dictionary*).

31.   Darwin to Fox, Down Farnborough Kent, 7 March (1853), CCDL, *LL*, 1:350.

32.   Darwin to Fox, Down Farnborough Kent, 7 March (1852), CCDL, *LL*, 1:350. For a further discussion of Darwin's views on the inheritance of illness see part 2, §1.

33.   Darwin to Hooker, Down Bromley Kent, 3 September (1857), DPL, Box 114.

34.   Darwin to Fox, Down Bromley Kent, 30 October (1857), CCDL.

35.   Darwin to Fox, Down Bromley Kent, 3 October (1856), CCDL.

36.   Ibid.

37.   Ibid.

38.   Dr. Henry Holland's collection of medical essays, *Medical Notes and Reflections*, had an essay "On Medical Evidence" which contained the following passage: "And here I must advert to another circumstance which renders strict attention to laws of evidence a matter of peculiar obligation at the present time. This is the tendency, so marked in modern physiology, to carry its researches into the more abstruse questions connected with vitality, the nervous power, and the relations of mental and material phenomena— inquiries justifiable in themselves, but needing to be fenced round by more than common caution as to testimony, and the conclusions thence derived. Yet here especially it is that such precautions have been disregarded;—partly, it may be, from the real difficulty and obscurity of the subject—still more, perhaps, from the incompetency of many of those who have taken it into their hands" (Henry Holland, *Medical Notes and Reflections*, 3d ed. [London, 1855], pp. 10–11). Opposite this passage, in the copy of this volume in Darwin's library, there is written in Darwin's handwriting "gully."

39. Darwin to Fox, Down Bromley Kent, 3 October (1856), CCDL.

40. Darwin to Fox, Down Bromley Kent, 22 February (1857), CCDL.

41. Ibid.

42. Darwin to Fox, Down Bromley Kent, 8 February (1857), CCDL. In *LL*, 1:467, this letter is dated as having been written in 1858. However, in this letter, Darwin writes to Fox: "It was a complete oversight that I did not write to tell you that Emma produced under blessed chloroform our sixth Boy almost 2 months ago." *Darwin's Journal* notes that Darwin's sixth son, Charles Waring Darwin, was born on 6 December 1856.

43. Darwin's *"Receipts"* and *"Memoranda"* Book contains an undated prescription, in Darwin's handwriting, for a mixture of muriatic acid and nitric acid, to be taken ten drops, twice a day, one hour before meals (appendix A, *Charles Darwin's Entries*, p. 39). Darwin would take a course of "nitro-muriatic acid" in early 1860; see part 1, §10, n. 2–3.

44. "As this acid [hydrochloric acid] has been discovered in the natural gastric juice, it is often proposed for use in morbid condidions of that secretion, especially when there is a deficiency of acid in it. Hydrochloric acid may be used in Phosphaturia; it has been employed by some in Putrid Fevers; and it may be given as an Alternative in the same cases as Nitric acid, doing most good when combined with the latter, so as to form Nitro-muriatic acid" (J. F. Royle and F. W. Headland, *A Manual of Materia Medica and Therapeutics*, 4th ed. [London: John Churchill, 1865], p. 51).

45. Darwin to Fox, Moor Park, Farnham, Surrey, Thursday (30 April 1857), CCDL. In this letter Darwin writes: "I have now been here for exactly one week." He was referring to having arrived at Moor Park on Thursday, 23 April 1857. For a discussion of the dating of Darwin's letters during his first sojourn at Moor Park see note 25, this section.

46. *The Rise and Progress of Hydropathy*, p. 57.

47. Darwin to Fox, Moor Park, Farnham, Surrey, Thursday (30 April 1857), CCDL.

48. Darwin to Hooker, Moor Park, Farnham, Surrey, Wednesday (29 April 1857), DPL, Box 114, *LL*, 1:449.

49. *Darwin's Journal*, p. 14.

50. Emma Darwin to her son Leonard, Basset, Sunday, 23 August (1874), *CFL*, 2:218. See also part 1, §10, n. 15.

51. Etty was at Moor Park for hydropathy in the summer of 1857; she recollects that when her father was at Moor Park he "was sometimes accompanied by my mother" (*CFL*, 2:165). Darwin, however, never mentions being with Emma in any of his extant letters from Moor Park.

52. Darwin to Fox, Down Bromley Kent, 30 October (1857), CCDL.

53. Darwin to Fox, Moor Park, Farnham, Surrey, Thursday (30 April 1857), CCDL.

54. Charles Darwin to his son William Erasmus Darwin, Moor Park,

Farnham, Surrey, Monday night (26 April 1858), DPL, Box 153. This letter may be dated 26 April 1858, for the following reasons: In this letter Darwin writes that he has met a Hungarian who will make observations on horses' stripes for him, and he further writes "I have been here since Tuesday." It is known, from his letter to Emma, that he met the Hungarian in April 1858 (*LL*, 1:471). In his *Journal* Darwin states that he was at Moor Park from Tuesday, 20 April, to Tuesday, 4 May.

55. Dr. Lane would be at Moor Park from 1854 to 1859, then at the hydropathy establishment of Sudbrook Park from 1860 into the 1870s. In the 1880s his address was in Harley Street, London. *The Times*, 13 July 1889, and the 1890 *Medical Directory* state that Dr. Lane died on 11 July 1889, age sixty-seven. (There are no obituaries of Dr. Lane in *Lancet*, *British Medical Journal*, or in medical biographical dictionaries, and little is known about the details of his life. The references to him are contained in the *Medical Directory*, 1865 and 1890; *The Times*, 15 June 1858, p. 11 and 13 July 1889, p. 1; and *The Rise and Progress of Hydropathy*, p. 57.)

56. Darwin to Fox, Moor Park, Farnham, Surrey, Thursday (30 April 1857), CCDL.

57. Darwin to Hooker, Moor Park, Farnham, Surrey, 25 June (1857), DPL, Box 114, *LL*, 1:460.

58. Edward W. Lane, *Hydropathy: Or, The Natural System of Medical Treatment. An Explanatory Essay* (London: John Churchill, 1857). A second edition was published in 1859 with an altered title, *Hydropathy or Hygienic Medicine: An Explanatory Essay*.

59. Darwin to Fox, Down Bromley Kent, 30 October (1857), CCDL. Darwin possessed a copy of this book, because he would write Fox: "I send you by this Post Dr. Lane's Book, which you can keep as long as you like" (Darwin to Fox, Down Bromley Kent, 7 May [1858], CCDL). Darwin's extant library (at Cambridge University Library and Down House) does not, however, contain a copy of Dr. Lane's book.

60. Edward W. Lane, *Hydropathy: Or, The Natural System of Medical Treatment. An Explanatory Essay* (London: John Churchill, 1857), pp. 85–86.

61. *Letter Read by Dr. B. W. Richardsom, F.R.S. at his Lecture on Chas. Darwin, F.R.S. In St. George's Hall, Langham Place, October 22nd, 1882*, by Edward Lane. This is a pamphlet of seven pages, without date or publisher, consisting of a letter from Dr. Lane to Dr. Richardson. Dr. Lane begins his letter by writing Dr. Richardson that "in accordance with your request, I gladly send you a few reminiscences of the late Mr. Darwin, derived from an intimate acquaintance with him during a period of several years." (A copy of this pamphlet is in DPL., Box 112.)

Sir Benjamin Ward Richardson (1828–96) was a physician who wrote fiction, biography, and scientific essays. In his book, *Disciples of Aesculapius*, Richardson had an essay on "Erasmus Darwin, M.D., F.R.S., and Darwinian Medicine." This essay indicates that Richardson had some correspondence with Charles Darwin about Dr. Erasmus Darwin, and about alcoholism (see part 1, §15, n. 72).

62.   Ibid., pp. 3–4. For a discussion of the effects of the *Beagle* voyage on Darwin's illness, see part 2, §1 and 2.

63.   See part 1, §15.

64.   *Letter Read by Dr. B. W. Richardson, F.R.S. at his Lecture on Chas. Darwin . . .*, pp. 5–6.

65.   Francis Darwin, "Reminiscences of my Father's Everyday Life," DPL, Box 140 (3), p. 86.

66.   *Letter Read by Dr. B. W. Richardson, F.R.S. at his Lecture on Chas. Darwin . . .*, pp. 5–6.

67.   Darwin to Fox, Down Bromley Kent, 30 October (1857), CCDL. In this letter Darwin writes: "I cannot say much for myself; I have had a poor summer, & am at last rather come to your theory that my Brains were not made for thinking, for twice I staid for a fortnight at Moor Park, & was so extraordinarily better that I can attribute the difference (& I fell back into my old state *immediately* I returned) to nothing but to mental work; & I cannot attribute the difference but in a very secondary degree to Hydropathy."

68.   Darwin to Hooker, Down Bromley Kent, 2 June (1857), DPL, Box 114.

69.   Darwin to Hooker, Down Bromley Kent, 15 January (1858), DPL, Box 114.

70.   Darwin to Fox, Down Bromley Kent, 16 April (1858), CCDL, *LL*, 1:469.

71.   *Darwin's Journal*, p. 14.

72.   Darwin to Syms Covington, Down Bromley Kent, 18 May (1858), *Notes and Records of the Royal Society of London* 14 (June 1959):26.

73.   Henrietta had already had hydropathy in Moor Park in the summer of 1857.

74.   Charles Darwin to Emma Darwin, Moor Park, Sunday (25 April 1858), *CFL*, 2:171–72. (This letter is dated "probably 1859" in *CFL*, 2:171. It has here been dated 25 April 1858 for the following reasons: In the letter Darwin writes: "Yesterday I was poorly: the Review and confounded Queen was too much for me; but I got better in the evening and am very well to-day." It is likely that this refers to Queen Victoria reviewing English troops at the military camp at Aldershot. The review took place on Friday, 23 April, and Saturday, 24 April, and was observed by spectators. Darwin liked to watch parades, and Aldershot was only about four miles from Moor Park. He may have written his Sunday letter to Emma after he had watched the Aldershot "Review" on Saturday. In his letter Darwin writes that he is only able to walk a little and that he is observing ants; he writes about these same things in his Monday, 26 April, letter to his son William [see n. 54, this section].)

75.   Charles Darwin to his son William Erasmus Darwin, Moor Park, Farnham, Surrey, Monday night (26 April 1858), and Monday (3 May 1858),

DPL, Box 153. Part of Darwin's 3 May 1858 letter is published in *CFL*, 2:165–66.

76. "I sat in the drawing-room till after eight, and then went and read the Chief Justice's summing up, and thought Bernard guilty" (Charles Darwin to Emma Darwin, Moor Park, Wednesday, April [1858], *LL*, 1:471). In *The Times*, Monday, 19 April 1858, there was a five-column article entitled "The Attempted Assassination of the Emperor of the French. Trial and Acquittal of Simon Bernard. Sixth Day." This mainly consisted of a very long speech, by the Lord Chief Justice, summarizing the evidence against Bernard. Bernard then said that, although he was against the rule of the French Emperor, he had not tried to assassinate him. After a deliberation of half an hour the jury stated that Bernard was "not guilty."

77. "I see at the last meeting of the Royal Soc. Claudet brought forward a wonderful new invention of throwing a pair of stereoscopic figures into a *single* magnified one on ground glass, and this image without any instrument stands out in relief and several people can view it at once" (Charles Darwin to his son William Erasmus Darwin, Moor Park, Farnham, Surrey, Monday night [26 April 1858]), DPL, 153). Antoine Francois Claudet (1797–1867) was a French photographer, residing in London, who was a fellow of the Royal Society. Claudet made many inventions in photography, as well as the application of the stereoscope to photography. On 10 March 1858, he communicated a paper to the Royal Society entitled "On the Stereoscopic Illusion" (*Royal Society Proceedings* 9 [1859]: 194–96).

78. Charles Darwin to Emma Darwin, Moor Park, Wednesday, April (1858), *LL*, 1:471.

79. Georgiana M. Craik, *Riverston*, 3 vols. (London: Smith, Elder, & Co., 1857).

80. Georgiana Marion Craik (1831–95), author of several works of fiction. *Riverston* seems to have been her first published work.

81. Charles Darwin to Emma Darwin, Moor Park, Wednesday, April (1858), *LL*, 1:471.

82. The authoress of "The Fair Carew," in *The Three Chances*, 3 vols. (London: Smith, Elder, & Co., 1858).

83. Charles Darwin to his son William Erasmus Darwin, Moor Park, Farnham, Surrey, Monday night (26 April 1858), DPL, Box 153.

84. Charles Darwin to his son William Erasmus Darwin, Moor Park, Monday (3 May 1858), DPL, Box 153, *CFL*, 2:166.

85. The military review at Aldershot—which occurred on Friday, 23 April, and Saturday, 24 April—was reported in *The Times*: 24 April 1858, p. 12, and 26 April 1858, p. 8.

86. The review at Aldershot has been supposed to be a "sham battle," but this had then been cancelled (presumably because of inclement weather) (*The Times*, 26 April 1858, p. 8). Darwin had intensely enjoyed the "sham battles"

at Cobham in 1854, and he may have anticipated a "sham battle" at Aldershot, and then been disappointed when this battle did not occur.

87.   Charles Darwin to Emma Darwin, Moor Park, Sunday (25 April 1858), *CFL*, 2:172.

88.   Darwin to Syms Covington, Down Bromley Kent, 18 May (1858), *Notes and Records of the Royal Society of London* 14 (June 1959):26.

89.   Charles Darwin to Emma Darwin, Moor Park, Wednesday, April (1858), *LL*, 1:471.

90.   Robert C. Stauffer, ed., *Charles Darwin's Natural Selection: Being the Second Part of His Big Species Book Written from 1856 to 1858* (Cambridge: Cambridge University Press, 1975), pp. 570–71. During most of his visits to Moor Park, Darwin would make notes on the vegetation of the Moor Park wood.

91.   Charles Darwin to Emma Darwin, Moor Park, Sunday (25 April 1858), *CFL*, 2: 172.

92.   Charles Darwin to his son William Erasmus Darwin, Moor Park, Farnham, Surrey, Monday night (26 April 1858), DPL, Box 153.

93.   Charles Darwin to Emma Darwin, Moor Park, Sunday (25 April 1858), *CFL*, 2:172.

94.   Robert C. Stauffer, ed., *Charles Darwin's Natural Selection: Being the Second Part of His Big Species Book Written from 1856 to 1858* (Cambridge: Cambridge University Press, 1975), pp. 368–69.

95.   Ibid., pp. 370–71; Charles Darwin, *The Origin of Species* (London: John Murray, 1859), p. 242.

96.   Charles Darwin to his son William Erasmus Darwin, Moor Park, Farnham, Surrey, Monday night (26 April 1858), DPL, Box 153.

97.   Charles Darwin to Emma Darwin, Moor Park, Wednesday, April (1858), *LL*, 1:471.

98.   Charles Darwin to his son William Erasmus Darwin, Moor Park, Farnham, Surrey, Monday night (26 April 1858), DPL, Box 153.

99.   Darwin to Fox, Down Bromley Kent, 7 May (1858), CCDL. Darwin also corresponded with Fox about the occurrence of stripes in horses.

100.   *LL*, 1: 469–71. In a letter to his son William, Darwin wrote: "I have just received your nice note and the hexagon, for which very many thanks, but I hope and think I shall not have to use it as I had intended, which was delicately to hint to one of the greatest mathematicians that he had made a blunder in his geometry, and sure enough there came a letter yesterday wholly altering what he had previously told me" (Charles Darwin to his son William Erasmus Darwin, Moor Park, Monday [3 May 1858], DPL, Box 153, *CFL*, 2: 165). The hexagon was to be used for the discussion on bees' cells in *The Origin of Species*.

101.   Charles Darwin to Emma Darwin, Moor Park, Sunday (25 April 1858), *CFL*, 2:172.

102. *Darwin's Journal*, p. 14, entry for 14 April 1858.

103. Darwin to Fox, Down Bromley Kent, 7 May (1858), CCDL.

104. Charles Darwin to his son William Erasmus Darwin, Moor Park, Monday (3 May 1858), DPL, Box 153, *CFL*, 2:166.

105. Darwin to Fox, Down Bromley Kent, 7 May (1858), CCDL.

106. Darwin to Hooker, Down Bromley Kent, 6 May (1858), DPL, Box 114, *LL*, 1:465.

107. Charles Darwin to his son William Erasmus Darwin, Down, 13 May (1858), DPL, Box 153.

108. Ibid.

109. Darwin to Syms Covington, Down Bromley Kent, 18 May (1858), *Notes and Records of the Royal Society of London* 14 (June 1959):26.

9 Illness and Writing
The Origin of Species

1. Darwin to Fox, King's Head Hotel, Sandown, Isle of Wight (postmark 22 July 1858), CCDL.

2. Darwin to Lyell, Down, 18 (June 1858), *LL*, 1:473.

3. Darwin to Lyell, Down, 26 (June 1858), *LL*, 1:475.

4. *LL*, 1:482.

5. Darwin to Fox, Down Bromley Kent, 24 June (1858), CCDL. (See also appendix A, *Emma Darwin's Entries*, n. 22.)

6. *CFL*, 2:162.

7. Darwin to Fox (Down), 2 July (1858), CCDL.

8. Ibid.

9. Darwin to Hooker, Down Bromley Kent, 5 July (1858), DPL, Box 114, *LL*, 1:482.

10. Darwin to Fox, King's Head Hotel, Sandown, Isle of Wight (postmark 22 July 1858), CCDL.

11. *Darwin's Journal*, p. 14.

12. Darwin to Hooker, Down Bromley Kent, 6 October (1858), DPL, Box 114.

13. *Darwin's Journal*, p. 14.

14. Darwin later recollected that the published Linnean Society papers "excited very little attention. . . . This shows how necessary it is that any new view should be explained at considerable length in order to arouse public attention" (*Autobiography*, p. 122).

15. Ibid.

16. Darwin to Fox, Down Bromley Kent, 13 November (1858), CCDL.

17. *Darwin's Journal* records that in 1858 he was at Moor Park from 25

October until 1 November, and that during this time he did the following work on his "abstract": "Oct. 25th Sect VI Difficulties finished Nov. 13 (Moor Park)." (This passage has been transcribed from the manuscript of *Darwin's Journal*, kept in RDC.)

18. Darwin to Fox, Moor Park, Farnham, Surrey, Saturday (12 February 1859), CCDL. In this letter Darwin writes that he has only two chapters of his "abstract" left to write; this should roughly date the letter February 1859. He then writes that he has been at Moor Park "a week & shall stay another." *Darwin's Journal* shows that in February 1859 he was at Moor Park from Saturday, 5 February, until Saturday, 19 February. Hence this letter may be dated 12 February 1859. This was Darwin's fiftieth birthday, but he makes no mention of this in his letter.

19. Pepsin had been discovered in 1839 by the German physiologist Theodor Schwann, and was then given—either in liquid or solid form—in cases of dyspepsia (J. F. Royle and F. W. Headland, *A Manual of Materia Medica and Therapeutics* [London: John Churchill, 1865], p. 713). In 1859 Dr. William Brinton, in his book on stomach diseases wrote:

> Pepsine has, I must confess, disappointed me in most of the cases of dyspepsia in which I have tried it; even after a careful selection of those which seemed best adapted for its use. Perhaps it is not often . . . that dyspepsia is caused by a mere deficiency of gastric juice; and certainly our existing means of diagnosis do not enable us to detect such cases with the accuracy that could be wished. While in many of those varieties of indigestion in which we are entitled to suspect graver and more constitutional causes, it is difficult to see how the scanty solution of a single alimentary constituent . . . can effect much benefit. Occasionally, indeed, I have found pepsine produces considerable disturbance, even in cases where no great irritability of stomach appeared to be present (William Brinton, *The Diseases of the Stomach* [London: John Churchill, 1859], p. 385).

20. *Darwin's Journal*, p. 15.

21. Francis Darwin, "Reminiscences of my Father's Everyday Life," DPL, Box 140 (3), p. 75.

22. George H. Darwin, "Recollections of my Father," DPL, Box 112, p. 24.

23. Darwin to Fox, 24 (March 1859), *LL*, 1:506.

24. During his later years Darwin would sometimes play billiards with his sons, some of whom were passionate billiard and pool players. In 1876 he built a billiard room in Down House, which was perhaps mainly intended for the use of his sons. After about a dozen billiard games this room was converted into Darwin's study (George H. Darwin, "Recollections of my Father," DPL, Box 112, p. 24). For more about the building of the 1876 billiard room see appendix A, *Charles Darwin's Entries*, n. 51.

25. Darwin to Hooker, Down Bromley Kent, 7 April (1859), DPL, Box 115.

26. Darwin to Hooker, Down Bromley Kent, 12 (April 1859), DPL, Box 115.

27. Darwin to Hooker, Down, 18 (May 1859), DPL, Box 115; *LL*, 1:513.

28.   Darwin to Hooker, Moor Park, Thursday (26 May 1859), DPL, Box 115; partially published in *LL*, 1:514.

29.   *Darwin's Journal*, p. 15.

30.   Darwin to Hooker, Down, 18 (May 1859), DPL, Box 115, *LL*, 1:513.

31.   Darwin to Hooker, Moor Park, Thursday (26 May 1859), DPL, Box 115, *LL*, 1:514.

32.   Darwin to Lyell, Down, 21 June (1859), *LL*, 1:515.

33.   *CFL*, 2:172.

34.   Darwin to Hooker, Down, 2 July (1859), DPL, Box 115.

35.   *Darwin's Journal*, p. 15.

36.   Darwin to Hooker, Down, 28 (July 1859), DPL, Box 115, *ML*, 1:126.

37.   Darwin to Hooker, Down Bromley Kent, 1 September (1859), DPL, Box 115; mostly published in *LL*, 1:518.

38.   Ibid.

39.   John W. Judd, *The Coming of Evolution* (Cambridge: Cambridge University Press, 1911), p. 117.

40.   Darwin to Hooker, Down, 11 (September 1859), DPL, Box 115, *LL*, 1:520.

41.   Darwin to Hooker, Down Bromley Kent, 1 September (1859), DPL, Box 115; mostly published in *LL*, 1:518.

42.   *The Rise and Progress of Hydropathy*, pp. 105–9. Ilkley would become a center of English hydropathy, rivaling Malvern.

43.   Darwin to Fox, Down Bromley Kent, 23 September (1859), CCDL.

44.   Ibid.

45.   Darwin to Miss Butler, Down Bromley Kent, 11 September (1859), Library American Philosophical Society, Philadelphia; published in part in P. Thomas Carroll, *An Annotated Calender of the Letters of Charles Darwin in the Library of the American Philosophical Society* (Wilmington, Del.: Scholarly Resources Inc., 1976), letter 168, p. 61. For an account of Darwin's contact with Miss Butler at Moor Park see part 1, §8.

46.   Darwin to Fox, Ilkley Wells House, Otley, Yorkshire, Thursday (5 October 1859), CCDL.

47.   *CFL*, 2:172.

48.   Darwin to Fox, Wells Terrace, Ilkley, Otley, Yorkshire, Wednesday (16 November 1859), CCDL.

49.   Ibid.

50.   Ibid.

51.   Darwin to Hooker, Wells Terrace, Ilkley, Otley, Yorkshire, Thursday (before 9 December 1859), DPL, Box 115.

52.   Darwin to Fox, Wells Terrace, Ilkley, Otley, Yorkshire, Wednesday (16 November 1859), CCDL.

53.   Ibid.

54.   Darwin to Hooker, Wells Terrace, Ilkley, Otley, Yorkshire, Thursday (before 9 December 1859), DPL, Box 115.

55.   Darwin to Fox, Down Bromley Kent, 25 December (1859), CCDL.

56.   Darwin to Fox, Ilkley Wells House, Otley, Yorkshire, Thursday (5 October 1859), CCDL.

57.   Darwin to Fox, Wells Terrace, Ilkley, Yorkshire, Wednesday (16 November 1859), CCDL.

58.   Dr. Edmund Smith (1804–64). Dr. Smith was M. D. Lambeth, 1858, and a member of the Royal College of Surgeons since 1827 (*London and Provincial Medical Directory*, 1860 and 1865; *The Rise and Progress of Hydropathy*, p. 107).

59.   Darwin to Hooker, Ilkley, Yorkshire (November 1859), *LL*, 2:24.

60.   Adam Sedgwick to Charles Darwin, Cambridge, 24 December 1859 (John W. Clark and Thomas M. Hughes, *The Life and Letters of Adam Sedgwick* [Cambridge, 1890], 2:356).

61.   Charles Darwin to Adam Sedgwick, Ilkley Wells House, Otley, Yorkshire, 26 November 1859 (John W. Clark and Thomas M. Hughes, *The Life and Letters of Adam Sedgwick* [Cambridge, 1890], 2:359).

62.   *Darwin's Journal*, p. 15.

63.   H. C. Watson to Charles Darwin, Thames Ditton, 21 November (1859), *LL*, 2:21.

64.   Edward B. Poulton, *Charles Darwin and the Origin of Species* (London: Longman's, Green, and Co., 1909), p. 214.

10   **Illness and**
The Origin **Controversy (I)**

1.   Darwin to Fox, Down Bromley Kent, 25 December (1859), CCDL.

2.   Dr. Frederick William Headland (1830–75), B.A., M.D., London University, physician to Charing Cross Hospital. Dr. Headland also wrote, in addition to his medical books, frequent political articles for Conservative newspapers (G. H. Brown, *Lives of the Fellows of the Royal College of Physicians of London, 1826–1925* [London, 1955], Munk's Roll, 1860, pp. 128–29).

3.   Darwin to Fox, Down Bromley Kent, 22 (March 1860), CCDL.

4.   Ibid.

5.   Darwin to Asa Gray, Down, 2 March (1860), Gray Herbarium of Harvard University, Cambridge.

6.   Darwin to Hooker, Down Bromley Kent, Saturday, 3 March (1860), DPL, Box 115, LL, 2:85.

7.   Darwin to Fox, Down Bromley Kent, 18 May (1860), CCDL.

8.   Ibid.

9.   Darwin to Hooker, Down Bromley Kent, 26 June (1860), DPL, Box 115.

10.   Sudbrook Park was used as a hydropathy establishment by a succession of individuals: Dr. Ellis from the 1840s to 1860; Dr. Lane 1860–77; then by a man named Borstal; then by a man named Hammond, after which its hydropathy use ceased (*The Rise and Progress of Hydropathy*, pp. 56–57).

11.   Darwin to Hooker, Sudbrook Park, Monday night (2 July 1860), DPL, Box 115, *LL*, 2:116.

12.   Ibid.

13.   Ibid. In the published transcription (*LL*, 2:117) the word "[health]" has been substituted for "stomach."

14.   Darwin to Huxley, Sudbrook Park, Richmond, 3 July (1860), Huxley Papers, Imperial College of Science and Technology, London; *LL*, 2:117.

15.   In 1873 Dr. Lane sent Darwin his book *Old Medicine and New*. In his letter of acknowledgment, addressed to "My dear Dr Lane," Darwin wrote: "I am very much obliged for the present of your little book, which I will read as soon as I have finished another in hand. I never forget how much I owe to Hydropathy, although the last time I tried it, it seemed to do me harm. The days which I spent at Moor Park have left a most pleasant recollection on my mind. I hope you & all your family are well, & I beg you to give my kind & grateful remembrances to Lady Drysdale & Mrs Lane" (Darwin to Dr. Edward W. Lane, Down Beckenham Kent, 23 June 1873, Library American Philosophical Society, Philadelphia; summarized in P. Thomas Carroll, *An Annotated Calender of the Letters of Charles Darwin in the Library of the American Philosophical Society* [Wilmington, Del.: Scholarly Resources Inc., 1976], letter 429, p. 154). *Old Medicine and New* is not in Darwin's extant library.

16.   *CFL*, 2:176.

17.   Darwin to Fox, Down Bromley Kent, 18 May (1860), CCDL.

18.   Darwin to Fox, 15 Marine Parade, Eastbourne, 18 October (1860), CCDL.

19.   Hooker suggested treating Etty with cod-liver oil; Darwin then wrote him for details of this treatment, and after Hooker sent these Darwin carried out the treatment on Etty (Darwin to Hooker, Down, 8 [February 1861]; Down Bromley Kent, 20 [February 1861]). Both letters are in DPL, Box 115.

20.   *CFL*, 2:163.

21.   Darwin to Fox, 15 Marine Parade, Eastbourne, 18 October (1860), CCDL.

22.   *LL*, 1:114.

23.   Holland came to see Etty first at Down in June, and then at Hartfield in July (Darwin to Hooker, Down Bromley Kent, 5 June [1860]; at Miss Wedgwood, Hartfield, 29 July [1860]). Both letters are in DPL, Box 115. In

August 1860, referring to the illness of Etty, Emma wrote Lady Lyell: "We had a visit from Sir Henry Holland, who cheered us again, and I believe his view is the true one. He has been so constantly kind, and taken so much trouble, that we feel very grateful" (Emma Darwin to Lady Lyell, Down Bromley Kent, 28 August [1860], *CFL*. 2: 177).

24. Darwin to Hooker, Down Bromley Kent, 26 (March 1861), DPL, Box 115.

25. In August 1862, Darwin began a letter to Asa Gray as follows: "We are a wretched family & ought to be exterminated." He then described the illnesses of himself and his family (Darwin to Asa Gray, Southampton, 21 August [1862]; Gray Herbarium of Harvard University, Cambridge; *LL*, 2: 175; *Calender of the Letters of Darwin to Gray*, pp. 45–46). In a September 1862 letter to Fox, Darwin, after mentioning that his brother Erasmus "is very far from strong," wrote: "All Darwins ought to be exterminated" (Darwin to Fox, Cliff Cottage, Bournemouth, Saturday night, 20 [September 1862]).

26. For Darwin's views on the hereditary nature of his illness see part 2.

27. Darwin to Hooker, Down Bromley Kent, 4 December (1860), DPL, Box 115.

28. Darwin to Hooker, Down Bromley Kent, 15 January (1861), DPL, Box 115.

29. Ibid., *LL*, 2:152.

30. Ibid.

31. Darwin to Hooker, Down Bromley Kent, 29 December (1860), DPL, Box 115.

32. *Autobiography*, pp. 237–38. The dating of this letter is uncertain. Emma may have written it in 1861, or before 1861.

33. Henslow had taught Darwin botany and natural history at Cambridge, gotten Darwin his position on the *Beagle*, and then (during and after the *Beagle* cruise) aided him in studying his *Beagle* collections (*Darwin and Henslow*, pp. 1–19).

34. Leonard Huxley, *Life and Letters of Sir Joseph Dalton Hooker* (London: John Murray, 1918), 2:60.

35. Darwin to Hooker, Down Bromley Kent, 23 (March 1861), DPL, Box 115.

36. Darwin to Hooker, Down Bromley Kent, 26 (March 1861), DPL, Box 115.

37. *Darwin and Henslow*, pp. 18–19, 200–216.

38. The Linnean Society, which was in London.

39. Darwin to Hooker, Down, 23 (April 1861), DPL, Box 115.

40. To get to Hitcham, Darwin would have to take a train to Charing Cross station in central London, then a train to Stowmarket, and then travel six miles by coach.

41. Darwin to Hooker, Down Bromley Kent, S.E., 18 (May 1861), *LL*, 2:165.

42.   Darwin to Hooker, Down Bromley Kent, 23 June (1862), DPL, Box 115.

43.   Darwin to Hooker, Down, 30 (June 1862), DPL, Box 115.

44.   Joseph D. Hooker to Brian Hodgson, 6 December 1862; Leonard Huxley, *Life and Letters of Sir Joseph Dalton Hooker* (London, 1918), 2:32–33.

45.   Darwin to Hooker, Down Bromley Kent, 12 ["10th" crossed out] November (1862), DPL, Box 115, *ML*, 1: 472.

In the 15 November 1860 issue of *The Chemist and Druggist; A Monthly Trade Circular,* there is an advertisement describing the London Company of "Condy Brothers" as "Drug Merchants," and manufacturers, importers, and exporters of "Essential Oils," "Fruit Essences, &c," and "Sundries." The same *Trade Circular* also has the following advertisement: "Condy's Patent Ozonised Water, for the bath and toilet, allays irritation of the skin, removes all secretions, destroys offensive odours, imparts a sensation of purity to the mouth, and has an effect on the frame at once purifying and exhilarating." There is no indication here that this "Ozonised Water" can be taken internally.

11   Illness and
The Origin Controversy (II)

1.   Richard Owen published an anonymously written, very critical review of *The Origin* in the *Edinburgh Review,* April 1860. After reading this Darwin wrote Lyell: "I have just read the Edinburgh, which without doubt is by Owen. It is extremely malignant, clever & I fear will be very damaging . . . it made me uncomfortable for one night; but I have got quite over it today. It requires much study to appreciate ["all" inserted] the bitter spite of many of the remarks against me; indeed I did not discover all myself. . . . It is painful to be hated in the intense degree with which Owen hates me" (Darwin to Lyell, Down Bromley Kent, 10 April [1860], Library American Philosophical Society, Philadelphia; published, with omission of Owen's name, in *LL,* 2:94).

2.   *Autobiography,* p. 105.

3.   "By the way one of my chief enemies (the sole one who has annoyed me) namely Owen, I hear has been lecturing on Birds, & admits that all have been descended from *one,* & advances his own idea that the oceanic wingless Birds have lost their wings by gradual disuse. He never alludes to me or only with bitter sneers & coupled with Buffon, & the Vestiges" (Darwin to Asa Gray, 23 July [1862], Down Bromley Kent, Gray Herbarium of Harvard University, Cambridge; *ML,* 1: 203; *Calender of the Letters of Darwin to Gray,* pp. 43–44).

4.   Hugh Falconer, "On the American Fossil Elephant of the Regions Bordering the Gulf of Mexico (*E. Columbi,* Falc.); with General Observations on the Living and Extinct Species," *Natural History Review* 3 (1863): 43–114. The "Introductory Remarks" of this essay (pp. 43–49) are devoted to a

discussion of Owen's conduct toward Falconer. A summary of the part of this article that disturbed Darwin is given in *ML*, 1:226–27.

5.   Darwin to Hooker, Down, 3 January (1863), DPL, Box 115; published in part with omission of Owen's name in *LL*, 2:189.

6.   Francis Darwin, "Reminiscences of my Father's Everyday Life," *LL*, 1:90. See also part 1, §2, n. 39.

7.   *ML*, 1:228. The editors of *ML*—Francis Darwin and A. C. Seward— explain that though this letter is dated "Dec. 10th," this date "must, we think, be a slip of the pen for Jan. 10th" (*ML*, 1:226).

8.   Darwin to Huxley, Down Bromley Kent, 10 December (1862), Huxley Papers, Imperial College of Science and Technology, London.

9.   Darwin to Fox, 6 Queen Anne Street, Tuesday evening (11 February 1863), CCDL.

10.   Darwin to Hooker, Down, 30 January (1863), DPL, Box 115.

11.   Darwin to Fox, 6 Queen Anne Street, Tuesday evening (11 February 1863), CCDL.

12.   Darwin to Hooker, Down Bromley Kent, 15 February (1863), DPL, Box 115.

13.   Darwin to Lyell, Down (4 January 1860), *LL*, 2:55.

14.   Darwin to Lyell, Down, 6 March (1863), *LL*, 2:196.

15.   Ibid., p. 197.

16.   Darwin to Huxley, Down, 26 (February? 1863), Huxley Papers, Imperial College of Science and Technology, London; *ML*, 1:239.

17.   Darwin to Hooker, Down Bromley Kent, 24 February (1863), DPL, Box 115, *LL*, 2:193.

18.   Darwin to Hooker, Down Bromley Kent, 15 May (1863), DPL, Box 115, *ML*, 1:241.

19.   Darwin to Hooker, Down, 5 March (1863), DPL, Box 115.

20.   Darwin to Asa Gray, Down Bromley Kent, 20 March (1863), Gray Herbarium of Harvard University, Cambridge; *Calender of the Letters of Darwin to Gray*, pp. 50–51.

21.   Asa Gray to Darwin, Cambridge, Mass., 20 April 1863, RDC; Jane Loring Gray, ed., *Letters of Asa Gray* (Boston: Houghton Mifflin & Co., 1893), 2:504–5.

22.   Darwin to Hooker, Down, 13 (March 1863), DPL, Box 115.

23.   Darwin to Hooker, Down Bromley Kent, 17 March (1863), DPL, Box 115.

24.   Darwin to Hooker, Down, 26 (March 1863), DPL, Box 115.

25.   James Startin (1806–72). Startin is described as "a noted skin specialist, directing his attention mainly to success without reference to dermatological science to which he added nothing. His out-patient room at Blackfriars was

crowded, and similarily his consulting room at 3 Savile Row was filled with
private cases, to whom he gave long and complex prescriptions so that neither
he nor anyone else knew which ingredient was effective" (*Plarr's Lives of the
Fellows of the Royal College of Surgeons of England*, revised by Sir D'Arcy
Power, with the assistance of W. G. Spencer and Professor G. E. Gask,
printed and published for the Royal College of Surgeons by John Wright &
Sons Ltd., Bristol, London: Simpkin Marshall Ltd., 1930, 11: 345–46). In
James Startin's little book, *A Pharmacopoeia for Diseases of the Skin*, 2d ed.
(London: Harrison and Sons, 1890), p. 32, under "Eczema," the following
prescriptions are given: "Alkaline and Iron Mixtures, Arsenic, Sulphur.
Local.—Lotions of Zinc and Bismuth, Lead Ointment, Glycerine of Sub-
acetate of Lead, Ointment of Diachylum Liq Carbonis Detergens, Zinc and
Bismuth Powders."

26.   Darwin to Hooker, Down, 26 (March 1863), DPL, Box 115.

27.   Ibid.

28.   Hooker, in addition to his dyspepsia and palpitations, also suffered from
eczema. (See part 1, §12, n. 6.)

29.   *Darwin's Journal* entries for April 1863 refer to his being "sick" and to
his "illness."

30.   *Darwin's Journal* records that in 1863 he saw "Dr. Jenner" on 20 April
and 22 April.

31.   Sir William Jenner (1815–98). In 1862 Jenner had become physician in
ordinary to Queen Victoria and, because of the failing health of Sir James
Clark (whom Darwin had consulted in 1837), he soon became responsible for
the immediate care of the queen. He then received the highest medical honors
and, "at the height of his powers, was the undisputed leader of his profession,
and he owed his supremacy to his mastery in two of its departments—those of
the practising consultant and of the clinical teacher" (*Dictionary of National
Biography*; G. H. Brown, *Lives of the Fellows of the Royal College of
Physicians of London, 1826-1925* [London: Published by the College, 1955],
p. 68).

32.   *Darwin's Journal*, p. 16. These visits are mentioned in Darwin to
Hooker, Down, 23 April (1863), DPL, Box 115.

33.   Darwin to Fox, Down Bromley Kent, S.E., 23 May (1863), CCDL.

34.   Darwin to Hooker, Down, 23 (June 1863), DPL, Box 115.

35.   Darwin to Fox, Down Bromley Kent, S.E., 23 May (1863), CCDL.

36.   Darwin to Hooker, Down Bromley Kent, 15 May (1863), DPL, Box 115.

37.   In June 1863, a deputation of Malvern inhabitants presented Dr. Gully
with an illuminated address, congratulting him and themselves on his
recovery from a severe (unspecified) illness. (I thank Miss Elizabeth Jenkins,
author of *Dr. Gully*, a novel [London, 1972], for telling me of this.)

38.   Darwin to Fox, Down Bromley Kent, S.E., 23 May (1863), CCDL.

39.   Darwin to Hooker, Down Bromley Kent, 25 (August 1863), DPL, Box 115. Francis Darwin has dated this letter September, but according to *Darwin's Journal*, from 2 September through the rest of September, he was at Malvern.

40.   Darwin to Fox, Villa Nuova, Malvern Wells, Friday, 4 (September 1863), CCDL. At this time the Darwin family lived in a different house, and a different section of Malvern, than they had lived in fourteen years previously.

41.   James Smith Ayerst was first a surgeon to the Royal Navy and a member of the Royal College of Surgeons of England, and then obtained his M.D. degree from Saint Andrews in 1856. In 1859 Ayerst, in conjunction with Dr. Gully, opened a hydropathic establishment at Wells House, Malvern Wells. He was described as "a successful homeopathic practitioner . . . a great hygienist, and believed as much in fresh air and sunlight as in water. Eventually he retired on account of ill health. This was some time before Dr. Gully's retirement" (*Medical Directory* [*Provincial*], 1865; *The Rise and Progress of Hydropathy*, p. 94).

42.   Emma Darwin to Fox, Malvern Wells, Tuesday (postmark 29 September 1863), CCDL.

43.   Ibid.

44.   Ibid.

45.   Darwin to Hooker, Down, Sunday and Monday (23 November 1863), DPL, Box 115.

46.   Darwin to Hooker, Malvern Wells, Sunday (6 October 1863), DPL, Box 115.

47.   Darwin's daughter Henrietta Litchfield wrote this memory of her father: "In the summer of 63 for the first time he had loss of memory ["mother says I am wrong as to this" inserted] & mother told me so as to be prepared that an epileptic fit was to be feared" (Henrietta Litchfield to Francis Darwin, Eastbourne, 18 March 1887, DPL, Box 112).

48.   Emma Darwin to Fox, Down Bromley Kent, S.E., 8 December (1863), CCDL.

49.   *Darwin's Journal*, p. 16.

50.   "I am distressed to hear of your being again ill. Busk has the most fertile brain of any man I know in regard to all such matters as your stomach, and I really think it might be worth while to consult him" (Hooker to Darwin, Thursday [August 1863], DPL, Box 152).

51.   George Busk (1807–86) studied at the College of Surgeons and for twenty-five years was surgeon to the hospital ship *Dreadnought*. In 1856 he retired from the practice of surgery and devoted himself solely to scientific work; microscopic studies of the Polyzoa and lower forms of life, and paleontological osteology. He was a close friend of Huxley and Hooker, and in 1864 was one of the nine eminent Victorian scientists who formed the X Club (*Proceedings of the Linnean Society of London*, 1875–88, pp. 36–38;

J. V. Jensen, "The X-Club: Fraternity of Victorian Scientists," *British Journal for the History of Science,* June 1970, pp. 63–72).

52. William Brinton (1823–67). Brinton made a special study of intestinal obstruction and diseases of the alimentary canal. His published books include *Pathology, Symptoms, and Treatment of Ulcer of the Stomach* (1857); *Lectures on the Diseases of the Stomach* (1859), a second edition appeared in 1864; *On Food and its Digestion* (1861). He became physician to Saint Thomas's Hospital in 1860 (*Dictionary of National Biography;* G. H. Brown, *Lives of the Fellows of the Royal College of Physicians of London, 1826–1925* [London: Published by the College, 1955], pp. 74–75).

53. Darwin to Hooker, Down, 10 (November 1863), DPL, Box 115, *LL,* 2:186–87.

54. In an enumeration of the causes of dyspepsia, perhaps undue intellectual exertion claims the first place. The influence of such exertion must not however be measured by its intensity; but rather by its rapidity, its duration, nay, even by the faculties it involves. The constructive mental efforts of genius are eminently wholesome ... because they demand a concord of faculties, a symmetry of mind, and an application of reason and judgment—in short, a moderate and varied exercise of all the mental powers. Conversely, I think dyspepsia may be caused by a deficiency of mental exertion;—a person accustomed to intellectual toil being rendered amenable to this malady by the loss of labour which habit had made pleasant, and comparatively healthy, to him (William Brinton, *The Diseases of the Stomach* [London: John Churchill, 1859], pp. 370–71).

Brinton then goes on to state: "Mental anxiety constitutes a cause of dyspepsia which though allied to the preceding, and often concurrent with it, is a far more efficient agent in producing gastric derangement ... one which sometimes renders the physician as powerless a ministrant to a dyspeptic stomach, as he would be to mind diseased' in the Shaksperian sense. How closely all the phenomena of digestion are connected with the mental states is a matter of common experience ... the chemistry of the stomach is subjected to the least material and palpable agents of our life, to that world of thought and emotion which works within every one of us" (p. 371).

55. Darwin to Hooker (13? November 1863), DPL, Box 115.

56. Dr. Gully retired from practice in 1872, after thirty years at Malvern, and died in March 1883 (*The Rise and Progress of Hydropathy,* chap. 5; Dr. James Gully, *Dictionary of National Biography*).

57. Darwin to Hooker, Down, 16 (November 1863), DPL, Box 115.

58. Darwin to Hooker, Down, Sunday and Monday (23 November 1863), DPL, Box 115.

59. Darwin to Hooker, Down, Saturday, 5 (December 1863), DPL, Box 115.

60. Emma Darwin to Fox, Down Bromley Kent, S.E., 8 December (1863), CCDL.

61. Ibid.

62.   Darwin had taken mineral acids in 1857 and 1860 (see part 1, §8, n. 42–44; §10, n. 2–3). Brinton had written as follows about the therapeutic use of acids: "*Acids* are regarded chiefly as tonics; with local effects . . . in furthering gastric secretion, as well as in aiding the solvent powers of the juice already poured out of the stomach. . . . They are contra-indicated by the great irritability of the stomach . . . such potent remedies should only be given in a small and dilute dose . . . during or immediately after a meal . . ." (William Brinton, *The Diseases of the Stomach* [London: John Churchill, 1859], p. 389).

63.   Darwin to Hooker, Down, Saturday, 5 (December 1863), DPL, Box 115.

64.   The hothouse had been built one year previously, in February 1863 (*Down: The Home of the Darwins*, pp. 29–30).

65.   Darwin to Hooker, Down, Monday (24 January 1864), DPL, Box 115.

66.   Darwin to Hooker, Down Bromley Kent, 5 April (1864), DPL, Box 115.

67.   Hooker to Darwin (February 1864); Leonard Huxley, *Life and Letters of Sir Joseph Dalton Hooker* (London: John Murray, 1918), 2:65.

68.   Darwin to Hooker, Down, Wednesday (1864), DPL, Box 115.

69.   Darwin to Hooker (Down), Saturday–Monday (22 February 1864), DPL, Box 115.

70.   "He has had a better week with much less sickness owing to a slight tightness of the chest & exema. The exema alas is gone & was hardly enough to affect him much but I am glad it is lurking about him" (Emma Darwin to Hooker, Down Bromley Kent, 12 March [1864], DPL, Box 115).

71.   Darwin to Asa Gray, Down Bromley Kent, 25 February (1864), Gray Herbarium of Harvard University, Cambridge; *Calender of the Letters of Darwin to Gray*, p. 53.

72.   Emma Darwin to Fox, Down Bromley Kent, Friday (postmark 6 May 1864), CCDL.

73.   Emma Darwin to Lady Lyell, Down Bromley Kent, 28 August (1860), *CFL*, 2:177.

74.   "On the sexual relations of the three forms of *Lythrum salicaria*," *Journal of the Linnean Society of London (Botany)* 8 (1865):169; "On the movements and habits of climbing plants," *Journal of the Linnean Society of London (Botany)* 9 (1867):1. (See *Darwin's Journal*, p. 16.)

75.   Asa Gray to Darwin, Cambridge, Mass., 16 February 1864, RDC; printed in part in Jane Loring Gray, ed., *Letters of Asa Gray* (Boston: Houghton Mifflin & Co., 1893), 2:522.

76.   Darwin to Hooker, Down Bromley Kent, 26 March (1864), DPL, Box 115.

77.   The indications of when, in cases of dyspepsia, to give alkalies were disputed. Dr. Frederick W. Headland wrote that "Dr. Pereira recommends alkalis in cases of dyspepsia and pyrosis, where there is an excess of acid secreted by the stomach. Yet this must not always be taken as an indication

for their employment." Dr. Headland then goes on to give his opinion that it is "a tolerable safe rule" to give alkali in those cases of dyspepsia which were thought to be due to "a gouty cause" or which were "accompanied by a marked lithic diathesia and excess of acid in the urine" (Frederick W. Headland, *The Action of Medicines in the System*, 4th American ed. [Philadelphia: Lindsay and Blakiston, 1863], p. 154). Dr. Brinton wrote:

> The alkalies . . . seem chiefly useful in cases in which the close of the diges-
> tive act is attended with much flatulence, regurgitation, and heartburn;
> where their immediate effects may be attributed to a neutralisation of those
> lactic and acetic acids, which the decomposition of the undigested food can
> produce. In other cases they . . . bring . . . general results at least as valu-
> able towards the cure of the malady: removing . . . the uric acid sediments
> associated with some of the more obstinate varieties of the malady; or pro-
> voking . . . the secretion of the liver, pancreas, or intestines . . . the admin-
> istration of alkalies should be limited to the latter part of the act of gastric
> digestion, and to the succeeding period of rest . . . these remedies should
> be regarded only as . . . temporary measures; and should not be pursued
> for a longer period than a few weeks at a time" (William Brinton, *The Dis-
> eases of the Stomach* [London: John Churchill, 1859, pp. 388–89).

78. Darwin to Hooker, Down, 13 April (1864), DPL, Box 115.

79. Emma Darwin to Fox, Down Bromley Kent, Friday (postmark 6 May 1864), CCDL.

80. Emma Darwin to Fox, Down Bromley Kent, 16 May (1864), CCDL.

81. Darwin to Hooker, Down Bromley Kent, Sunday morning (27 March 1864), DPL, Box 115.

82. Darwin to Hooker, Down, 13 April (1864), DPL, Box 115.

83. Darwin to Hooker, Down, 25 April (1864), DPL, Box 115.

84. Darwin to Hooker, Sunday (15 May 1864), DPL, Box 115.

85. Ibid.

86. Darwin to Asa Gray, Down Bromley Kent, 28 May (1864), Gray Herbarium of Harvard University, Cambridge; *Calender of the Letters of Darwin to Gray*, pp. 54–55.

87. Darwin to Hooker, Down, 25 (June 1864), DPL, Box 115.

88. Darwin to Hooker (Down), Friday evening (1864), DPL, Box 115.

89. Hooker to Darwin, DPL, Box 152, p. 197. Jenner did become an F.R.S. in 1864. Hooker had become a fellow of the Royal Society in 1847, was then active in the affairs of the Royal Society, and served as president from 1873 to 1878.

90. Huxley to Darwin, Royal School of Mines, Jermyn Street, 18 April 1864; Leonard Huxley, *Life and Letters of Thomas H. Huxley* (New York, 1913), 1:270.

91. Asa Gray to Darwin, Cambridge, Mass., 11 July 1864, RDC.

92. Darwin to Asa Gray, Down Bromley Kent, S.E., 13 September (1864),

Gray Herbarium of Harvard University, Cambridge; *Calender of the Letters of Darwin to Gray*, p. 55.

93.   *Darwin's Journal*, p. 16.

94.   Darwin to Hooker, Down Bromley Kent, 23 September (1864), DPL, Box 115, *LL*, 2:212.

95.   Darwin to Hooker, Down, 22 October (1864), DPL, Box 115. All of this letter, omitting the word "vomiting," is published in *ML*, 1:251–52.

96.   Lyell's wife had no formal medical training and no scientific interest in medicine. However, she was sympathetic to ill persons, and she prescribed medicines for her servants when they were ill—they had great faith in her medical wisdom—and probably suggested medicines for her family. (I thank Professor Leonard G. Wilson, who is preparing a three-volume biography of Sir Charles Lyell, for writing me a letter about Lady Lyell.)

97.   Darwin to Asa Gray, Down Bromley Kent, S.E., 29 October (1864), Gray Herbarium of Harvard University, Cambridge; *Calender of the Letters of Darwin to Gray*, p. 56. Gray's reply to this letter has been lost.

98.   "Syrup of Phosphate of Iron was introduced in a paper read to the Medical Society of London in 1851 by Dr. Routh, and Mr. Greenish subsequently described to the Pharmaceutical Society the process by which it was prepared. The formula was afterwards improved by Mr. Gale, and his process was adopted in the B.P. It has since been modified" (A. C. Wootton, *Chronicles of Pharmacy*, 1910, 1:405). In England, in the 1860s, there were several preparations of phosphate of iron. A frequently used preparation was blue phosphate—a salt of the oxides of iron and phosphorous—which was used medically as "a mild Chalybeate. . . . Dr. Prout used it in Diabetes. The presence of Phosphoric Acid with the Iron has caused it to be recommended, on theoretical grounds, in rickets, scrofula, and nervous disorders" (J. F. Royle and F. W. Headland, *A Manual of Materia Medica and Therapeutics* [London: John Churchill, 1865], pp. 155–56).

99.   Darwin to George Busk, Down Bromley Kent, S.E., 4 December (1864), Burndy Library, Norwalk, Conn.

100.   Darwin to Fox, Down Bromley Kent, S.E., 30 November (1864), CCDL.

12   **Illness and**
The Origin **Controversy (III)**

1.   Darwin to Hooker, Down, 7 January (1865), DPL, Box 115.

2.   Ibid.

3.   For a discussion of the concept of "suppressed gout," see part 2, §1, n.7, 8.

4.   Hooker to Darwin (January 1865); Leonard Huxley, *Life and Letters of Sir*

Joseph Dalton Hooker (London: John Murray, 1918), 2:72.

5. Darwin to Hooker, Down, 2 (February 1865), DPL, Box 115.

6. "I hope you are better—I am pretty well, but somehow not overstrong &
bothered with Eczema in the lobes of the ear, for which I am put upon
Mercury & Iodide of Iron by Startin" (Hooker to Darwin, Kew, 3 February
1865, DPL, Box 102).

7. Darwin to Hooker, Down, 9 February (1865), DPL, Box 115.

8. Darwin to Hooker, Down, 6 April (1865), DPL, Box 115.

9. "I am in truth sorry that you had trouble & gave Busk trouble by writing to
him; for there was no hurry; & I feel sure I must bear my load of daily discomfort, & be thankful that I can occupy myself for a few hours daily" (Darwin to
Hooker, Down, 10 March [1865], DPL, Box 115).

10. *Darwin's Journal*, p. 17.

11. Darwin to Hooker, Down, Monday (2 May 1865), DPL, Box 115.

12. Darwin to Hooker, Down, 4 May (1865), DPL, Box 115.

13. Ibid.

14. *Autobiography*, p. 76.

15. Darwin to Dr. John Chapman, Down Bromley Kent, S. E., 16 May
(1865); Darwin Evolution Collection, University of Virginia Library, University of Virginia, Charlottesville. It is not known what caused Dr. Chapman to
send Darwin a copy of his book. Darwin's library does not contain the book.

16. F. N. L. Poynter, "John Chapman (1821–1894): Publisher, Physician and
Medical Reformer," *Journal of the History of Medicine*, winter 1950, pp. 1–22.

17. John Chapman, *Functional Diseases of the Stomach. Part 1. Sea-
Sickness: Its Nature and Treatment* (London: Trubner and Co., 1864), pp. 5–6.

18. Darwin to Dr. John Chapman, Down Bromley Kent, S.E., 16 May
(1865); Darwin Evolution Collection, University of Virginia Library, University of Virginia, Charlottesville.

19. Emma.

20. This is a page with writing on both sides, which is kept in a folder
headed "1865 May 20," Darwin Evolution Collection, University of Virginia
Library, University of Virginia, Charlottesville. Hereafter cited as "Darwin's
Medical Notes, 1865 May 20."

21. Emma Darwin to Hooker (Down, 18 July 1865), DPL, Box 115.

22. Dr. Chapman finished reading *The Origin of Species* on 21 February
1860—three months after *The Origin* had been published—and he then wrote
in his "Diary": "It impresses me as one of the most important books of this
century, and is likely to effect an immense mental revolution. The sagacity,
knowledge and candour displayed in the work are unusually great and
wonderful" (Gordon S. Haight, *George Eliot & John Chapman, with
Chapman's Diaries* [New Haven: Yale University Press, 1940], p. 237).

23.   Darwin to Dr. John Chapman, Down Bromley Kent, S.E., 7 June 1865; Darwin Evolution Collection, University of Virginia Library, University of Virginia, Charlottesville.

24.   Darwin to Hooker, Down, 1 June (1865), DPL, Box 115.

25.   Darwin to Dr. John Chapman, Down Bromley Kent, S.E., 7 June 1865; Darwin Evolution Collection, University of Virginia Library, University of Virginia, Charlottesville.

26.   Darwin to Hooker, Down, Monday (12 July 1865), DPL, Box 115.

27.   Emma Darwin to Hooker (Down, 18 July 1865), DPL, Box 115.

28.   John Chapman, *Neuralgia and Kindred Diseases of the Nervous System* (London, 1873). This is the only book of Dr. Chapman's which is in Darwin's library. Darwin's copy (today kept at Down House) contains no annotations, only the following inscription on the front flyleaf: "Charles Darwin Esq F.R.S. Etc Etc With the Authors respects."

29.   Darwin to Hooker, Down, Monday (12 July 1865), DPL, Box 115.

30.   "I have had a shocking month with much sickness & have done nothing" (Darwin to Hooker, Down, 1 June [1865], DPL, Box 115).

31.   R. C. Olby, "Charles Darwin's Manuscript of Pangenesis," *British Journal for the History of Science* 1 (1963):250–63. Olby transcribes and dates Darwin's essay.

32.   Darwin to Lyell, Down, 22 August (1867), *LL*, 2:255.

33.   Darwin to Huxley, Down Bromley Kent, S.E., 27 May (1865), Huxley Papers, Imperial College of Science and Technology, London; *LL*, 2:228.

34.   Huxley to Ernst Haeckel, Royal School of Mines, Jermyn Street, London, 7 June 1865; Leonard Huxley, *Life and Letters of Thomas H. Huxley* (New York, 1913), 1:288.

35.   Darwin to Hooker, Down, Saturday (18 July 1865), DPL, Box 115.

36.   Emma Darwin to Hooker (18 July 1865), DPL, Box 115.

37.   *CFL*, 2:183.

38.   "My wife for a couple of months has been suffering much from headaches" (Darwin to Fox, Down Bromley Kent, 3 January [1855], CCDL).

39.   "Emma has suffered much from headaches of late; but I hope will soon be better" (Darwin to Fox, Down Bromley Kent, 23 September [1859], CCDL). "My wife is fairly well but suffers much from repeated headaches" (Darwin to Fox, Down Bromley Kent, 6 February [1867], CCDL).

40.   *CFL*, 2:164.

41.   *CFL*, 2:171–72. See part 1, §8, n. 73–74.

42.   Darwin to Hooker, Down Bromley Kent, S.E., 16 August (1865), DPL, Box 115.

43.   Darwin to Hooker, Down Bromley Kent, Thursday, 27 (September 1865), DPL, Box 115.

44. Jacob Rosenbloom, "An Appreciation of Henry Bence Jones, M.D., F.R.S., 1814–73," *Annals of Medical History* 2 (1919):262–64; N. G. Coley, "Henry Bence-Jones, M.D., F.R.S. (1813–1873)," *Notes and Records of the Royal Society of London* 28 (1973):31–56.

45. Darwin to Fox, Down Bromley Kent, S.E., 25 October (1865), CCDL.

46. Darwin to Huxley, Down Bromley Kent, S.E., 4 October (1865), Huxley Papers, Imperial College of Science and Technology, London.

47. *Darwin's Journal*, p. 17.

48. Darwin to Hooker, Down Bromley Kent, S.E., 22 December (1865), DPL, Box 115.

49. *Darwin's Journal*, p. 17.

50. Emma Darwin to Fanny Allen, Queen Anne Street (London), Sunday (28 April 1866), *CFL*, 2:184–85.

51. Darwin to Fox, Down Bromley Kent, S.E., 24 August (1866), Burndy Library, Norwalk, Conn.

52. *CFL*, 2:195.

53. N. G. Coley, "Henry Bence-Jones, M.D., F.R.S. (1813–1873)," *Notes and Records of the Royal Society of London* 28 (1973):50.

54. Darwin to Fox, Down Bromley Kent, 6 February (1867), CCDL.

55. N. G. Coley, "Henry Bence-Jones, M.D., F.R.S. (1813–1873)," *Notes and Records of the Royal Society of London* 28 (1973):50.

56. Darwin to Fox, Down Bromley Kent, 6 February (1867), CCDL.

57. Darwin to Huxley, Dumbola Lodge, Freshwater, Isle of Wight, 23 July (1868), Huxley Papers, Imperial College of Science and Technology, London.

58. Darwin to Fox, Down Bromley Kent, S.E., 21 October (1868), CCDL.

59. Darwin to Hooker, Dumbola Lodge, Freshwater, Isle of Wight, Saturday, 17 (July 1868), DPL, Box 94.

60. William Allingham (1824–89) is today noted for his poems about Ireland, and for his diary, which revealed "something of Boswell's sharp eye and ear for detail" and gave "many detailed accounts of famous Victorian men and women." This was the only occasion on which he saw Darwin (Alan Warner, *William Allingham* [Lewisburg, Pa.: Bucknell University Press, 1975), pp. 11, 66–78).

61. At this time Hooker was president of the British Association for the Advancement of Science, and he was working on an address that he would make at the association meeting in August 1868, in Norwich.

62. *William Allingham's Diary* (introduction by Geoffrey Grigson) (Fontwell, Sussex: Centaur Press, Ltd., 1967), p. 184.

63. "God knows whether my strength and spirit will last out to write a chapter versus Mivart and others; I do so hate controversy, and I feel I should do it so badly" (Darwin to Wallace, Down Beckenham Kent, 12 July 1871;

James Marchant, *Alfred Russel Wallace: Letters and Reminiscences* [New York: Harper and Brother, 1916], p. 221).

64.   Peter J. Vorzimmer, *Charles Darwin: The Years of Controversy* (Philadelphia: Temple University Press, 1970), p. 287, n. 4 (chap. 10).

65.   Charles Darwin, *The Origin of Species* (New York: New American Library, 1958), p. 200.

66.   Darwin clearly went on believing in the validity of natural selection. How effective his answers to Mivart were, however, has been recently debated. According to Peter Vorzimmer, Mivart's attacks "badgered" Darwin into a "state of frustrating confusion" (Peter J. Vorzimmer, *Charles Darwin: The Years of Controversy* [Philadelphia: Temple University Press, 1970], p. 251). According to Michael T. Ghiselin, Darwin's "vastly superior learning and imagination provided immediate and effectual answers" to Mivart's attacks (Michael T. Ghiselin, "Mr. Darwin's Critics, Old and New," *Journal of the History of Biology*, spring 1973, p. 161).

67.   Darwin to Hooker, Down Beckenham Kent, 4 August (1872), DPL, Box 94.

13   Improved Health, Old Age

1.   Darwin to Mrs. Haliburton, Down, 1 November (1872), *LL*, 2:352.

2.   Francis Darwin, "Reminiscences of my Father's Everyday Life," *LL*, 1:106.

3.   John W. Judd, *The Coming of Evolution* (Cambridge: Cambridge University Press, 1911), p. 118. See, also, page 92, this section.

4.   Francis Darwin, "Reminiscences of my Father's Everyday Life," *LL*, 1:107.

5.   Darwin to Fox, Down Beckenham Kent, 29 October (1872), CCDL.

6.   Darwin to Fox, Down Beckenham Kent, 29 October (1872), CCDL.

7.   Darwin to Asa Gray (Sevenoaks), 22 October (1872), *LL*, 2:495; *Calender of the Letters of Darwin to Gray*, p. 60.

8.   Emma Darwin to her aunt Fanny Allen, Down, Tuesday (27 September 1872), *CFL*, 2:210.

9.   *Darwin's Journal*, p. 19.

10.   Darwin to Hooker, Down Beckenham Kent, 12 September (1873), DPL, Box 95.

11.   Sir Andrew Clark, Bart., M.D. (1826–93). For obituaries on Clark see *Lancet*, 11 November 1893, and *British Medical Journal*, 11 November 1893.

12.   *Lancet*, 11 November 1893, p. 1224.

13.   Emma Darwin to her aunt Fanny Allen, Down, Friday (1873), *CFL*, 2:214.

14.   Emma Darwin to her daughter Henrietta Litchfield, Tuesday evening (1873), *CFL*, 2:215.

15. Darwin to Hooker, Down Beckenham Kent, 12 September (1873), DPL, Box 95.

16. Leonard Huxley, *Life and Letters of Thomas H. Huxley* (New York, 1913), 1:402. Huxley was a patient of Dr. Andrew Clark, a friend and patient of Dr. Henry Bence Jones, and an "acquaintance" of Dr. John Chapman (Darwin to Huxley, Down Bromley Kent, S.E., 27 May [1865], Huxley Papers, Imperial College of Science and Technology, London). There is, however, no definite evidence that Huxley influenced Darwin to consult any of these three doctors. In Darwin's extant letters to Huxley there are only occasional accounts of his illness, and these lack the intimacy and detail of his accounts to Hooker and Fox.

17. Darwin to Huxley, Down Beckenham Kent, 5 December (1873), Huxley Papers, Imperial College of Science and Technology, London.

18. This was a diary from 1874–82 containing cursory notations by Darwin about sums of money, the progress of his manuscripts, and his trips from and back to Down. There are occasional references to Darwin's health, and to Dr. Clark and the latter's treatments.

19. Dr. Clark prescribed what were called "Clark's pills," which contained strychnine, or quinine and strychnine (John H. Winslow, *Darwin's Victorian Malady* [Philadelphia: American Philosophical Society, 1971], p. 34).

20. Darwin to Hooker, Down Beckenham Kent, 4 March (1874), DPL, Box 95.

21. *Darwin's Journal*, pp. 19–20.

22. Darwin to Maxwell Masters, Down Beckenham Kent, 10 July (1875), Burndy Library, Norwalk, Conn.

23. Charles Darwin to his son George Darwin, Down, 13 July (1876), *CFL*, 2:224.

24. Darwin to an unidentified correspondent, Down Beckenham Kent, 22 September 1876, Burndy Library, Norwalk, Conn.

25. *Darwin's Journal*, p. 21. During this visit Darwin stayed at the home of his daughter Henrietta Litchfield, 4 Bryanston Street, London.

26. Darwin to Hooker, 4 Bryanston Street (London) (2–5 March 1878), DPL, Box 95.

27. Henrietta Litchfield to Francis Darwin, Eastbourne, 18 March 1887, DPL, Box 112.

28. "Henrietta Litchfield manuscript," pp. 1, 11. This is a fifteen-page untitled manuscript by Mrs. Henrietta Litchfield which gives a detailed and moving account of her father's last illness and death. The manuscript is kept at Down House, and is quoted in Sir Hedley Atkins' book *Down: The Home of the Darwins*, pp. 37–40. I thank the Royal College of Surgeons of England, and Sir Hedley Atkins, for permission to quote from this manuscript; and Sir

Hedley for sending me a copy. Hereafter I shall refer to it as "Henrietta Litchfield manuscript."

29.   Darwin's daughter, Henrietta Litchfield, wrote as follows to her brother Francis Darwin: "Mother is very strong how much better his [Darwin's] health was the last ten years of his life. She said that she did not think he ever had a very distressing fit of sickness. . . . I think mother thinks simply to say that his health was very much better; ["she says he had" inserted] much less distressing symptoms, & that he kept much steadier to his work" (Henrietta Litchfield to Francis Darwin, Eastbourne, 18 March 1887, DPL, Box 112).

30.   A "near neighbor" of Darwin at Downe (during the last decade of Darwin's life) writes: "I remember once, during an illness, inquiring of the butler how Mr. Darwin was, when he said: 'Master's illnesses nowadays are nothing to what they used to be. About thirty years ago many's a time when I was helping to nurse him, I've thought he would die in my arms' " (L.A. Nash, "Some Memories of Charles Darwin," *Overland Monthly*, San Francisco, 1921, 77:27). A year after his master's death, Darwin's butler told an American visitor at Down House that "For the first twenty years after Mr. Darwin's return from South America, his health was very bad, much more so than later" (David Starr Jordan, *The Days of a Man: Being Memories of a Naturalist, Teacher, and Minor Prophet of Democracy* [Yonkers-on-Hudson, N.Y.: World Book Co., 1922], 1:272).

31.   Darwin to J. M. Herbert, Down Beckenham Kent, 25 December 1880; Sir Gavin de Beer, ed., "The Darwin Letters at Shrewsbury School," *Notes and Records of the Royal Society of London*, 23 (June 1968):74.

32.   Darwin to Fox, Down Beckenham Kent, 11 May (1874), CCDL.

33.   Francis Darwin, "Reminiscences of my Father's Everyday Life," *LL*, 1:94–95.

34.   See note 7, this section.

35.   In February 1875, when he was writing his book, *Insectivorous Plants,* Darwin told Hooker: "You ask about my book, & all that I can say is that I am ready to commit suicide: I thought it was decently written, but find so much wants rewriting. . . . I begin to think that every one who publishes a book is a fool" (Darwin to Hooker, Down Beckenham Kent, 10 February [1875], *LL*, 2:501).

36.   Francis Darwin, "Reminiscences of my Father's Everyday Life," *LL*, 1:108.

37.   Darwin to J. M. Herbert, Down Beckenham Kent, 25 December 1880; Sir Gavin de Beer, ed., "The Darwin Letters at Shrewsbury School," *Notes and Records of the Royal Society of London* 23 (June 1968):74.

38.   Leonard Darwin, "Memories of Down House," *The Nineteenth Century, and After,* 106 (July–December 1929):120.

39.   *Autobiography,* p. 46.

40. Darwin to Mrs. Haliburton, Down, 1 November (1872), *LL*, 2:352. For Darwin's views on the illnesses of his children see part 2, §1.

41. *CFL*, 2:204–5.

42. Darwin to Fox, Down Beckenham Kent, 2 December (1877), CCDL.

43. Charles Darwin to his son George Darwin, Down, 13 July (1876), *CFL*, 2:224.

44. *Autobiography*, p. 97.

45. Francis Darwin, "Reminiscences of my Father's Everyday Life," *LL*, 1:135.

46. *CFL*, 2:254.

47. Francis Darwin, "Reminiscences of my Father's Everyday Life," *LL*, 1:135.

48. John W. Judd, *The Coming of Evolution* (Cambridge: Cambridge University Press, 1911), p. 118.

49. Francis Darwin, "Reminiscences of my Father's Everyday Life," *LL*, 1:106.

50. *Autobiography*, pp. 96–97.

14   The Final Illness

1. *Darwin's Journal*, p. 21.

2. Emma Darwin (Patterdale), Sunday (June 1881), *CFL*, 2:247.

3. Darwin to Hooker, Glenrhydding House, Patterdale, Penrith, 15 June 1881, DPL, Box 95, *ML*, 2:433.

4. Darwin to Wallace, Down Beckenham Kent, 12 July 1881; James Marchant, *Alfred Russel Wallace: Letters and Reminiscences* (New York: Harper and Brother, 1916), p. 261.

5. Sir Arthur Salusbury MacNalty, "The ill health of Charles Darwin," *Nursing Mirror*, 4 December 1864, p. ii. There is no mention of Dr. F. C. MacNalty in Darwin's letters, *Darwin's Journal*, or the "Private Diary."

6. *Darwin's Journal*, p. 21.

7. *LL*, 2: 527–28.

8. Emma Darwin to her daughter Henrietta Litchfield, Friday morning (London, December 1881), *CFL*, 2:250.

9. John H. Judd, *The Coming of Evolution* (Cambridge: Cambridge University Press, 1911), pp. 158–59.

10. Darwin to Anthony Rich, Down, 4 February 1882, *ML*, 2:446–47.

11. "Henrietta Litchfield manuscript," p. 1; *Down: The Home of the Darwins*, p. 38.

12. *CFL*, 2:251.

13. "Henrietta Litchfield manuscript," p. 2; *Down: The Home of the Darwins*, p. 38.

14. *Down: The Home of the Darwins*, p. 38.

15. "Henrietta Litchfield manuscript," p. 2.

16. "Henrietta Litchfield manuscript," p. 2; *Down: The Home of the Darwins*, p. 38.

17. Ibid.

18. "He [Darwin] felt the *strongest gratitude* to Dr. Clark & wd not hear of anything that might mortify him" ("Henrietta Litchfield manuscript," p. 5; underlining in original). Seventeen days after Clark's visit, Darwin partially expressed his anger by writing: "Dr. Clark's kindness is unbounded to me, but he is too busy to come here" (Darwin to Huxley, Down, 27 March 1882, *LL*, 2:529).

19. "Henrietta Litchfield manuscript," p. 3; *Down: The Home of the Darwins*, p. 38.

20. Sir Thomas Lauder Brunton introduced amyl nitrite to treat angina pectoris in 1867, and it was widely used in the 1880s. Brunton wrote that "amyl nitrite appears to arrest the spasm of the vessels in Angina Pectoris by causing paralysis of the vessels themselves or the peripheral ends of the vasomotor nerves" (Thomas Lauder Brunton, *A Textbook of Pharmacology, Therapeutics and Materia Medica* [London: Macmillan and Co., 1885], p. 212).

21. Sir Norman Moore (1847–1922) had been associated with Saint Bartholomew's Hospital, London, since 1872. He would become an eminent clinician and medical writer, teacher, and historian. Since his student days at Cambridge he had shown "a keen interest in natural history." (For an obituary on Moore see *British Medical Journal*, 9 December 1922.) Darwin had seen Moore previously and then said he did not have confidence in him ("Henrietta Litchfield manuscript," p. 1; *Down: The Home of the Darwins*, p. 38).

22. "Henrietta Litchfield manuscript," p. 3; *Down: The Home of the Darwins*, p. 38.

23. Ibid.

24. Mr. Charles H. Allfrey (1839–1912) obtained his M.D. degree from Edinburgh University in 1861, and became a fellow of the Royal College of Surgeons in 1867. He practiced in partnership with Dr. Heckstall Smith at Saint Mary Cray, and took an active part in founding the Chislehurst and Cray Valley Hospital (*Plarr's Lives of the Fellows of the Royal College of Surgeons of England*, 1930, 1:18).

25. "Henrietta Litchfield manuscript," p. 5, underlining in original; *Down: The Home of the Darwins*, pp. 38–39.

26. Nux vomica was an extract from the fruit of an East Indian tree, which contained two active alkaloids—strychnine and brucine. It was used as a tonic and stimulant.

27. "Henrietta Litchfield manuscript," pp. 5–6; *Down: The Home of the Darwins*, pp. 38–39.

28. Ibid.

29. This appears to be a letter, or part of a word, which Darwin wrote and then crossed out.

30. "Henrietta Litchfield manuscript," pp. 7–8; *Down: The Home of the Darwins*, p. 39.

31. Ibid.

32. "Henrietta Litchfield manuscript," p. 8.

33. Dr. Walter Moxon (1836–86), a noted and brilliant London physician, associated with Guy's Hospital, who in 1881 delivered the Croonian Lectures at the Royal College of Physicians (Munk's Roll, *Lives of the Fellows of the Royal College of Physicians 1826–1925* [London: Published by the College, 1955], p. 164).

34. "Henrietta Litchfield manuscript," p. 9.

35. Francis Darwin to Huxley, Down, Thursday (20 April 1882), Huxley Papers, Imperial College of Science and Technology, London. In this letter, written the day after Darwin died, Francis Darwin gives a brief account of his father's final illness.

36. "Henrietta Litchfield manuscript," p. 10.

37. Francis Darwin to Huxley, Down, Thursday (20 April 1882), Huxley Papers, Imperial College of Science and Technology, London.

38. "Henrietta Litchfield manuscript," p. 10.

39. Ibid.; *Down: The Home of the Darwins*, p. 39.

40. Francis Darwin to Huxley, Down, Thursday (20 April 1882), Huxley Papers, Imperial College of Science and Technology, London.

41. "Henrietta Litchfield manuscript," pp. 10–11; *Down: The Home of the Darwins*, pp. 39–40.

42. *British Medical Journal*, 29 April 1882, p. 628. Darwin does not seem to have had an autopsy.

15 Symptom, Treatments, Habits

1. Darwin to Hooker, Down, 13 (March 1863), DPL, Box 115.

2. "Darwin's Medical Notes, 1865 May 20."

3. *Darwin's Journal*, p. 9; Darwin to Hooker, Down, 10 (November 1863), DPL, Box 115, *LL*, 2:186–87.

4. Darwin to Hooker, Down, 23 (June 1863), DPL, Box 115.

5. Darwin to Hooker, Down Bromley Kent, 23 June (1862), DPL, Box 115.

6. Sir Joseph Hooker, "Reminiscences of Darwin," *Nature*, 22 June 1899, p. 188.

7.   Darwin first seems to have used the word "fit" to describe some of his episodes of eczema in the 1860s.

8.   Darwin to Fox, The Lodge, Malvern, 24 (March 1849), CCDL.

9.   For a description of the animals that were kept at Down see *Down: The Home of the Darwins*, pp. 78–84.

10.   That Darwin may have had "a severe allergy, possibly to pigeons," has been suggested by Gruber and Barrett, *Darwin on Man*, p. 44, n. 15. For a discussion of this see part 2, §6.

11.   "Darwin's Medical Notes, 1865 May 20."

12.   That Darwin may have had idiopathic paroxysmal tachycardia has been suggested by Dr. C. E. Dent, "Darwin's Health," *British Medical Journal*, 24 April 1965, p. 1129.

13.   *Autobiography*, p. 115.

14.   Darwin to Fox, Malvern, Thursday (27 March 1851), CCDL.

15.   Darwin to Hooker (30 October 1863), DPL, Box 115.

16.   Darwin to Hooker, Down, 27 (November 1863), DPL, Box 115.

17.   Darwin to Hooker, Sevenoaks, 22 October (1872), DPL, Box 95.

18.   *CFL*, 2:212.

19.   Darwin to Hooker, 16 Montague Street, Portland Square (London), Sunday night (6 April 1873), DPL, Box 95.

20.   Darwin to Huxley, Down Beckenham Kent ["19th" crossed out] 23 (April) 1873, Huxley Papers, Imperial College of Science and Technology, London; Leonard Huxley, *Life and Letters of Thomas H. Huxley* (New York, 1913), 1:394–95.

21.   Darwin to Huxley, Down Beckenham Kent, 28 April (1873), Huxley Papers, Imperial College of Science and Technology, London.

22.   "Huxley is here & is wonderfully pleasant & jolly—He says that he is quite well; but his face is very thin, & he eats suspiciously little" (Darwin to Hooker, Down Beckenham Kent, 25 October [1873], DPL, Box 95).

23.   Leonard Darwin, "Memories of Down House," *The Nineteenth Century and After* 106 (July–December 1929):121.

24.   *CFL*, 2:169.

25.   Francis Darwin, "Reminiscences of my Father's Everyday Life," *LL*, 1:112. Soon after his father died, Leonard Darwin described him as follows: "The evident interest with which he listened to anyone who talked sense (or even nonsense), the brightness and animation of his face when he joined in himself and spoke of anything that he felt an interest in, the wonderful simplicity and kindness of his manner, especially when talking to young people, made listening to a conversation where he was quite delightful" (Margaret Keynes, *Leonard Darwin 1850–1943* [Cambridge: Privately printed at the Cambridge University Press, 1943], p. 43).

26. Adolphe Quetelet (1796–1874). Belgian mathematician, astronomer, and statistician.

27. Darwin to Fox, Down Farnborough Kent, 4 September (1850), CCDL, LL, 1:341.

28. Leonard Darwin, "Memories of Down House," *The Nineteenth Century and After* 106 (July–December 1929):121.

29. *Autobiography*, p. 140. In the 1870s Darwin described himself as follows: "I am essentially a very poor critic, as I have often found to my cost.—I am always inclined to believe all I read & differ only after long reflection" (Darwin to an unidentified individual, Down Beckenham Kent, 9 June [1871–75], Library American Philosophical Society, Philadelphia; summarized in P. Thomas Carroll, *An Annotated Calendar of the Letters of Charles Darwin in the Library of the American Philosophical Society* [Wilmington: Del.: Scholarly Resources Inc., 1976], letter 408, p. 148).

30. Francis Darwin, "Reminiscences of my Father's Everyday Life," *LL*, 1:99–100; Darwin to Fox (Shrewsbury), Wednesday (25 December 1828), CCDL.

31. *Darwin and the "Beagle,"* p. 206.

32. Emma Wedgwood to Charles Darwin, Maer, Sunday (30 December 1838), DPL, RDC.

33. Darwin to Hooker, Down, 10 April (1846), *ML*, 1:416.

34. Darwin to Fox, The Lodge, Malvern, 24 (March 1849), CCDL.

35. Darwin to Henslow, The Lodge, Malvern, 6 May 1849; *Darwin and Henslow*, p. 163.

36. Robert M. Stecher, "The Darwin-Innes Letters," *Annals of Science* 17 (December 1961):256.

37. Ibid.

38. *LL*, 1:110.

39. *Down: The Home of the Darwins*, p. 98.

40. "It is very disheartening for me, that all the wonderful good which Moor Park did me at the time, has gone all away like a flash of lightning, now that I am at work again. And eheu, eheu, I have left off snuff for nothing!" (Charles Darwin to his son William Erasmus Darwin, Down, 13 May [1858], DPL, Box 153).

41. Francis Darwin, "Reminiscences of my Father's Everyday Life," DPL, Box 140 (3), p. 8.

42. Ibid., pp. 13–14.

43. Ibid., p. 8.

44. Charles Darwin to Susan Darwin (Malvern, Monday, 19 March 1849), DPL.

45. Darwin to Henslow, The Lodge, Malvern, 6 May 1849; *Darwin and Henslow*, p. 163.

46. Darwin to Hooker, Down, 10 April (1846), *ML*, 1:416.

47. Francis Darwin, "Reminiscences of my Father's Everyday Life," DPL, Box 140 (3), p. 31.

48. John W. Judd, "Darwin and Geology," in A. C. Seward, ed., *Darwin and Modern Science* (Cambridge: Cambridge University Press, 1909), p. 379.

49. The Analytical Sanitary Commission, "Snuff and Its Adulteration," *Lancet* 2 (1853):508–12, 532–36; J. J. Gregeen, "Case of Lead Poisoning Caused by the Use of Snuff," *Medical Times & Gazette* 2 (1861):443; Dr. Weaver, "Lead-Poisoning by Snuff," *British Medical Journal* 1 (1885):77; Robert Ormsby, "Aphonia Caused by Lead Poisoning Contracted by the Abuse of Snuff," *New York Medical Journal* 52 (1890):552.

50. Goodman and Gilman, *The Pharmacological Basis of Therapeutics* (New York: Macmillan Co., 1955), pp. 620–23.

51. Francis Darwin, "Reminiscences of my Father's Everyday Life," DPL, Box 140 (3), p. 8.

52. Charles Darwin to Caroline Darwin, Buenos Ayres, 20 September (1833); *Darwin and the "Beagle,"* p. 91.

53. *"Beagle" Diary*, 9 September 1833, p. 176.

54. Francis Darwin, "Reminiscences of my Father's Everyday Life," DPL, Box 140 (3), pp. 14–15.

55. Francis Darwin, "Reminiscences of my Father's Everyday Life," *LL*, 1:99.

56. *Autobiography*, p. 60.

57. Francis Darwin, "Reminiscences of my Father's Everyday Life," *LL*, 1:96.

58. Sir Mountstuart E. Grant Duff, *Notes from a Diary, 1892–1895* (London: John Murray, 1904), 1:80–81.

59. Darwin to Hooker, Down Farnborough Kent, 29 (May 1854), DPL, Box 114, *ML*, 1:78.

60. Darwin to Hooker, Down, 23 (1855?), DPL, Box 114.

61. Darwin to John Lubbock, Thursday (before 1857), *LL*, 1:497. Underlining in the original.

62. Darwin to Fox, Down Bromley Kent, 22 (March 1860), CCDL. See §10.

63. Darwin to Hooker, Malvern Wells, Sunday (6 October 1863), DPL, Box 115. See §11.

64. "Darwin's Medical Notes, 1865 May 20." See §12.

65. Sir Buckstone Browne, "Darwin's Health," *Nature*, 2 January 1943, p. 15.

66. Francis Darwin, "Reminiscences of my Father's Everyday Life," *LL*, 1:96.

67. Francis Darwin, "Reminiscences of my Father's Everyday Life," 10, DPL, Box 140 (3).

68. Ibid., pp. 10–11.

69. *Autobiography*, p. 224.

70. Desmond King-Hele, *Erasmus Darwin* (New York: Charles Scribner's Sons, 1963), pp. 14, 32–33.

71. *Autobiography*, p. 36.

72. Sir Benjamin Ward Richardson, "Erasmus Darwin, M.D., F.R.S., and Darwinian Medicine," in *Disciples of Aesculapius* (New York: E. P. Dutton & Co.; London: Hutchinson & Co., 1901), 2:693.

73. "As a rule he [Darwin] put small faith in doctors, and thus his unlimited belief in Dr. Darwin's medical instinct and methods of treatment was all the more striking" (Francis Darwin, "The Darwin Family," *LL*, 1:10).

74. *Autobiography*, p. 144. For a discussion of the energizing effects of Darwin's eczema, see part 2, §7.

75. Leonard Darwin, "Memories of Down House," *The Nineteenth Century and After* 106 (July–December 1929):121.

76. *William Allingham's Diary* (introduction by Geoffrey Grigson) (Font-well, Sussex: Centaur Press, Ltd., 1967), p. 184. See §12.

77. For further comments on Sir George's theory of the causation of Darwin's illness, see part 2, §6.

78. Sir George Pickering, *Creative Malady* (London: George Allen & Unwin, Ltd., 1974), p. 23.

79. *Autobiography*, pp. 82–85.

80. *Autobiography*, p. 144.

81. Darwin to Hooker, Down Bromley Kent, 2 June (1857), DPL, Box 114. See §8.

82. Darwin to Fox, Down Bromley Kent, S.E., 30 November (1864), CCDL. See §11.

83. Henrietta Litchfield to Francis Darwin, Eastbourne, 18 March 1887, DPL, Box 112.

84. Darwin to Mrs. Haliburton, Down, 1 November (1872), *LL*, 2:352.

85. Frederic Harrison, *Autobiographic Memoirs* (London: MacMillan & Co., Ltd., 1911), 2:112.

86. "Certainly of Darwin, perhaps of Browning, almost of Dickens, we feel that the whole best in the man was realised, that there was no wastage of energy. But of how many Victorians can we say this?" (Esme Wingfield-Stratford, *Those Earnest Victorians* [New York: William Morrow & Co., Inc., Paperback Apollo Editions, n.d.], p. 260).

87. Phyllis Greenacre, *The Quest for the Father: A Study of the Darwin-Butler Controversy, as a Contribution to the Understanding of the Creative Individual* (New York: International Universities Press, Inc., 1963), pp. 90–91. For a further discussion of Dr. Greenacre's views on Darwin, see part 2, §3.

2

Theories of the Origins of the
Illness

1   The Theories of Darwin and
His Doctors

1.   "Darwin's Medical Notes, 1865 May 20." See part 1, §12.

2.   *Letter Read by Dr. B. W. Richardson, F.R.S., at his Lecture on Chas. Darwin, F.R.S. in St. George's Hall, Langham Place, October 22nd, 1882,* by Edward Lane (n.d., n.p.), p. 3.

3.   "The Late Charles Darwin," *British Medical Journal,* 29 April 1882, p. 628.

4.   Darwin to Hooker, Down, 7 January (1865), DPL, Box 115; "Darwin's Medical Notes, 1865 May 20." See part 1, §12. The diagnosis of "suppressed gout" seems to have been made by Drs. Brinton and Jenner.

5.   Darwin to Fox, Down Farnborough Kent, 6 February (1849), CCDL. See part 1, §6.

6.   "The Late Charles Darwin," *British Medical Journal,* 29 April 1882, p. 628.

7.   "Gout has been called retrocedent when the sudden subsidence of the gouty inflammation has been followed by sudden affection of some internal organ or function. Such affection is no doubt liable to occur whenever the local inflammation is repelled without the constitution being adequately relieved" (J. C. Forbes, "Gout," *The Cyclopaedia of Practical Medicine* [London, 1833], 2:378). "Retrocedent gout" was defined as "a term applied to the metastasis of gout to some internal organ or organs, whereby, on the sudden cessation of the inflammation of the joint, grave symptoms referable to the nervous or circulatory or digestive system appear" ("Gout, retrocedent" in Henry Power and Leonard W. Sedgwick, *The New Sydenham Society's Lexicon of Medicine and the Allied Sciences* [London, 1888], vol. 3).

8.   "Suppressed gout" was defined as "a term applied to those cases in which symptoms of disturbance of internal organs is supposed to depend upon a gouty condition, in which the external articular inflammation is imperfectly developed" ("Gout, suppressed," in Henry Power and Leonard W. Sedgwick, *The New Sydenham Society's Lexicon of Medicine and the Allied Sciences* [London, 1888], vol. 3).

9.   Henry Holland, *Medical Notes and Reflections* (London, 1855), p. 240.

10.   Ibid., p. 233.

11.   James Copeland, *A Dictionary of Practical Medicine* (London, 1858), 1:1044.

12.   Sir Alfred Baring Garrod, M.D., F.R.S., 1819–1907. For a summary of Dr. Garrod's work on gout, see "Sir Alfred Baring Garrod, FRS," *Journal of*

the American Medical Association 224 (1973):663–65; W. S. C. Copeman, *A Short History of the Gout, and the Rheumatic Diseases* (Berkeley and Los Angeles: University of California Press, 1964), pp. 106–8.

13.   Alfred Baring Garrod, *The Nature and Treatment of Gout and Rheumatic Gout*, 2d ed. (London, 1863), p. 263.

14.   Ibid., p. 264.

15.   Ibid., p. 265.

16.   Ibid., p. 491.

17.   Ibid., p. 490.

18.   W. S. C. Copeman, *A Short History of the Gout, and the Rheumatic Diseases* (Berkeley and Los Angeles: University of California Press, 1964), p. 107.

19.   Henry Holland, *Medical Notes and Reflections* (London, 1855), p. 239.

20.   When Dr. Erasmus Darwin was forty-eight he reported that he had an attack of acute gout "with much pain, and tumour, and redness about the joint of the toe." He had two more attacks when he was forty-nine. When he was fifty-six he wrote that he "had a little gout . . . the top of the foot and right toe swelled considerably" (Desmond King-Hele, *Erasmus Darwin* [New York: Charles Scribner's Sons, 1963], p. 35).

21.   When Dr. Robert Darwin was almost sixty-three he "had a bad fit of the gout together with a good deal of fever," and he was "confined to his bed for a week" (Darwin to Fox [Shrewsbury], 2 January 1829, CCDL). When Dr. Robert ·Darwin was almost seventy-nine "his leg . . . suddenly inflamed & was very painful" (Darwin to Fox, Down Bromley Kent, Thursday [14? February 1845?], CCDL). This may have been an attack of acute gout.

22.   Dr. Erasmus Darwin described the health of Charles Howard, the maternal grandfather of Dr. Robert Darwin, as follows: "The late Mr. Howard was never to my knowledge in the least insane, he was a drunkard both in public and private—and when he went to London he became connected with a woman and lived a deba[u]ched life in respect to drink, hence he had always the Gout of which he died but without any the least symptom of either insanity or epilepsy, but from debility of digestion and Gout as other drunkards die" (Dr. Erasmus Darwin to his son Dr. Robert Darwin, Derby, 5 January [1792], *Autobiography*, p. 224).

23.   See §4 of this part.

24.   Gruber and Barrett, *Darwin on Man*, pp. 104, 266.

25.   Darwin's copy of this volume is today preserved in the Cambridge University Library; the title page has the signature "Charles Darwin 1839."

26.   Henry Holland, *Medical Notes and Reflections* (London, 1839), p. 22.

27.   TN, 4:183.

28.   Charles Darwin, *The Variation of Animals and Plants under Domestication* (London: John Murray, 1868), 2:7. On the same page, note 12, Darwin

lists some of the works on hereditary disease which he has read: "Dr. Prosper Lucas's great work, 'Traité de l'Hérédité Naturelle', 1847. Mr. W. Sedgwick, in 'British and Foreign Medico-Chururg. Review,' April and July, 1861: Dr. Garrod on Gout is quoted in these articles. Sir Henry Holland, 'Medical Notes and Reflections', 3rd edit., 1855. Piorry, 'De l'Hérédité dans les Maladies,' 1840. Adams, 'A Philosophical Treatise on Hereditary Peculiarities', 2nd edit., 1815. Essay on 'Hereditary Diseases', by J. Steinan, 1843. *See* Paget, in 'Medical Times', 1857, p. 192, on the inheritance of Cancer; Dr. Gould, in 'Proc. of American Acad. of Sciences,' Nov. 8, 1853, gives a curious case of hereditary bleeding in four generations. Harlan, 'Medical Researches,' p. 593."

29.   Ibid., p. 404.

30.   "Darwin's Medical Notes, 1865 May 20." See part 1, §12.

31.   *LL*, 1:197.

32.   Darwin to Mrs. Haliburton, Down, 1 November (1872), *LL*, 2:353.

33.   Darwin was deeply interested in studying the offspring of consanguineous marriages (Darwin to John Lubbock, Down, 17 July 1870, *LL*, 2:309).

34.   See part 1, §8.

35.   Charles Darwin to his brother Erasmus Darwin, Down, 30 June 1864, *ML*, 1:247.

36.   James Hague, "A Reminiscence of Mr. Darwin," *Harper's New Monthly Magazine*, October 1884, p. 759.

37.   Titus Munson Coan (1836–1921). American physician, author of many literary, critical, and medical publications (*Who's Who in America*, vol. 1, 1897–1942; *Appletons' Cyclopaedia of American Biography*, vol. 1, 1888).

38.   Titus Munson Coan, "Darwin," *The Library Table*, November 1876, p. 143.

39.   A clipping of the article cited in note 38 is preserved in the Darwin Papers in the Cambridge University Library (DPL, Box 140). The only marking on the article is the word "Philosophy," written in Darwin's handwriting. This refers to a part of the article which states that the concept of evolution was present in Greek philosophy, and which quotes (in Greek) an evolutionary passage from the Greek comedian Aristophanes. Nothing is known about the relations between Darwin and Titus Munson Coan, or the source of Dr. Coan's information about Darwin's seasickness.

40.   *LL*, 1:197. In 1882 Francis Darwin told Darwin's friend, the Reverend J. Brodie Innes: "I think my father did not agree with the usually received opinion as to . . . [seasickness] undermining his health" (Francis Darwin to the Reverend J. Brodie Innes, 23 June 1882, in Robert M. Stecher, "The Darwin-Innes Letters," *Annals of Science* 17 [1961]:257).

41.   Wilhelm Preyer (1842–97) became an early convert to the Darwinian

theory, corresponded with Darwin, and wrote articles on Darwin and the Darwinian theory for Germans.

42. Wilhelm Preyer, "Charles Darwin," *Das Ausland*, 2 April 1870, p. 316.

43. Charles Darwin to Wilhelm Preyer, Down Beckenham Kent, 15 May 1870, published in Wilhelm Preyer, *Darwin: Sein Leben und Werfen* (Berlin: Ernst Hofmann & Co., 1896), pp. 149–50. This letter is published in German translation without the English original.

44. *LL*, 1:198.

45. Gruber and Barrett, *Darwin on Man*, p. 282.

46. "It [purposeless vivisection of animals] is a subject which makes me sick with horror, so I will not say another word about it, else I shall not sleep to-night" (Darwin to Professor Ray Lankester [22 March 1871], *LL*, 2:378).

47. Darwin to Hooker, Down Bromley Kent, 29 December (1860), DPL, Box 115. See part 1, §10.

48. Darwin to Francis Galton, November 1879, *LL*, 2:414.

2 Several Different Theories, and a Comparison of Darwin's Illness with the Illnesses of His Relations and Children

1. "Charles Darwin," *British Medical Journal*, 29 April 1882, p. 635.

2. "Charles Robert Darwin, F.R.S.," *Lancet*, 29 April 1882, p. 714.

3. "Charles Robert Darwin," *The Times*, 21 April 1882.

4. G. W. Bacon, *The Life of Charles Darwin, with British Opinion on Evolution* (London, 1882), p. 9.

5. L. C. Miall, *The Life and Work of Charles Darwin* (Leeds, 1883), p. 20.

6. *LL*, 1:198.

7. Part 1, §8.

8. George J. Romanes, "Charles Darwin. Character and Life," in *Charles Darwin. Memorial Notices Reprinted from Nature* (London, 1882), p. 14.

9. "Darwin's Life and Letters—I," *The Nation*, 17 November 1887, p. 401.

10. Thomas H. Huxley, *Darwinian Essays* (New York, 1912), p. 293.

11. Leonard Huxley, *Charles Darwin* (New York: Greenberg Publishers, 1927), p. 112.

12. Sir Buckston Browne, "Darwin's Health," *Nature*, 2 January 1943, p. 15.

13. Leonard Darwin, "Memories of Down House," *The Nineteenth Century and After* 106 (July–December 1929):121.

14. *LL*, 1:135.

15. Dr. William Waring Johnston, 1843–1902 (Kelly and Burrage, *Dictionary of American Medical Biography* [New York, 1928]).

16. W. W. Johnston, "The Ill Health of Charles Darwin: Its Nature and Its Relation to His Work," *American Anthropologist* (*N.S.*) 3 (1901):158.

17. John C. Nemiah, "Neurasthenic Neurosis," in A. M. Freedman, H. I. Kaplan, B. J. Sadock, eds., *Comprehensive Textbook of Psychiatry–II* (Baltimore: Williams and Wilkins Co., 1975), 1:1264–67; A. P. Noyes and L. C. Kolb, *Modern Clinical Psychiatry* (Philadelphia: W. B. Saunders Co., 1963), pp. 411–13.

18. W. W. Johnston, "The Ill Health of Charles Darwin: Its Nature and Its Relation to His Work," *American Anthropologist* (*N.S.*) 3 (1901):157.

19. John C. Nemiah, "Neurasthenic Neurosis," in A. M. Freedman, H. I. Kaplan, B. J. Sadock, eds., *Comprehensive Textbook of Psychiatry–II* (Baltimore: Williams and Wilkins Co., 1975), 1:1264–67.

20. Dr. George Milbry Gould, 1848–1922 (Kelly and Burrage, *Dictionary of American Medical Biography* [New York, 1928]).

21. George M. Gould, "Charles Darwin," in *Biographic Clinics* (Philadelphia, 1903), p. 103.

22. Ibid., pp. 91–94.

23. Ibid., pp. 102–3.

24. This was the opinion of two ophthalmologists to whom I described Darwin's symptoms.

25. *Letter Read by Dr. B. W. Richardson, F.R.S., at his Lecture on Chas. Darwin, F.R.S. in St. George's Hall, Langham Place, October 22nd, 1882*, by Edward Lane (n.d., n.p.), p. 5.

26. *LL*, 1:496.

27. Francis Darwin, "Reminiscences of my Father's Everyday Life," DPL, Box 140 (3), pp. 7–8.

28. "What an incomparably good fellow you are to send me the eye-glass: I have now got it with a string round my neck, and practice every now and then, making horrible contortions, to keep it to my eye. I believe with practice I shall at last succeed, and that it will be *very* useful; and again I say that you are an incomparably good fellow" (Charles Darwin to his son William E. Darwin, Down, 26 April [1862], DPL, Box 153. In this letter Darwin writes "To day, thank Heaven, I finished last revise of my accursed little orchid book." In his *Journal* he records that he finished his orchid book on 28 April 1862. Hence this letter must have been written on 26 April 1862.). Darwin would wear this pince-nez low down on his nose, and carry it suspended around his neck on a ribbon (Francis Darwin, "Reminiscences of my Father's Everyday Life," DPL, Box 140 [3], pp. 7–8).

29. Francis Darwin, "Reminiscences of my Father's Everyday Life," DPL, Box 140 (3), p. 7.

30. Ibid., p. 8.

31. "Sir Arthur Keith (1866–1955)/Keith-Flack Node," *Journal of the American Medical Association* 200 (1967):164–65.

32. Sir Arthur Keith, *Darwin Revalued* (London, 1955), p. 214.

33. Walter C. Alvarez, born 22 July 1884 ("Dr. Walter Alvarez: A Medical Legend Nears 90," *Modern Medicine*, 8 July 1974, pp. 32–39).

34. Dr. Alvarez has commented on Darwin's illness in the following publications: Books: *Nervousness, Indigestion, and Pain* (New York and London: Paul Hoeber, Inc., 1943), pp. 240–43; *Practical Leads to Puzzling Diagnoses: Neuroses that Run through Families* (Philadelphia and Montreal: J. B. Lippincott Co., 1958), pp. 246–47. Articles: "The Nature of Charles Darwin's Lifelong Ill-Health," *New England Journal of Medicine* 261 (1959): 1109–12; "Why the Nervous Ill Health of Charles Darwin?" *Modern Medicine*, 12 January 1970, pp. 103–4; "Manic-Depressive Insanity Related to Genius," *Modern Medicine*, 26 January 1970, pp. 100–102. Letters: *New England Journal of Medicine* 262 (1960):421–22; *Medical Tribune*, 11–12 July 1964. Dr. Alvarez's view of Darwin's illness—especially the hereditary nature of the illness and the presumed similarity of Darwin's symptoms to the symptoms of his relatives—is summarized by Philip Marshall Dale, M.D., in "Charles Darwin: 1809–1882," in *Medical Biographies: The Ailments of Thirty-three Famous Persons* (Norman: University of Oklahoma Press, 1952), pp. 196–98.

35. "Dr. Walter Alvarez: A Medical Legend Nears 90," *Modern Medicine*, 8 July 1974, p. 34.

36. Walter C. Alvarez, "The Nature of Charles Darwin's Lifelong Ill-Health," *New England Journal of Medicine* 261 (1959):1112.

37. Ibid., p. 1108.

38. Ibid., p. 1110.

39. Ibid., pp. 1111–12.

40. "The 'Mauve Factor' in Schizophrenia," *Medical World News*, 14 December 1973, p. 49.

41. The illness of Darwin's great-grandfather, Charles Howard, and the gouty illness of his grandfather, Dr. Erasmus Darwin, have been described in part 2, §1, n. 20, 22.

42. Dr. Erasmus Darwin to his son Dr. Robert Darwin, Derby, 5 January (1792), *Autobiography*, p. 224; Anna Seward, *Memoirs of the Life of Dr. Darwin* (London: J. Johnson, St. Paul's Church-Yard, 1804), pp. 12–14.

43. See §4 of this part.

44. R. B. Litchfield, *Tom Wedgwood: The First Photographer* (London: Duckworth and Co., 1903), pp. 23–24.

45. Ibid., p. 179.

46. Anna Seward, *Memoirs of the Life of Dr. Darwin* (London: J. Johnson, St. Paul's Church-Yard, 1804), p. 407.

47. Ibid., pp. 405–6; Charles Darwin, *"The Life of Erasmus Darwin,"* together with an Essay on his Scientific Works by Ernst Krause (New York: D. Appleton and Co., 1880), pp. 71–76.

48. Francis Galton, *Memories of My Life* (London: Methuen & Co., 1908),

p. 79. For further details on the early symptoms of this illness, see D. W. Forrest, *Francis Galton: The Life and Work of a Victorian Genius* (New York: Taplinger Publishing Co., 1974), p. 22.

49. Ibid., p. 155.

50. Karl Pearson, *The Life, Letters and Labours of Francis Galton* (Cambridge: Cambridge University Press, 1924), 11:179.

51. *Autobiography*, p. 42.

52. Darwin to Fox, Down Bromley Kent, 8 February (1857), CCDL.

53. Ague was acute fever; also paroxysms consisting of cold, hot, and sweating stages.

54. Erasmus Darwin to his brother Charles Darwin, 23 November (1859), *LL*, 2:29.

55. Darwin to Fox, Down Bromley Kent, 22 (March 1860), CCDL.

56. *Darwin and Henslow*, p. 13, n. 1.

57. Darwin to Fox, Down Beckenham Kent, 11 May (1874), CCDL.

58. Darwin to Fox, at H. Wedgwood's, Hopedone, Dorking, 26 May (1876), Pearce Collection, Woodward Biomedical Library, University of British Columbia, Vancouver, Canada.

59. Darwin to Fox, Down Beckenham Kent, 2 December 1877 (this letter is not in Darwin's handwriting), CCDL.

60. *CFL*, 2:243, 281.

61. Walter C. Alvarez, "The Nature of Charles Darwin's Lifelong Ill-Health," *New England Journal of Medicine* 261 (1959):1112.

62. See part 1, §8, 9.

63. Darwin to Fox, Malvern, Thursday (27 March 1851), CCDL.

64. See part 1, §7.

65. See part 1, §8–10; appendix A, *"Receipts" and "Memoranda,"* pp. 20–22 (original pagination).

66. Gwen Raverat, *Period Piece* (New York: W. W. Norton, 1952), p. 124.

67. Darwin noted both of these illnesses in his *Journal* (*Darwin's Journal*, p. 13).

68. Darwin to Fox, Cliff Cottage, Bournemouth, 12 September (1862), CCDL.

69. "Our poor Boy had the rare case of second rash & sore throat, besides mischief in Kidneys; & as if this was not enough a most serious attack of Erysipelas with Typhoid symptoms. I despaired of his life, but this evening he has eaten one mouthful & I think has passed the crisis" (Darwin to Asa Gray, Down Bromley Kent, 23 July [1862], Gray Herbarium of Harvard University, Cambridge; mostly published in *ML*, 1:202).

70. In the summer of 1857 Etty had hydropathy at Moor Park (Darwin to Fox, Moor Park, Farnham, Surrey, Thursday [1 May 1857], CCDL; Darwin

to Fox, Down Bromley Kent, 30 October [1857], CCDL; *Darwin's Journal*, p. 14).

71.   Darwin to Fox, Down Bromley Kent, 24 June (1858), CCDL. See also part 1, §9, 10.

72.   Darwin to Fox, 15 Marine Parade, Eastbourne, 18 October (1860), CCDL.

73.   Darwin to Hooker, at Miss Wedgwood's, Hartfield, Tonbridge Wells, 29 July (1860), DPL, Box 115.

74.   Darwin to Fox, 2 Hasketh Crescent, Torquay, 8 July (1861), CCDL.

75.   Darwin to Fox, Down Bromley Kent, 18 May (1860), CCDL.

76.   *CFL*, 2:176.

77.   Darwin to Reverend J. Brodie Innes, Down Bromley Kent, 1 May (1862) (Robert M. Stecher, "The Darwin-Innes Letters," *Annals of Science* 17 [1961]: 209–10).

78.   Darwin to Fox, Down Bromley Kent, 23 May (1863), CCDL.

79.   Darwin to Fox, Down Bromley Kent, 30 October (1857), CCDL.

80.   Darwin to Hooker, Down Bromley Kent, 6 October (1858), DPL, Box 114.

81.   Darwin to Fox, Down Bromley Kent, 23 September (1859), CCDL.

82.   Darwin to Reverend J. Brodie Innes, Down Bromley Kent, 24 February (1862) (Robert M. Stecher, "The Darwin-Innes Letters," *Annals of Science* 17 [1961]:212).

83.   Ibid.

84.   See part 1, §15.

85.   Gwen Raverat, *Period Piece* (New York: W. W. Norton, 1952), p. 123. This book, by a granddaughter of Darwin, gives vivid portraits of six of Darwin's children—Henrietta, George, Francis, Leonard, Horace, and William— as adults. William Darwin appears to have been relatively healthy and unconcerned about illness. For a discussion of this book, and the hypochondriasis of the Darwin children, see Dr. Douglas Hubble, "The Life of the Shawl," *Lancet*, 27 February 1954, pp. 1351–54.

86.   Horace Darwin was described as having "really had weak health"; when he was forty-two; "after years of ill health, he was at last successfully operated on by Sir Frederick Treves for *typhlitis*, as appendicitis was then called" (Gwen Raverat, *Period Piece* [New York: W. W. Norton, 1952] p. 204). Francis Darwin was described as "always apt to suffer from fits of depression"; he once said about himself, "I don't like myself very much as I am, and I really could not bear the thought of going on for ever." Some of his depression may have been accentuated by the death of his young wife (after giving birth to a first child) when he was twenty-eight (Gwen Raverat, *Period Piece* [New York: W. W. Norton, 1952] pp. 189, 191). Leonard Darwin was described as having "long suffered from incapacitating sick headaches"; when he was forty

he resigned from the army "partly on the grounds of health"; when he was forty-five he wrote his mother about his digestive difficulties: "I wish I lived in the days of Pickwick when one could get blind drunk without moral or physical inconvenience, instead of in these degenerate days when an extra help of curry or a strong cup of coffee has worse effects." His disposition has been described as follows: "he had not his father's demonstrative nature, nor his high spirits and capacity for intense enjoyment, being of a quieter, more contemplative, temperament" (Margaret Keynes, *Leonard Darwin 1850–1943* [Cambridge: Privately printed at the Cambridge University Press, 1943], pp. 13, 33. Margaret Keynes was a niece of Leonard Darwin.).

87.   Sir Francis Darwin, "Memoir of Sir George Darwin," in *Scientific Papers of Sir George Howard Darwin* (Cambridge at the University Press, 1916), 5:xiv. Sir Francis had medical training and was the younger brother of Sir George.

88.   Sir George Pickering, *Creative Malady* (London: George Allen & Unwin, Ltd., 1974), p. 9.

89.   Sir Francis Darwin, "Memoir of Sir George Darwin," in *Scientific Papers of Sir George Howard Darwin* (Cambridge at the University Press, 1916), 5:xiv.

90.   Ibid.

91.   Gwen Raverat, *Period Piece* (New York: W. W. Norton, 1952), p. 187.

92.   George Darwin was born in 1845, and died from cancer in 1912. He became Plumian professor of astronomy and experimental philosophy at Cambridge, and published papers on problems of mathematical cosmogony which have been regarded as "a milestone in the development of cosmogony" (Zdenek Kopal, "George Howard Darwin," in Charles C. Gillispie, ed., *Dictionary of Scientific Biography* [New York: Charles Scribners, 1971]), 3: 582–84.

93.   Darwin to Hooker, Down Bromley Kent, 26 (March 1861), DPL, Box 115. See part 1, §10.

3   Psychoanalytic Theories

1.   Edward J. Kempf, born 1885.

2.   Edward J. Kempf, "Charles Darwin—The Affective Sources of His Inspiration and Anxiety Neurosis," *Psychoanalytic Review* 5 (1918):151–92. The *Psychoanalytic Review* first appeared in 1913, and was the first psychoanalytic periodical in English. Kempf's essay on Darwin was then reprinted, with the same title, as a section in his big book *Psychopathology* (St. Louis: C. V. Mosby and Co., 1920), pp. 208–51.

3.   Imre Hermann, "Charles Darwin," *Imago* 13 (1927):57–82.

4.   Dr. Douglas Hubble: "Charles Darwin and Psychotherapy," *Lancet*, 30 January 1943, pp. 129–33; "The Evolution of Charles Darwin," *Horizon*

14 (1946):74–85; "The Life of the Shawl," *Lancet*, 26 December 1953, pp. 1351–54; "The Life of the Shawl," *Lancet*, 27 February 1954, p. 467; "The Autobiography of Charles Darwin," *Lancet*, 5 July 1958, pp. 37–39. Dr. Rankine Good: "The Life of the Shawl," *Lancet*, 9 January 1954, pp. 106–7; "The Origin of 'The Origin': A Psychological Approach," *Biology and Human Affairs*, October 1954, pp. 10–16.

5.   Erasmus Darwin Barlow, "The Dangers of Health," *The Listener*, 23 August 1956, pp. 265–67.

6.   Phyllis Greenacre, *The Quest for the Father: A Study of the Darwin-Butler Controversy, as a Contribution to the Understanding of the Creative Individual* (New York: International Universities Press, Inc., 1963), p. 128.

7.   Dr. Edward Kempf, "Charles Darwin—The Affective Sources of His Inspiration and Anxiety Neurosis," *Psychoanalytic Review* 5 (1918):167.

8.   Imre Hermann, "Charles Darwin," *Imago* 13 (1927):69–72.

9.   Dr. Douglas Hubble, "The Life of the Shawl," *Lancet*, 27 February 1954, p. 467.

10.   Dr. Phyllis Greenacre, *The Quest for the Father*, p. 33.

11.   Dr. Rankine Good, "The Life of the Shawl," *Lancet*, 9 January 1954, p. 106. This is a short letter to *Lancet*. Dr. Good presents his views on Darwin's illness, in more detail, in "The Origin of 'The Origin': A Psychological Approach," *Biology and Human Affairs*, October 1954, pp. 10–16.

12.   "To my deep mortification my father once said to me, 'You care for nothing but shooting, dogs, and rat-catching, and you will be a disgrace to yourself and all your family.' But my father, who was the kindest man I ever knew, and whose memory I love with all my heart, must have been angry and somewhat unjust when he used such words." "My father ... was very properly vehement against my turning an idle sporting man, which then [1827] seemed my probable destination" (*Autobiography*, pp. 28, 56).

13.   Dr. Douglas Hubble, "The Evolution of Charles Darwin," *Horizon* 14 (1946):84.

14.   Dr. Phyllis Greenacre, *The Quest for the Father*, p. 90.

15.   Ibid.

16.   See note 12 of this section.

17.   See part 1, §2.

18.   Sir Arthur Keith, *Darwin Revalued* (London: Watts & Co., 1955), p. 222.

19.   Gruber and Barrett, *Darwin on Man*, pp. 266–75.

20.   In the first pages of his third *Transmutation Notebook* (written July 1838–October 1838) Darwin writes "father" once and "Father" twice. In his 1876 *Autobiography* the word *father* appears seventy times in reference to Dr. Robert Darwin: forty-nine times it is given a small *f* and twenty-one times a capital *F*. (For a psychological interpretation of this see Douglas Hubble, "Before Our Time," *Lancet*, 5 July 1958, p. 39.)

21. See part 1, §6. When his father died Darwin seems to have inherited about £45,000 (Sir Arthur Keith, *Darwin Revalued* [London: Watts & Co., 1955], p. 225).

22. *LL*, 1:11.

23. Ibid.

24. See part 1, §3.

25. John Bowlby, "Darwin's Health," *British Medical Journal*, 10 April 1965, p. 999.

26. Susannah Darwin is said to have been an "invalid," and to have had "a long decline" in her health (*Autobiography*, p. 22; Eliza Meteyard, *A Group of Englishmen* [London, 1871], p. 360). Nothing is known about the details of her illness. Two individuals who saw her, several years before her death, make no mention of her being ill. In June 1815 Mrs. Josiah Wedgwood visited the Mount and then commented: "I always enjoy the society of Mrs. Darwin" (Mrs. Josiah Wedgwood to her sister Emma Allen (The Mount), Shrewsbury, 28 June 1815, *CFL*, 1:68). Mr. F. Gretton, a companion of young Charles Darwin, recollects visiting the Mount around 1814–17: "Mrs. Darwin I distinctly remember, a pleasant, courteous, somewhat retiring lady" (F. E. Gretton, *Memory's Harkback, through Half-a-Century* [London: Richard Bentley & Son, 1889], p. 36). It is possible that Susannah Darwin was suffering from a subacute illness and that, when seeing visitors, she concealed her illness.

27. *LL*, 1:9.

4   The Possibility of Chagas' Disease, Other Possible Medical Causes

1. Professor George Gaylord Simpson, "Charles Darwin in Search of Himself," *Scientific American* 199 (August 1958):117–22.

2. "Naturalist's Evolution," *MD*, September 1959, p. 141.

3. Dr. Phyllis Greenacre, *The Quest for the Father*, p. 32.

4. Professor Saul Adler (1895–1966). Obituary in *New York Times*, 26 January 1966. Dr. Adler was born in Russia, and educated in Leeds University in England and the School of Tropical Medicine in Liverpool. In 1933 he received the Chalmers gold medal of the Royal Society of Tropical Medicine and Hygiene, and (at the time of his death) he was the only Israeli member of the British Royal Society. In Israel he became the head of the parasitology department, Hebrew University, Jerusalem.

5. Professor Saul Adler, "Darwin's Illness," *Nature*, 10 October 1959, pp. 1102–3.

6. Lawrence A. Kohn, "Charles Darwin's Chronic Ill Health," *Bulletin of the History of Medicine* 37 (1963):239–56.

7. Sir Gavin de Beer, *Charles Darwin: Evolution by Natural Selection*

(Garden City, N.Y.: Doubleday & Co., Inc., 1964), pp. 115–17.

8. Peter B. Medawar, "Darwin's Illness," *New Statesman*, 3 April 1964, pp. 527–28. This essay was reprinted in *Annals of Internal Medicine*, October 1964, and then in P. B. Medawar, *The Art of the Soluble* (London: Methuen & Co., Ltd., 1967).

9. James A. Brussel, "The Nature of the Naturalist's Unnatural Illness: A Study of Charles Robert Darwin," *Psychiatric Quarterly Supplement*, pt. 2, 1966, pp. 1–17.

10. "Darwin's Illness," *Canadian Medical Association Journal*, 26 December 1964, pp. 1371–72; Julian Huxley and H. B. D. Kettlewell, *Charles Darwin and his World* (New York: Studio Book, Viking Press, 1965), p. 66.

11. Douglas Hubble, "Darwin's Illness," *New Statesman*, 10 April 1964, p. 561. Dr. Hubble wrote this letter as a reply to Medawar's article.

12. A. W. Woodruff, "Darwin's Health in Relation to His Voyage to South America," *British Medical Journal* 1 (1965):745–50. (This article has been reprinted, under the same title and with some changes, in Arnold Sorsby, ed., *Tenements of Clay: An Anthology of Medical Biographical Essays* [London: Julian Friedmann Publishers, Ltd., 1974], pp. 215–30). A. W. Woodruff, "The Impact of Darwin's Voyage to South America on His Work and Health," *Bulletin of the New York Academy of Medicine* 44 (1968):661–72.

13. A. W. Woodruff, "Darwin's Health in Relation to His Voyage to South America," *British Medical Journal* 1 (1965):747–48.

14. Ibid., p. 10.

15. It has been shown that Chagas' disease causes severe destruction of cardiac tissue, leading to cardiac impairments and "sudden cardiac deaths with or without congestive failure" ("New Light on Chagas' Disease," *Lancet*, 29 May 1965, pp. 1150–51).

16. A. W. Woodruff, "The Impact of Darwin's Voyage to South America on His Work and Health," *Bulletin of the New York Academy of Medicine* 44 (1968):668–70.

17. A. W. Woodruff, "Darwin's Illness," *British Medical Journal* 1 (1965): 1380.

18. A. W. Woodruff, "Darwin's Health in Relation to His Voyage to South America," *British Medical Journal* 1 (1965):749.

19. Saul Adler, "Darwin's Illness," *British Medical Journal* 1 (1965):1249–50.

20. Michael Kelly, "Darwin Really Was Sick," *Journal of Chronic Diseases* 20 (1967):341.

21. Sir Gavin de Beer states that the clinical picture of Chagas' disease "matches Darwin's symptoms in detail." J. G. Crowther infers that Chagas' disease "may be" the cause of Darwin's "peculiar illness." John Chancellor writes: "The most readily accepted diagnosis appears now to be that Darwin had a genuine illness, aggravated by his hypochondria. The illness was

probably Chaga's Disease.... The symptoms of Chaga's Disease correspond perfectly with Darwin's medical history from the time when he landed in England from the *Beagle* until his death. The trypanosoma invades the heart muscle of its victim, leaving him very tired; it also invades other parts of the body, causing lassitude, gastro-intestinal discomfort and heart trouble, of which Darwin died" (Sir Gavin de Beer, "Charles Robert Darwin," in Charles C. Gillispie, ed., *Dictionary of Scientific Biography* [New York: Charles Scribners, 1971], 3:566; J. G. Crowther, *Charles Darwin* [London: Methuen, 1972], p. 37; John Chancellor, *Charles Darwin* [London: Weidenfeld and Nicolson, 1973], p. 122). Sir Gavin, Mr. Crowther, and Mr. Chancellor take no cognizance of any of the objections to Chagas' disease. Two biographers of Darwin, Robert C. Olby and Paul-Emile Duroux, discuss Professor Woodward's criticisms of Chagas' disease, and then conclude that Darwin's illness was most likely "psychosomatic" (Robert C. Olby, *Charles Darwin* [Oxford University Press, 1967], pp. 47–48; Paul-Emile Duroux, *Les Darwin* [Paris: Editions Universitaires, 1972], pp. 13–14).

22.   "Naturalist's Evolution," *MD*, September 1959, p. 141.

23.   Lawrence A. Kohn, "Charles Darwin's Chronic Ill Health," *Bulletin of the History of Medicine* 37 (1963):251.

24.   Ibid., pp. 241, 251.

25.   Ibid., p. 252.

26.   Francis Darwin, "Reminiscences of my Father's Everyday Life," *LL*, 1:96–97.

27.   Ibid., pp. 100–101; see part 1, §5.

28.   DeWitt Stetten, Jr., "Gout," *Perspectives in Biology and Medicine*, winter 1959, pp. 194–95.

29.   Hyman J. Roberts, "Reflections on Darwin's Illness," *Journal of Chronic Diseases* 19 (1966):723–25; "Reflections on Darwin's Illness," *Geriatrics*, September 1967, pp. 160–67.

30.   Hyman J. Roberts, "The Syndrome of Narcolepsy and Diabetes, Idiopathic Edema, Cerebral Dysrhythmias and Multiple Sclerosis (200 Patients)," *Journal of the American Geriatrics Society*, October 1964, pp. 926–76. Pages 926–30 summarize the clinical features of this syndrome.

31.   Francis Darwin, "Reminiscences of my Father's Everyday Life," *LL*, 1:99–100.

32.   Francis Darwin, "Reminiscences of my Father's Everyday Life," *DPL*, Box 140 (3), p. 9; Sir Buckston Browne, "Darwin's Health," *Nature*, 2 January 1943, p. 15.

33.   Francis Darwin, "Reminiscences of my Father's Everyday Life," *DPL*, Box 140 (3), p. 12.

34.   Dr. Torben K. With is associated with the Central Laboratory, Svendborg County Hospital, Svendborg, Denmark. He has published many

articles on porphyria, including the following: "Acute Intermittent Porphyria: Diagnosis Four Years Post Mortem by Chemical Studies in Relatives," *Scandinavian Journal of Clinical and Laboratory Investigation* 16 (1964):465–69; "The Porphyrias in the Light of Danish Observations," *Danish Medical Bulletin*, October 1969, pp. 257–67; "The Clinical Chemistry of the Porphyrias," *Clinical Biochemistry* 1 (1968):224–42.

35. Desmond King-Hele, *Erasmus Darwin* (New York: Charles Scribner's Sons, 1963), p. 21. See part 2, §2, for an account of Mrs. Mary Darwin's illness.

36. Dr. With mentioned his porphyria theory to Mr. Desmond King-Hele; the latter, in his second book on Dr. Erasmus Darwin, then wrote this passage: "Mary Darwin's disease is not known, but Dr. T. K. With has suggested that it may have been acute intermittent porphyria. Whatever it was, the disease seems to have been hereditary, for somewhat similar symptoms appeared in several of her descendants, including her grandson Charles Darwin" (Desmond King-Hele, ed., *The Essential Writings of Erasmus Darwin* [London: MacGibbon & Kee, 1968], pp. 18–19). I thank Dr. With and Mr. King-Hele for answering my queries, and informing me how Dr. With developed his theory.

37. Described in part 2, §2.

38. "Darwin's Medical Notes, 1865 May 20." See part 1, §12.

39. Ibid.

5 The Possibility of Arsenic Poisoning

1. John H. Winslow, *Darwin's Victorian Malady: Evidence for its Medically Induced Origin* (Philadelphia: American Philosophical Society, 1971).

2. Lawrence A. Kohn, "Charles Darwin's Chronic Ill Health," *Bulletin of the History of Medicine* 37 (1963):252.

3. John H. Winslow, *Darwin's Victorian Malady: Evidence for its Medically Induced Origin* (Philadelphia: American Philosophical Society, 1971), p. 74.

4. Ibid., p. 73.

5. Kenneth P. Dubois and E. M. K. Geiling, *Textbook of Toxicology* (New York: Oxford University Press, 1959), pp. 134–35.

6. "Darwin's Medical Notes, 1865 May 20." See part 1, §12.

7. Darwin to Hooker, Down Farnborough Kent, 12 October (1849), DPL, Box 114, *LL*, 1:347.

8. Darwin to Hooker, Moor Park, Farnham, Surrey, Wednesday (29 April 1857), DPL, Box 114, *LL*, 1:449.

9. See part 1, §11, 12.

10. See part 1, §7.

11.   See part 1, §12.

12.   John H. Winslow, *Darwin's Victorian Malady: Evidence for its Medically Induced Origin* (Philadelphia: American Philosophical Society, 1971), pp. 61–62.

13.   Dr. W. D. Foster writes that after studying this photograph, in his copy of Lady Barlow's edition of Darwin's *Autobiography*, "I was not able to convince myself of the existence of 'corn-like elevations', and they are certainly not to be seen on the original photograph at Down" (W. D. Foster, "Book Reviews," *Isis* 63 [1972]:591–92).

14.   *CFL,* 2:60.

15.   Francis Darwin, "Reminiscences of my Father's Everyday Life," *LL,* 1:89.

16.   Henry Fairfield Osborn, "Charles Darwin," in *Impressions of Great Naturalists* (New York and London: Charles Scribner's Sons, 1928), p. 51.

17.   *William Allingham's Diary* (introduction by Geoffrey Grigson) (Fontwell, Sussex: Centaur Press, Ltd., 1967), p. 184. See part 1, §12.

18.   Darwin to Fox, The Lodge, Malvern, 24 (March 1849), CCDL.

19.   *LL,* 2:356.

20.   John Spencer Clark, *The Life and Letters of John Fiske* (Boston and New York: Houghton Mifflin Co., 1917), 1:478–79.

21.   Haeckel's description of Darwin is quoted in G. T. Bettany, *Life of Charles Darwin* (London: Walter Scott, 1887), pp. 147–48.

22.   Professor Ferdinand Cohn, *Breslauer Zeitung,* 23 April 1882.

23.   Osler's description of Darwin is written inside the cover of his copy of the July 1858 Darwin-Wallace Linnean Society Papers. It was published in *Bibliotheca Osler* (Oxford, 1929), p. 155.

24.   W. D. Foster, "Book Reviews," *Isis* 63 (1972):592.

25.   John H. Winslow, *Darwin's Victorian Malady: Evidence for its Medically Induced Origin* (Philadelphia: American Philosophical Society, 1971), p. 68.

26.   Ibid. See also "The Late Charles Darwin," *British Medical Journal,* 29 April 1882, p. 628.

27.   Darwin to Asa Gray, Down, 2 March (1860), Gray Herbarium of Harvard University, Cambridge. See part 1, §10.

28.   Darwin to Hooker, Down Bromley Kent, Saturday, 3 March (1860), DPL, Box 115, *LL,* 2:85. See part 1, §10, n. 5, 6. On 20 April 1853 Darwin reported, in his *Diary of Health,* that he had a cold, mild fever, and "chest-pain." The nature of this "chest-pain" was not specified and it seems to have lasted for only one day. (See part 1, §7, n. 38.)

29.   John H. Winslow, *Darwin's Victorian Malady: Evidence for its Medically Induced Origin* (Philadelphia: American Philosophical Society, 1971), pp. 66–67.

30.   Ibid., p. 67.

31.   The source that Dr. Winslow gives for the assertion that Darwin "mentioned growing bald at the age of twenty-eight" is a letter that Charles Lyell wrote to Darwin, when the latter was twenty-eight, in which Lyell said: "Do not flatter yourself that you will be believed till you are growing bald like me, with hard work and vexation at the incredulity of the world" (*LL*, 1:294). When Darwin was about twenty-eight he commented that his face was "already beginning to wrinkle," but he said nothing about the state of his hair (*Autobiography*, p. 234).

32.   The portrait of Darwin by George Richmond. (Reproduced in Geoffrey West, *Charles Darwin: A Portrait* [New Haven: Yale University Press, 1938], p. 152.)

33.   A portrait reproduced in *Darwin and Henslow*, p. 149.

34.   A photograph reproduced in *Autobiography*, p. 111.

35.   A portrait reproduced in Sir Gavin de Beer, *Charles Darwin: Evolution by Natural Selection* (New York, 1964), p. 164.

36.   John H. Winslow, *Darwin's Victorian Malady: Evidence for its Medically Induced Origin* (Philadelphia: American Philosophical Society, 1971), p. 66.

37.   *Darwin and the "Beagle,"* pp. 167–68. What "great teeth" refers to is obscure: it could refer to Darwin's teeth, or to teeth (animal or human) which he had collected.

38.   Darwin to Fox, Down Farnborough Kent, 24 (October 1852), CCDL, *LL*, 1:352. (See appendix B, n. 19.)

39.   Darwin to Hooker, Down Bromley Kent, 26 (March 1861), DPL, Box 115. (See part 1, §10, n. 23.)

40.   "Darwin's Medical Notes, 1865 May 20." See part 1, §12.

41.   Leonard Darwin, "Memories of Down House," *The Nineteenth Century and After* 106 (July–December 1929):121. See part 2, §2. Sir Buckston Browne, in his account of Darwin's *Diary of Health*, states that Darwin had "pyorrhoea and sore gums"; but this is not indicated in the *Diary*, and no other source is given for it (Sir Buckston Browne, "Darwin's Health," *Nature*, 2 January 1943, p. 14).

42.   Francis Darwin, "Reminiscences of my Father's Everyday Life," DPL, Box 140 (3), p. 9.

43.   Sir Buckston Browne, "Darwin's Health," *Nature*, 2 January 1943, p. 14.

44.   John H. Winslow, *Darwin's Victorian Malady: Evidence for its Medically Induced Origin* (Philadelphia: American Philosophical Society, 1971), p. 67.

45.   Darwin to Fox, Down Farnborough Kent, 19 March (1855), CCDL, *LL*, 1:407. See part 1, §8, n. 1.

46.   Darwin to Fox, Down Bromley Kent, 20 October (1856), CCDL.

47.   Darwin to Hooker, Down, Monday (24 January 1864), DPL, Box 115. See part 1, §11, n. 65.

48.   "Darwin's Medical Notes, 1865 May 20." See part 1, §12.

49.   W. D. Foster, "A Contribution to the Problem of Darwin's Ill-Health," *Bulletin of the History of Medicine* 39 (1965):477–78.

50.   John H. Winslow, *Darwin's Victorian Malady: Evidence for its Medically Induced Origin* (Philadelphia: American Philosophical Society, 1971), pp. 68–69.

51.   See part 1, §7.

52.   See part 1, §11, n. 47; part 2, §2.

53.   J. M. Herbert to Francis Darwin, 12 June 1882, DPL, Box 112. See part 1, §1.

54.   Charles Darwin to Susan Darwin (London), Friday morning (9 September 1831), *Darwin and the "Beagle,"* p. 48. See part 1, §2.

55.   Charles Darwin to Susan Darwin (London), Friday morning (9 September 1831), *Darwin and the "Beagle,"* p. 48. See part 1, §2.

56.   James M. Gully, *The Water Cure in Chronic Disease* (New York: Wiley & Putnam, 1847), pp. 43–44.

57.   William Brinton, *The Diseases of the Stomach* (London: John Churchill, 1859), pp. 393–94.

58.   Edward W. Lane, *Hydropathy: Or the Natural System of Medical Treatment* (London: John Churchill, 1857), pp. 36–41.

59.   J. F. Royle and F. W. Headland, *A Manual of Materia Medica and Therapeutics* (London: John Churchill, 1865), p. 227.

60.   See part 1, §10.

61.   James Startin, *A Pharmacopoeia for Diseases of the Skin,* 2d ed. (London: Harrison & Sons, 1890), pp. 30–35.

62.   See part 1, §11. Some physicians prescribed arsenic, "given in quite small doses," as "the remedy for chronic ekzema in adults" ("Domestic Medicine and Surgery," by a member of the College of Surgeons of England, in Ross Murray, *The Modern Householder* [London, 1872], p. 584).

63.   John H. Winslow, *Darwin's Victorian Malady: Evidence for its Medically Induced Origin* (Philadelphia: American Philosophical Society, 1971), p. 34.

64.   See part 1, §13, n. 19.

65.   See appendix A, *"Receipts" and "Memoranda,"* pp. 1, 3.

66.   *Darwin and the "Beagle,"* p. 184.

67.   Charles Darwin to Caroline Darwin, 13 October 1834, *Darwin and the "Beagle,"* p. 107.

68.   Henry Holland, "On Mercurial Medicines," in *Medical Notes and Reflections* (London, 1855), pp. 531–39. See note 71 this section.

69.   John H. Winslow, *Darwin's Victorian Malady: Evidence for its Medically Induced Origin* (Philadelphia: American Philosophical Society, 1971), p. 26.

70.   See appendix A, *"Receipts" and "Memoranda,"* pp. 6, 11, 14, 22.

71.   This calomel controversy, and the shift in the opinions of many English doctors on the effectiveness and safety of calomel, is mentioned in Edward W. Lane, *Old Medicine and New* (London, 1873), pp. 32–37. Dr. Henry Holland steadily maintained his belief in the effectiveness of calomel in the three editions of his book, *Medical Notes and Reflections*. In the first, 1839, edition of this book Dr. Holland wrote: "The dread prevailing in France and Germany as to the use of Calomel, and the reprobation of English practice on this score, are well known. Unless partial cases of abuse be admitted as argument, such as may occur in the case of any other medicine, it cannot be allowed that there is much justification for these harsh views. It may indeed be affirmed, (and I state this on my own observation,) that the judgment is formed mainly on hearsay, and has gained weight by mere repetition" (Dr. Henry Holland, "On Mercurial Medicines," in *Medical Notes and Reflections* [London, 1839], pp. 247–48). Dr. Holland kept this passage in the 1840 and 1855 editions of his book.

72.   James Startin, *A Pharmacopoeia for Diseases of the Skin*, 2d ed. (London: Harrison & Sons, 1890), pp. 30–35.

73.   F. W. Headland, *An Essay on the Action of Medicines in the System* (London: John Churchill, 1852), p. 315. Dr. Headland reaffirmed his belief in the efficacy of calomel in the fourth American edition (1863) of this *Essay*.

74.   James M. Gully, *The Water Cure in Chronic Disease* (New York: Wiley & Putnam, 1849), pp. 43–44.

75.   William Brinton, *The Diseases of the Stomach* (London: John Churchill, 1859), pp. 393–94.

76.   Edward W. Lane, *Hydropathy: Or the Natural System of Medical Treatment* (London: John Churchill, 1857), pp. 36–41.

77.   "We thank you sincerely for your kind sympathy about poor Etty, who about a fortnight ago had three terrible days of sickness & was given loads of calomel which I always dread" (Darwin to Hooker, Down Bromley Kent, 4 February [1861], DPL, Box 115).

6   Recent Theories

1.   Gruber and Barrett, *Darwin on Man*, p. 44, n. 14.

2.   See part 1, §15.

3.   Eliza Meteyard, *A Group of Englishmen* (London, 1871), p. 357.

4.   George H. Darwin, "Recollections of my Father," DPL, Box 112, pp. 14–15. Darwin stopped raising pigeons after the publication of *The Origin of*

Species. The house, which served as a pigeon aviary, remained standing (but unused) for several decades.

5. Pigeon allergy causes pulmonary fibrosis with symptoms of cough, dyspnea, and (sometimes) fever. This allergy does not cause gastrointestinal or skin symptoms.

6. "My own interest in Charles Darwin dates back to the time when I used to pay frequent visits to Downe village in the years between the two world wars. It also stems to some extent from heredity. My great-great-grandfather, the Wesleyan preacher Jabez Bunting, was an intimate friend of both the Darwin and the Wedgwood families. His grandson Percy, who was the founder and editor of the *Contemporary Review* and my father's cousin, was intensely interested in Darwinism and visited Darwin at Downe on a number of occasions during the latter days of the great man's life. It is from their writings that I have culled some of the information contained in this book" (James Bunting, *Charles Darwin* [Folkestone: Bailey Brothers & Swinfen, Ltd., 1974], pp. 7–8).

7. Ibid., p. 8.

8. Ibid., p. 105.

9. Sir Hedley Atkins, *Down: The Home of the Darwins: The Story of a House and the People Who Lived There* (Published under the auspices of the Royal College of Surgeons of England, Lincoln's Inn Fields, London, 1974). Sir Hedley lives in Down House with his wife and family, and is curator of the Down House Estate.

10. George Pickering, *Creative Malady: Illness in the Lives and Minds of Charles Darwin, Florence Nightingale, Mary Baker Eddy, Sigmund Freud, Marcel Proust, Elizabeth Barrett Browning* (London: George Allen & Unwin Ltd., 1974).

11. *Down: The Home of the Darwins*, p. 70.

12. George Pickering, *Creative Malady* (London: George Allen & Unwin, Ltd., 1974), p. 91.

13. Ibid., p. 86.

14. C. D. Darlington, *Darwin's Place in History* (Oxford: Basil Blackwell, 1959), pp. 47–48.

7 The Evidence for
Psychological Causation

1. John H. Winslow, *Darwin's Victorian Malady: Evidence for its Medically Induced Origin* (Philadelphia: American Philosophical Society, 1971), p. 23.

2. Darwin to J. M. Herbert, Down Beckenham Kent, 25 December 1880; Sir Gavin de Beer, ed., "The Darwin Letters at Shrewsbury School," *Notes and Records of the Royal Society of London* 23 (1968):74. See part 1, §13.

3. Francis Darwin, "Reminiscences of my Father's Everyday Life," *LL*, 1:107.

4. *Autobiography*, p. 115. See part 1, §5.

Appendixes

Appendix A
The "Receipts" and
"Memoranda" Book

1.   I thank the Royal College of Surgeons of England, and Sir Hedley Atkins, for permission to transcribe this book. I also thank Miss Jessie Dobson—past curator of the Hunterian Museum of the Royal College of Surgeons, London— and Miss Elizabeth Allen—present curator of the Hunterian Museum—for sending me copies of The *"Receipts" and "Memoranda" Book*, and for answering my queries.

2.   *CFL*, 2:165.

3.   "Please to send me in a Box a Vulcanized Indian-Rubber Enema of medium size.—The one which I had from you & which suits me, is 4 1/4 inches ["in height" inserted] from the base to the upper part of the wooden rim which receives the bone nozzle—" (Darwin to an unidentified individual, Down Beckenham Kent, 8 November [1871–75], Library of the American Philosophical Society, Philadelphia; mentioned in P. Thomas Carroll, *An Annotated Calender of the Letters of Charles Darwin in the Library of the American Philosophical Society* [Wilmington, Del.: Scholarly Resources Inc., 1976] letter 410, p. 149. I thank Mr. Carroll for informing me of this letter before it was published.).

4.   In ascertaining the authors of the different entries in *"Receipts" and "Memoranda"* I have been greatly aided by Mr. Karl Aschaffenburg, hand-writing expert, to whom I showed manuscript letters of Dr. Robert W. Darwin, Catherine Darwin, Susan Darwin, Caroline Darwin, Erasmus Alvey Darwin, Charles and Emma Darwin, Francis Darwin, and Mrs. Henrietta Litchfield. After studying these letters Mr. Aschaffenburg was able to identify the authors of almost all of the writings in *"Receipts" and "Memoranda."*

Dr. Robert Darwin's Prescriptions

1.   T. P. Bythell, "Dr. Darwin (March 26th, 1884)," *Salopian Shreds and Patches*, 9 April 1884, p. 27. In 1833 Dr. Darwin ended a brief letter to his son Charles as follows: "You know I never write any thing besides answering questions about medicine and therefore as you are not a patient I must conclude" (Dr. Robert Darwin to Charles Darwin [Shrewsbury], 7 March 1833, *Darwin and Henslow*, pp. 70–71).

2.   *Darwin and the "Beagle,"* p. 11.

3.   Eliza Meteyard, *A Group of Englishmen* (1795 to 1815) (London: Longmans, Green, and Co., 1871), p. 265.

4.   "He [Dr. Erasmus Darwin] once thought inoculation for the measles might, as in the small-pox, materially soften the disease; and after the patriotic example of lady Mary Wortley Montague, he made the trial of his *own* family, upon his youngest son, Robert, now Dr. Darwin of Shrewsbury, and upon an infant daughter, who died within her first year. Each had, in consequence, the disease so severely, as to repel, in their father's mind, all future desire of repeating the experiment" (Anna Seward, *Memoirs of the Life of Dr. Darwin* [London, 1804], pp. 60–61).

5.   Calomel, mercurous chloride, was a medicine which, in the early nineteenth century, was "more extensively and more usefully employed than almost any other article of the materia medica . . . it moreover imparts force to many of the mild, and moderates the severity of drastic medicines . . . it appears to be particularly eligible in diseases of children; and it is singular that infants can generally bear larger doses of it than adults" (J. A. Paris, *Pharmacologia* [New York, 1825], 2:200–201). It was used in a wide variety of diseases, including syphilis, some inflammations, and gastrointestinal disorders. In large doses it was used as a purgative, and it was thought that "by proper management it may be made to increase, in a remarkable manner, almost any of the secretions or excretions" (Andrew Duncan, *The Edinburgh New Dispensatory*, 12th ed. [Edinburgh, 1830], p. 809).

6.   For bleeding, see note 24 in this section.

7.   Antimonial wine was a solution of tartar emetic (see part 1, §1, n. 7) and sherry wine (J. A. Paris, *Pharmacologia* [New York, 1825], 2:355). "Of late the use of tartar-emetic has been extended to almost all inflammatory diseases, chiefly by the Italians and French, as a controstimulant, or to depress the system." It was given in the form of solutions (Andrew Duncan, *The Edinburgh New Dispensatory*, 12th ed. [Edinburgh, 1830], p. 763).

8.   See note 39 of this section.

9.   See note 13 of this section.

10.   Charles Darwin to his son William at Rugby, Down, 29 (1855 or 1856), *CFL*, 2:157.

11.   "Carbonate of Potash" was potassium carbonate. See also note 37 this section.

12.   Tolu was a balsam which was obtained by incision from the bark of the Tolu tree. It existed in the form of "Syrup of Balsam of Tolu" and "Syrup of Tolu." It was used to give an agreeable flavor to medicines (Andrew Duncan, *The Edinburgh New Dispensatory*, 12th ed. [Edinburgh, 1830], pp. 723–24).

13.   In March 1855 Darwin wrote Fox: "With respect to ourselves, I have not much to say; we have just now a terribly noisy house with the Hooping cough: but otherwise are all well" (Darwin to Fox, Down Farnborough Kent,

19 March [1855], CCDL, *LL*, 1:407). Two months later he wrote Fox: "My wife is away from home at Rugby, nursing Willy, who has had your dreadful enemy the Scarlet Fever, rather badly, but yesterday & today's letters make me perfectly easy: but I think I shall go in a few days, & relieve guard. We are in a terrible perplexity about contagion, for here *all* the children have the Hooping cough which Willy has not had" (Darwin to Fox, Down Farnborough Kent, 23 May [1855], CCDL). In 1851 Darwin had written his son William: "What a curious thing infection is, yesterday Backy [Francis Darwin] and Lizzie [Elizabeth Darwin] plainly had got the mumps, and this was about as long since you had them, as your attack was from the time the Hensleighs [Hensleigh Wedgwood and wife] were here. They have had it very slightly, even slighter than you, Etty [Henrietta Darwin] and Georgy [George Darwin]" (Charles Darwin to his son W. E. Darwin, Down, 1 March [1851], DPL, Box 153).

14.   Croup was any affection of the larynx in children characterized by difficult and noisy respiration and a cough.

15.   Chalk was calcium carbonate.

16.   Rhubarb was an extract from the plant of the genus *Rheum*. It was used as "a mild cathartic which operates without violence or irritation, and may be given with safety even to pregnant women and to children.... Besides its purgative quality, it is celebrated as an astringent, by which it increases the tone of the stomach and intestines, and proves useful in diarrhoea and disorders proceeding from laxity" (Andrew Duncan, *The Edinburgh New Dispensatory*, 12th ed. [Edinburgh, 1830], p. 582).

17.   Compound chalk was powdered chalk mixed with fragrant and/or appetizing substances such as cinnamon and pepper (J. F. Royle and F. W. Headland, *A Manual of Materia Medica and Therapeutics* [London: John Churchill, 1865], p. 121).

18.   Sal volatile was a solution of ammonium carbonate. It was used as an antacid, stimulant, antispasmodic, in "acid dyspepsia," convulsions, fainting, and depressed states (J. F. Royle and F. W. Headland, *A Manual of Materia Medica and Therapeutics* [London: John Churchill, 1865], p. 67).

19.   See note 39 this section.

20.   Thrush was a mild infection of the mouth.

21.   "In disease, opium is chiefly employed to mitigate pain, diminish morbid sensibility, procure sleep, allay inordinate actions, and to check diarrhoea, and other excessive discharges" (Andrew Duncan, *The Edinburgh New Dispensatory*, 12th ed. [Edinburgh, 1830], p. 541).

22.   Treacle was molasses.

23.   *Autobiography*, p. 30.

24.   Bleeding, as a treatment for different illness, was much used in the first half of the nineteenth century. In the second half of the nineteenth century the practice of bleeding underwent a gradual and sure decline. In England, due to

the influence of Sir William Jenner and Sir William Gull, it was discarded about 1860 (Fielding H. Garrison, "The History of Bloodletting," *New York Medical Journal,* 1 and 8 March 1913, pp. 23, 27).

25. Dr. Erasmus Darwin had written about the use of blisters as follows: "But a blister acts with more permanent and certain effect by stimulating a part of the skin, and thence affecting the whole of it, and of the stomach by association, and thence remove the most obstinate heartburns and vomitings. From this the principal use of blisters is understood, which is to invigorate the exertions of the arterial and lymphatic vessels of the skin, producing an increase of insensible perspiration, and of cutaneous absorption; and to increase the action of the stomach, and the consequent power of digestion; and thence by sympathy to excite all the other irritative motions: hence they relieve pains of the cold kind, which originate from defect of motion; not from their introducing a greater pain, as some have imagined, but by stimulating the torpid vessels into their usual action; and thence increasing the action and consequent warmth of the whole skin, and of all the parts which are associated with it" (Erasmus Darwin, *Zoonomia; or, The Laws of Organic Life* [London, 1796], 2:700–701). In the early nineteenth century, blisters were produced to act as a "Counter-irritation": an irritation which was meant to "diminish, counteract, or remove some other irritation or inflammation existing in the body" (C. J. B. Williams, "Counter Irritation," in *The Cyclopaedia of Practical Medicine* [London, 1833], 1:484).

26. A handkerchief of a fine white linen, originally made at Combray in Flanders. (Also an imitation made of handspun cotton yarn.)

27. "I am grieved to hear my father, who is kindness itself to him [Willy], thinks he [Willy] looks a very delicate child. I felt quite ashamed at finding out, what I presume you did not know any more than I, that he has had *half a cup of cream* every morning, which my father (who seemed rather annoyed) says he believes is one of the most injurious things we could have given him. When we are at home we shall be able to look more after him. Only conceive, Susan found him when he started in the carriage with his stockings and shoes half wet through; my father says getting his feet wet on the grass, when afterwards changed, is rather a good than a bad thing, but to allow him to start on a journey in that state was risking his health. Last night Susan went into Doddy's [Willy's] room and found no water by his bedside. I tell you all these disagreeablenesses that you may feel the same necessity that I do of our own selves looking and not trusting anything about our children to others" (Charles Darwin to Emma Darwin at Maer Hall [Shrewsbury, 1 July 1841], *CFL,* 2:59).

28. Senna was an extract from the leaves of a small shrub, belonging to the genus *Cassia.* "Senna is a very useful cathartic, operating mildly, and yet effectually; and if judiciously dosed and managed, rarely occasioning the bad consequences which too frequently follow the exhibition of the stronger purges. The only inconveniences complained of in this drug are, its being apt

to gripe, and its nauseous flavour. These are best obviated by adding to the senna some aromatic substance, as cardamom, ginger, cinnamon, &c. and by facilitating its operation by drinking plentifully of any mild diluent" (Andrew Duncan, Jr., *The Edinburgh New Dispensatory*, 11th ed. [Edinburgh, 1826], p. 286).

29.   Scammony was a milky extract from the roots of scammony convolvulus, a climbing perennial plant. It was used as "an efficacious and powerful purgative" (Andrew Duncan, Jr., *The Edinburgh New Dispensatory*, 11th ed. [Edinburgh, 1826], p. 318).

30.   "Compound Powder of Senna" contained both senna and scammony. "The scammony is used as a stimulus to the senna powder; the quantity of the latter necessary for a dose, when not assisted by some more powerful substance, being too bulky to be conveniently taken in this form" (Andrew Duncan, *The Edinburgh New Dispensatory*, 12th ed. [Edinburgh 1830], pp. 1007–8).

31.   It was held that some wines, used in moderation, improved appetite and digestion and were good for general health (J. A. Paris, *Pharmacologia* [New York, 1825], 2:349–55).

32.   The *"Receipts" and "Memoranda"* entries of Dr. Robert Darwin, Charles Darwin, and Emma Darwin contain references to different iron medicines. In Europe and in the British Isles iron was much used by physicians during the eighteenth and nineteenth centuries. In his *Manual of the Medicinal Preparations of Iron*, published in 1864, Henry N. Draper of Dublin listed sixty-four forms in which iron could be prescribed. Speaking of iron he said: "of repute in the treatment of certain diseased conditions from almost the earliest period from which history hands us down any record of medicine, it has continued to acquire popularity, until in our own time we find it holding among therapeutic agents a position not second to that of any other substance." Charles Phillips of Edinburgh, a leading authority on therapeutics and materia medica of the later part of the nineteenth century, was skeptical about the efficacy of iron in curing some cases of anemia. Phillips, however, stated that iron was of benefit in the treatment of hemorrhage, leukorrhea, prolonged lactation or too frequent pregnancies, rheumatism, dyspepsia, and other illnesses, especially if the cause were removed (Leonard J. Goldwater, "A Short History of Iron Therapy," *Annals of Medical History*, n.s., 7 [1935]:265). (See, also, note 62 this section.)

When Dr. Robert Darwin prescribed "Rust of Iron Chalk" he may have referred to a mixture of iron oxide and iron carbonate. This was prepared by exposing iron wire to water and air until it was corroded into rust, which was then triturated into a powder (J. A. Paris, *Pharmacologia* [New York, 1825], 2:171; Andrew Duncan, *The Edinburgh New Dispensatory*, 12th ed. [Edinburgh, 1830], p. 778). Dr. Erasmus Darwin had prescribed "rust of iron, filings of iron, salt of steel" for some conditions of the liver, stomach, and viscera (Erasmus Darwin, *Zoonomia; or, The Laws of Organic Life* [London,

1796], 2:737). In 1802 James C. Madison of Virginia had published his doctor's thesis entitled, "Observations on the Medical Properties of Iron." In this he wrote that "the physicians of this country are much in the habit of using the limatura ferri (filings) as well as the rust," and that "iron rust has been given in the amounts of one ounce in twenty four hours," although the usual dose was one dram. He mentions no ill effects from the use of the very large doses (Leonard J. Goldwater, "A Short History of Iron Therapy," *Annals of Medical History*, 7 [1935]:264–65).

33.   Mr. Edgar Cockell, a Downe surgeon. See part 1, §6, n. 1.

34.   Aromatic chalk preparations would be described as having the following uses: "Antacid and Cordial. Useful in Diarrhoeas, and an excellent addition to Rhubarb and Magnesia, and such powders, for children" (J. F. Royle and F. W. Headland, *A Manual of Materia Medica and Therapeutics* [London: John Churchill, 1865], p. 121). See notes 15 and 17 of this section.

35.   An extract from the Logwood (Lignum) tree grown in Jamaica. At the end of the eighteenth century Dr. Erasmus Darwin classified it as a medicine which affected the absorption of the intestines (Erasmus Darwin, *Zoonomia; or, The Laws of Organic Life* [London, 1796], p. 2; "Catalogue of the Sorbentia," p. 737). In the early nineteenth century logwood was regarded as an "astringent"—a medicine which caused contraction of the tissues—and a watery infusion of logwood was prescribed in "protracted diarrhoeas, and in the later stages of dysentery" (J. A. Paris, *Pharmacologia* [New York, 1825], 2:184; Andrew Duncan, *The Edinburgh New Dispensatory*, 12th ed. [Edinburgh, 1830], p. 461). In 1859 infusions of logwood would be prescribed in cases of dyspepsia with a "tendency to diarrhoea or pyrosis" (William Brinton, *The Diseases of the Stomach* [London: John Churchill, 1859], p. 386).

36.   The cinnamon bark and compound may have been used here because of their soothing effects on the stomach (see note 48 this section), and as an aromatic to cover the taste of the logwood (Andrew Duncan, *The Edinburgh New Dispensatory*, 12th ed. [Edinburgh, 1830], p. 499).

37.   The medical uses of potassium carbonate were described as follows: "In cases where an alkali is indicated, this preparation offers an agreeable and efficient remedy . . . . In disordered states of the digestive functions alkalies frequently act with surprising effect; in calculous affections their value has already been noticed . . . and the stomach appears to bear the protracted exhibition of the carbonate of potass or soda with more temper than it does of any other alkaline combination" (J. A. Paris, *Pharmacologia* [New York, 1825], 2:273). For further comments on this prescription see part 1, §4.

38.   The word "narcotic" was synonymous with the words "sedative," "anodyne," "hypnotic," and "soporific." Narcotics were defined as "substances which in moderate dose, occasion a temporary increase of the actions of the nervous and vascular systems, but which is followed by a greater

depression of the vital powers than is commensurate with the degree of previous excitement, and which is generally followed by sleep" (J. A. Paris, *Pharmacologia* [New York, 1825], 1:104).

39.   Henbane was derived from a plant (*Hyoscyamus niger*), which was "an annual plant, which grows in great abundance in most parts of Britain, by the road sides, and among rubbish, and flowers in July." Henbane's medicinal principal—obtained from the plant's seeds and leaves—was the alkaloid hyoscyamus. It was applied locally for pains, to dilate spasms of the rectum, urethra, and cervix, and to dilate the eye. It was given systemically in diseases where it was "desirable either to allay inordinate action, or to mitigate pain." It was most commonly given in the form of a tincture; then as a powder, an extract from its leaves or seeds, and an "infusion prepared by digesting the bruised leaves in olive oil." It does not seem to have been commonly used in the form of pills (Andrew Duncan, *The Edinburgh New Dispensatory*, 12th ed. [Edinburgh, 1830], pp. 473–75; J. A. Paris, *Pharmacologia* [New York, 1825], 2:204).

40.   A closely similar preparation was also called "Ward's Essence for the Head-ach" or "Linimentum Camphore Compositum," and its composition was as follows: camphor two, liquor ammonia six, spirits of lavender sixteen parts. Liquor ammonia and camphor were strong stimulants, and this essence was called "highly stimulating" (J. A. Paris, *Pharmacologia* [New York, 1825], 2:218). This "Ward's Essence," and the one prescribed by Dr. Darwin, were (presumably) rubbed into the skin of the head and neck to act as counterirritation in cases of headache. (For the internal uses of ammonia and camphor sees notes 18 and 47 this section, and note 44 in the next section.) External application of liniments was still used to treat headaches in the later nineteenth century (see "Domestic Medicine and Surgery," by a member of the College of Surgeons of England, in Ross Murray, *The Modern Householder* [London, 1872], p. 598).

41.   See note 22 this section.

42.   What was called "Common distilled Vinegar" was mainly acetic acid (J. A. Paris, *Pharmacologia* [New York, 1825], 2:13–14).

43.   Laudanum was tincture of opium.

44.   Ipecacuan was an extract from a root and its main medicinal action was to stimulate the stomach. In large doses it acted as an emetic, in smaller doses it was thought to increase appetite and digestion. It was most directly effective in the form of a powder (J. A. Paris, *Pharmacologia* [New York, 1825], 2:208–11). Ipecacuanha wine was a mixture of the root of ipecacuan with Spanish white wine (Andrew Duncan, *The Edinburgh New Dispensatory*, 12th ed. [Edinburgh, 1830], p. 976).

45.   Benzoin was a resinous substance obtained from the *Styrax benzoin*, a tree of Sumatra. Medically it was used as an expectorant, and for its pleasant odor (J. A. Paris, *Pharmacologia* [New York, 1825], 2:92).

46.   Peruvian bark, also called *Cinchona*, was first used in the treatment of intermittent fevers; it was then used in the treatment of a wide variety of illnesses, including "periodical pain, inflammation, haemorrhage, spasm, cough, loss of external sense, &c." *Cinchona*, when given in powdered form, sometimes caused feelings of gastric oppression, and even vomiting. In these cases it was then administered in the form of its infusion or decoction, with the addition of its tincture (J. A. Paris, *Pharmacologia* [New York, 1825], 2:115–20; Andrew Duncan, *The Edinburgh New Dispensatory*, 12th ed. [Edinburgh, 1830], pp. 383–87). This may explain why Dr. Darwin prescribed, together, both the decoction and tincture of Peruvian bark.

47.   Subcarbonate of ammonia was a "stimulant, antispasmodic . . . antacid . . . and in large doses . . . [an] emetic" (J. A. Paris, *Pharmacologia* [New York, 1825], 2:43). A mixture of decoction and tincture of *Cinchona*, and spirits of ammonia—similar to the prescription of Dr. Darwin—was used as a "tonic" (J. A. Paris, *Pharmacologia* [New York, 1825], 1:268).

48.   "Cinnamon is a very elegant and useful aromatic, more grateful both to the palate and stomach than most other substances of this class. Like other aromatics, the effects of cinnamon are stimulating, heating, stomachic [improving appetite and digestion], carminative [relieving flatulence], and tonic" (Andrew Duncan, *The Edinburgh New Dispensatory*, 12th ed. [Edinburgh, 1830], p. 499). (See, also, note 41 in the next section.)

49.   "Cortex Aurantii" is Latin for orange peel. "The rind [of orange] proves an excellent stomachic and carminative, promoting appetite, warming the habit, and strengthening the tone of the viscera" (Andrew Duncan, *The Edinburgh New Dispensatory*, 12th ed. [Edinburgh, 1830], p. 388).

50.   Dilute sulphuric acid had many medicinal uses, including that of stimulant in cases of "relaxation of the digestive organs" (J. A. Paris, *Pharmacologia* [New York, 1825], 2:32).

51.   The sulphate of quinine was used where *Cinchona* was used, especially in intermittent fevers, acute rheumatism, and hemmorhages and fluxes (Andrew Duncan, *The Edinburgh New Dispensatory*, 12th ed. [Edinburgh, 1830], p. 998). Some doctors classified quinine as a "bitter" (see part 1, §6, n. 11) and held that it was especially effective in some cases of dyspepsia (William Brinton, *The Diseases of the Stomach* [London: John Churchill, 1859], p. 386). "As a tonic in simple debility, and loss of appetite from atonic dyspepsia Quinine is unrivalled. It is rarely given where there is much irritation of the stomach" (Henry Beasley, *The Book of Prescriptions* [London, 1859], p. 404).

52.   *LL*, 1:10.

53.   The combination of ipecacuanha and opium was thought to enhance the diaphoretic effects of ipecacuanha (J. A. Paris, *Pharmacologia* [New York, 1825], 2:211).

54.   Cream of tartar was a salt of potassium and antimony. See part 1, §1, n. 7, and note 7 this section.

55.   The wearing of a flannel shirt was held, by some, to have a medicinal value: "A flannel shirt, to one who has not been in the habit of wearing one, stimulates the skin by its points, and thus stops vomiting in some cases; and is particularly efficacious in checking some chronical diarrhoeas, which are not attended with fever; for the absorbents of the skin are thus stimulated into greater action, with which those of the intestines consent by direct sympathy" (Erasmus Darwin, *Zoonomia; or, The Laws of Organic Life* [London, 1796], 2:438).

56.   The Shrewsbury chemist. See part 1, §6, n. 5.

57.   Borax, in the form of a powder, was applied locally to ulcers. It was regarded as a "detergent" for ulcerous states (J. A. Paris, *Pharmacologia*, [New York, 1825], 2:310).

58.   Before being applied to an ulcer, borax powder was, usually, mixed with honey. Oil of almonds may have been a substitute for the honey.

59.   In the nineteenth century, different medicines were combined, physically, to form pills. Soap was very frequently used for the formation of such pills because it protected some medicines from the effects of the gastric juice (J. A. Paris, *Pharmacologia* [New York, 1825], 1:240–41). Opium pills were prepared by heating a mixture of soap, water, and powdered opium (Frank D. Foster, *An Illustrated Encyclopaedic Medical Dictionary* [New York, 1891]). Pills could be made in the home. Henrietta Darwin, in her memories of life at Down, recalls the "delight of rolling rhubarb pills" (*CFL*, 2:165).

60.   A cordial has been defined as "a medicine, food, or beverage which invigorates the heart and stimulates the circulation" (*The Shorter Oxford English Dictionary*).

61.   Peppermint water was a "carminative and antispasmodic" and a vehicle "for other medicines to correct their operation, or to disguise their flavour" (J. A. Paris, *Pharmacologia* [New York, 1825], 2:235).

62.   Muriated tincture of iron was iron chloride. It was regarded as an "astringent" and "tonic" (J. A. Paris, *Pharmacologia* [New York, 1825], 2: 173; J. F. Royle and F. W. Headland, *A Manual of Materia Medica and Therapeutics* [London: John Churchill, 1865], p. 147). See also note 32 this section.

63.   Quassia, an extract from the wood of the Jamaica quassia tree, belonged to the class of vegetable medicinal substances known as "bitters" (see part 1, §6, n. 11) and was used to treat gastrointestinal disorders, fevers, cachexia, gout, dropsies, and vaginal discharges (J. A. Paris, *Pharmacologia* [New York, 1825], 2:207; Andrew Duncan, *The Edinburgh New Dispensatory*, 12th ed. [Edinburgh, 1830], pp. 574–75).

Charles Darwin's Entries

1.   Darwin to Asa Gray, Down Bromley Kent, S.E., 29 October (1864), Gray Herbarium of Harvard University, Cambridge; *Calender of the Letters of Darwin and Gray*, p. 56. See part 1, §11, n. 96–98.

2.   See part 1, §6, 8, 12.

3. See part 2, §1.

4. See, for instance, part 1, §12, n. 47, 48.

5. Unidentified

6. Squill was obtained from *Urginea maritima*, a bulbous plant that grows on the shores of the Mediterranean. It was used medically, since the sixth century B.C., to treat many different illnesses. (For the history of squill see "Symposium on Squill," *Bulletin of the New York Academy of Medicine*, June 1974.) In Victorian England, tincture of squill was chiefly used as an expectorant in cases of chronic bronchitis and catarrh where there was not much fever. In larger doses it was an emetic, but it was rarely used as such (Henry Beasley, *The Book of Prescriptions* [London, 1859], p. 445; J. F. Royle and F. W. Headland, *A Manual of Materia Medica and Therapeutics* [London: John Churchill, 1865], pp. 629–30). See, also, note 16 in the next section.

7. "Sweet Spirit of Nitre" was a mixture of ether, nitrous acid, and alcohol. It was used as a stimulant and antispasmodic (J. F. Royle and F. W. Headland, *A Manual of Materia Medica and Therapeutics* [London: John Churchill, 1865], pp. 675–77).

8. "Probatum est" is Latin for "is improbable." Darwin sometimes used Latin to express strong feelings.

9. Mr. Engleheart was a Downe village doctor. He cared for Darwin's son Leonard, and was aided financially by Darwin. He lost his life in Africa, crossing a swollen river to attend a patient (*CFL*, 2:182, n. 1). After Engleheart's death Darwin wrote: "Mr. Englehart's lungs (& I fear purse also) failed him; & he is to us a fearful loss as a doctor" (Darwin to Reverend J. Brodie Innes, Down Beckenham Kent, S.E., 18 October 1869; Robert M. Stecher, "The Darwin-Innes Letters," *Annals of Science*, 17 [1961]:231).

10. Nitre was potassium nitrate, also known as saltpeter. It was used to bring down fever, and as a diuretic (J. F. Royle and F. W. Headland, *A Manual of Materia Medica and Therapeutics* [London: John Churchill, 1865], pp. 87–89).

11. "Reach" meant to spit or bring up bronchial or stomach contents, or to make efforts to vomit.

12. "Aperient" was a laxative to open the bowels so as to expel an unwanted intestinal content. This aperient consisted of three purgatives: *rhubarb* (see note 16 in previous section); *Jalap*, from the root of *Ipomoea purga*, a Mexican plant, "an active drastic cathartic, producing copious watery evacuations. It irritates the intestine and may cause nausea and griping"; and *sulphate of potash*, "a mild laxative" frequently combined with rhubarb to act as a cathartic (Henry Beasley, *The Book of Prescriptions* [London, 1859], pp. 300, 399–400).

13. "Mr. Edwards" was, perhaps, a Downe neighbor. Darwin once sold him a mare, and then failed to sell him another horse (Darwin to Reverend

J. Brodie Innes, Down Bromley Kent, 28 December [1860]; Robert M. Stecher, "The Darwin-Innes Letters," *Annals of Science*, 17 [1961]:207). Charles Darwin to his son William Erasmus Darwin, Down, 11 [n.d.]; Down, 7 July [1850]; DPL, Box 153).

14.   The source of this reference is not clear. In the eleventh and twelfth editions of Duncan's *New Dispensatory* there are no references to Ceratum Resinae on page 831. In the twelfth edition of *The New Dispensatory* the composition of Ceratum Resinae is described as follows: a pound each of yellow resin and yellow wax and one pint of olive oil; "melt the resin and wax together with a slow fire; then add the oil, and strain the cerate, while hot, through linen" (Andrew Duncan, *The Edinburgh New Dispensatory*, 12th ed. [Edinburgh, 1830], p. 1037).

15.   Corrosive sublimate, bichloride of mercury, was used locally and systemically in secondary syphilis and cutaneous diseases. Many considered it a poison and were against its systemic use (J. F. Royle and F. W. Headland, *A Manual of Materia Medica and Therapeutics* [London: John Churchill, 1865], p. 212). Henry Holland, however, wrote about it as follows: "Bichloride of Mercury . . . under discreet employment is one of the most valuable remedies we possess. . . . I have seen its influence in augmenting and improving the secretions—procuring the absorption of morbid growths—altering the state of the skin in many cutaneous disorders—and changing the character of morbid actions generally throughout the system—in cases where I believe no other medicine, or combination of medicines, would have had equal effect. . . And though otherwise held by common opinion, I think it on the whole as safe a medicine as Calomel in the hands of the practitioner" (Sir Henry Holland, *Medical Notes and Reflections* [London, 1855], pp. 539–40).

16.   Collodion was a solution of pyroxylin in ether and alcohol. When this solution was applied to the skin and left exposed to the air, it dried rapidly, by evaporation of the ether and alcohol, and left the pyroxylin adherent to the skin as a thin transparent film which was impervious to air (J. F. Royle and F. W. Headland, *A Manual of Materia Medica and Therapeutics* [London: John Churchill, 1865], p. 317). Collodion was invented in 1847, was first used to form "artificial skin" over small wounds, and then to cover larger wounds, sores, and inflamed skin. In the 1860s it was held that collodion was especially efficacious in erysipelas, and that "its anti-inflammatory effect was due to its impermeability to the air (air was considered essential for the production of animal heat, an excess of which caused inflammation)." Collodion was also thought to be a valuable treatment for several systemic diseases, including typhoid and cholera (John K. Crellin, "Collodion as a Nineteenth-Century Dressing and Panacea," *M&B Pharmaceutical Bulletin*, July/August 1964, pp. 41–44).

17.   For the uses of muriatic (hydrochloric) acid and nitric acid in gastric disease, see part 1, §8, n. 44.

18.   Darwin's writing of the name of this doctor is indistinct. "Dr. Trout" is

unidentified. "Dr. Prout" may refer to Dr. William Prout (1785–1850), who published papers on physiological chemistry and who, in 1823, discovered the existence in the stomach of free hydrochloric acid (*Dictionary of National Biography*).

19. "Effervescing mixture," a mixture which gives off bubbles of gas.

20. Carbonate of soda was used as an antacid in "dyspepsia, heartburn, flatulence, gouty and rheumatic affections, and cases of lithic deposit in the urine.... It is diuretic and diaphoretic" (Henry Beasley, *The Book of Prescriptions* [London, 1859], p. 461).

21. Citric acid was a crystallizable acid prepared from the juice of the lemon or lime. It was used as an antalkaline, to lower temperature, as an antiscorbutic, and a substitute for lemon juice (J. F. Royle and F. W. Headland, *A Manual of Materia Medica and Therapeutics* [London: John Churchill, 1865], pp. 327–29).

22. Prussic acid, also called hydrocyanic acid, existed in two forms: a poison; and then a form which was weaker and which was known as "medicinal or diluted hydrocyanic acid." This second form was used in a variety of illnesses: "in Chronic Coughs and affections of the Heart, in painful Neuralgia, and Stomach complaints.... Externally as a wash to allay pain and irritation in Chronic Skin Diseases" (J. F. Royle and F. W. Headland, *A Manual of Materia Medica and Therapeutics* [London: John Churchill, 1865], pp. 416–20).

23. Darwin to W. & J. Burrow, Ltd., Down Beckenham Kent, 18 July 1881; *Notes and Records of the Royal Society of London* 14 (1959):60.

24. The page reference "p. 8112" cannot be identified. Darwin was sometimes imprecise in his references to publications, and his entry may refer to the following article: W. B. O'Shaughnessy, "Extract from a Memoir on the Prescription of the Indian Hemp, or Gunhaj, (Cannabis Indica) Their Effects on the Animal System in Health, and Their Utility in the Treatment of Tetanus and Other Convulsive Diseases," *Journal of the Asiatic Society of Bengal*, no. 91, July 1839, pp. 838–51. In this article O'Shaughnessy first reported the effects of hemp (marijuana) in animals, and then in a number of human illnesses. He reported a case of hydrophobia in which, although the patient died, hemp greatly alleviated his suffering, and also cases of tetanus in which hemp relieved suffering and seemed to cure the disease. He suggested that hemp was of use in treating cholera. He concluded his article by saying that his observations were preliminary, and he urged the medical profession to give hemp "the most extensive and the speediest trial." In a few years, as a result of this and subsequent articles by O'Shaughnessy, hemp came to be widely used in England and America as a "wonder drug," capable of alleviating a "wide variety of ailments, from menstrual cramps and excessive menstrual bleeding to inflamed tonsils and migraine headaches" (Gabriel G. Nahas, *Marihuana—Deceptive Weed* [New York: Raven Press, Publishers, 1973], p. 7).

25.   In England, during the nineteenth century, there was a fear of cholera and several cholera epidemics. In June 1832, Fox in England reported to Darwin aboard the *Beagle*: "The cholera is now spread all over England, and tho not the very dreadful scourge we were led to expect it to be is very awful in many places. It began I fear at Derby last week, and is now in many of the larger towns, clearly making progress in England and Scotland and Ireland" (Fox to Darwin, Upperstone near Nottingham, 30 June 1832, RDC). This was the beginning of a large English cholera epidemic. Cholera was epidemic in London in 1853 and 1854, and pandemic in England in 1866 (Arthur R. Pollitzer, *History of Cholera* [Geneva: World Health Organization, 1959], monograph series, no. 43). The medications for "cholera with diarrhoea" varied but generally consisted in giving opium, cathartics, and fluids. It was important that medications be given early ("Domestic Medicine and Surgery," by a member of the College of Surgeons of England, in Ross Murray, *The Modern Householder* [London, 1872], pp. 559–60).

26.   Magnesia was "one of the most frequently used of all purgative medicines" (Henry Beasley, *The Book of Prescriptions* [London, 1859], p. 322).

27.   Unidentified.

28.   "Sickness," in Darwin's vocabulary, usually denoted vomiting. See part 1, §15.

29.   Magnesia, in addition to being a purgative, was given as an antacid in "dyspepsia, heartburn, pyrosis, gouty and lithic disorders" (Henry Beasley, *The Book of Prescriptions* [London, 1859], p. 318).

30.   "Lime Water" was a solution of hydrate of lime (hydrate of calcium oxide) in water. It was used as an antacid in dyspepsia (J. F. Royle and F. W. Headland, *A Manual of Materia Medica and Therapeutics* [London: John Churchill, 1865], pp. 116–18).

31.   Cassia was from the bark of a tree—resembling cinnamon yet different from it (Cassia was called "spurious cinnamon")—which was used as a stimulant and to relieve flatulence (J. F. Royle and F. W. Headland, *A Manual of Materia Medica and Therapeutics* [London: John Churchill, 1865], pp. 580–82).

32.   Sir Benjamin Collins Brodie (1783–1862), English physiologist and surgeon.

33.   Unidentified.

34.   Darwin's sister.

35.   Quinine disulphate. Quinine and its salts, in addition to previously mentioned uses (note 51 in the previous section), were used in "neuralgia and other affections when marked by periodicity" (Henry Beasley, *The Book of Prescriptions* [London, 1859], p. 404).

36.   Dilute nitric acid.

37. "Tinct. Aurantii" was "Tincture of Orange" (see note 49 in the previous section). This was frequently used as a "tonic adjunct to draughts and mixtures" (J. F. Royle and F. W. Headland, *A Manual of Materia Medica and Therapeutics* [London: John Churchill, 1865], p. 322).

38. Quinae Disulph.   3 ss
    Acid. Nit. dil.   3 iij
    Tinct. Aurantii,
    Syrupi Zingibi., ana 3vj.
    Misce. Capiat ex. cyath. aquae cochl. min. j. bis.

                                                        terve quotidie
                                                        Mr. J. Morgan

This prescription was used to treat the "Cachexy of Children" (published in Henry Beasley, *The Book of Prescriptions* [London, 1859], p. 411, prescription 2417).

39. A "Tonic" was defined as a medicine "possessing the power of gradually increasing the tone of the muscular fibre when relaxed, and the vigor of the body when weakened by disease. . . . When a Tonic is fitly prescribed, as in a case of debility, its effects are gradually perceived; the energy of the stomach and the appetite are increased, digestion is facilitated, the force of the circulation is augmented . . . the respiration becomes fuller and more vigorous. . . . Secretions become more natural . . the senses and all the faculties become more active and the strength increased . . . the patient . . . is restored to pristine health and energy" (J. F. Royle and F. W. Headland, *A Manual of Materia Medica and Therapeutics* [London: John Churchill, 1865], pp. 746–47). It was postulated that "tonics" produced their "invigorating effects" by acting through the blood and enabling the nervous system to "secrete the nervous influence by which the whole frame is strengthened" (F. W. Headland, *The Action of Medicines in the System*, 4th American ed. [Philadelphia: Lindsay and Blakiston, 1863], p. 162). Referring to the use of tonics in the treatment of dyspepsia, Dr. William Brinton wrote: 'The substances termed *tonics* are often remarkably useful: indeed, unless contra-indicated by great irritability of stomach, may be regarded as almost indispensable" (William Brinton, *The Diseases of the Stomach* [London: John Churchill, 1859], p. 385). Dr. Henry Holland, however, held that "the theory and uses of tonic medicines—exceedingly vague, it must be owned, in every part of practice—are not least so in their relation to disorders of digestion" (Henry Holland, *Medical Notes and Reflections* [London, 1855], p. 228). Many different substances were regarded as acting as tonics: these included vegetable bitters (see part 1, §6, n. 11), fruits such as oranges and lemons, *Cinchona* and quinine (see note 51 in the previous section), and minerals. Thus several of Dr. Robert Darwin's prescriptions which contain no indications for use— Peruvian bark (*Cinchona*), ammonia, cinnamon tea, orange peel, sulphuric acid, and sulphate of quinine—may have been intended as tonics and for use in dyspepsia, and may have been used by Charles Darwin for these purposes.

40.   Iron existed in the form of many different compounds; oxides, tartrates, sulphates, carbonates, phosphates, iodides, malates, lactates, and chlorides were some of the more commonly used preparations. Iron citrate was described as "a mild preparation, pleasant to the taste, and useful for children and weak persons" (J. F. Royle and F. W. Headland, *A Manual of Materia Medica and Therapeutics* [London: John Churchill, 1865], p. 162). Iron was commonly regarded as a tonic. Dr. William Brinton wrote about its use as follows: "Various metallic substances ordinarily classed as tonics are also extremely useful in dyspepsia. Especially may we notice the preparations of iron . . . in general useful, not only in proportion to the anaemia and general derangement of nutrition present, but in proportion as the habits and circumstances of the patient have prevented his getting that due share of light, air, and exercise, the want of which aggravates (if not causes) so much of the dyspepsia of civilized life. Hence it is more useful in females than in males; more in the sedentary dyspeptic than in the florid over-fed subjects of indigestion whom you will occasionally meet within country practice. That it has other uses in this malady than those of a mere aliment and tonic can, however, scarcely be doubted: increasing . . . both the gastric and intestinal secretions by a specific determination to the mucous structures which furnish them. . . . Of its various preparations, the modern citrate is perhaps more readily borne than any, and in an effervescent form, will sometimes agree with the most delicate stomach. . . . The carbonate, phosphate, sulphate, and sesquichloride, form a scale of increasingly irritative preparations: and therefore demand, not only a diminished dose, but an increased dilution. . . . The oxide of iron, as well as iron filings or raspings, which used formerly to be given in treacle, are now . . . almost obsolete" (William Brinton, *The Diseases of the Stomach* [London: John Churchill, 1859], pp. 386–87). Dr. Henry Holland, although critical of the theory of tonic medicines (see note 39, this section) had written that "ammoniated iron with an aloetic medicine" and "sulphate of iron in solution with the sulphate of magnesia or soda" were "beneficial" in the treatment of dyspepsia (see part 1, §4, n. 9). However it was held by some that iron compounds were not really tonics because "they are not of use in cases of simple debility, except when attended with paleness, or Anaemia. . . . Iron is the only direct remedy which can be employed in Anaemia and its kindred disorders, as Chlorosis, Amenorrhoea, &c." (J. F. Royle and F. W. Headland, *A Manual of Materia Medica and Therapeutics* [London: John Churchill, 1865], p. 139).

41.   In the 1860s, as in 1830 (see note 48 in the previous section), cinnamon was regarded as a "tonic" and a "stomachic," and was used in "low states of the constitution" and to "check Nausea, relieve Flatulence, and Cramps." "Oil of Cinnamon" was described as "a grateful but powerful Stimulant" (J. F. Royle and F. W. Headland, *A Manual of Materia Medica and Therapeutics* [London: John Churchill, 1865], pp. 579–80, 747).

42.   "Spirits of Vine" perhaps refers to the juice of the grapevine which was

used in "making syrups and sherbets," and had previously been used in medicines (J. F. Royle and F. W. Headland, *A Manual of Materia Medica and Therapeutics* [London: John Churchill, 1865], p. 339).

43.   Madder, also called *Rubia*, was from the roots of the plant *Rubia tinctorum*. It was used as a diuretic, and "esteemed" by some doctors as an "emmenagogue"—a medicine which has the power of promoting the menstrual discharge when this had been interrupted (Henry Beasley, *The Book of Prescriptions* [London, 1859], p. 428).

44.   Camphor was an extract from the wood of the camphor tree. It was a "sedative, antispasmodic, and diaphoretic. It produces slight exhilaration without quickening the pulse; quiets nervous irritation and restlessness" (Henry Beasley, *The Book of Prescriptions* [London, 1859], p. 148).

45.   Julep was a liquid sweetened with sugar or syrup which could be used as a vehicle for medicines.

46.   "Myrh" is a misspelling of "myrrh" (or myrrha). Myrrh was a gum resin from the *Balsamodendron myrrha* tree. "It acts upon the mucous tracts in the same manner as the balsams, checking their secretions when inordinate in quantity. It is also tonic and antispasmodic. It is given in atonic dyspepsia, in chlorosis, in amenorrhoea, and in chronic bronchitis" (Henry Beasley, *The Book of Prescriptions* [London, 1859], pp. 341–42).

47.   Arnica was an extract from a plant which was an "Acrid stimulant" and an irritant to the intestine. Diluted with water, it was applied locally to bruises and swellings (J. F. Royle and F. W. Headland, *A Manual of Materia Medica and Therapeutics* [London: John Churchill, 1865], pp. 501–2).

48.   Alum was aluminum sulphate and potassium oxide. It was applied locally to sores and ulcers, and used as a gargle in sore throat and infections of the mouth (Henry Beasley, *The Book of Prescriptions* [London, 1859], p. 46).

49.   Darwin to Reverend J. Brodie Innes (1848), in Robert M. Stecher, "The Darwin-Innes Letters," *Annals of Science* 17 (1961):203.

50.   The Shrewsbury chemist. (See part 1, §6, n. 5.)

51.   Perhaps Thomas Hayter Lewis (1818–98), architect. Over the years Lewis did repairs in Down House. He is mentioned in several letters. "Lewis came up to mend the pipes, and from first dinner to second dinner was a first-rate dispensary [dispensation] as they [the Darwin children] never left him" (Charles Darwin to Emma Darwin [Down], Monday night, February 1845, *CFL*, 2:93). "We have just begun the horrid mess of plastering the new rooms; for *all* the outside plaistor had to be stripped off. Lewis found the floor boards so damp, that he could not lay down the floor in any of the rooms; and the ceilings are so damp that they cannot be white-washed" (Charles Darwin to his son William Darwin [Down], Tuesday night [before 1858], DPL, Box 153).

  In the fall of 1876 Darwin planned to alter Down House by building a billiard room, with a bedroom and dressing room above. He had a "Mr. Deards,"

"Mr. Laslett," and Lewis give him estimates of the cost of this work. He then accepted Deards' estimate—because it was cheaper than those of Laslett and Lewis—and he repaid Laslett and Lewis for the expenses involved in making their estimates (P. Thomas Carroll, *An Annotated Calender of the Letters of Charles Darwin in the Library of the American Philosophical Society* [Wilmington, Del.: Scholarly Resources Inc., 1976], letters 499–501, pp. 173–74). Perhaps these *"Receipts" and "Memoranda"* "Estimates" concern this 1876 period of Down House building.

52.   Hurdles were portable rectangular frames, like field gates, used to form temporary fences.

53.   When water, or moisture, was added to lime the latter disintegrated; this was called slacking.

54.   "E. Cresy Jun.," may be Edward Cresy, Jr., "principal assistant clerk at the Metropolitan Board of Works, and architect to the fire brigade," who died in 1870 at the age of forty-seven. For his father, Edward Cresy, see part 1, §6, n. 2 (Edward Cresy in *Dictionary of National Biography*; obituary notice of Edward Cresy, Jr., in *The Times* 15 October 1870).

55.   A thrill was the pole or shaft by which a wagon, cart, or other vehicle was attached to the animal drawing it.

56.   "Ox gall," from the entrails of the ox, was commonly used for manufacturing glue.

57.   Moritz Rugendas (1799–1858) was a German artist who traveled through South America a decade before Darwin's visit there, sketching the land and the people. The following account of his travels was published: *Voyage pittoresque dans le Bresil*, by Maurice Rugendas, trans. M. de Colbery (Paris: Engelman, 1835). Two of Rugendas' pictures are reproduced in Robert S. Hopkins, *Darwin's South America* (New York, 1969), pp. 51, 71.

58.   Charles Othon Frederic Jean Baptiste Comte de Clarac (1777–1847), French archaeologist, who from 1815 to 1818 went to Brazil and South America with the Brazilian embassy of the Duke of Luxembourg. From this South American trip he brought back many pictures of South American flora and fauna.

59.   Darwin had, presumably, seen engravings of the Brazilian forest drawings of Moritz Rugendas and Le Compte de Clarac at some time before he went on the *Beagle* voyage; he may have seen these in the home of his then Cambridge teacher J. S. Henslow. Then, on 8 April 1832, as he was entering a Brazilian forest, he wrote in his pocket notebook: "Mimosa Forest—natural veil, but more glorious than those in the engraving." He elaborated on this in his *Diary*: "We entered a forest which in the grandeur of all its parts could not be exceeded. As the gleams of sunshine penetrate the entangled mass, I was forcibly reminded of the two French engravings after the drawings of Maurice Rugendas & Le Compte de Clavac [Clarac]; in these is well represented the infinite number of lianas & parasitic plants & the contrast of the flourishing

trees with the dead & rotten trunks. I was at an utter loss how to sufficiently admire this scene." After returning from his exploration of the forest he told his sister Caroline: "I advise you to get a French engraving, Le Foret du Brasil; it is most true and clever." He then wrote Henslow: "Your engraving is exactly true, but understates, rather than exagerates the luxuriance [of the Brazilian forest].—I never experienced such intense delight" (*Darwin and the "Beagle,"* pp. 158–59; *"Beagle" Diary*, 8 April 1832, p. 50; Charles Darwin to Caroline Darwin, Botofogo Bay, 25 April [1832], *Darwin and the "Beagle,"* p. 64; Darwin to Henslow, Rio de Janeiro, 18 May 1832, *Darwin and Henslow*, p. 55).

Emma Darwin's Entries

1.   *CFL*, 1:266.

2.   See part 1, §12, n. 38–41. On at least one occasion Emma suffered "dreadfully" from both "toothache and headache" (Charles Darwin to Catherine Darwin, Sunday [July 1842], *ML*, 1:33).

3.   *CFL*, 2:267.

4.   Ibid., pp. 163–65.

5.   See part 1, §8 and 10.

6.   Darwin to Reverend J. Brodie Innes (1848), in Robert M. Stecher, "The Darwin-Innes Letters," *Annals of Science* 17 (1961):203.

7.   The source for this statement about the supposed action of citric acid has not been identified.

8.   For the medicinal uses of quassia see *Dr. Robert Darwin's Prescriptions*, n. 63.

9.   Zinc oxide formed "a mild cooling ointment," which was "applied to wounds, to ring-worm of the scalp, impetiginous pustular eruptions, and tarsal opthalmia" (Henry Beasley, *The Book of Prescriptions* [London, 1859], p. 516).

10.   Lard was hog's fat (with the salt removed) which was used as a basis for various cerates and ointments (J. F. Royle and F. W. Headland, *A Manual of Materia Medica and Therapeutics* [London: John Churchill, 1865], pp. 711–12).

11.   Glycerine was "a sweet principle obtained from fats and fixed oils." It had a soothing effect on the skin, was applied to chapped hands and sores, and was mixed with other skin medications (J. F. Royle and F. W. Headland, *A Manual of Materia Medica and Therapeutics* [London: John Churchill, 1865], pp. 518–19).

12.   Erasmus Darwin seems to have been ill for most of his adult life (see part 2, §2). In later years Erasmus lived in London, and would visit Down House during the summer, or join Charles Darwin and his family on a holiday. Then, gradually, Erasmus became disinclined to travel, stopped his visits to

Down, and could only be seen in his London home (Francis Darwin, "Reminiscences of my Father's Everyday Life," DPL, Box 140 [3], p. 46).

13. Francis Darwin, 1848–1925.

14. Benzoin was the balsamic resin of the *Styrax benzoin*, a tree from Sumatra. Compound tincture of benzoin was used as a "Stimulant Expectorant" (J. F. Royle and F. W. Headland, *A Manual of Materia Medica and Therapeutics* [London: John Churchill, 1865], pp. 510–13; Henry Beasley, *The Book of Prescriptions* [London, 1859], pp. 123–24). See *Dr. Robert Darwin's Prescriptions*, n. 45.

15. Syrup of poppies was a narcotic medicine from the capsule of the poppy plant (which produced opium); it was similar to opium, but not as powerful, and used in some cases where opium was used. The poppy existed in corn (red), white (albus), and black forms (J. F. Royle and F. W. Headland, *A Manual of Materia Medica and Therapeutics* [London: John Churchill, 1865], pp. 280–83; Henry Beasley, *The Book of Prescriptions* [London, 1859], pp. 367–68).

16. "Oxymel" was a drink compounded of honey and vinegar which was used as an expectorant and diaphoretic (J. F. Royle and F. W. Headland, *A Manual of Materia Medica and Therapeutics* [London: John Churchill, 1865], p. 698). Oxymel was combined with squill to form oxymel scillae, which was used as an expectorant and diuretic (Henry Beasley, *The Book of Prescriptions* [London, 1859], p. 445). See note 6 in the previous section.

17. See note 14 in this section.

18. See note 46 in the previous section.

19. See note 16 in this section.

20. See *Dr. Robert Darwin's Prescriptions*, n. 43.

21. Unidentified.

22. In June 1858 Darwin's daughter Etty suffered from an illness which Darwin first described as "an attack very like diptheria," and "a modified form of that horrid new complaint, Diptheria" (Darwin to Fox, Down Bromley Kent, 24 and 27 June [1858], CCDL). Etty soon recovered from this diptherialike attack, and then became ill in a chronic and different form. (See part 2, §2, n. 70–76.)

23. "Tincture of steel. *Tinctura Martis cum sale ammoniaco.* Residuum in subliming iron filings with ammoniac q. p. S.V.R. q. s. to extract the tincture, evaporate to one half, and add a little spirit of salt" (Samuel Frederick Gray, *A Supplement to the Pharmacopoeias* [London, 1818], p. 267).

24. See note 11 in this section.

25. Perhaps Dr. Norman Moore, of St. Bartholomew's Hospital, London, who was Darwin's last physician (part 1, §14, n. 21). There are, however, many "Dr. Moore's" listed in Victorian medical directories.

26. For the signs of croup see *Dr. Robert Darwin's Prescriptions*, n. 14.

27. "Ipecac": an abbreviation of ipecacuanha or ipecacuan (see *Dr. Robert Darwin's Prescriptions*, n. 44).

28. Muriated iron was iron chloride. It was, perhaps, intended to be a tonic. See *Dr. Robert Darwin's Prescriptions*, n. 62 and *Charles Darwin's Entries*, n. 39.

29. Unidentified.

30. A bunion was an inflamed swelling on the foot, especially on the inside of the ball of the great toe.

31. For laudanum, see *Dr. Robert Darwin's Prescriptions*, n. 43.

32. Goulard's cerate (named after Thomas Goulard, an eighteenth-century French physician) was a mixture of subacetate of lead, white wax, camphor, and olive oil, which was used as a soothing ointment for inflamed and irritated areas (J. F. Royle and F. W. Headland, *A Manual of Materia Medica and Therapeutics* [London: John Churchill, 1865], p. 184).

33. Lint was a soft material, made by scraping or raveling old linen cloths, used for dressing wounds or tender surfaces.

34. Acetate morphia, made by dissolving pure morphine in acetic acid and evaporating to form crystals, could then be taken orally, but had an "intensely bitter taste" (J. F. Royle and F. W. Headland, *A Manual of Materia Medica and Therapeutics* [London: John Churchill, 1865], p. 292). Emma's prescription, because it further diluted acetate of morphia with water and acetic acid, may have lessened this bitter taste.

35. Unidentified.

36. Bran was the husk of wheat, barley, oats, and so on, separated from the flour after grinding.

37. Muslin was a coarse, heavy, cotton material.

38. A contemporary account of how "to wash coloured prints, cretonnes, etc.," stated: "Put a little bran into lukewarm water; wash quickly through; rinse *in cold* water also quickly. Hang to dry in a room without fire or sunshine. Iron with not *too* hot an iron. Use no soap" (Ross Murray, *The Modern Householder* [London, 1872], p. 414).

39. *CFL*, 2:164.

40. The Reverend William Kirby, 1759–1850, was a well-known entomologist. Darwin possessed Kirby's *Monographia Apum Angliae, &c*, 2 vols. (Ipswich, 1802), and Kirby and Spence, *An Introduction to Entomology*, 4 vols. (London, 1818–27); he used the latter in writing *The Variation of Animals and Plants under Domestication* and *The Descent of Man*.

Entries Whose Authors Are Unidentified

1. Castor oil was a purgative which was thought to act quickly and to cause little irritation of the intestine (J. F. Royle and F. W. Headland, *A Manual of*

Materia Medica and Therapeutics [London: John Churchill, 1865], pp. 591–92).

2. Dr. Henry Letheby was a well-known chemist, toxicologist, and sanitarian. He was lecturer on chemistry and toxicology in the Medical School of the London Hospital, and medical officer of health to the London City Commissioners of Sewers. He died on 29 March 1876 (*Medical Times and Gazette*, 22 April 1876, p. 447; *British Medical Journal*, 8 April 1876, p. 451).

3. John Horsley was elected a fellow of the College of Surgeons in 1856. He died in March 1888.

4. The Terling typhoid epidemic broke out on 13 November 1867, and was reported to have waned about the end of December 1867 (House of Commons Papers, Commissioners Reports, 1874, 33). However, according to Attfield's 18 June 1868 letter in *The Times*, the Terling epidemic was still active in the spring of 1868.

5. Sir Arthur Keith, *Darwin Revalued* (London, 1955), p. 43.

6. John Attfield, 1835–1911, was professor of practical chemistry to the London School of Pharmacy and Pharmaceutical Society, author of numerous publications in chemistry and pharmacy, and one of the most notable personalities in English pharmacy ("The Late Dr. Attfield," *Pharmaceutical Journal and Pharmacist*, 25 March 1911, p. 396).

Appendix B
Darwin and the Early Use
of Chloroform Anesthesia

1. Francis Boott, M.D. (1792–1863). Born in Boston of British parents and holding friendships in both America and England, he received his M.D. degree from the University of Edinburgh in 1824, and then settled in London in 1825. He first practiced successfully as a physician in London from 1825 to 1832. He then largely gave up medical practice and devoted himself to the study of botany, ancient and modern literature, and the affairs of the London Linnean Society. (There is an obituary of Dr. Boott in the *Gardeners' Chronicle and Agricultural Gazette*, 16 January 1864, pp. 51–52.) Dr. Boott was a friend of Hooker, and a friend of Darwin from 1838 until his death in 1863 (*LL*, 1:264).

2. This seems to be the only time that Darwin writes "Chloriform" with an *i* instead of an *o*.

3. Darwin to Dr. Francis Boott, Athenaeum Club (London), Saturday, 20 August 1848 (Charles Hamilton, auction no. 59, 29 June 1972).

4. Myrtle Simpson, *Simpson the Obstetrician* (London: Victor Gollancz, Ltd., 1972), pp. 131–33.

5. Ibid., pp. 133–37.

6. Ibid., pp. 140–42.

7. Ibid., pp. 141–42.

8. Ibid., pp. 141–55.

9. "What a beautiful instance Chloroform is of a discovery made from *purely* scientific researches, afterwards coming almost by chance into practical use" (Darwin to Henslow, Down Farnborough Kent, Sunday night, 1 April 1848, *Darwin and Henslow*, p. 159).

10. See part 1, §4, n. 45–46.

11. Darwin to the Reverend J. Brodie Innes (1848), in Robert M. Stecher, "The Darwin-Innes Letters," *Annals of Science* 17 (1961):203. (See appendix A, *Charles Darwin's Entries*, n. 49.)

12. Darwin to Fox, Down Farnborough Kent, Thursday (January 1850), CCDL.

13. J. H. Ashworth, "Charles Darwin as a Student in Edinburgh, 1825–1827," *Proceedings of the Royal Society of Edinburgh* 60 (1934–35):98. Darwin's class-cards for this year were not preserved.

14. Darwin to Henslow, Down Farnborough Kent, 17 January (1850), *Darwin and Henslow*, p. 166.

15. Darwin to Hooker, Down Farnborough Kent, 3 February (1850), DPL, Box 114.

16. Darwin to Hooker, Down Farnborough Kent, 17 January (1854), DPL, Box 114.

17. Darwin to Henslow, Down Farnborough Kent, 17 January (1850), *Darwin and Henslow*, p. 166.

18. Darwin to Fox, Down Farnborough Kent, Thursday (May 1850), CCDL.

19. Darwin to Fox, Down Farnborough Kent, 24 (October 1852), CCDL, *LL*, 1:352. This June 1852 tooth extraction under chloroform is reported in Darwin's *Diary of Health*. See part 2, §5, n. 38.

20. Darwin to Hooker, Down Farnborough Kent, 26 (March 1861), DPL, Box 115. See part 2, §5, n. 39.

21. Darwin to Fox, Down Farnborough Kent, 24 (October 1852), CCDL, *LL*, 1:352.

22. Cecil Woodham-Smith, *Queen Victoria* (New York, 1972), p. 328.

23. Ibid.

24. "Sir James Young Simpson," *Encyclopaedia Britannica* 20 (1968):555.

25. Darwin to Fox, Down Bromley Kent, 8 February (1857), CCDL.

26. *Autobiography*, p. 48.

27. Darwin to his daughter Henrietta Litchfield, 4 January 1875, *LL*, 2:380.

28. E. Westacott, *A Century of Vivisection and Anti-Vivisection* (Ashingdon, Rochford, Essex, England: C. W. Daniel Co., Ltd., 1849), p. 75.

Index

Abinger Hall, 89
Acetic acid, 163
Acid medicines. *See* Acetic acid; Citric
    acid; Mineral acid; Nitric acid; Prus-
    sic acid; Sulphuric acid
Adam Bede (George Eliot), 65
Adler, Professor Saul, 127, 129–30. *See
    also* Chagas' disease
Agassiz, Louis, 25, 32, 33
Aldershot, Darwin sees Queen Victoria
    review troops, 61
Alkalies (also called alkaline medi-
    cines), 78, 101, 144, 158. *See also*
    Ammonia carbonate; Chalk; Potas-
    sium medicines; Soda, carbonate of;
    Soda water
Allbutt, Sir Clifford, 121
Allen, Fanny, 85
Allfrey, Mr. Charles, 94, 95, 96
Allingham, William, 87, 105, 134
Almonds, oil of, 155
Aloes, 46
Alum, 159
Alvarez, Dr. Walter C., 117, 120, 121,
    122
Amebiasis, 127
American Anthropologist, 114
American Philosophical Society, Mem-
    oirs of the, 132
American Psychoanalytic Association,
    122
Ammonia, liquid (also called liquor
    ammonia), used to test for arsenic,
    165. *See also* Ammonia medicines
Ammonia carbonate, Darwin experi-
    ments with actions on roots and
    leaves, 93. *See also* Ammonia med-
    icines
Ammonia medicines: carbonate of am-
    monia, 78, 105; liquor of ammonia,
153; sal volatile (carbonate of am-
    monia), 150, 156, 157; subcarbonate
    of ammonia, 154
Amyl nitrite, 94, 95
Antimony medicines: antimonial wine,
    149, 150, 156, 162; antimony powder,
    155; tartar, cream of, 155; tartar
    emetic, given by Darwin to patients,
    4, 100; tartar emetic ointment, given
    by Darwin to himself, 45, 101
Antiquity of Man, The (Lyell), 73–74
Aperient, 157
Argentina, 11, 12, 103, 127
Arnica, tincture of, 159
"Arnic [arnica] gargle," 159
Arsenic: as a medicine, 7, 8, 9, 101,
    132–39; in wreaths and dresses, 164–
    65. *See also* Darwin, Charles, works
    about, *Darwin's Victorian Malady*;
    Winslow, Dr. John H.
Aschaffenburg, Mr. Karl, ix, 148, 255,
    n. 4
Athenaeum Club, 15
Atkins, Mr. (unidentified), gives pre-
    scription for "continued sickness,"
    158
Atkins, Sir Hedley, ix, 140–41
Attfield, Professor John, letter to the
    editor of *The Times*, 166–67
Aurant, tinct. cort., 154. *See also* Or-
    ange peel, tincture of
Aurantii, tinct., 158
Ayerst, Dr. James, 75

Bacon, G. W., 113
Barlow, Dr. Erasmus Darwin (Darwin's
    great-grandson), 122
Barlow, Lady Nora (Darwin's grand-
    daughter), xi, 134
Barnacles, 32, 50, 52, 54, 98, 116

277